PRENTICE-HALL

HISTORY OF MUSIC SERIES

H. WILEY HITCHCOCK, editor

TWENTIETH-CENTURY
MUSIC
An Introduction

third edition

TWENTIETH-CENTURY MUSIC
An Introduction

ERIC SALZMAN

Composer

PRENTICE HALL, ENGLEWOOD CLIFFS, NEW JERSEY 07632

Library of Congress Cataloging-in-Publication Data

Salzman, Eric. date
  Twentieth-century music.

  (Prentice-Hall history of music series)
  Includes bibliographies and index.
  1. Music—20th century—History and criticism.
I. Title.   II. Title: 20th century music.   III. Series.
ML197.S77 1988   780'.904   87-19292
ISBN 0-13-935057-8

Printed in the United States of America

20 19 18 17 16 15 14 12 11 10 9 8 7 6 5 4 3

©1988, 1974, 1967 by Prentice Hall
A Division of Simon & Schuster
Englewood Cliffs, New Jersey 07632

Cover photo: Albert Gleize's cubist portrait "IGOR STRAVINSKY," 1914. Collection of Richard S. Zeisler, New York.

Music: from Stravinsky's *Le Sacre du Printemps*. Copyright by Edition Russe de Musique. Copyright assigned 1947 to Boosey and Hawkes for all countries of the world. Reprinted by permission.

PRENTICE-HALL INTERNATIONAL (UK) LIMITED, *London*
PRENTICE-HALL OF AUSTRALIA PTY. LIMITED, *Sydney*
PRENTICE-HALL CANADA INC., *Toronto*
PRENTICE-HALL HISPANOAMERICANA, S.A., *Mexico*
PRENTICE-HALL OF INDIA PRIVATE LIMITED, *New Delhi*
PRENTICE-HALL OF JAPAN, INC., *Tokyo*
SIMON & SCHUSTER ASIA PTE. LTD., *Singapore*
EDITORA PRENTICE-HALL DO BRASIL, LTDA., *Rio de Janeiro*

FOREWORD

Students and others interested in the history of music have always needed books of moderate length that are nevertheless comprehensive, authoritative, and engagingly written. The Prentice-Hall History of Music Series was planned to fill these needs. It seems to have succeeded: revised and enlarged second editions of books in the series have been necessary, and now a new cycle of further revisions is underway, toward third editions.

Six books in the series present a panoramic view of the history of music of Western civilization, divided among the major historical periods—Medieval, Renaissance, Baroque, Classic, Romantic, and Twentieth-Century. The musical culture of the United States, viewed historically as an independent development within the larger Western tradition, is treated in another book; and one other deals with music in Latin America. In yet another pair of books, the rich folk and traditional musics of both hemispheres are considered. Taken together, these ten volumes are a distinctive and, we hope, distinguished contribution to the history of the music of the world's peoples. Each volume, moreover, may of course be read singly as a substantial account of the music of its period or area.

The authors of the books in the Prentice-Hall History of Music Series are scholars of international repute—musicologists, critics, and teachers of exceptional stature in their respective fields of specialization. Their goal in contributing to the series has been to present works of solid, up-to-date scholarship that are eminently readable, with significant insights into music as a part of the general intellectual and cultural life of man.

H. WILEY HITCHCOCK, *Series Editor*

PREFACE

Previous editions of this book began with the statement "Any consideration of the music of the twentieth century must begin with the reminder that a good deal of it has not yet been written." Now, in fact, most of this century's music *has* been written. The projection of twentieth-century music as the unfolding of two large cycles (each beginning with a period of revolution and ending with synthesis) and the appearance of "post-modern" styles as the logical outcome of the second cycle—both predicted in the earlier editions—have become facts rather than hypotheses. Twentieth-century music, which conveniently began somewhere around 1900, threatens to run its course by the end of the century.

The history of culture can be thought of in many ways: as a succession of events (the way we tend to think about ancient history), as the movement of great historical forces (the way we think about the Renaissance and Reformation), in terms of social, political, and economic realities (our view of the Middle Ages and of the Baroque and Rococo-Classical periods as well), or in terms of creative personalities (the Romantic view). As this series of books itself can testify, these conceptions need not be mutually exclusive, and none of them need preclude an understanding of cultural history as a history of ideas. Without, I hope, entirely forgetting any of the former, it is the last-named that I have tried to write: the creative development of musical ideas in the last eighty-five years understood against and as distinct from the past, in the variety and unity of its own growth and in its potential for the future.

It is my hope and belief that a book of this kind can bring the reader towards the musical experience itself, in terms of the greatest variety and richness of ideas and expression, a richness itself characteristic of the twentieth-century musical experience. Towards this end, certain sacrifices have consciously been made. Detailed biographical information will have to be sought elsewhere (such things are, except in the cases of the very youngest composers, available in standard reference works). Analytic material has been relegated to an appendix consisting of a few indicative examples—it is always to be assumed that, on every page of this book, the reader is being actually referred to the music itself. No attempt has been made to achieve the illusory goal of completeness, and long lists of also-rans have been avoided. I am well aware that Schmitt, Schreker, Ghedini, Grainger and Glière, Weiner and Weinberger, Alfven, Zemlinsky, and a host of greater and lesser lights do not appear and that others, particularly—but not exclusively—composers of only national or local significance, receive brief consideration. I am also conscious of the fact that the work of certain composers—particularly since World War II—inevitably receives a certain emphasis because it lends itself easily to verbal analysis or description, qualities which do not necessarily correspond to artistic values. The deficiencies of this book with respect to American music are, fortunately, compensated for by the inclusion in this series of a volume of H. Wiley Hitchcock devoted entirely to the subject: *Music in the United States*. It is the intention here to treat the development of American music in our century in terms of the general development of twentieth-century ideas everywhere; it is, surprisingly enough (and limited as it is), one of the first such attempts. In any case, I can only hope that, in a book intended to be devoted to essentials, the essentials are there.

Although the first edition of this book was published in 1967, the bulk of it was written on a boat to Europe in the spring of 1964. This moment had more than symbolic value for me; it marked a change in direction for me as a composer beginning with my *Foxes and Hedgehogs*, on texts from John Ashbery's "Europe." The culture change—the clash in values from Old World to New—scored out in that piece as the structure of a music drama has come to serve as a metaphor for the vast upheavals and changes of the 1960's through the 1980's.

Change has continued to overtake music and the arts as it has the whole of society; new forces have been set in motion and the outcome is hardly in sight. Of necessity, one's own work and thought has also evolved. The two decades that have elapsed are difficult to write about, not only because the events set in motion are still in progress, but also because the author himself has played a part in their unfolding.

The first version of this book marked off a distinct period; we can, with certain neatness, refer to it as the period of modern music. There were loose ends, of course, and even certain ideas that were clearly prophetic of what was to come. Approaching a second, and now a third edition, I had two obvious choices; leave the book as it was or rewrite it completely, reflecting the state of the art and the currency of my own thought. However, I have chosen a third course. The earlier parts of the book have been left essentially intact. There are minor revisions—corrections, emendations, a few rephrasings and clarifications, an occasional re-evaluation—and the specimen analyses have been relegated to an appendix. But the final section of the book has been rewritten for a second time and now constitutes an entire new section on post-modernism. It was my aim not merely to bring the book "up-to-date"—although the events of the past decades have been sketched and an attempt made to assess their significance—but also to establish a firmer conceptual framework for the whole post-war period.

Inevitably, certain differences of approach in this final section will become apparent. There is a much greater emphasis on social and technological change as a background for understanding the artistic events, and there is a greater emphasis on the interactions between the arts. This in part reflects the evolution of my own ideas, in part our closeness to the events (musical synthesis takes greater time and distance), and in part the nature of the period.

One or two additional points need to be amplified here. The problem of providing dates for works is not always as simple as it might appear. Dates given in reference works, programs, chronologies, biographies, or scores often differ and may (when accurate) refer to the date of completion, copyright, publication, or first performance. The attempt here has been to give, as closely as possible, the actual dates of composition. Hopefully, any factual errors or imprecisions which remain undiscovered do not affect the basic premises of the book.

The intent in organizing the musical examples as an appendix is the make the book more continuously readable and less forbidding to the general, non-specialist reader. The examples are, in any case, only intended to suggest approaches for the reader who wishes to pursue more analytical studies. The illustrations—including Gleize's cubist portrait of Stravinsky reproduced on the cover of the volume—have been chosen with the idea of bringing together a series of portraits which are themselves works of art.

It is not possible to acknowledge more than a very few of the many intellectual and spiritual debts incurred in writing a book like this. Among those which cannot be omitted, I would like to include H. Wiley Hitchcock, the understanding and skillful editor of this series and the author of the volume on American music without which any grasp of the twentieth century is necessarily incomplete; my principal teachers, Roger Sessions and Milton Babbitt; Edgard Varèse, who never taught but was, in the true sense, always a teacher; Ross Parmenter, former Music Editor of *The New York Times*, who was almost entirely responsible for my writing career in music; Marjorie Samoff, co-founder with me of the American Music Theater Festival; Michael Sahl, my long-term collaborator on six music-theater works, several recordings, and a handbook of American harmony called *Making Changes*; Paul Wittke, my collaborator at G. Schirmer; Suzanne La Plante, who was my invaluable assistant on the third edition, and who should be credited with most of the new bibliographical matter; Anna Rubin of the American Music Center and the staffs at the Center and the Research Division of the New York Public Library at Lincoln Center; and finally, that extraordinary younger generation of performers and creators—in music and the other performing arts—who have made possible the beginnings of a new, vital cultural life.

ERIC SALZMAN

CONTENTS

TWENTIETH-CENTURY
MUSIC
An Introduction

part one

Introduction

ONE

TWENTIETH-CENTURY MUSIC AND THE PAST

The music of the twentieth century seems so fundamentally different from the music of the past and so varied and wide-ranging in itself that it is difficult to realize that it has deep roots in what came before and, at the same time, a pervasive unity that distinguishes it from its past.

The creative history of Western music since 1900 is inconceivable without the evolution of Western culture in the preceding centuries; our musical institutions and, indeed, our whole way of thinking about music are inheritances from the recent and not-so-recent past, and in certain fundamental ways the tradition has continued to exert its influence even on the greatest innovators.[1] Nevertheless, a distinctly twentieth-century viewpoint emerges from the fact that nearly all the creative musical thinking of our century—even that which is described as "conservative"—has participated

---

[1] When traditional historians talk about "modern" European history, they mean "since the French Revolution." Similarly, "modern art" surveys used to begin with David and Goya. Only in music has there been general agreement not to treat this time span as one period.

1

in the search for new expressive structures. The old forms, the old expressive structures, can be implied by the term "functional tonality" understood in its broadest traditional sense, embracing ideas and "expression" on the one hand and underlying structural, organizing principles on the other. After 1900 the old propositions ceased to function as *a priori* assumptions; related to the tradition or not, tonal or non-tonal, conservative or revolutionary, all twentieth-century musical art has to establish its own expressive and intellectual premises.

In spite of technological, social, and esthetic upheaval, our musical ideals are still communicated in the context of a musical life whose structure, means, and institutions are largely derived from the late eighteenth and nineteenth centuries.[2] This is true of our concert and operatic institutions, of our instruments (most old violins have been so largely rebuilt that they can be considered nineteenth-century instruments), and of instrumental technique. It is true of the modern orchestra, of our chamber music ensembles, of our operatic forms, of the virtuoso soloist, and of the solo recital. Similarly, the bulk of our musical repertory, our techniques of teaching the practice and theory of music (and the institution of the conservatory itself), as well as most of our artistic and esthetic notions and assumptions about what music is and what it ought to do—all these things reached their full development between 1700 and 1900 and have been bequeathed to us surprisingly intact.

Some of our most fundamental ways of thinking about music and musical creation are also inheritances from the recent past. Indeed, our whole notion of "art" and artistic creation as a unique and separable human activity is a relatively modern Western idea, by no means universal in human experience, and one which strongly links the "Romantic" era with the twentieth century. The notion of the creation and experience of music for its own sake is one that entered Western musical culture at a fairly recent date, and in spite of many attempts in the last decades to modify this rather special conception of the role of music in our society, we still tend to think of the highest forms of music making as the purest—that is, the most isolated and detached from other forms of human activity. Like our nineteenth-century forebears, we think of the composer as a creative individual communicating personal, original, and unique thoughts in a distinctive style and with a particularized point of view and expression. This lingering concept of the

---

[2] This is not a book that deals with the development of musical ideas in relationship to general history. Clearly, however, two world wars and the social, political, technological, and scientific revolutions of the twentieth century have had a meaning for contemporary culture parallel to the impact that the fall of the *ancien régime*, Napoleon, the Industrial Revolution, and the new bourgeois society had on the life and thought of the nineteenth. Attempts will be made now and then—particularly in the final section—to annotate the as yet unwritten social history of new music.

composer as a romantic culture hero has led us to place greater emphasis than ever on creative individuality, originality, and freedom. Finally, the nineteenth century taught us to understand the work of art as conditioned by its historical and cultural context while, at the same time and without contradiction, regarding it as an individual expression of artistic uniqueness. The very notion of "the avant-garde" as it is usually understood is a nineteenth-century, Romantic conception.[3]

We can expect, then, to comprehend a great deal of what has happened in the twentieth century in terms of the past. Just as the historical personalities of Beethoven and Wagner remain decisive in the formation of our conceptions of the role of the composer in society, so does the music of these two composers suggest the development of ideas and techniques which evolved into characteristic twentieth-century modes of musical thought. The modulatory freedom in Beethoven's music stands in a direct relationship to the chromatic freedom and incipient "atonality" of *Tristan und Isolde*. In turn, Wagner's expanded palette of orchestral, harmonic, and contrapuntal techniques can be clearly traced in the music of composers like Richard Strauss, Gustav Mahler, and even César Franck, Gabriel Fauré, and Claude Debussy. The revival and refinement of classical organizational principles and the close relation of these to modern structural ideas of a music that is totally organic and interrelated are already basic in the music of Brahms. The resources of harmonic and melodic patterns that lie outside of the major-minor functional tonality system are suggested by the music of composers like Mussorgsky and even Dvořák. The "back-to-Bach" movement and the rediscovery of "pre-Bach" music and musical forms were accomplished facts long before 1900. In short, chromaticism; the extended and freer use of dissonance; the establishment of harmonic and melodic freedom; the use of harmonic, melodic, and structural ideas derived from folk music and early Western music; the concept of the structural interrelationships between all the parts of a musical composition; the discovery of the distant past and of non-Western music; the vast expansion of instrumental technique and color; the new freedom, complexity, and independence of rhythm, dynamics, and tone color—all these modern ideas have roots deep in the last century.

Less obvious, perhaps, but equally important is the persistence of certain underlying modes of musical thought, especially those dealing with large statement and structure—complex and subtle ideas built up over the course of many generations and not easily dissipated even by revolutionary changes on the surface. There is a central development of musical thinking connecting Haydn directly with Mahler in a line of structural conceptions that constantly increase in size and scope. This kind of thinking remains

---

[3] *Gebrauchsmusik* and the social ideals of the 1930s represented significant attempts to break with these Romantic notions. And the traditional view of art has again been challenged in the last years; see the final chapter of this book.

surprisingly operative in the twentieth century—in the many attempts to revive and renew "sonata form," for example, or, in a more profound way, in the development of chromatic and twelve-tone structures in the work of the Viennese, the direct inheritors of the "main line" tradition.

More than anything else, however, the Romantic notion of the artist as an individualist has helped to form the modern impulse towards originality and uniqueness. In a sense, the vast and swift changes in all modern art can be seen as an intensification of a historical process of change that has long been operative in Western culture. But even if we accept the premise that the vast expansion of vocabulary and means in this century is part of an overall process that has taken place over the past centuries, there is reason to believe that, after a point, the character of the process itself changed and quantitative distinctions became clearly qualitative. For our purposes, we can define that point as the moment when traditional tonality ceased to provide the fundamental expressive and organizational foundation of musical thought and was replaced by other modes of musical expression and organization. This change actually occurred in the years around 1900, and it is this fact that enables us to speak distinctively of the music of the twentieth century.

Western music between about 1600 and 1900 was distinguished by the development of a characteristic kind of musical thinking that has been called "functional tonality." The word "tonality" can be defined in a rough way as a representation of a basic scale formation within which certain hierarchies prevail—expressed as points of stability and instability. Certain tones and combinations of tones represent goals and suggest stability and rest, while others imply motion to or away from these goals. Tonality in its traditional form presents a principle of order in musical thought which implies that every formation of horizontal and vertical (that is, melodic and harmonic) tones has a definable relationship to every other such formation. In other words, every musical event has a "function" or a functional role which relates it to what has come before and what will happen next. The basic psychological principle here is expectation; the basic musical technique is that of direction and motion. Out of this grow the characteristic ways in which musical lines will rise and fall and the ways in which simultaneous musical lines will relate to one another in harmonic patterns. The idea of expectation suggests the use of resolution and non-resolution; of so-called dissonance and consonance; of intensity and relaxation; of cadence, accent, and articulation; of phrase and punctuation; of rhythm and dynamic; even of tempo and tone color.

Out of these apparently simple psychological and musical facts evolved one of the most complex and sophisticated modes of artistic expression that man has ever developed. The concept of primary goals suggested the possibility of secondary goals—the idea of "modulation," in which musical motion could turn away from its primary centers of gravity to secondary centers, which could then serve to reinforce the motion back to the primary ones. This made possible the complex structures of eighteenth- and nineteenth-century music, which, with their web of relationships, unfolding in time, tie every note of a piece firmly to every other note. When we say that Beethoven's "Eroica" Symphony is in E♭, we are saying much more than the fact that its first and last harmonies are E♭ major triads; we are implying a whole way of thinking about the organization of sound, which determines every aspect of our experience of the music.[4]

Characteristic forms of tonal expression, contrast, interrelationship, and structure guided musical thinking for three centuries. Except to a limited degree in certain forms of folk and popular music, they are no longer operative; since the opening years of this century, composers have ceased to accept the unquestioned validity of these concepts. Wagner's extreme chromatic freedom, "atonal" as it may seem at times, is still based on the listener's expectation that one musical event implies another—much of *Tristan* is built on the very idea of the defeat of expectation. The music of Debussy, Schoenberg, and Stravinsky, however, no longer depends on that expectation but sets forth new kinds of definitions and relationships. Even the most conservative twentieth-century music establishes forms of motion and rest with new means. When Beethoven uses the familiar dominant-tonic cadence, it has a formal and expressive significance that is inseparable from the entire fabric and structure of the musical thought; when the same musical event occurs in Prokofiev, it is a local incident whose significance must be understood in other terms. While certain underlying universal principles have retained their force and validity, since 1900 there has no longer been the necessity to assume that any generally accepted premise precedes the fact of musical composition or that any one musical realization must follow or be derived from any other.

The development of creative musical thought since 1900 has been rich and complex, full of remarkable achievements, remarkable and unremarkable failures, enormous and continuing promise, and seemingly endless contradiction. There is some reason to believe that developments of the last twenty years or so mark a more definitive break with the past—for better or for worse—than anything accomplished previously. But all twentieth-century music can be comprehended as a unity if it is understood against the background of the past and the dominating tonal ideas of the past. Once this unity, essentially negative in its nature, has been grasped, we can begin to understand the positive ways in which contemporary creative thought has redefined its intellectual, expressive, and creative aims.

---

[4] The vexed question of "classical" tonality is obviously not so simple; the foregoing is intended to be suggestive rather than definitive. Most modern views about the encompassing function of the old tonality derive from the writings of the Austrian theorist Heinrich Schenker.

The history of music in the twentieth century can be understood in terms of two great cycles: first, the abandonment of functional tonality after 1900, the explorations of vast new materials before and after World War I, and the new tonal and twelve-tone syntheses that followed; and second, the very different but parallel set of rejections, new beginnings, explorations, analyses, and syntheses following World War II. The bond that connects all of twentieth-century music grows out of the fact that each composer—and each piece—has had to establish new and unique forms of expressive and intellectual communication. To understand the music of this century, we must examine these forms.

BIBLIOGRAPHICAL NOTES

Out of a growing number of surveys on music of the twentieth century that can be found on library shelves, only a few need be cited here (none of these cover the whole period). William Austin's *Music in the 20th Century* (New York, 1966) and Peter Yates's *Twentieth-Century Music: Its Evolution from the End of the Harmonic Era into the Present Era of Sound* (New York, 1967) are both limited largely to the period before World War II; Arnold Whittal's *Music Since the First World War* (London, 1977) is limited roughly to a fifty-year period. Three more recently written surveys concentrate on the music composed since World War II: Michael Nyman's *Experimental Music: Cage and Beyond* (New York, 1974), Reginald Smith Brindle's *The New Music: The Avant Garde Since 1945* (London, 1975), and Paul Griffiths's *Modern Music: The Avant Garde Since 1945* (London, 1981). More specialized studies dealing with composers from particular countries can be found in the bibliographical notes for Chapter 8. Two important source collections are limited largely to the first half of the century: *Contemporary Composers on Contemporary Music*, eds. E. Schwartz and B. Childs (New York, 1967; repr. New York, 1978) and *The American Composer Speaks: A Historical Anthology, 1790–1965*, ed. Gilbert Chase (Baton Rouge, 1966). See also the discussions of composers by other composers in Henry Cowell's *American Composers on American Music: A Symposium* (New York, 1933; repr. 1962) and *Perspectives on American Composers*, eds. B. Boretz and E. T. Cone (New York, 1971), largely a "Princeton perspective". Nicolas Slonimsky's astonishing year-by-year documentary *Music Since 1900* now has a supplement (through July 1986) to its fourth edition (New York, 1971). Slonimsky has also revised *Baker's Biographical Dictionary of Musicians* (7th ed., New York, 1984) to include a wide range of twentieth-century composers, even some of the younger figures. *The New Grove Dictionary of Music and Musicians*, ed. Stanley Sadie (London, 1980) does the same on a still wider scale; *The New Grove Dictionary of American Music*, eds. H. Wiley Hitchcock and Sadie (New York, 1986) not only supersedes the American-music entries in *The New Grove* of 1980 but is indispensable for all kinds of music in the United States up to early 1986. John Vinton compiled a

Dictionary of Contemporary Music (New York, 1974), in which the entries on the various parameters of musical sound are particularly strong. Mention should be made of the volume *Aspects of Twentieth-Century Music*, ed. Gary Wittlich (Englewood Cliffs, N.J., 1975), a "theoretical" discussion but one which examines the changes in the various parameters of musical sound during the twentieth century.

Several attempts have been made to produce generalized studies of twentieth-century materials and methods to serve as theoretical statements or teaching matter; only one or two of these, connected with the work of particular composers, will concern us (see the relevant chapters of this book). The following specialized periodicals—several of them no longer in existence—contain all sorts of matter pertaining to the history, criticism, documentation, esthetics, theory, and practice of twentieth-century music: *Modern Music* (New York, 1924–1946); *Tempo* (London, 1946–   ); *Music Survey* (High Holborn, W.C., 1947–1952); *Music Today* (Int. Soc. for Contemporary Music, London, 1949–1959?); *The Score* (London, 1949–1961); *Journal of Music Theory* (New Haven, 1957–   ); *Die Reihe* (Vienna; Eng. tr. Bryn Mawr, PA, 1958–1968); *Darmstädter Beiträge zur Neuen Musik* (Mainz, Germany, 1958–   ); *Perspectives of New Music* (Princeton, 1962–   ); *Electronic Music Review* (Trumansburg, NY, 1967–1968); *Source: Music of the Avant Garde* (Davis, CA, 1967–1973); *Contact: Contemporary Music Magazine* (Birmingham, later Heslington, Yorks., England, 1971–   ); *NUMUS-West: North America's New Music Journal* (Mercer Island, WA, 1972–1975); *Soundings* (Los Angeles, 1972–   ); *Interface: Journal of New Music Research* (Lisse, Netherlands, 1972–   ); *Xenharmonikon: An Informal Journal of Experimental Music* (Rahway, later Highland Park, NJ, 1974–1975); *Analog Sounds* (New York, 1974–1979); **Asterisk: A Journal of New Music* (Ann Arbor, 1974–   ); *Melos/Neue Zeitschrift für Musik* (from 1978 as *Neue Zeitschrift für Musik*, Mainz, Germany, 1975–   ); *Ear Magazine* (New York, 1973–   ); and *Computer Music Journal* (Menlo Park, CA, 1977–   ).

part two

The Breakdown of Traditional Tonality

TWO

THE SOURCES

More than anything else, the expansion of the use and meaning of chromatic inflection led to the development of the large tonal canvases of the eighteenth and nineteenth centuries. The structural use of modulation produced the large instrumental forms that are the great intellectual achievement of traditional tonality. Chromaticism pre-dates classical tonality, of course, but through the pattern of changing key relationships it came to play a particular structural role in the growth of tonal forms. In the evolution of things, it was modulation and chromaticism—and their local allies, secondary dominants and altered chords—that ultimately undermined that very tonality. Modulation, aided by the universal acceptance of equal temperament, helped create convincing, dramatic structures of large scope by delaying and ultimately reinforcing the musical motion of a piece towards home base. In the Classic and Romantic symphony, modulation and chromaticism were essential in the formation of large structures. With many of the Romantic composers, Chopin and Liszt for example, chromaticism played its major role in matters of expressive detail; in Brahms and, especially, in the gigantic structures of the Wagnerian music drama, it functioned both as detail and as the basis for structural prolongation. *Tristan und Isolde* is still part of the Classic-Romantic tradition in that its extreme chromaticism is still based on expectation defeated by "false" and evasive resolution, harmonic delay, and long-range suspension. Nevertheless, in parts of *Tristan* and *Parsifal* we are at the point where a quantitative development is very nearly a qualitative one, where the distinction between "tonal" and "atonal" chromaticism becomes a fine psychological line.

    Tristan und Isolde was first performed in 1865, but, in a way, its influence did not become decisive until the end of the century. None of the direct heirs of the Wagner tradition—Bruckner, Strauss, even Mahler— was primarily concerned with the development of Tristanesque chromatic procedures, although each of them employed the new harmonic, melodic, and modulatory freedom as the basis for a late-Romantic, tonal style. The only post-Wagnerian who used a complex chromatic idiom was Max Reger (1873–1916), but Reger's chromaticism is carefully systematized and based on eighteenth-century forms and procedures derived from Bach and Mozart. Reger had a certain influence—mainly theoretical—on Hindemith; otherwise his significance for the twentieth century is small.

    The composer who most directly and completely connects late Wagner and the twentieth century is Arnold Schoenberg (1874–1951). The inventor of twelve-tone music began his career in perfect Tristanesque Wagnerianism, and in works like *Verklärte Nacht* (1899), the *Gurrelieder* cycle (1901; orchestration completed 1911), *Pelleas und Melisande* (1902–1903), and the First and Second String Quartets (1905, 1908) the implications of *Tristan* and *Parsifal* are carried forward, eventually beyond the realm of tonal expectation and tonal form. By contrast, Richard Strauss (1864–1949) and Gustav Mahler (1860–1911) absorbed *Tristan* chromaticism into their composing equipment without any special effort to develop further in this direction.

    Strauss developed few new techniques and, essentially, he found no new universal forms. His style up to and perhaps including *Der Rosenkavalier* (1909–1910) suggests not so much a development from as a thorough exploration of the implications of the Wagnerian revolution. It is impossible to deny the impact of works like *Salome* (1903–1905) and *Elektra* (1906– 1908) on the early development of twentieth-century music, but it is difficult today to assess the significance of that impact. Perhaps the relationship is clearest on the dramatic-psychological plane; we would call it Freudian and trace its influence on the development of "expressionist" musical theater in works like Schoenberg's *Erwartung* and Berg's *Wozzeck* and *Lulu*. Musically, we can see two important contributions. In the small, Strauss finds it possible—in a way that Wagner never did—to delay or even omit the resolution of harmonic and melodic "dissonance"; in the large, he extends this principle of free, "dissonant" motion to produce "free association" forms which often defeat the natural and expected phrase-motion with breaks in the continuity of thought and with abrupt confrontations and juxtapositions obviously deriving from dramatic-psychological considerations. However, Strauss never really abandons functional tonality; it is somehow still operative, and, at the very moment when he seemed to be on the point of destroying it, he turned— first in *Der Rosenkavalier* and then definitively in *Ariadne auf Naxos* (1911–1912)—to classical forms and techniques in a clear attempt to reinstate it. *Ariadne* is, in effect, the first piece of neo-Classicism; it predates Stravinskyan neo-Classicism by a number of years. But, as we shall see, Stravinsky's neo-tonality is synthetic; Stravinsky actually had to go through the process of destroying functional tonality and then inventing a new kind of tonality to replace it. Strauss never went that far; he went to the edge of the abyss and then turned back. He redefined his own limits as those of functional tonality. Strauss lived through nearly half of the twentieth century, long enough to become the only significant composer who still fully accepted and believed in those limitations.[1]

The case of Mahler is still more complex. To some extent, he can be said to have duplicated the Wagnerian revolution in symphonic music, partly by adapting the symphonic tradition to a vocal and lyric-dramatic conception of musical discourse (achieved largely through the intermediate forms and techniques of the late-Romantic lied as represented, for example, in the work of a composer like Hugo Wolf). Mahler's basic language is the common practice of the nineteenth century—securely tonal, even fundamentally diatonic. Through the long, long extension of lyric, melodic lines, an ever-extended delay of the cadence, a magnificent long-range harmonic motion, careful planning and pacing of dynamic and rhythmic curves, and extensive and skillful modulation, he extended relatively simple and apparently limited ideas into enormous and powerful structures. Mahler, in fact, built entire structures on a complex interrelationship of tonal areas to the point where, although detail is always clearly set forth in terms of tonal function, the long-range motion builds up in new tonal shapes; these large-scale compositions move successively through wider and wider ranges of tonal areas and often resolve in tonal regions far from those in which they have set out. Mahler's work, consisting almost entirely of symphonies and orchestral songs, makes extensive use of folk song and, in fact, synthesizes many aspects of nineteenth-century style. At the same time Mahler, like Charles Ives, articulated a crisis of traditional values and a world-view which became widely understood only later through the massive intervention of technology in cultural

---

[1] Conscious "classicism" can be found in many Strauss works after *Der Rosenkavalier*; a good case can be made for a kind of new tonal synthesis in some of the composer's late works, parallel in some important respects to Schoenberg's "non-tonal" synthesis; see especially the *Metamorphosen* for 23 solo strings of 1945.

Bust of Gustav Mahler by Rodin, which is on display in Philharmonic Hall, Lincoln Center for the Performing Arts. © 1965, Lincoln Center for the Performing Arts. Photographed by Bob Serating Photo, New York.

life. The essentially new view of tonal form, the remarkable expansion of phrase-structure, the use and expansion of modulation and color, the very scope and range of the large-scale, multi-faceted music, and its simultaneous character of involvement and detachment all have had an important influence in the twentieth century. Mahler seems at first to have escaped the tonal upheavals of the early years of the century, but the underlying spiritual crisis is nonetheless explicit in his work. Indeed, it is Mahler's achievement that he made this crisis his subject matter; this itself has kept his music alive and relevant in the latter part of the century.[2]

One important late-Romantic remains to be mentioned here: the enigmatic Ferruccio Busoni (1866–1924). In his teaching and writing about music, notably in the *Sketch of a New Esthetic of Music* published in 1907, the famous piano virtuoso anticipated part of the development of contemporary ideas with visionary clarity. But his own vast output escapes the late nineteenth century only occasionally: in the use of chromatic, expressive dissonance in a few late works like the *Elegies* for piano of 1907 and in the intense contrapuntal chromaticism of some of the other keyboard works. Busoni's chromatic practice, like Reger's, was as much a return to eighteenth-century ideals as a derivation from Wagner; however, the idea of a "neo-Classical" chromaticism seems to have had no important development (except for a few works of Schoenberg, to be discussed later).

The tonal tradition in its most typical forms is Italo-German, and it can be said to have declined in Central Europe by virtue of its own inner, contrapuntal, chromatic development. Elsewhere this tonal tradition was much weaker, and once the overwhelming domination of Italian and German style had been shaken off, other, older traditions could rise to the surface and lead to new ideas. In Eastern Europe, for example, the Romantic rediscovery of folk music had a decided impact on tonal ideas. While the folk music of Germany, Austria, and Italy actually seems to have accommodated itself over the years to classical tonal organization,[3] the traditional music of Hungary and the Slavic countries always maintained its modal independence, and even the so-called Hungarian-Gypsy music of Liszt and Brahms[4] suggests certain melodic usages (and a harmonic carry-over) at variance with common diatonic tonal usage. Eastern modal ideas show up in the work of composers

---

[2] Mahler had a more direct and superficial influence, most notably on the modern Russian symphony but also on Kurt Weill, Leonard Bernstein, and certain kinds of music theater.

[3] For pre-tonal forms in German folk music, see early chorale settings; in Italy, a pre-tonal folk music has persisted outside of the main urban centers.

[4] Both of these composers had, of course, a direct influence on posterity. Schoenberg has written eloquently of the intellectual impact of Brahms on modern musical thought; Liszt, who was an innovator in practically every musical domain, has been said to have prefigured nearly everyone from Wagner to Berg but, ironically, his late music, innovative to the point of atonality, seems to have had little direct influence.

like Dvořák and the Russian "Five" (although tonally accommodated); in the case of a Mussorgsky, such ideas were decisive in forming a melodic and harmonic style which often contradicted prevailing contrapuntal-tonal notions. (The performing editions of Rimsky-Korsakov and other well-wishers were designed to eliminate or smooth out such "crudities.")

One highly developed Western art-music tradition has consistently remained somewhat outside the central development: that of France. Although the classical abstract formulation of tonal usage derives from the theoretical writings of Rameau, the actual evolution of French practice has taken place quite independently of the Italian-German tonal evolution. Characteristic of this independence is a metrical, rhythmic, and phrase flexibility closely related to the free, non-accentual character of the French language. This relative freedom from "tonic" accent confers on French music a quality of fluid, poetical prose as opposed to the metrical "verse" construction of Italian and German music; in turn, French music often seems much less directional and much more coloristic. The independence was very persistent in the eighteenth century; it was less noticeable in the nineteenth, when French composers—Berlioz was a notable exception—tended to accept classical Italian and German rhythmic and structural forms. The influence of Wagner was as decisive in the latter part of the century as that of the classical masters had been earlier, but Wagner at least could suggest fluid prose and expressive color, and the French version of Wagnerian chromaticism is a very distinct if minor development with consequences for the twentieth century. One characteristic form of Wagnerian chromaticism came to France by way of Belgium through the work and influence of César Franck (1822–1890). Franck and the Franckophiles, Vincent d'Indy (1851–1931) and Ernest Chausson (1855–1899; d'Indy's pupil, Albert Roussel [1869–1937], carried the line into still another generation) used extensive schemes of chromatic modulation combined with a flexible, asymmetrical sense of line and a tendency for rich, chromatic harmonies to shade off into color inflections in a very French way. Henri Duparc (1848–1933; who corresponds somewhat to Hugo Wolf), Guillaume Lekeu (1870–1894; another Belgian), and Emmanuel Chabrier (1841–1894; at different times the most Wagnerian and the most anti-Wagnerian of French composers) all made their Bayreuth pilgrimages. Equally important, the literary influence of Wagner, particularly as transmitted through the work of the "symbolist" poets, played no small role in creating the rather special esthetic and intellectual atmosphere of *fin-de-siècle* Paris.

The tendency towards a flexible melodic style joined to a rich, sensuous, subtle harmonic palette is most highly developed (and most free of Wagnerism) in the work of Gabriel Fauré (1845–1924), a composer who developed his poetic, evanescent chromaticism within the bounds of a complex, refined sense of tonal structure. Fauré, like Reger and Mahler, never left the confines of functional tonality, and his influence on later developments was only peripheral, but the freedom and subtlety of his style represent the artistic climate in France in the late nineteenth century and suggest, in a way parallel to Debussy's, the coming tonal revolutions.

BIBLIOGRAPHICAL NOTES

The sources of contemporary music have only recently received serious attention. One of the few classic studies in this field, Ernst Kurth's *Romantische Harmonik und ihrer Krise in Wagner's "Tristan"* (2nd ed., Berlin, 1923), has never been translated into English. Elliott Zuckerman's *The First Hundred Years of Wagner's "Tristan"* (New York, 1964) is stronger on literary than musical matters; the same is true for the more recent study by Anne D. Sessa, *Richard Wagner and the English* (Rutherford and London, 1979). Carl Dahlhaus's *Between Romanticism and Modernism: Four Studies in the Music of the Later Nineteenth Century* (trans. Mary Whittal, Berkeley, CA, 1980) discusses both the literary and musical influences of Wagner; J. Peter Burkholder's brief article "Viewpoint: Brahms and Twentieth-Century Classical Music" (*Nineteenth-Century Music* 8/1 [1984], 75–83) suggests that the breakdown of tonality was a crisis of purpose rather than musical language. Jim Samson's often illuminating study *Music in Transition: A Study of Tonal Expansion and Atonality 1900–1920* (New York, 1977) deals in part with the reinterpretation of tonality by Liszt and other late-Romantic composers as well as by Busoni, Debussy, Bartók, and Stravinsky.

More specialized books include Dika Newlin's *Bruckner, Mahler, Schoenberg* (2nd ed., London, 1979); David B. Greene's *Mahler: Consciousness and Temporality* (New York, 1984; a psychoanalytical/phenomenological approach to the life and music of Mahler); Henry-Louis de La Grange's *Mahler* (vol. I, Garden City, NY, 1973; the French multi-volume publication has been updated [1979, 1983, 1984] to incorporate many new facts discovered since 1971); Donald Mitchell's multi-volume study *Gustav Mahler: The Early Years* (London and Boston, 1980), *The Wunderhorn Years* (London, 1975), and *Songs and Symphonies of Life and Death, Interpretations and Annotations* (Berkeley, 1985); and Norman Del Mar's three-volume study *Richard Strauss* (London, 1962, 1969, 1973). The literature on Busoni includes a biography by Edward J. Dent (London, 1933, repr. 1974); Larry Sitsky's recent study *Busoni and the Piano* (Westport, CT, 1986), and Daniel M. Raessler's article "Schoenberg and Busoni: Aspects of Their Relationship" (*Arnold Schoenberg Institute Journal* 7/1 [June 1983], 6–27). The Busoni *Sketch* is available in English translation (reprinted in *Three Classics in the Aesthetic of Music*, New York, 1962), as are the various writings of Schoenberg: *Theory of Harmony* (Berkeley, CA, 1978; paperback ed., 1983) and *Style and Idea* (ed. Leonard Stein, trans. Leo Black, paperback ed., with revisions, Berkeley, CA, 1984).

On the French background there is Martin Cooper's *French Music from the Death of Berlioz to the Death of Fauré* (London, 1951), Serge Gut and Daniele Pistone's *La musique de chambre en France de 1870 à 1918* (Paris, 1978), and Laurence Davies's *César Franck and His Circle* (London, 1970). Romain Rolland's *Musicians of Today* (Paris, 1908; Eng. trans. New York, 1915) has the status of a document. Recent biographies of French composers include Robert Orledge on Fauré (New York, 1982) and Ralph S. Grover on Ernest Chausson (Lewisburg and London, 1980).

THREE

THE REVOLUTION: PARIS

In the late nineteenth century, Paris regained its old position as intellectual and artistic center of the West. Native musical tradition was not strong: the Opéra reigned supreme and the operatic tradition was that of Meyerbeer, Offenbach, and the Italians tempered by the genteel sentimentalities of Gounod; there was a revival of symphonic and chamber music, but it was dominated by a watered-down classicism. The answer to this "philistinism" and "academicism" was Wagnerism; Wagner had an overwhelming impact on French intellectual life not yet absorbed or overcome. But the Paris of the post-Prussian War period had an enormous intellectual and artistic vitality of its own, especially in the visual arts (academic and impressionist) and in literature; the line that descends from Baudelaire to Mallarmé and to the twentieth century also left deep traces on the history of music. *Fin-de-siècle* esthetics and a conscious search for new forms and new means combined with a rather special French refinement and a subtle, abstracted sensuality. We recognize the kind of sensibility that we find in Mallarmé also in Fauré and, especially, in Debussy.

There was another aspect to the intellectual style of the times: a mordant, dry, ironic wit. In the visual arts, it appears in the work of an artist like Toulouse-Lautrec; in music, it turns up in Chabrier as a conscious antidote to Wagnerism. But its most important musical exponent was Erik Satie (1866–1925), a remarkable innovator who displayed more genius than talent. Satie came to music late and struggled to find the form for his ideas. His remarkable inventions were almost offhand: casual, amusing discoveries

Erik Satie by Jean Cocteau. Meyer Collection, Paris. Reproduction forbidden.

which took shape as literary-musical wit. Satie constructed aphorisms and then turned them into simple musical expressions. As often as not, the point is in the idea, the title: "Cold Pieces," "Three Pieces in the Form of a Pear," "Truly Flabby Preludes," "Automatic Descriptions," "Disagreeable Impressions." However, the larger works (the ballets *Parade* [1917] and *Relâche* [1924] and the remarkable setting from Plato, *Socrate* [1918]) as well as a few of the shorter pieces display a quality of simple invention that transcends many of the shortcomings and reflect the extraordinary originality of Satie's mind.

Satie was by no means the only example of a French composer at the turn of the century who tried to break with the past in an attempt to make music a vehicle for some kind of literary taste; the thing was in the air. And, ultimately, although Satie had both an immediate and a long-range influence, a great deal of his work was in fact produced in the shade of composers better fitted than he to accomplish the break with traditional formal techniques, a break he so clearly foreshadowed. But he continues to occupy a special place in the history of recent music not only as the godfather to a generation of composers but also as a spiritual grandfather of some latter-

Left to right: Stravinsky, Diaghilev, Cocteau, and Satie (dated 1917). Sketch by M. Larionov. Meyer Collection, Paris. Reproduction forbidden.

day avant-gardism. He was the first to *use* sound—disconnected, static, objectified sound—in an abstract way, essentially divorced from the organizational and structural principles of tonal form and development.

DEBUSSY

The problem of finding new modes of discourse, of replacing classical developmental-variational principles of tonality with new content and new expressive form, occupied the best musical minds in the decades around 1900. In Germany and Austria, the process had a strongly evolutionary aspect, growing out of the inner development of the tradition itself. In France, where classical tonality was much less firmly rooted or perhaps more artificially cultivated, the break occurred earlier and with greater ease and thoroughness. We have discussed a number of people who helped to bring this about, but by far the most important was Claude Debussy. Debussy was, from the start, further removed from Bach and Beethoven than Schoenberg ever could be; *La Mer* has less to do with fugues and sonatas than even the most radical works of the Viennese.

Debussy (1862–1918), like most French composers, was intensively trained in the Central European classical tradition. The Paris Conservatoire, where he spent eleven years, has—since its directorship, 1821–1841, by an Italian, Luigi Cherubini—specialized in the very principles, techniques, and forms which have not been especially characteristic of French musical creativity.[1] To some extent, French music has been stifled by this, but for Debussy it was a source of strength. All the first great innovators of the twentieth century—Debussy, Stravinsky, Ives, the Viennese—met the challenge of the classical tradition and the classical disciplines in one way or another. But it is a curious fact that Debussy was the only one to have had an intense classical conservatory training. For Schoenberg, the tradition provided an intellectual model and suggested underlying universal principles; for Debussy, it was a matter of *métier*, of fluency, and of complete, natural control.

Debussy's innovations, while expressed in great part in instrumental works, were based to some extent on the special and subtle inflections of French language and poetry; on the character and length of sound (as opposed to strong metrical and rhythmic accent); on the fluid and non-symmetrical organization of French meter, rhythm, accent, and phrase. Debussy extended this kind of rhythmical and phrase organization into every aspect of music;

---

[1] This is not so surprising as it might seem. In the history of art, theory generally *follows* practice and codification is most easily performed, not by a practitioner, but by someone on the outside—in space or time—looking in.

Claude Debussy. Sketch by Henri Detouche. Meyer Collection, Paris. Reproduction forbidden.

thus melodic, harmonic, rhythmic, and timbral ideas are blended and unified in essentially new ways and become different aspects of a single basic conception. Sounds and sound patterns are related to one another by arbitrary and sensual aural criteria rather than by the old necessities of motion and resolution governed by linear, tonal logic. Debussy was able—and this was his genius—to organize these new relationships into new forms which retain their psychological validity and structural logic without depending on previously accepted conventions of tonal language and structure. In *Tristan*, even ultra-chromaticism and the most extended false resolutions are still governed by the laws of tonal motion and expectation; in *Pelléas et Mélisande*, no such criteria are operative. Debussy's vocabulary of sound is chosen for its empirical (i.e., "sensual") qualities, and the motion from one sound pattern to the next is built on intervallic relationships and on parallelisms of structure, using very clear, immediate, and localized aural and psychological insights. In Debussy's earlier work, the simple and classical patterns of contrast and return still govern the large forms; later even these vanish, to be replaced by ongoing associative forms which depart from one point and, without the necessity of substantive recapitulation, arrive at another. In a sense, this non-narrative, non-cyclical form—achieved by Debussy in a work like the ballet *Jeux* of 1912—represents the larger intellectual tendency of the pre-World War I revolutions which we call "atonal." While our experience of complex chromatic forms over the last sixty or seventy years allows us to accept the new tonal relationships in Debussy as unexceptional, there is no question that works like *La Mer* and *Jeux* mark as thorough and significant a break with the tonal tradition as any of the most complex works of Schoenberg or his colleagues.

Like many of his contemporaries, Debussy was influenced not only by the free rhythmic flow of the French language but also by the prevailing literary culture of France. Its esthetic, partly Wagnerian in origin, was allied with the late-Romantic ideal of expressive musical poetry, and until his last few works, Debussy was generally concerned with expressive subjects, programs, and texts closely associated with the work of the "symbolist" poets: the *Prélude à l'après-midi d'un faune* of 1892–1894 (after Mallarmé), *La Mer* of 1902–1905, *Images* for orchestra of 1905–1912, the various sets of piano pieces written between the 1880s and 1910, and, of course, the songs and theatrical works. It is a mistake to ignore the importance of non-musical, poetic ideas on the development of Debussy's musical ideas and the forms of his musical thought, but it is equally important to realize that his expressive and poetic intent can be understood in musical terms as well

If is often suggested that the whole-tone scale forms the basis of Debussy's musical technique, with the implication that the old seven-note major-minor scale hierarchies were replaced by the ambiguities of the six-note whole-step scale. However, in point of fact, whole-tone relationships are used by Debussy in conjunction with, or as part of, much more complex melodic and harmonic usages—interlocking pentatonic forms, for example—based on a fundamental principle of symmetry. The whole-tone scale itself is, of course, symmetrical, as are most of the harmonies associated with it (e.g., the augmented triad). But there are many Debussyan patterns based on symmetrical structures that are not necessarily derived from whole-tone scales at all; some of these are individual events, others are combinations of events generally arranged in parallels. Characteristic are chains of triads, of seventh, ninth, or eleventh chords, or of related structures built on fourths or major seconds arranged in pentatonic, whole-tone, diatonic, or chromatic patterns, the last-named including free, sliding chromatic shifts based on "secondary-function" chords but often arrived at through parallel or sequential motion. This parallel, symmetrical (rather than contrapuntal, contrary) motion has its counterpart in the rhythmic and phrase structure, also built on parallelism and symmetry. Thus the principle which obtains in the choice of chord and melodic line extends to the broad melodic and harmonic movement of Debussy's music and ultimately determines the larger motion and form of each piece (see Appendix; Example 3-1).

The fine, elegant tonal imagination of Debussy is thus given a much wider and more profound field of action and expression. In traditional tonality, the musical motion, expression, and, ultimately, structure are all interrelated functions of the unequal and fundamentally asymmetrical character of the basic material—the major-minor scales and triads, with their unequal intervals and hierarchies of motion and value. Debussy was the first composer to substitute successfully another set of values, a musical thought based on symmetrical patterns and structures with a highly weakened directional motion and thus a very ambiguous sense of tonal organization. Debussy consciously exploits this ambiguity. He sets floating, symmetrical ideas against clear, tonal cadences. Identical repeated phrases and harmonies seem to change meaning according to content. Traditional tonal devices such as sequences delay or extend the feeling of suspended tonality even further, eventually establishing more than one area of tonal ambiguity; the music seems to hover between suspended polarities. In Debussy's music, these ambiguities are built into the structure of the musical thought.

One result of this ambiguity of tonal relationships is that rhythm, phrase, dynamics, accent, and tone color are largely freed from direct dependence on tonal motion; they tend to gain an importance in the musical process almost equal to that of melody and harmony. This development was as significant in a positive sense as the breakdown of the old tonality was in a negative one. The rhythmic and phrase forms, the dynamics, the articulation, and the tone color are as basic in the music of Debussy as the actual choice of pitches, or very nearly so. In a sense, the qualities of the musical ideas are often so interdependent that the various components of the sound seem to shade off into one another; that is, under certain circumstances, pitch almost functions as color, color takes the place of line (there is often a clear "rhythm" of color changes), dynamics and articulation provide rhythmic and phrase impetus, and so forth. There are individual sound patterns and even isolated sounds—each endowed in equal part with pitch, a dynamic, accent, rhythm, and color—which seem to create their own context and which form the basic ideas of each piece. These ideas are valid, so to speak, in their own terms, for their value as sound and perhaps for their psychological effect—not for their position in a directional development or ongoing variations. They build up in relatively static structures organized in the juxtaposition of linked and parallel ideas. Tonal centers are ultimately established, not by linear motion, but by the focusing and refocusing of shifting, fluctuating patterns which in themselves are fluid yet unified and full of specific, identifiable character, and which combine through analogy, juxtaposition, and symmetry. An analogy might be drawn from one of Debussy's own musical "subjects": the sea, whose waves form a powerful surge of undulating motion in varying crests and troughs without necessarily any real movement underneath.

The development of Debussy's style can be traced with a great deal of clarity from the derivative, even Wagnerian sound of his early music to the final, remarkable abstract pieces of the war years. The Baudelaire songs of 1890, the String Quartet of 1893, and the *Prélude à l'après-midi d'un faune* are the first mature works. The composer's style is completely established in his opera based on Maeterlinck, *Pelléas et Mélisande* (1893–1902), in the *Chansons de Bilitis* and in the Verlaine songs of the period 1898–1904, the *Estampes* and *Images* for piano of 1903, 1905, and 1907, and the orchestral *La Mer* and *Images*. A still greater broadening of techniques and resources can be found in works around 1910: the *Trois Ballades de François Villon*, the two sets of *Préludes* for piano, the music for d'Annunzio's *Le Martyre de St. Sébastien*, and the ballet *Jeux*. The last works of 1915–1917—the twelve *Etudes* for piano and the sonatas for cello and piano, for flute, viola, and harp, and for violin and piano—suggest striking new directions. For the first time since the String Quartet, Debussy abandoned literary associations. In the *Etudes*, Debussy set himself quite literally a series of specifically technical-creative problems to solve, problems which lie at the very root of new musical organization and communication. In the sonatas, he similarly attacked questions of musical structure and of the organization of thought projected onto broader, simpler planes of large, neo-tonal form and intimate, precise communication.

AFTER DEBUSSY

The musical manner of Debussy has been widely imitated, and an attempt has been made to elevate this manner into a style or school which has, by analogy with the terminology of art history, been dubbed "impressionism." Musical impressionism seems to imply certain kinds of colorful "tone painting" based on Debussy's harmonic and melodic palette and, especially, on a range of shimmering, blended instrumental colors.[2] His originally rather subtle and esoteric manner quickly became adapted to the functions of background music, partly because of the easy identification of coloristic

---

[2] A much better and more precise analogy could be drawn between the music of Debussy and the organic forms and sensual esthetic of Art Nouveau and related literary movements.

resources, partly because the fluidity and non-assertive character of the style made it an ideally unobtrusive and psychologically apt material for dramatic accompaniment, and partly because the static ambiguity of the tonal motion made it easy to create musical materials of flexible length without assertive beginning, middle, or end.

Nevertheless, in spite of the fact that there has been—and continues to be—a good deal of Debussyism in a superficial sense, there has never been any real Debussy school. If the minor imitators and movie-music pastiches are ruled out, the "impressionist" movement boils down to Debussy himself, a few early works of Maurice Ravel (1875–1937), and a handful of pages in the work of a few outlanders. Ravel's early style does derive from Debussy although, in a few cases, Ravel's development seems parallel to or even in advance of Debussy. It is in his piano music, especially, and in his music for the theater that Ravel's originality and independence from Debussy can be best understood. *Jeux d'eau* of 1901, *Miroirs* of 1904–1905, and *Gaspard de la nuit* of 1908 (all for piano), the one-act comic opera *L'Heure espagnole* of 1907–1909, and the ballet *Daphnis et Chloé* of 1909–1912 are the works in which Ravel remains closest to Debussy and the conventional notions of "impressionism"; but, already in these pieces, the more classical orientation of Ravel is evident. Ravel is fastidious as to surface detail and closely concerned with a recognizable frame of external structure; he is involved with line, clarity of articulation, brilliant, idiomatic writing, and careful tonal organization. In the end, Ravel may be classified as a classicist; his particular contribution might be described as a unique ability to combine the rich harmonic and melodic vocabulary of ninths and elevenths with free motion of parallel chords and chromatic sidesteps, all animating simple forms which are themselves the result of a new and clear sense of tonal movement.

There is scarcely another composer of note who can be described as "impressionist." Paul Dukas (1865–1935), an elegant and fastidious composer of very limited output, was influenced by Debussy, and the very prolific Florent Schmitt (1870–1958) has sometimes been classified in this way. The English composer Frederick Delius (1862–1934), who lived a good part of his life in France, evolved something of an original version of the Debussy manner, and the style is represented in America by the talented Charles Griffes (1884–1920), who died just at a point when he was developing a personal idiom, free of Debussyism. The list is hardly longer than that; as we have seen, Debussy himself was hardly a "Debussyiste" by the end of his life.

Nevertheless, Debussy's influence on the music of this century was incalculable, and it has hardly ended. The techniques which he evolved are most obviously in evidence in the work of a number of non-Germanic composers—most notably Vaughan Williams but also De Falla, Bartók and Kodály, Ernest Bloch, Respighi and Puccini, one or two of the Russians—who were all in one way or another interested in establishing some kind of new tonal-modal style based on a particular local musical tradition or language that lay outside of or broke the bonds of classical tonality. For them, the new Debussyan vocabulary offered a set of expressive and formal resources within which a great variety of ideas and materials could be expanded, integrated, and made expressive in terms of a high artistic style. Also, the new free harmonic techniques could often be combined with modal melodic tradition—a fact which Debussy himself exploited and which suggested a natural way of using folk material without squeezing it into pre-cut tonal patterns.

The long-range influence of Debussy has, however, been even more profound. The disassociation of the individual sound event, the elevation of timbre and articulation to a point equal to harmony and melody, the use of constructions free from tonal patterns and based on symmetry, and the consequent building up of new static and associative forms are all important twentieth-century ideas which find a point of origin in the work of Debussy. In this broader sense, the French composer's influence is traceable in the developing ideas of Schoenberg, Berg, and Webern as well as of Stravinsky, Bartók, and Varèse; indeed, it can be found in most of the principal trends of the century and is still significant in the work of certain latter-day avant-gardists, notably Pierre Boulez.

THE RUSSIANS

The role of Paris as an international artistic and intellectual center in the years preceding World War I was enhanced by the presence in the French capital of a considerable number of foreign artists. Of the musicians resident in or closely associated with Paris, the Russians were the most important. Russian musical thought had, throughout the nineteenth century, maintained some independence from that of Central Europe, and the continuing vitality of older folk and liturgical traditions was a continuous challenge to classical tonality. The Russianism of "The Five" provided non-Western elements that were occasionally more than decorative; in Mussorgsky's music the Russian materials are deeply felt and penetrate to the core of the style. Mussorgsky's so-called crudities were in reality departures from the accepted Western tonal norms; even Rimsky-Korsakov could not conventionalize Mussorgsky's forms.

At the beginning of this century, Russian art was in the vanguard of European development and it continued to be so well into the Soviet period. The Stalinization of Soviet music and the subsequent insistence on a national and popular symphonic style have served to obscure the work and the very existence of an important and original group of Russian composers active in

Pablo Picasso and Igor Stravinsky by Jean Cocteau. Meyer Collection, Paris. Reproduction forbidden. "After the reprise of 'Sacre' and 'Parade' [Satie ballet for which Picasso did the decor], Picasso comforts Stravinsky. He drank too much vodka."

the first quarter of the century, including the remarkable Nikolay Roslavets (1881–1944), who anticipated aspects of twelve-tone music, and Alexander Mosolov (1900–1973), a kind of Soviet Varèse who experimented with percussion materials.

The first Russian composer, however, to influence the course of Western musical thought was Alexander Skriabin (1872–1915). A little younger than Debussy, two years older than Schoenberg, and influenced by both,

Stravinsky playing *Le Sacre du printemps*, 1913. Sketch by Jean Cocteau. Meyer Collection, Paris. Reproduction forbidden.

Skriabin was an original creative mind who never quite found new forms for his profoundly new ideas. He was an excellent pianist who started out as a Chopinist and used the piano all his life as the medium for his most original and successful creations.[3] He was a declared visionary, and the gradual suspension of tonality in his music was associated with a kind of post-Wagnerian chromatic mysticism. Whatever its mainsprings, his style eventually evolved into a kind of exotic modality (based on a scale of three whole steps, minor third, and a minor second) and, finally, into a crystalline, motionless atonality built on harmonies compounded in fourths. Some of the early theorists of contemporary music (including Schoenberg) attempted to systematize the use of harmonic structures built in fourths by analogy with the old constructions in thirds. But the parallels are misleading and we can see today that the major "theoretical" significance of the fourth lies in the fact that, along with the minor second, it is the basic unit of a series

---

[3] Skriabin was influenced by Chopin and Liszt; he was, like them, a performing musician who linked Eastern European origins with a Central European style and (to a point) French taste, to produce a series of innovations and, in the end, a style of great originality. Skriabin's influence might seem greater if we knew more about chromatic music in the Soviet Union.

which generates the complete tempered chromatic scale. In any case, Skriabin's use of fourths was based on symmetrical structures and clearly derived from an intensified, dissonant "impressionistic" chromaticism.

Skriabin toured a great deal as a pianist and lived for periods in Paris and other parts of Western Europe, but he died before the Revolution forced the fateful split between Russian expatriate and Soviet artist. Sergey Prokofiev (1891–1953), after producing a series of highly original works based on a kind of dissonant, rhythmical, sophisticated primitivism, left (Czarist) Russia for Paris, where he elaborated a symphonic and theatrical style of considerable scope. He later went back to (Soviet) Russia to develop a lyric-symphonic popular Soviet manner. On the other hand, Stravinsky (1882–1971), who derived from Rimsky-Korsakov and started out as a purveyor of stylized Russian and Eastern exoticisms in Paris, never went back but settled in the West, developing a mature style which was to become the dominant influence in Western music for more than a quarter-century. Stravinsky's first important works were written under the influence of his teacher, Rimsky-Korsakov, tempered by a little Debussy and a decidedly original and volatile imagination. Only the use of orchestral color and a few piquant harmonies and rhythms amid the genteel exoticism of *L'Oiseau de feu* of 1909–1910 and the picturesque and wry, fantastic humor of *Petrouchka* of the following year suggest what was to follow: the violence of *Le Sacre du printemps* and the establishment of a new kind of tonality.

Le Sacre was completed in 1912,[4] the same year that Debussy composed his *Jeux* and Schoenberg his *Pierrot lunaire*. Just as *Jeux* suggests the crisis of form and *Pierrot* that of harmonic and melodic organization, *Le Sacre* marks a definitive break with the old rhythm-phrase-accent structures. In Stravinsky's pivotal ballet score, rhythm and accent are clearly divorced from their old dependence on melodic and harmonic tonal organization and motion; indeed, if anything, the harmonic sense of the music is actually closely dependent on the rhythmic and accentual organization. The way things happen in *Le Sacre* is determined by the almost kinesthetic impact of violent rhythmic articulation and accents organized in asymmetrical, shifting patterns. The harmonic structures and simple melodic patterns—many of them derived from Russian and other folk sources—are virtually isolated; "chords" and melodic bits appear as individual static objects; they relate to each other often only by virtue of patterns of repetition and of shifting metrical accent. Ideas based on simple, insistent repetition gain long-range power and significance through the juxtaposition of contrasting patterns and planes and through their constant rhythmic and metrical reinterpretation (see Appendix; Example 3-2).

---

[4] Stravinsky did not move to Paris until 1920, and *Le Sacre* was composed in French Switzerland, where the composer lived between 1910 and 1920. But it is with the Paris of the Russian Ballet that the work is inextricably associated.

Everything in *Le Sacre* is asserted; nothing falls into place naturally or by expectation. This is a piece of high artifice in the best sense: the idea that it is a "primitive" work is misleading; it is about primitivism, but is not itself primitive at all. The quality of disassociated insistence, combined with a striking use of chordal, non-contrapuntal dissonance, produces the effect of an arbitrary motionless, elemental power, but in actual fact every gesture is carefully calculated and the dynamic articulation of the whole is almost schematic. *Le Sacre* is less obviously "atonal" and seemingly more primitive than corresponding works of the Viennese school only because it is not linear-chromatic in the German tradition. But it presents and resolves some very complex psychological and musical problems. Disassociated ideas appear as artifacts, set into block structures built up in layers. The piece unfolds in time, not through forward motion in the old manner, but by way of the explosive rhythmic release of confined and volatile musical energies. *Le Sacre* is a work that takes shape, not through the extension of line and counterpoint, but through the juxtaposition of static levels of sound and statement, dividing up and punctuating psychological time with rhythm and accent, statement and articulation. For Stravinsky, *Le Sacre* was in many ways a beginning, middle, and end; he quickly went on to other things. Nevertheless, many of his characteristic and fundamental techniques first appeared in this work.

BIBLIOGRAPHICAL NOTES

For the intellectual climate in late nineteenth-century France, see A. G. Lehmann, *The Symbolist Aesthetic in France* (Oxford, 1950), and the more recent articles by Jean-Michel Nectoux, "Musique, symbolisme, et art nouveau: notes pour une esthétique de la musique française fin de siècle," in *Art nouveau, Jugendstil, und Musik*, ed. Jürg Stenzl (Zurich, 1980), pp. 13–30, and Rey M. Longyear, "Towards the Fin de Siècle: Stylistic Change and Symbolist Connotations in French Music" (*Miscellanea Musicologica* 13 [1984], 75–96). The two standard biographies of Erik Satie are by Pierre-Daniel Templier (trans. L. French and David S. French, Cambridge, MA, 1969) and Rollo Myers (New York, 1968). *The Writings of Erik Satie* (collected and trans. by Nigel Wilkens, London, 1980) provide a revealing glimpse into Satie's persona. Alan M. Gilmore's "Erik Satie and the Concept of the Avant Garde" (*Musical Quarterly* 69/1 [1983], 104–19) traces his influence on later composers.

Robin Holloway's *Debussy and Wagner* (London, 1979) and Carolyn Abbate's article "Tristan in the Composition of *Pelléas*" (*Nineteenth-Century Music* 5/2 [Fall 1981], 117–41) discuss similarities between the two operas, as well as borrowings of Debussy from Wagner. Edward Lockspeiser's two-volume study *Debussy: His Life and Mind* (5th ed., London, 1980) paints a psychosociological portrait of the composer. The writings of Debussy, many under the pen name M. Croche, can be found in *Debussy on Music. The Critical Writings of the Great French Composer* (collected and introduced by François Lesure, trans. and ed. by Richard Langham Smith, New York, 1977). Recent contributions to the scholarly literature on Debussy and his works include Robert Orledge's *Debussy and the Theatre* (Cambridge, England, 1982) and Roy Howat's *Debussy in Proportion: A Musical Analysis* (Cambridge, England, 1983). The analysis of *Jeux* by Herbert Eimert (in Vol. 5 of *Die Reihe*) is still a classic. For discussions of Debussy's tenuous connection with the impressionist movement, see Stefan Jarocinski's *Debussy: Impressionism and Symbolism* (London, 1976) and Ronald Byrnside's article "Musical Impressionism: The Early History of the Term" (*Musical Quarterly* 66/4 [1980], 522–37). For modern views of Debussy's importance and influence, see *Debussy et l'évolution de la musique au XXe siècle*, ed. Edith Weber (Paris, 1965), and Christopher Palmer's *Impressionism in Music* (New York, 1973). For one view of the relationship between Debussy and Ravel, see Charles Rosen's "Where Ravel Ends and Debussy Begins" in the May 1959 issue of *High Fidelity*. A more thorough study can be found in Werner Keil's *Untersuchungen zur frühen Klavierstils von Debussy und Ravel* (Wiesbaden, 1982).

Well-documented biographies exist for both Ravel and Griffes: see Arbie Orenstein's *Ravel: The Man and Musician* (New York, 1975) and Edward Maisel's *Charles T. Griffes: The Life of an American Composer* (updated, with a new introduction and notes, New York, 1984). There is also a descriptive catalogue of Griffes's works, compiled by Donna K. Anderson (Ann Arbor, 1983).

Only recently has there been any substantial work on Skriabin in English. James M. Baker's *The Music of Alexander Scriabin* (New Haven, 1986) is part of the new series Composers of the Twentieth Century. Faubion Bowers's *The New Scriabin: Enigma and Answers* (New York, 1973) and Hugh MacDonald's *Skriabin* (Oxford, England, 1978) are both geared towards the amateur rather than the student or scholar. An interesting study on mysticism in the Russian arts at the turn of the century is Martin Cooper's "Aleksandr Skryabin and the Russian Renaissance" (*Studi Musicali* 1/2 [1972], 327–56). The most thorough monograph on Skriabin is in French: Manfred Kelkel's *Alexandre Scriabine: sa vie, l'ésotérisme, et le langage musical dans son oeuvre* (Paris, 1978).

Two books recently translated from the Russian throw light on Stravinsky's Russian-derived early works: Boris Asaf'yev's *A Book About Stravinsky* (Leningrad, 1929; trans. Richard F. French, Ann Arbor, 1982) and Irina Vershinina's *Stravinsky's Early Ballets* (Moscow, 1967; trans. Larry G. Heien, Ann Arbor, 1986). For the background of Stravinsky's *Le Sacre du printemps*, see especially Richard Taruskin's "Russian Folk Melodies in *The Rite of Spring*" (*Journal of the American Musicological Society* 33/3 [Fall 1980], 501–43). Stravinsky's own *Chronicles of My Life* (London, 1976) and the many volumes of conversations with Robert Craft (*Conversations with Igor Stravinsky* [1959], *Memories and Commentaries* [1960], *Expositions and Developments* [1962], *Themes and Episodes* [1966], *Dialogues and a Diary* [1968], *Retrospectives and Conclusions*

[1969]) contain, according to Taruskin, "much willful distortion and myth-making" but nevertheless are an important source for Stravinsky's views. Analyses of *Le Sacre* can be found in *Relevés d'apprenti* by Pierre Boulez (Paris, 1966; English trans., New York, 1968) and Allen Forte's *The Harmonic Organization of the Rite of Spring* (New Haven, 1978). Stravinsky's sketches (1911–1913) for *Le Sacre* have been published in a facsimile edition (London, 1969) with commentary by Robert Craft.

FOUR

THE REVOLUTION: VIENNA

At the turn of the twentieth century, Paris had only one rival as the capital of Europe: Vienna, the seat of the Austro-Hungarian Empire and still a cultural crossroads. Vienna had once been the meeting place of the musical North and South, where the contrapuntal and instrumental techniques of the Germans mingled with the operatic and instrumental styles of Italy; the child of that Viennese marriage was the classical symphony. At the opening of this century, Vienna—the city of Freud and Schnitzler, of the Secessionist movement and Gustav Mahler—was to become the center of the transformation of that very classical tonality which had produced some of her greatest musical achievements.

SCHOENBERG

The author of that transformation, Arnold Schoenberg, was born in Vienna in 1874 (he was to die in Los Angeles in 1951). Schoenberg was essentially self-taught and always remained outside the powerful Vienna musical "establishment," but he entirely mastered traditional technique and he remained all his life involved in the study and teaching, not only of the classical disciplines but also of the profoundest and most universal aspects of the tradition. Schoenberg's starting point was, of course, Wagner—specifically the Wagner of *Tristan* and *Parsifal*—but his real intellectual antecedents were Bach, Beethoven, and Brahms. He began with the Wagnerian chromatic vocabulary, but from the start his basic concerns were with that intellectual integrity and totality of conception which—as he himself did so much to show—were basic to the classical tradition. Schoenberg's music is steeped in contrapuntal principles, in notions of the complex interrelationships between the vertical and the horizontal, and in concepts of total form; and it is through these ideas, older and more universal than classical tonality itself, that we can understand his development. He was also a thoroughgoing Hegelian; that is, he believed that music, like all aspects of human life, is part of a process of change and that there are universal and inevitable principles which control history and historical change. For Schoenberg the classical tradition of form—the concept of an all-pervasive intellectual organization—represented a universal principle, while the development of chromaticism represented a principle of change and evolution. The growth of equal temperament, chromaticism, and modulation had made possible the historical rise of functional tonality in the seventeenth and eighteenth centuries and destroyed it in the twentieth; thus tonality contained within itself from the start the seed of its own destruction.

Schoenberg's *Verklärte Nacht*—originally written for string sextet, later recast for string orchestra—and his massive *Gurrelieder* (orchestrated in 1910–1911), for soloists, chorus, and large orchestra, are still, in spite of their great originality, within the Wagnerian orbit. The works of the years 1902–1906—including the symphonic poem *Pelleas und Melisande* (after Maeterlinck and written at about the time that Debussy completed his operatic version), the First String Quartet in D minor, and the *Kammersymphonie*—show a steady but marked expansion of chromatic and contrapuntal techniques with the effect of delaying tonal resolutions over longer and longer periods. This is particularly true of the Chamber Symphony, in which whole-tone patterns and melodic and harmonic constructions in fourths appear. These techniques, related to those of Debussy, represent aspects of the total chromatic material: adjacent whole-tone scales as well as cycles of fourths will generate the complete chromatic gamut; also, half-step, whole-step, and fourth patterns have important characteristics of symmetry which distinguish them from the unbalanced, "hierarchical" structures of major-minor triads and scales. But Schoenberg was never primarily interested in working out the harmonic implications of these kinds of structures; his instinct (later formalized) was to seek out the meaning of harmonic structures in their relationship to line, and the technique of most of his later music (with some exceptions) is based on complex, chromatic, contrapuntal thinking with motivic and, increasingly, intervallic construction carried out within smaller and smaller revolutions of the total chromatic cycle. The Second String Quartet (completed 1908) shows the germ of the process within a single work; the composition begins well within the bounds of a contrapuntal, chromatic tonality, organized thematically, and then proceeds towards a linear chromaticism in which motives and intervals assume the structural force exerted formerly by tonal expectation and function. With a quotation of the popular Viennese tune "Ach, du lieber Augustin," Schoenberg bids an ironic farewell to tonality; the unexpected appearance of the human voice in the last two movements introduces a new conceptual universe with the words of Stefan Georg, "I feel a breath of air from other planets."

In the work which followed, the Three Piano Pieces, Op. 11 (completed 1909), the new non-tonal motivic chromaticism is completely dominant. The opening phrases still have a thematic function, but they also form fundamental sound matter which accounts for a good deal of what happens in the piece. There is, of course, simple thematic statement and development. But this must now function entirely without the aid of tonal motion, support, or superstructure. For the first time, every sound, every interval, every event has a unique and independent value, free of the hierarchies of tonal discourse—and equally free of the meanings formerly invested in them. Thematic development remains, but totally abstracted from its old contexts. But this was not enough for Schoenberg; it was necessary for him to transform all the musical materials so that the old balance and interaction between all aspects of the musical matter and discourse were restored in some new artistic synthesis. His solution, from the start, was to affirm a basic unity between linear and vertical events and to assert (not merely assume but aggressively assert, through the music itself) the fundamental identity of the individual elements of the tempered, chromatic scale (see Appendix; Example 4-1).

The piano pieces of Op. 11 were followed by a series of important works including the song cycle from Stefan George's "Book of the Hanging Gardens" (Op. 15, completed in 1908); the *Five Orchestral Pieces*, Op. 16, of 1909; the operas *Erwartung* and *Die Glückliche Hand* of 1909 and 1913; the *Six Little Piano Pieces*, Op. 19 (1911), *Herzgewächse* for soprano, celesta, harmonium, and harp, Op. 20 (also 1911); *Pierrot lunaire*, Op. 21, of 1912; and the *Four Orchestral Songs*, Op. 22, of 1913–1916. In all of these works, chromatic motion functions without tonal controls to indicate direction or to set up long-range relationships. There is a definite impulse towards the highest chromatic density and, as a result, a strong tendency towards the constant and repeated use of all twelve notes on an even and revolving basis. The pieces hold together not only through the extended use of motives in the thematic sense but also through the play of distinctive pitch combinations which give characteristic sound and shape to each work. The writing is contrapuntally conceived; but harmonic, articulative, timbral, and rhythmic statement may all be decisive in the character of the ideas and their organization. Thus, although we now see that the rhythmic and phrase structures of these works come out of their immediate late-tonal predecessors, these structures are not governed by a more basic (tonal) impulse but themselves give motion to the music.[1] Similarly, dynamics, accent, articulation, and coloration are indicated with unprecedented exactness and detail; nothing could be assumed any more from context; every event and every aspect of every event had a new and independent meaning. Each of the pieces sets forth its own musical, expressive, and formal premises. Every event is unique and each piece becomes the particular development and realization of unique and independent events which interrelate through the formal premises established by the piece itself.

Each of these works represents some very specific discoveries and explorations of new and distinctive aspects of musical experience. Some of these experiences are timbral; there is an enormous expansion of instrumental and orchestral technique in these works (as in comparable works of Berg and Webern), parallel to the expansion of materials and resources in the other musical domains. Instrumental colors formerly considered exceptional (mutes, *sul ponticello*, harmonics, fluttertonguing, etc.) are normal here, and techniques formerly of great rarity (*col legno battuto* and *tratto*, harmonics on the piano, etc.) are common. Instruments are used in extreme and unusual registers and dynamic levels, while an enormous variety of instrumental combinations are employed. The movement of the *Five Orchestral Pieces* entitled "Farben" is realized completely in terms of a series of subtle harmonic and timbral changes rung on a chordal structure. In the monodrama *Erwartung*, Schoenberg even abandons thematic-motivic structure in order to create a psychological-dramatic form based on ongoing chromatic line, on an articulation of changing intensities, and on an athematic intervallic structure; the kaleidoscopic orchestral treatment—in a consistent state of flux—is used to project a single, long psychological form and motion. Yet at the same time, in the *Three Pieces* for chamber ensemble, the last left unfinished in 1910, Schoenberg, like Webern, used an entirely different concept of the orchestra as an interweaving of solo sounds used to project miniature form. Conversely, the sound of a solo instrument is "scored" in timbral terms in a work like the *Six Little Piano Pieces*, Op. 19—studies in concise, aphoristic expression, each one of which articulates some brief, precise aspect of the chromatic experience.

---

[1] This is one reason why this aspect of this music, which today seems the most related to the past, appeared for a long time as the most difficult and impenetrable.

Nearly all of the techniques of Schoenberg's early period (including even brief reminiscences of tonality) are present in his *Pierrot lunaire*, twenty-one poems by Albert Giraud in a German translation, set for *Sprechstimme* and chamber ensemble. Characteristically, the work is severely patterned in a symmetrical and prophetically serialized arrangement: the poems, strict *rondeaux*, are grouped in three sets of seven each, and the chamber instrumentation is varied from song to song to obtain maximum differentiation. Motivic and intervallic constructions of every kind are used, incorporated into complex linear textures employing some of the classical canonic forms, sometimes closely organized, sometimes free. The vocal line, for the most part, is not actually sung but declaimed according to the *Sprechstimme* or "speech-song" technique first used by Schoenberg in his *Gurrelieder*: fixed pitches are indicated but the vocalist is directed only to approximate the curve of the notated line in a manner somewhere between song and speech. These songs—like many early works of Schoenberg—show an exceptional sensitivity to texture, and indeed the most basic and compelling formal aspect of the composition is its underlying organization in fluid, flashing, chromatic textures set into patterns of great severity and profundity.

It is not insignificant that the early pivotal works of Debussy, Stravinsky, and Schoenberg were involved with some kind of theatrical or literary statement; in Schoenberg's case, we can easily infer the importance of "expressive intent" in his chromatic revolution. But none of the great innovators of the twentieth century—least of all Schoenberg—was exclusively concerned with expressive detail, and the key problem was how to derive meaningful form out of the new materials generated by an expressive upheaval. Schoenberg was eventually to solve this problem in a characteristic and significant way, but in the meantime he devised a series of interim solutions which grew organically out of a remarkable series of new materials and new experiences. It is interesting to note, in the light of our latter-day new music—as it has emerged from a strict and intellectual serialism derived from the later work of Schoenberg and Webern—that their earlier explorations and approaches seem more remarkable and meaningful than ever.

BERG AND WEBERN

Schoenberg was the only one of the major composers of the early part of the century to have had important pupils, and two of these, Alban Berg (1885–1935) and Anton Webern (1883–1945), have a major place in the development of modern creative ideas. Convenient historical niches have been found for both: Berg has been described as an instinctual lyricist whose music links with tradition, while Webern has been seen as the intellectual, numerical abstractionist and the prophet of the avant-garde. Like most such generalizations, these labels cover a rich reality with a thin tissue of truths. Over half of Webern's output is vocal, for example, and many aspects of his work are a deliberate re-casting of traditional patterns in a new aphoristic style often conceived in terms of an underlying lyricism. In certain ways, Berg's music is actually more independent of tradition. It is true that Berg did not take up Schoenberg's twelve-tone idea with as much enthusiasm as

Alban Berg by Franz Rederer. Reproduced by permission of the Music Division of The New York Public Library.

Webern, but on the other hand, Berg was the most numerologically inclined of the three; his works are full of the most elaborate—often arbitrary—number sequences, precise and fearful symmetries carried out in every dimension and domain. Berg was the kind of "instinctualist" who placed great faith in elaborate, mystical, and arbitrary systems.

Berg's early songs and his Piano Sonata, Op. 1 (1906–1908), come out of a post-Wagnerian tradition touched by Debussy and the contrapuntal genius of Schoenberg. The sonata, with its chromatic lines pulsing in a

Portrait of Anton Webern by Oskar Kokoschka. Reproduced by permission of Annie Knize.

continual ebb and flow, is, by courtesy, tonal, but the shifting Skriabinesque harmonic impact of lines never articulates an organic tonal structure with any clarity. The piece resolves itself on its B-minor point of tonal departure, but the resolution is imposed. The real structure of the piece—like that of the related String Quartet, Op. 3 (1910)—is a complex of unresolved motions deriving from an inner web of motives and motivic intervals which never seem to articulate or be articulated by the ongoing harmonic flux. In a sense, these were the problems and contradictions with which Berg was to wrestle all his life; in the end, he was able to deal with them by recognizing the contradictions and building his music on the very concept of conflict and opposition.

The Four Songs, Op. 2, written between 1909 and 1910, derive from the late-Romantic lied tradition and from Wagnerian harmony tinged with not a little Debussy; yet the mixture is personal, and in the end it brings Berg close to an expressive atonality. The *"Altenberg" Lieder*, Op. 4, for soprano and orchestra (1912), are the first fully mature works in consistency and quality of invention and expression; they have Berg's characteristically intense linear-melodic style combined with a remarkable sense of color as an organic part of his conception. Berg's pieces grow out of an interplay between line (the concept of line and phrase which comes out of the tradition) and the play of color and texture (the most original and far-reaching aspect of his work).

Both the Clarinet and Piano Pieces, Op. 5 (1913), and the Three Orchestra Pieces, Op. 6 (1914–1915), achieve expressive form through a complex interplay of line, register, color, and texture. Op. 5 is a set of miniatures, closely related to contemporaneous pieces by Schoenberg and Webern. The pieces of Op. 6 are at the opposite extreme in scope and specific gravity, although their enormous contrapuntal density ends up by communicating analogous structures made out of timbre and sonority as well as line. The first movement is an early and exceptional example of a piece framed in percussion sound (but see Webern's Op. 6, No. 4); and the long, contrapuntal pile-up of the march-like third movement is built up through accumulations of orchestral sound. All of these works depend in great part on the effect of a complex irresolution. The Piano Sonata is virtually the last word in chromatic tonality, built up in shifting, oscillating, ambiguous harmonic structures which, nevertheless, are still presumed to have tonal and directional functions. In the following works, tonal functions persist only obliquely, and, in the Op. 6 pieces, ideas are expressed in dense, insistent lines weighted down with a tremendous expressive baggage and are almost impossible to clarify in performance. At times, Berg seems actually to be composing in textures and densities whose inner detail is complex, very free and variable, and not at all clearly defined aurally. The music is formed by the process of accumulation; Berg replaces the directional movement of tonality with a new and simpler kind of directionality based on the accumulation of tension and texture.

In *Wozzeck*, written between 1914 and 1922, Berg used the whole range of techniques found in his early works but now enormously expanded by the simultaneous use of a complex of dramatic, literary, and classical musical forms. Berg arranged a remarkable series of fragments by Georg Büchner into a kaleidoscopic libretto about a wretched army orderly who kills his unfaithful mistress and drowns himself. *Wozzeck* is, from one point of view, a social document cast in the theatrical and musical idiom of the early part of the century known as "expressionism." But on a profounder level, *Wozzeck* is about the human condition. The seemingly brutalized Wozzeck is a character of a certain grandeur; a visionary who, in his essential uniqueness and humanity, has just what the other characters lack—some natural nobility. Similarly, the music has a range and grandeur even in the almost touching sordidness and literalness of certain details. The intentionally vulgarized stage music stands next to a whole series of chamber and symphonic patterns which are sketched out underneath. Berg has imposed a classical shape or procedure on each of the fifteen scenes, and the larger forms of the acts are arranged as a series of interconnected formal patterns and symmetries; even in small details, number and system play a surprisingly decisive role. Berg, whose musical style was complex, free, and fluid, set himself rigid frameworks as if to give his musical imagination something solid from which to push off. In a sense, these rigid patterns serve something of the same function (on a simpler level, to be sure) as the twelve-tone conception in Schoenberg's later work. *Wozzeck* is, of course, in no sense twelve-tone—it was completed before Schoenberg's first twelve-tone pieces—but it does contain a prominent theme made up of all twelve notes (as does, for that matter, Strauss's *Also sprach Zarathustra* of 1895–1896), and there is often a striking tendency towards a total chromatic density. Indeed, the techniques run from simple triadic writing to the most intense "atonality," from *Sprechstimme* to lyric line, from diatonic melody to chromatic parlando, from chamber-ensemble counterpoint to broad orchestral strokes, from complex, busy motion to static intensity, from isolated, aphoristic punctuation to broad ongoing development. There are sonata and variation forms, *Leitmotiv* development, bits of popular song, small closed forms, and big, open psychological ones that ultimately determine the shape of the whole. The famous orchestral interlude that precedes the final scene takes on the function of summation; it universalizes the trivial and sordid tragedy. *Wozzeck* thus becomes more than a proletarian tragedy and more than the cumulative effect of a series of expressive and immediately comprehensible musical strokes. It remains the only post-Wagnerian, post-tonal work written in a heavily dissonant, chromatic style to have had a consistent theatrical success, and it remains the classic example of chromatic, "atonal" style combined with classical, closed forms applied, uniquely and with great psychological validity, to a modern, intense, dramatic expression.

Whereas Berg expanded Schoenberg's chromatic vision into large forms, dependent on tradition and psychological insight, Webern worked almost from the first in an opposite direction—towards the isolation of the single event, the disassociation of adjacent events within a context of the total interrelationship of the whole. Webern is at once the simplest and the most difficult of composers: the most and least intellectual, the easiest to take apart yet the hardest to follow, the most esoteric yet the most comprehensible, the most classical yet the most advanced, the most individual and personal yet the most influential and widely imitated. It is the simplicity of Webern's esthetic which explains the paradoxes. Webern's music consists of few notes set forth over a very short period of time; he reduced the problem of expressive form to the isolated, individual event and in so doing made every interpretation of the single event a possible one. It is from this point of view that Webern can be said to have re-invigorated a "classical" view of form while, at the same time, completing the destruction of tonal thinking.

Webern achieved his mature style very quickly, and his later development took place almost entirely within the narrow limits of his personal esthetic of clarity and concision. His principle is that of maximum variety within an extremely tight and condensed unity. Theme, development, and structural motion and relationship appear as a single sound or event. The unit is the interval between adjacent or simultaneous sounds—isolated, carefully defined, and packed with the maximum possible expressive and intellectual content. This concept of the interval had, even before the formulation of twelve-tone principles, the notion of succession as its fundamental principle. This linear-melodic basis of Webern's music (even its harmonic structure is a matter of the simultaneity of musical events whose origin can be found in linear succession) is reflected in the fact that over half of his works are vocal; among the early compositions, Op. 2, 3, 4, 8, 12, 13, 14, and 15 are for voices. All of these works employ traditional pitched singing— Webern never used *Sprechstimme*—and most of them use solo voices with piano and instruments in the tradition of the German lied.

Webern's detached, intense way of building up phrases by linking isolated tones and intervals and relating small groups of "melodic" tones also carries over into his early instrumental pieces as a way of unfolding very abstract and static formal conceptions in real time. These works are characterized by intense brevity, a pure, even lyric, quality, and a carefully constructed unity. The pitch successions, whether isolated or grouped in small cells, form a series of points which tend to fill up a distinct and very carefully defined musical space. Thus a succession will be divided between various registers and between various instruments and instrumental groupings. Colors and registers form a succession equally important to that of the pitches themselves, and all elements are closely grouped in clear and close relationships.

Already in the *Five Movements* for string quartet, Op. 5, of 1909, Webern applied elaborate principles of complex unity within a vastly restricted space. The *Six Pieces*, Op. 6, of the same year constitute a comparatively large work for a comparatively large orchestra, but the other works written from 1910 to 1914 turn again towards miniaturization: *Four Pieces* for violin and piano, Op. 7; *Six Bagatelles* for string quartet, Op. 9; *Five Pieces for Orchestra*, Op. 10; *Three Small Pieces* for cello and piano, Op. 11. There is, to be sure, more than a trace of late-Romantic statement still remaining— Mahler in an atonal nutshell! Some of the movements of Op. 5, 6, and 10 are comparatively large in scope and even the briefest gestures are full of intense, expressionist-Romantic *Angst*; indeed, the concentration and the intensity of the concentration itself are a result of the enormous, unreleased energies inherent in the laconic ideas and terse forms.

Webern's principle is always "maximization of the minimum": an intentionally limited collection of pitches, registers, colors, rhythms, accents, and articulations is revealed in its greatest possible variety. Portions of the complete chromatic gamut are filled in by half-steps (or, by the analogy of octave equivalence, by major sevenths and minor ninths) or, secondarily, by short figures arranged in whole-steps, thirds, and sixths; a good example of this is the first of the *Bagatelles*, Op. 9. The single event becomes striking and, most significantly, the single repetition, identity, or association becomes crucial; perhaps the most extreme example here is Op. 11, three movements in a bare handful of measures, a few tiny gestures, mere seconds of isolated sound emerging briefly from the silence that becomes, for Webern, a basic condition of the musical experience. The fourth piece of Op. 10 consists of six measures with only forty-eight separate note indications, about half of which are repeated notes (see Appendix; Example 4-2).

Webern did not pursue this line any further for a number of years; in the rest of his early period, up through his first twelve-tone works, he returned to vocal and polyphonic forms. Between 1915 and 1927—from his Op. 12 to Op. 19—he wrote exclusively for solo voices with instruments, recreating, often with considerable complexity, the forms of the polyphonic lied in terms of expressive chromatic ideas and dense, carefully controlled dissonant counterpoint.[2] Webern's "historical" contribution was certainly his elaboration—and eventually refinement and systemization—of techniques of construction through the isolation of the individual event and the tightly bound relationship of pitch, duration, intensity, and color, all expressed in terms of the maximum differentiation within the most minimal, economic sequence of events in the briefest, most compressed structural time span.

---

[2] It should be remembered that Webern was a trained musicologist whose doctoral dissertation, written under the guidance of Guido Adler, was on the music of the Renaissance composer Heinrich Isaac (ca. 1450–1517), one of the masters of polyphonic song.

But Webern, like Berg, had first to follow Schoenberg in the reconstruction of a complex counterpoint, based on the classical relationships but systematically chromatic and free of tonal implications. This symmetrical, chromatic, complex polyphony was, of course, to provide the basis for the twelve-tone consolidation to follow.

BIBLIOGRAPHICAL NOTES

For the background on this important period, see the writings by Schoenberg cited at the end of the last chapter, as well as his letters (ed. Erwin Stein, trans. Eithne Wilkens and Ernst Kaiser, New York, 1965). Charles Rosen's short monograph on Schoenberg (New York, 1975) paints an interesting portrait of Viennese musical life and attitudes towards contemporary music at the turn of the century and after. Hans H. Stuckenschmidt's biography of Schoenberg has been translated into English (New York, 1977); see also Willie Reich's *Schoenberg: A Critical Biography* (New York, 1971). Allen Forte's "Schoenberg's Creative Evolution: The Path to Atonality" (*Musical Quarterly* 64/2 [1978], 133–76) traces Schoenberg's change in compositional style through the use of set-theory analysis. The *Journal* of the Arnold Schoenberg Institute (Los Angeles, 1976–   ) is a prime source for articles on many aspects of Schoenberg's music and career; it also includes articles on Berg and Webern.

Willi Reich's biography of Berg (New York, 1965) supplants the often-cited biography by Redlich; it contains articles by Berg himself on Schoenberg and on "atonality" which are important documents of the period. Douglas Jarman's *The Music of Alban Berg* (paperback ed., Berkeley and Los Angeles, 1985) contains many expert analyses of the music and also reveals certain details of Berg's life and work that have come to light only within the past ten years.

Webern's *Path to the New Music* (trans., Bryn Mawr, PA, 1963; repr., New Jersey, 1975) consists of transcriptions of lectures given during the "twelve-tone period," but the historical transition from tonality to atonality in pre-World War I Vienna is also discussed. Walter Kolneder's *Anton Webern: An Introduction to His Works* (Berkeley, 1968) discusses all of the early works. See also the Webern issue of *Die Reihe* (No. 2, 1955, trans. Bryn Mawr, 1958) for articles and analyses of this composer's works. Hans and Rosaleen Moldenhauer's biography of Webern (London, 1978) is based to a large extent on manuscripts, diaries, and other writings donated by the composer's daughter to the Moldenhauer Archives. There is an annotated bibliography of works about Webern, compiled by Zoltan Roman (Detroit, 1983).

George Perle's *Serial Composition and Atonality* (5th ed., Berkeley, 1982) and Jim Samson's *Music in Transition* (cited on p. 15) contain specific discussions of pre–twelve-tone works. See also Allen Forte's *The Structure of Atonal Music* (2nd ed., New Haven, 1977) for one theoretical explanation of structure in the music of this period.

part three

The New Tonalities

FIVE

STRAVINSKY AND NEO-CLASSICISM

The result of new musical developments everywhere in the early years of the century was the weakening or the destruction of the accepted implications of traditional functional tonality. The cumulative effect, not only of the work of the "atonal" Viennese but also of Debussy, of Strauss's *Elektra* and *Salome*, of *Le Sacre du printemps*, of the early works of Bartók and the folklorists, and of a dozen lesser developments, has so permeated our musical consciousness that, except in certain very limited areas of folk and popular music, the old tonal way of thinking is no longer operative. Even in pop and traditional jazz, where triadic tonality is still a dominant feature, we accept the triad with added tones or even more complex structures as consonant. Contrapuntal voice-leading is generally replaced by parallel harmonic structures including chains of unresolved sevenths and ninths. Modal inflections outweigh the purely tonal impulses, and forms of the subdominant or even the submediant—rather than the dominant—often lead the cadences. The final cadence is replaced by the fade-out. Only the diatonic, four-measure melodic structures seem to reflect the strong functional hierarchies of the old tonal music; and even these often give way to more complex forms.

In the more complex and serious forms of pop music and jazz as well as in nearly every form of concert and operatic music—even the most conservative—the old tonal forms can no longer be taken for granted, and they have often been totally replaced by some kind of *new* tonal conception. Of the major figures who participated in the tonal revolutions before the First World War, only Strauss backed away, first into a kind of proto–neo-Classicism and later into a quiet absorption with traditional techniques and forms. Debussy, at the time of his death, was on the verge of creating new tonal forms; in fact, such new forms and techniques came into existence within a few years of the end of World War I. All of these were synthetic: none depended on traditional tonal functions but instead synthesized anew—even from piece to piece—their tonal structures. To put it another way, the tonal works of the past had been specific instances of processes that can be generalized; the new tonal works established their general processes as part of their individual creative statement.

A large body of the new tonal music, centered on the work of Igor Stravinsky, has been known as "neo-Classical"; a more logical and inclusive term might be "neo-tonal." Much of this music has been concerned with forms and materials derived from the classical tradition, but a great part of it also derives from an earlier or a more recent past or no particular past at all. For Stravinsky himself, the uses of the past are very significant; but restrictive and essentially polemical terms like "neo-Classicism" cannot serve to indicate the range of Stravinsky's "past"—from Dufay and Isaac to Tchaikovsky and Webern—or the essential interiorization of that past, radically transformed into something new and essentially Stravinskyan. The essence of Stravinskyan "neo-Classicism" lies in the thorough rebuilding of tonal practice independent of the traditional functions which had first established those forms.[1]

After the first performance of *Le Sacre* in 1913 with its famous *succès de scandale*, Stravinsky returned to an unfinished theater work, his opera *Le Rossignol*, which he completed in 1914 in a manner markedly at variance with the original Debussy/Rimsky-Korsakov conception. Stravinsky could not return to the colorful semi-tonal world of the beginning of the work after the experience of *Le Sacre*, but a generalized tonal sense still seems to linger in the much more spare and dissonant character of the later parts of the opera. More significantly, however, Stravinsky composed a number of short instrumental and instrumental-vocal works between 1912 and 1920—two sets of pieces for piano four-hands, two works for string quartet, three pieces

---

[1] There are many parallels with Picasso and the two forms of cubism—analytic and synthetic—separated by a period of neo-classicism. The analogy to tonality (which can be pushed surprisingly far) would be "realistic" perspective.

for solo clarinet, sets of songs for voice and instruments—which correspond roughly with the slightly earlier tendencies towards miniaturization in the music of Schoenberg and Webern. These neglected pieces are interesting because they employ tiny bits of the gigantesque, dissonant vocabulary of *Le Sacre* in brief, aphoristic forms based on nearly motionless ostinatos. This tendency towards clear, static, ostinato-based forms is also clearly evident in the last two works based largely on Russian materials: the burlesque opera *Renard* of 1915–1916 and the "choreographic scenes," *Les Noces*, written between 1914 and 1917 but given final and characteristic instrumental setting (for four pianos and percussion) only in 1923. Both of these works use a high degree of static "color" dissonance combined with and set off from diatonic, "neo-Russian" melodic ideas. Even a cursory glance at *Le Sacre* will reveal that these techniques are actually already present in that score, but they are fully realized in *Les Noces*. *Les Noces* is the first of Stravinsky's works to re-establish an ancient and thoroughgoing tonal principle—tonality by assertion. These remarkable choral sketches of a Russian peasant wedding employ a simple yet effective melodic technique which juxtaposes brief melodic motives with ornamented figures and insistent choral chants, all set in cyclical patterns of repetition turning around one or two insistent pitches. The ritualistic quality of this writing, much enhanced by the remarkable piano-and-percussion orchestration, is further emphasized by a basic structural technique of juxtaposition of alternating and contrasting static layers of sound patterns. This technique, already present in *Le Sacre*, is the basis for the so-called "additive" construction which Stravinsky was to use throughout his life—big building-blocks of sounds and sound patterns, often based on static ostinatos, set against one another in repetitive, alternating cycles which, although assertive and unyielding in nature, gain vitality and even a sense of motion by being constantly re-interpreted in shifting overlaps of accent, rhythm, meter, and phrase.

Les Noces is one of many Stravinsky works which proved a source of inspiration to other composers but not—except in the basic ways suggested above—to Stravinsky himself. Stravinsky's next work, *L'Histoire du soldat* (1918), uses Russian folklore, but it contains few musical Russianisms;[2] up-to-date popular, dance, and jazz materials are enclosed in small forms. *L'Histoire* was conceived for a small travelling theater and it employs a narrator, mimed or danced action, and an ensemble of seven instruments including an important percussion part.[3] It is, in effect, the first of Stravinsky's "neo-Classic" pieces, although in fact it contains nothing more Classical than a pair of off-key chorales, a few simple, closed dance forms, and a dependence on the triad (used as an articulative rather than Classical tonal device).

---

[2] The recurring three-note cadential phase in the violin solo is very close to one in a Russian pop song, "Moscow Nights"; a common source would be suggested.

[3] The musicians are to be visible; they play roles equal to those of the other performers.

Nevertheless, *L'Histoire* is the prototype for later "neo-Classical" works in its sometimes overt references to other music, its spare but vigorous lines and colors, its shifting rhythmic and accentual organization, its use of small closed forms, its ironic wit, and its method of achieving tonal centers of gravity through assertion and juxtaposition.

Stravinsky's "neo-Classic" period is generally dated from 1919, the year he began work on the ballet *Pulcinella*, after Pergolesi. To the extent that music by Pergolesi (or whoever really wrote the music Stravinsky used as source material) actually appears, the work might be said to be tonal in the old sense. Heard in this way, *Pulcinella* becomes an eccentric set of arrangements of and intrusions on eighteenth-century style. But it is nothing of the sort, of course; Pergolesi has been transformed at every moment into something quite new. The Baroque progessions are no longer representatives of a musical direction and motion; they are literally sound objects or blocks of sound which gain new meanings from new contexts. A progression or melodic pattern may begin from the middle, so to speak, or stop at some point short of a satisfactory "resolution"; such patterns are set into the typical overlapping cycles of repetition with shifting accents and metrical values; and all of this is reinforced by a clear and brilliant if restrained orchestration in which color functions analogously to rhythm and phrase.

Almost simultaneously with this derivative and "neo-Classical" work, Stravinsky composed the most original and independent of his instrumental compositions, the *Symphonies of Wind Instruments* (1920). This important if neglected work, dedicated to the memory of Debussy, is as un-Classical as it is un-Debussyesque (although perhaps it owes something both to the great tradition and to the work of the French master in its absolute clarity and its originality of form, which moves from one block sonority to another through the juxtaposition of static rhythm and texture). Again, this work— although it looks back and ahead—remains isolated in Stravinsky's output; it is, like many Stravinsky works, typical only of itself.

Stravinsky's other instrumental compositions of this period show a marked tendency to develop the kind of rhythmic and harmonic vitality within closed, static forms found in *L'Histoire*: the *Ragtime* for eleven instruments of 1918, the *Three Pieces* for solo clarinet of 1919, the Concertino for string quartet and the *Piano Rag-Music* of 1920, the Suite for chamber orchestra and the remarkable *Five-Fingers* piano pieces (whose melodies turn out to be simple permutations of *Le Sacre*-like themes) of 1921, the important Octet for winds of 1923, the Concerto for piano and winds of 1923–1924, the fine Piano Sonata of 1924, and the *Sérénade en La* for piano of 1925 move almost step by step toward the re-establishment of tonal form without a single instance of traditional tonal structure.

Parody is a word that can be used in reference to these works if the term is understood in its original sense, not necessarily implying satire.

Parody technique—that is, the use and transformation of pre-existing material—was a recognized way of writing music during the Renaissance, and much more recently, a similar procedure can be found in the other arts: the use of Homeric materials in James Joyce, the quotes and references of T. S. Eliot, Picasso's paintings after Delacroix. Stravinsky's esthetic is, to some extent, that of art removed to the second degree; that is, art about art or, more to the point, about the experience of art.[4] Stravinsky's own musical experience—never limited merely to the so-called "Classical" period—is the subject matter, taken in hand and transformed with the most careful and brilliant art and artifice; the entire range of musical experience, Renaissance to ragtime, is the material for a new and entirely contemporary commentary, sometimes witty, sometimes merely elegant and decorative, sometimes kinetic and "tangible" in its rhythmic pulse, sometimes concerned with formal patternings, often dealing at a deeper level with very real problems of expressive structure and communication.

Through it all, Stravinsky is never anything less than precise. This very precision and the clarity and dryness of his style, taken in conjunction with certain polemical remarks by the composer himself, have led to the facile conclusion that Stravinsky's music is "inexpressive" (apparently in contradistinction not only to the Romantic tradition but also to the contemporary Viennese "expressionists"); it is, supposedly, intended to "express" or communicate nothing at all. Stravinsky was largely responsible for the introduction of what we might call the "cabinet-maker" theory of the composer's role in society: the composer, like his colleague the joiner, creates beautiful things that have no more or less meaning than the beautiful curve on the leg of a fine chair. A chair, of course, has a function (and the curve may express something about that function); thus to some extent Stravinsky, and to a larger extent Hindemith and others, attempted to re-establish music as a "functional" art (just as they attempted to construct new tonalities with new musical hierarchies or "functions"). Nevertheless, Stravinsky's art is by no means exclusively craftsmanship, and Stravinsky himself subsequently denied that he ever meant to say that his music is in no sense "expressive." That his music is the product of a refined craftsmanship there can be no doubt, but that it is no more than a simple flat statement which is the mere aggregate of its parts is never true. Nor is it merely decorative or merely constructivist—any more than is the cubism of Picasso. Just as cubism is a poetic statement about objects and forms, about the nature of vision and the way we perceive and know forms, and about the experience of art and the artistic transformation of objects and forms, so Stravinsky's music is a poetic statement about musical objects and aural forms, about the way we hear and

---

[4] In a very different context, the notion of "second degree" has returned in the recent vogue for quotation and transformation (see Chapter 18).

the way we perceive and understand aural forms, about our experience of musical art and the artistic transformation of musical materials, always measured in that special domain of musical experience, time.

In 1921–1922, Stravinsky wrote the one-act opera *Mavra*, dedicated to the memories of Glinka, Pushkin, and Tchaikovsky; six years later he wrote a ballet, *Le Baiser de la fée*, which so thoroughly absorbs and transforms music of Tchaikovsky that it is often virtually impossible to tell where Tchaikovsky leaves off and Stravinsky begins. These works shocked those followers of Stravinsky who understood classicism as a historic and esthetic principle. In actual fact, Stravinsky can be said to have derived his neo-Classical taste directly from his nineteenth-century predecessors; Tchaikovsky himself, for example, wrote a prototype of a neo-Classical work in a suite based on Mozart. The very close relationship between Stravinsky's music and the nineteenth century is often overlooked. Stravinsky's real musical inheritance from the immediate past has, after the early ballets, little to do with Romantic exoticism or lushness and nothing at all to do with Wagnerian music drama and a giant symphonic style; but it has a great deal to do with the *salon* and the fashionable theater of the ballet and French-Italian opera. The *salon* and ballet traditions preserved certain classical ideas of closed form and a simple, closed melodic-harmonic style which are in fact to be found (suitably transformed, of course) in *Le Baiser de la fée*, in the Piano Sonata and *Sérénade en La*, in the *Four Etudes* for orchestra (completed in 1928), in the *Capriccio* for piano and orchestra of 1929, in the *Duo Concertant* for violin and piano of 1931–1932, and, along with certain classical derivations, in the ballet *Apollon musagète* of 1928. To be sure, like any musical ideas used by Stravinsky, these elements are treated in typical Stravinskyan fashion. The essence of the technique always lies not in the source of the ideas but in the character and technique of the transformations.

Beginning with the Piano Concerto of 1923–1924, another element enters into many of Stravinsky's works: we might characterize it as a tendency (related to that of "synthetic cubism") to construct prototypical, abstracted materials and forms. This is particularly true of the whole series of symphonic and concerted works written in the 1930's and 1940's, but it is already fully developed in the big opera-oratorio based on Sophocles's *Oedipus Rex* (1927). The text, by Jean Cocteau, consists of a series of short and simple spoken narrations in the vernacular which punctuate big arias, duets, and choruses written originally in French but translated into a solemn, dead, hierarchical, and prototypical language: Latin. *Oedipus Rex* is not tragedy or even, in the ordinary sense, drama—nothing actually happens except what we are told about between the scenes—but it contains an abstracted idea of mythic-ritual musical drama refined almost down to the skeletal framework. The simplest possible diction is everywhere employed, and this laconic declamation is organized into blocked-out set-speeches and choruses. The narrator stands apart in modern clothes; the characters, although costumed and masked, have neither individuality nor the power to act—they are not even symbolic in the conventional sense but merely abstracted, particular manifestations of a human condition. There is no motion, because whatever transpires is pre-ordained; all that is necessary is to reveal it. The motion lacking on the stage is offered by the music in the form of rhetorical gesture, and almost every gesture—like the elements of the myth itself—is familiar. The music of *Oedipus* is neither really operatic nor dramatic but represents the "idea" of these things. The very conventionality of the musical figures (Creon's trombone triad tune, the Verdiana in Jocasta's aria and the following duet with Oedipus, the grand-opera music of the "Gloria," the suggestions of Handelian oratorio) suggest detachment, abstraction, and generalization; but these materials are also redefined through the musical and literary associations. Out of all this arises a kind of reconstruction of what is traditionally referred to as "style"—what Stravinsky calls "manner." The familiar and conventional gestures are thus redefined and given a certain new and powerful inevitability in their new environment. *Oedipus* is not Verdian or Handelian any more than it is Greek tragedy. It is not "about" the tragedy of a Greek hero or of anyone at all but about tragedy itself—the form and artistic experience of tragedy in its grandest operatic-oratorio guise.

In the same way, the subject matter of the Violin Concerto of 1931 is the conception of the concerto—the relationship between solo and tutti. The concerti grossi of 1937–1938 and 1946, the important symphonies of 1939–1940 and 1942–1945, the minor *Danses concertantes* of 1941–1942 and *Scènes de ballet* of 1944, and even the *Ebony Concerto* of 1945 are all in some sense archetypical. Only the theater works of the period—*Perséphone* of 1933–1934, with its mixture of narration (text by André Gide) and dance, the ballets *Jeu de cartes* of 1936 and *Orpheus* of 1947, with its subtle neo-Baroque forms—show an independent line of thought. Stravinsky's last major "neo-classical" works are, in widely differing ways, again prototypical: the *Mass* for men's and boys' voices and ten instruments (1944–1948), with its medieval evocations, and the opera *The Rake's Progress* of 1948–1951 (to an ironic "classical" libretto by W. H. Auden and Chester Kallman), with its recreation of operatic gesture, convention, and pattern. *The Rake's Progress* is a kind of meta-opera, a second-degree opera whose subject matter is largely opera itself. It is also, among other things, a compendium of Stravinskyan style and form and the last gasp of neo-Classicism; with the *Cantata* of 1951–1952 Stravinsky began again to move in new directions.

It is important to realize that these "second-order" forms stand outside Classical procedure, to which they are no more bound than Stravinsky's melodic ideas—even when explicitly borrowed—are committed to Classical continuations. Classical forms and types are based on process; they evolve according to tonal principles and it is through this process of evolution that they come to be. Stravinsky's types are not involved with process and tonal function; they come into being through statement and assertion. Classical music defines its time span through a chain of processes and developing relationships; Stravinsky organizes his time spans by precise, given articulations and rhythmic divisions. As we have said, Classical form is the result of the ongoing process of functional tonality; with Stravinsky, form is prior and itself creates the tonality.

Stravinsky himself has spoken of his technique of "composing by interval" and of his use of "polarity" as a tonal organizing principle. In Classical usage there is a network of contrapuntal motion away from and back towards goals that are partly defined culturally, partly by the nature of this motion itself. In Stravinsky, tonality is represented by the emphasis, the repetition, or the sustaining of chords or chordal patterns; by a stated, fixed set of relationships between tones that remains constant for a movement or a piece. There is nothing inevitable about the tonal centers in Stravinsky's music; they are present and effective because they are stated and asserted to be so; and the means of assertion—repetition, ostinato, pedal point, juxtaposition of melodic and harmonic levels on specific tones and intervals, accent and articulation, rhythmic and metrical displacement—provide the basis for both the tonality and the form (see Appendix; Example 5-1).

Stravinsky's music is nearly always art to the second degree, art about art. In the absence of a wider social context (out of which traditional craftsmanship grew) Stravinsky chose Western culture itself—not in the historical sense but as a contemporary phenomenon—as his subject matter. In so doing he could not help expressing the crisis of traditional culture even as he defined a musical sensibility that is still very much part of our contemporary awareness.

BIBLIOGRAPHICAL NOTES

The development and change in Stravinsky's views over the years would require a text unto itself; to the sources already given at the end of Chapter 3, the important *Poetics of Music* (Cambridge, MA, 1947) should be added. Like all of Stravinsky's public statements, this was written with a collaborator (the Russo-French esthetician Pierre Souvtchinsky) but is hardly less significant for that.

Out of the mass of Stravinskyana, two works might be mentioned: Roman Vlad's *Stravinsky* (3rd ed., London, 1978) and Charles M. Joseph's *Stravinsky and the Piano* (Ann Arbor, 1983). Several collections of essays honoring Stravinsky have appeared at different periods of his life: Merle Armitage, ed. (New York, 1936); Edwin Corle, ed. (New York, 1949), adopting material from the

Armitage book; the 75th anniversary issue of *The Score* (London, May–June 1957); the 80th birthday issue of *The Musical Quarterly* (New York, 1962; also paperback, New York, 1963); Benjamin Boretz and Edward T. Cone, eds., *Perspectives on Schoenberg and Stravinsky* (revised ed., New York, 1972), and special 1971 issues of *Melos* (Mainz), *Perspectives of New Music* (Princeton, NJ), and *Tempo* (London). Arthur Berger's "Problems of Pitch Organization in Stravinsky" (*Perspectives of New Music* 2/1 [Fall/Winter 1963]) foreshadowed the most current controversy concerning Stravinsky analysis: the predominance of the octatonic scale in his music. On the pro-octatonic side there is Pieter van den Toorn's *The Music of Igor Stravinsky* (New Haven, 1983) and Richard Taruskin's "Chernomoor to Kaschei: Harmonic Sorcery; or Stravinsky's 'Angle' " (*Journal of the American Musicological Society* 38/1 [Spring 1985], 72–142). The opposing view is held by both Allen Forte in his *The Harmonic Organization of the Rite of Spring* (cited on page 32) and Joseph Straus in his 1981 Yale University dissertation, "A Theory of Harmony and Voice Leading in the Music of Igor Stravinsky" and the article "Stravinsky's Tonal Axis" (*Journal of Music Theory* 26 [1982], 261–90). Other analytic views appear in Pierre Boulez's *Notes of an Apprenticeship* (New York, 1968; a poor translation with many errors). A discussion of the "neo-Classical" problem appears in Edward T. Cone's "The Uses of Convention: Stravinsky and His Models" (*Musical Quarterly* [July 1962], 287–99) as well as in Alan Lessem's "Schoenberg, Stravinsky, and Neo-Classicism: The Issues Reexamined" (*Musical Quarterly* [October 1982], 527–42). Eric Walter White's *Stravinsksy: The Composer and His Works* (2nd ed., Berkeley, CA, 1980) is, in spite of some shortcomings, a substantial reference work. Robert Craft's and Vera Stravinsky's *Stravinsky in Pictures and Documents* contains extended commentary by Craft.

SIX

NEO-CLASSICISM AND
NEO-TONALITY IN FRANCE

Classicism can be defined historically as a return to certain periods of high accomplishment and style and esthetically as the use of certain strict intellectual standards of form and form-enclosed content. It has always been an important element in French culture, a situation emphasized by the fact that French tradition itself lies somewhat outside the organic development of classical norms. The classical impulse which periodically recurs in French painting right up to Picasso has always been based on a rationalization of the external trappings of the antique as transmitted by the masters of the Italian Renaissance and early Baroque. Similarly, French musical classicism through the nineteenth and well into the twentieth century was not based on French music itself—French tradition is not strong on symphonic-tonal practice, and France produced little important "classical" instrumental music—but on an external, rational synthesis of the practice of the Central European masters. This kind of classicism was extensively taught at the Paris Conservatoire and constantly recurred in French music even through the crisis of

Wagnerism that shook French music at the end of the nineteenth century. It was by no means very deeply concerned with the fundamental techniques of Classical tonality but rather with its external manifestations. Thus, paradoxically, the Classical system, never deeply rooted in French musical thought, was rather easily undermined and replaced by Debussy and Stravinsky; yet, on the other hand, non-Classical and neo-Classical tonal practice is an essential and strong part of modern French music up until recently.[1]

RAVEL

As pointed out earlier, the notion of an impressionist "school" in French music is of dubious validity. Even in his earlier and most Debussyesque works, Ravel maintains a certain independence from the complex, shifting sonorities and ambiguous tonal relationships of the older composer. Ravel was always more of a Classicist than Debussy, yet paradoxically his musical thinking was always far less abstract. He was, in his way, a far more brilliant orchestrator than Debussy, yet his orchestration was imposed from the outside and was never as organic as that of Debussy. Ravel produced no independent, abstract orchestral music except for two piano concertos; virtually everything else stems from the theater or the dance, or is orchestrated from piano works. The strong strain of Classicism in Ravel's work is present from his earliest period; in his later years it became a dominant factor in his music. The early *Menuet antique* and the famous *Pavane pour une infante défunte*, the String Quartet of 1902–1903 and, to a lesser extent, the song cycles *Shéhérazade* (1903) and *Histoires naturelles* (1906), with their refined elegance, all show not only Classical forms but also a notable tendency to enrich the traditional harmonic and color vocabulary while remaining close to the constraints and conditions of Classical practice. The one-act comic opera, *L'Heure espagnole* (1907–1909), uses the shifting ninth and eleventh chords, parallel structures, tonal ambiguities, and color phrases of impressionism, but even where obvious Classical form is not used, the clarity of texture and line, the directionality of the musical motion, as well as the dry, detached wit (and even the use of popular, Spanish elements) suggest the strong influence of certain aspects of Classical tradition.

Most of Ravel's other pre-war works, culminating in the ballet *Daphnis et Chloé* (1909–1912), are much more clearly related to Debussy; indeed

---

[1] This is equally true of another country in which the classical tradition was even weaker—the United States. On the one hand, this country could produce Ives and a strong avant-garde position outside the European tradition; on the other, the United States also produced a late-blooming "neo-tonal" style in the works of Copland and others whose commitment and influence remained strong over a period of years.

Maurice Ravel at the seashore, Saint-Jean-de-Luz, near his native village of Ciboure on the Basque coast of France. Sketch by Alexandre Benoit. Meyer Collection, Paris. Reproduction forbidden.

they have served as better prototypes of "impressionism" than any works of Debussy. However, even before the war (and hence even before Stravinsky), Ravel began to simplify his style in the direction of greater clarity of means and economy of expression. The *Trois Poèmes de Stéphane Mallarmé* of 1913 uses voice, piano, string quartet, two flutes, and two clarinets, and the Piano Trio of 1914 shows a careful and deliberate attempt to revive old or create new "classical" forms. *Le Tombeau de Couperin*, first written for piano in 1914–1917 and later orchestrated (1919) makes explicit its relationship to eighteenth-century practice.

Ravel's post-war music, beginning with *La Valse* of 1919–1920, shows an enormous expansion of technique within the clearly formed stylistic lines of his earlier music; works like the Sonata for violin and cello of 1920–1922 and the *Chansons madécasses* for voice, piano, flute, and cello of 1925–1926 use freely dissonant harmonic and linear combinations in ways that go far beyond the old tonal and even "impressionist" techniques. The popular *Boléro* of 1928 is exceptional in Ravel's works for its intentionally primitive style, but its primitivism conceals a great deal of art; the obsession with a single idea and the assertive, unrelenting C-major tonality which breaks just before the end serve to highlight the distinctive instrumentation. Following the charming *L'Enfant et les sortilèges* (1920–1925; text by Colette)—virtually a "number opera" with its succession of picturesque arias and ensembles—Ravel's important late works are two piano concertos written in 1929–1931, one in D for the left hand alone, the other in G for two hands. These works, worlds away from "impressionism," represent new directions for Ravel. Both show elements of jazz and create tonal feeling by the use of added tones and appoggiatura chords; the effect of these new values that have been attached to the concepts of consonance and dissonance is somewhat analogous to that of Debussy's last sonatas, and it is exactly that achieved by certain modern jazz musicians who violate functional tonality at every chord yet in some sense also recreate it out of a new set of conventions. It is perhaps significant that although, of all the major masters of the century, Ravel had the least influence on the development of new music, he had possibly the greatest influence on the popular musical imagination.

"LES SIX"

Ravel's neo-Classicism was essentially a refinement of and a growth out of his Debussyism, modified by a refined original temperament, a taste for jazz and for Spanish music, and an ability to assimilate new ideas. The composers of "Les Six," on the other hand, were strongly anti-Debussy from the start (not to mention anti-Wagner, anti-Fauré, and anti-d'Indy as well), and they cultivated light popular, music-hall, and café style as well as jazz. There was actually never any consistent or coherent esthetic position taken by the six young composers; they were named as a group almost accidentally, through an obvious analogy with the Russian nationalist "Five." Satie was their sponsor, however, and they were strongly influenced by his formidable musico-literary irreverence and irrelevance. To some extent, the literary and artistic movements of Dada and surrealism are also reflected in their music; but it is curious that the nihilist, anti-art of the Dadaists and the intense, associative and disassociative psychological techniques of the surrealists found little echo in their music beyond a mild if witty use of quotation and parody.

Two of "Les Six," Louis Durey (1888–1979) and Germaine Tailleferre (1892–1983), wrote little of importance; a third, Georges Auric (1899–1983), composed one notable ballet score and a good deal of latter-day film music. Arthur Honegger (1892–1955), a Swiss, had little relation stylistically to the rest of the group and must be considered separately. The music of "Les Six" today is represented almost entirely by the work of Darius Milhaud (1892–1974) and Francis Poulenc (1899–1963).

The creative output of Milhaud is immense, and it is almost impossible to make any effective generalizations about it. Milhaud had the most rigorous classical training at the Conservatoire; this, added to his natural proficiency, produced a composing technique of the utmost facility. In general he used a rich harmonic vocabulary, derived from pile-ups of thirds and triads, combined with a very simple, flexible melodic sense. Milhaud developed a kind of free counterpoint of triads and triad-like formations which in turn suggested a counterpoint of tonal areas. The idea of the manipulation of simultaneous tonalities—"polytonality"—already employed before World War I by Bartók (the *Bagatelles* for piano) and Charles Ives (the choral *67th Psalm*) achieved a certain importance in the 1920s. This expansion of tonal thought seemed to offer new possibilities for known materials and structures: Milhaud made a conscious attempt to create polytonal movement and form in early works such as *Les Choéphores* (1915) and *Saudades do Brasil* (for piano; 1920–1921). The notion of "polytonality" as such, however, had little further development; in a sense, the concept of different yet simultaneous tonalities is self-contradictory. The derivation and perceptibility of harmonic structures made out of interlocking or juxtaposed triads may be unquestionable, but long strings of these "polychords"—no matter how separated in space and timbre—cannot meaningfully establish simultaneous, contradictory tonal centers. Indeed, the significance of "polytonality" in Milhaud's music is neither formal nor systematic but is to be found rather in the use of separate bands or layers of sound which, in works like the ballet *L'Homme et son désir* (1918), actually form a polyphony made up of densities of sound. Often the use of diatonic ideas which clash with and contradict each other has a specifically witty intent. The forms are generally small, derived from vocal and dance patterns, and full of quotes and parodies of popular, dance, folk, jazz, café, and music-hall music. A great number of these pieces are "occasional" in nature, written with some specific purpose in mind; others seem like mere idle amusement for composer or performer. There is an offhand quality about much of Milhaud's music that goes beyond the inevitable unevenness of a prolific composer and takes on the character of an esthetic position.

Milhaud wrote also a great quantity of extended and serious instrumental work, mainly for chamber combinations, but his most important contributions have undoubtedly been in the theater, where he collaborated with writers of the stature of Paul Claudel, Cocteau, and Franz Werfel. Milhaud always responded imaginatively to the theatrical situation. His "Orestes" trilogy, written with Claudel and including most notably *Les Choéphores*, makes striking use of a number of new and combined techniques including narration and rhythmic speaking-chorus with percussion. The ballet *L'Homme et son désir* employs instrumental forces disposed in particular spatial arrangements, a prophetic idea. The famous *Le Boeuf sur le toit* of 1919 is a compendium of popular tunes, mostly South American in origin (Milhaud had been an attaché in the French embassy at Rio de Janeiro during World War I) and treated in a noisy, rattling, racy manner. *La Création du monde*, a ballet of 1923, often considered Milhaud's masterpiece, is the first major composition to make extensive, serious, and subtle use of jazz. Milhaud did not actually "write" jazz, but the music is imbued with the sound and style of the jazz of that day.

The list could be extended. *Le Pauvre matelot* of 1926 is a curiously grim but effective piece of verismo opera with a text by Cocteau. At another extreme are the infinitesimal *"opéras minutes"* to librettos by Henri Hoppenot of the following year with their absurdly condensed bits of classical tragedy. And the *Christophe Colomb* of 1928 presents still another huge contrast; it is a very grand symbolic opera with an allegorical text by Claudel and a musical and dramatic apparatus of considerable weight and power.

The pairing of Milhaud with his contemporary Francis Poulenc has obvious historical and even some esthetic justification, but they are in fact two vastly different musical personalities. Milhaud, the intensely trained "natural" musician, was brought up in the classical tradition and rejected it or used it to his own ends with the utter ease of a fluent and prolific master. Poulenc, virtually self-taught, slowly and painstakingly re-created tradition in a series of small, witty, elegant, and fastidious pieces, carefully worked out almost from note to note. One side of Poulenc's musical personality is shown by *buffo* works like *Le Bal masqué* (1932), the Concerto for two pianos (1932), and *Les Mamelles de Tirésias* (1944), where wrong notes, movie music, barroom ballads, and sentimental chansons jostle each other in racy profusion. But there is another Poulenc who was a direct heir to the nineteenth-century neo-Classical and salon tradition—a durable factor in French musical life. A work like the Organ Concerto (1938), although superficially derived from Bach, is really a direct descendant of the lyric, popular classicism of composers like Viotti and Saint-Saëns. Traces of this lyric gift are present even in the most outrageous of the parody-and-quote pieces, and a simple, *cantabile* expression can be found in a good deal of the piano and chamber music. It is already present in early works like the ballet *Les Biches* (1923); it is the dominant musical speech in the simple, effective *Dialogues des Carmélites* (1953–1956), which crosses Duparc with Mussorgsky, and in choral works like *Stabat Mater* (1950), *Gloria* (1959), and the *Sept Répons des ténèbres* (1961). Poulenc's gift for lyric line is most evident in his songs, among which are his most attractive and successful works, and which, apart from the very different case of Strauss, represent a clearer continuation or reinstatement of the tradition than any other music we shall be discussing in this book.

The third important member of "Les Six" scarcely belongs with the others at all. Honegger's connection with the group really came about through his association with his fellow-pupil Milhaud and through the intellectual and moral patronage of Satie. Honegger's starting point was the Central European tradition up to and including even early Schoenberg but tempered considerably by Debussy and the Russians. His first reputation was based on the dramatic psalm *Le Roi David* (1921) and on several picturesque orchestral works: *Pastorale d'été* (1920), *Pacific 231* (the famous musical railroad train of 1923), and *Rugby* (1928). His early reputation as a composer of picturesque, noisy, avant-garde tone poems was, however, to prove misleading. *Le Roi David*—originally conceived, like *L'Histoire du soldat*, as a stage work with spoken narration and dialogue, mime, and dance—is scored for a chamber ensemble and intentionally built around a simple, almost popular melodic style. Even in the later concert version for large orchestra, the essentially simple closed forms remain unaltered, and the modified, unsystematic modal tonality remains fundamental to the effect; only the big contrapuntal choruses that close the main sections of the piece use extended classical form. Honegger returned to this genre in 1934–1935 with the popular *Jeanne d'Arc au bûcher*; *Le Roi David* itself is the prototype for a widespread popular choral style built on simple modal tonality, modest choral counterpoint, local color, and small, easily apprehended forms. Honegger himself was concerned with the expansion of these techniques (minus the pseudo-Orientalisms of *Le Roi David*) into a more complex, contrapuntal symphonic and chamber style: in the list of his later works, large-scale symphonic and chamber works predominate. Long lines, moving across large, free diatonic and modal areas, with harmonic structures built on accumulations of thirds and added diatonic tones, and a highly accented but basically regular, even motoric rhythm are the hallmarks of this style; it accommodated the classical tradition to a modified, conservative, and accessible modern idiom with a good deal of expressive effect. Like the much more consistent and highly organized tonal style developed by Hindemith in his later years, the idiom had considerable influence over a period of about a quarter of a century. Honegger's work represents a strong and serious recasting of tradition in a manner that has, in spite of serious formal defects (structures far too extended for the light tonal supports), a certain amount of scope and purpose; as such it served as one of the starting points for twentieth-century tonal symphonic tradition.

BIBLIOGRAPHICAL NOTES

In addition to the material on Ravel noted at the end of Chapter 3, mention might be made of a view from the avant-garde: Pierre Boulez's "Trajectories: Ravel, Stravinsky, Schoenberg," an essay of 1949 reprinted in English translation in *Notes of an Apprenticeship* (New York, 1968). Material on "Les Six" may be found in Henri Hell's *Francis Poulenc* (trans. Edward Lockspeiser, New York, 1959; an updated version is available only in French; Paris, 1978), Darius Milhaud's autobiographical *Notes Without Music* (New York, 1953); and, in French, Honegger's *Je suis compositeur* (Paris, 1951). The most thorough study of Milhaud is by Paul Collaer but is available only in French (Geneva and Paris, 1982), but see also Christopher Palmer's *Milhaud* (London, 1976). Keith W. Daniel's *Francis Poulenc: His Artistic Development and Musical Style* (Ann Arbor, 1982) and Vivian Lee Poates Wood's *Poulenc's Songs: An Analysis of Style* (Jackson, MS, 1979) concentrate on the composer's musical style, while Pierre Bernac's *Francis Poulenc: The Man and His Songs* (trans. Winifred Radford, New York, 1977) discusses matters of interpretation. Two recent studies on Honegger are available only in German: Kurt von Fischer's short monograph on the composer, his esthetic, and musical style (Zurich, 1978), and Hans Dieter Voss's study of the oratorio *Le roi David* (Munich and Salzburg, 1983).

SEVEN

NEO-CLASSICISM AND NEO-TONALITY OUTSIDE OF FRANCE

HINDEMITH AND GEBRAUCHSMUSIK

The most highly developed of the new tonal styles was that of Paul Hindemith (1895–1963). Hindemith was the youngest of the first group of major twentieth-century pioneers, and his artistic development follows the general pattern of the early decades but at a distance of some years. Thus his early work, written at about the time of World War I and shortly there-after, comes out of the Central European line—the tradition of Brahms and Reger, however, rather than that of Wagner. Like Reger, Hindemith extended the chromatic range with great mastery, always in terms of the great contrapuntal tradition; to the end of his life, he remained a contrapuntist. With the early string sonatas of 1917–1919 (Opus 11), we are already in the composer's first mature phase. A long series of important works followed: the one-act operas of 1919–1921, *Cardillac* of 1926, *Hin und Zurück* and

Neues vom Tage of 1927 and 1929, the song cycles *Die junge Magd* and *Das Marienleben* of 1922 and 1923, more sonatas for strings, a series of string quartets, a number of works for piano, the famous *Kleine Kammermusik* for winds (Op. 24, No. 2) of 1922, and a group of concerted works with chamber orchestra. All of this music has a contrapuntal aggressiveness and a free use of dissonance that led to its being described initially as "atonal"; it now seems neither systematically tonal nor really atonal. The harmonic sense and the big construction of the lines, though often extremely chromatic, nearly always suggest a clear but undefined sense of underlying tonal shape and direction; a rather intense, expressive invention dominates the surface. Works like *Das Marienleben* (in its original version) come very close in many ways to the Viennese expressionists; on the other hand, pieces like the *Suite 1922* for piano and some of the *Kammermusik* compositions show a wit and an irreverent boisterousness that approach and even—in matters of satire and irony—outdo "Les Six."

About 1927, Hindemith began to change his musical style and outlook in the direction of simplicity and clarity, and towards a careful new tonal style which was to characterize his music until his death. In the end, his style was conditioned by a number of factors, nearly all of which derived from his extraordinary musicality. Hindemith was an exceptional type of "natural" musician; he composed with extraordinary facility and he was active as a violist and conductor. Almost all of his works of the 1920's (including the operas) were conceived for chamber performance, often with the composer himself playing the violin, viola, or viola d'amore; and he was one of the first modern musicians to explore—through performance as well as research—the vast areas of early music. He was a well-known teacher and an influential theorist. In 1927, Hindemith formulated a definitive statement of his conception of the role of the composer in society; like Stravinsky, he placed great emphasis on the composer as craftsman, but he also stressed the importance of the relationship between the composer and the performer. In the late 1920's and early 1930's he wrote a series of ensemble and solo works for amateur and student performance, including a musical play for children and a whole day's worth of music written for young students at a school. On a more advanced level came a long series of sonatas for virtually every important instrument and a further series of concerted works for solo instruments with small and large orchestras. This so-called *Gebrauchsmusik* or "music for use" represents in part a return—or at least an idealization— of the relationships that had existed between composers, performers, patrons, and audiences before the nineteenth century. The Romantic composer was presumably inspired by an inner compulsion, by a need to communicate something; Hindemith was inspired by a commission, by the presence of a performer (himself perhaps), and by the reality of an actual performing situation. It is probable that the re-establishment of the composer-performer

Paul Hindemith by Rémusat. Meyer Collection, Paris. Reproduction forbidden.

relationship, and of the significance of the realities of performance and the performance situation, was Hindemith's most enduring theoretical contribution.

As a theorist, however, Hindemith wanted to accomplish a great deal more than that. Coincident with the establishment of the *Gebrauchsmusik* ideal came the simplification of his style and the definitive return to tonal ways of thinking. This is clear not only in the solo and chamber works but also in the major compositions of the 1930's and 1940's, beginning with the *Konzertmusik* for strings and brass of 1930 and continuing with the opera *Mathis der Maler* (1934–1935), the symphony extracted from it, a pair of concertos for orchestra, and several ballet scores. During this period Hindemith also began to systematize his ideas; this ultimately resulted in a series of theoretical works (never wholly completed) and in the big, didactic cycle of fugues and interludes for piano published in 1943 as *Ludus Tonalis*. Hindemith consciously attempted to formulate a new tonal system which, growing out of certain acoustical principles and some fundamental notions of linear counterpoint, was to include a complete range of chromatic expression. The basic conception was that of the weight and tension of individual intervals, determined by an acoustic and psychological classification and revealed through a system of harmonic and melodic necessity (derived in part from the overtone series). Hindemith's music after the late 1920's was increasingly based on such ideas. Tonal centers are established by a kind of gravitational melodic movement and a harmonic motion based on chords of greater and lesser tension; the triad remains primary, the focal point of cadence and rest.[1] This remarkable parallel to the old tonal system—based, not on tradition and usage, but on presumed acoustical and psychological validities—was adopted by the composer in such a thoroughgoing manner that he even returned to some of his important older works and revised them in order to make them conform more closely to his later thinking, e.g., *Das Marienleben*, settings of texts on the life of the Virgin by Rainer Maria Rilke, revised in 1948 and its outlines softened, its harmonic and melodic movement more rationalized, more goal-directed. (See Appendix; Example 7-1.)

Although Hindemith thought of his theoretical ideas and method of teaching as a synthesis, they have in fact proved to be relevant only to certain kinds of music—principally Hindemith's own. For Hindemith himself, however (less so perhaps for his pupils and imitators), they provided a way of achieving a coherent kind of musical speech which could sustain invention and produce consistent and large-scale forms in an individual and contemporary tonal language. Hindemith's later works fit the patterns thus

---

[1] Hindemith's classification of chordal structures, of intervals, and of triadic relationships has been described as a tonal system without the notion of "key." The classical system would then be, presumably, a special case of this wider theoretical principle.

established—his opera based on the life of Kepler, *Die Harmonie der Welt* (1956–1957); his opera based on Thornton Wilder's *The Long Christmas Dinner* (1960); his setting of Whitman's *When Lilacs Last in the Dooryard Bloom'd* (1946); the *Octet* (1957–1958); and the later choral works. Hindemith tried to synthesize the great linear tradition with a kind of chromatically accented tonality; in doing so he created an individual style with its unmistakable sound of major and minor seconds, fourths and fifths. Everything works, everything is under perfect control. The music lies well for the instruments; within a narrow rhythmic compass, energy, impulse, and forward motion generate larger periods which are woven into large-scale forms through a carefully controlled use of intervallic tension and succession. Hindemith's music can be expressive; it is always idiomatic, if sometimes routine. He himself considered his later work as a logical and maturing development, but his major creative powers seem better expressed in the freer earlier work; certainly the early versions of the revised works are preferable.

There is unquestionably a logic and—up to a point at least—an inner development in Hindemith's work. Unlike other prolific composers, Hindemith was never uncritical about his own work; his standards of craftsmanship never flagged, only his inspiration. When his imagination was equal to his craft—as it tended to be especially in his dramatic works—he was able to turn his personal synthesis of theory and practice into the highest artistic communication.

THE DIFFUSION OF NEO-CLASSICISM

Neo-Classicism or neo-tonality in one form or another became the dominant international idea in the 1930's and 1940's. Neo-Classicism as such hardly constituted a "style" or a "school," and the broadest impact of the new tonal techniques was on the development of the national styles to be discussed in the next chapter. There remain, however, a number of composers and works to be mentioned here whose outlook, essentially international in character, was strongly conditioned by classic ideals as re-expressed through new tonal forms.

In France, there are several lesser figures who, while officially outside of "Les Six," were related to them in style and temperament. The most important of these are Jacques Ibert (1890–1962) and Jean Françaix (b. 1912), two witty, minor talents whose esthetic ranges from a kind of neo-impressionism (Ibert's *Escales* of 1922) to a musical jollity that is very close to Poulenc and Milhaud (Ibert's wind quintet, 1930; Françaix's Concertino for piano and orchestra, 1932). Mention should also be made of the later work of Vincent d'Indy (1851–1931). D'Indy, who derived from Franck, was an important pedagogue, and the Schola Cantorum, of which he was director from its inception in 1900 to his death, was an important center of new ideas as well as of the revival of old ones. Under d'Indy's direction, the Schola pioneered in the authentic performance of old music; it also evolved new techniques of teaching composition. D'Indy's own work is a curious mixture of a rich Franck-Wagner late nineteenth-century symphonic style, a sense of classical technique and form, an expanded modern chromatic palette somewhat cautiously used, and a love of folk song and folk-song-like simplicity. Some of these ideas were carried further by d'Indy's pupil Albert Roussel (1869–1937), who, starting with a kind of amalgamation of d'Indy and Debussy, achieved an individual neo-Classical style whose development seems parallel to rather than directly influenced by the work of a composer like Stravinsky.

Outside of France, certain composers in Italy, Germany, Russia, England, and the United States contributed to an essentially international movement.

The classical tradition was, in great part, Italian, but neo-Classicism as an intellectual or expressive idea has had a relatively minor role in modern Italian musical life, with one major exception. Alfredo Casella (1883–1947), a once influential but now neglected composer, developed a tonal style based on a free use of the seven diatonic steps combined with traditional forms derived from the Monteverdi-Scarlatti tradition. Casella was an important figure in Italian musical life, and he played a major role in the revival of Italian instrumental music; he also helped to create a modern Italian tonal idiom and to insure that ultra-chromatic, atonal, and twelve-tone ideas would not penetrate Italian musical life—as, indeed, they did not until after his death. The most important younger Italian neo-Classicist was Goffredo Petrassi (b. 1904) who, until his involvement in serialism, wrote a number of works in a serious, colorful, abstract, limber tonal style.[2]

In most of Europe "neo-Classicism" was long considered by many as a form of musical intellectualizing and even ultra-modernity. In Germany, however, a number of composers picked up some of the simpler aspects and techniques of Stravinsky, Hindemith, and the French to synthesize an accessible, popular, neo-tonal style. The most important of these is Carl Orff (1895–1982), whose blocky, triadic theater music is built on obsessively repeated harmonic structures, semi-chanted, repetitious melodic figurations, and a simple, colorful orchestration based on percussion sounds, most of it quite clearly derived from Stravinsky, especially from *Les Noces*. Orff has applied some of these materials to a kind of creative-play teaching method for children which has had a great deal of success in Germany and elsewhere.

---

[2] The work of other "neo-tonal" Italians—Respighi, Pizzetti, Malipiero—is considered in Chapter 8.

Werner Egk (1901–1983), whose name and music were often linked with Orff's, writes a more elaborate kind of piece, based on popular types and influenced by French style. Egk's music has simple direction and development; Orff's intentionally has none. Orff's music stands as virtually the last and simplest representative of an esthetic of simplicity which had considerable influence in European and American music between the wars.[3]

In his "Classical" Symphony and in many of his later works as well, Prokofiev achieved something of a tonal synthesis which constitutes an authentic and—by and large—convincing "neo-Classicism"; the same is true (but to a much lesser degree) of the work of Dmitri Shostakovich (1906–1975). In England, a work like William Walton's *Façade* is very close in wit and intent to the French style of the period, especially in its original form with Edith Sitwell's poetry recited to a chamber accompaniment. All of Benjamin Britten's highly original tonal music could be placed here; and important American works like the early music of Roger Sessions, the *Short Symphony* (1932–1933) and other pieces of Aaron Copland, the Gertrude Stein settings of Virgil Thomson, earlier works of Elliott Carter, Lukas Foss, and Arthur Berger, most of the music of Irving Fine, many compositions by Walter Piston and Roy Harris, as well as a large group of works by younger composers show a strong neo-Classical or neo-tonal bent of one kind or another.

"Neo-Classicism" petered out in a series of modest styles, eclectic in nature and severely limited in scope. Composers like Stravinsky and Hindemith could re-create tonal forms out of which big pieces could be made, works which were at once clever, craftsmanlike, clear and even accessible, idiomatic and full of vitality, allied with tradition but essentially new and capable of assimilating with ease such divergent elements as quotes from the classics, folk music, and jazz; parody, wit, and elegance; and a great deal of serious intellectual thought and communication about the nature of musical form, craft, art, and experience. The experience was, after a certain point, too limiting, too restricted for another generation—indeed, even for Stravinsky himself. If tonality were to retain vitality, it was clear that it had to find new forms.

BIBLIOGRAPHICAL NOTES

There is little or no general literature on "neo-Classicism," a fact which may be due partly to the inadequacy of that useful but misleading and catch-all term. For Hindemith, the composer's own *Craft of Musical Composition* (New

[3] There is a link between Orff and some of the American composers active in the 1930's and 1940's—Virgil Thomson, Harry Partch, early John Cage, Lou Harrison, and others. This music, in turn, relates to latter-day minimalism (Glass, Reich, et al.; see Chapter 19).

York, 1941, 1942) and *A Composer's World* (Cambridge, 1952) are fundamental. Most of the secondary literature on Hindemith has been available only in German; only recently have important sources become available in English: David Neumeyer's *The Music of Paul Hindemith* (New Haven, 1986; one in a new series of books devoted to composers of the twentieth century) and Andres Briner's biography of the composer, which has recently been translated into English (Zurich, 1971; London, 1983). Geoffrey Skelton's biography (London, 1975) avoids discussion of the music, but covers some interesting details of the composer's life. There are annuals devoted to both Hindemith (Mainz, 1971–   ) and Albert Roussel (Brussels, 1978–   ), and the April 1929 issue of *La revue musicale* is a "numéro spécial" on Roussel. Howard Pollack's recent study of Walter Piston (Ann Arbor, 1982) surveys that composer's music and writings after the first two biographical chapters. Allen Forte's *Contemporary Tone Structures* (New York, 1955) is a rare and serious attempt to discuss twentieth-century tonal ideas.

EIGHT

NATIONAL STYLES

The development of national styles outside of Central Europe and the general international evolution of twentieth-century music are closely related. The discovery of folk music, particularly that of Eastern Europe, was one of the factors that broadened the horizons of Western music. At the same time, no extensive independent developments of great significance could take place until the dominance of the central, "common practice" tonal system was ended. In general, some new kind of tonal framework was needed within which distinctly national idioms—derived from the small forms of folk and dance music—could be expanded into larger means of creative communication. Thus, outside of Germany and France, a whole series of local styles developed, adapting to local modes of musical speech influences first from Debussy and Ravel, later from Stravinsky, Hindemith, and others. In spite of the fact that the principal ideological opposition in the first part of the twentieth century was between Stravinskyan "neo-Classicism" and Schoenbergan chromatic and twelve-tone ideas, it was rather the strong local and national styles which proved to be the principal bulwark against atonal and twelve-tone ideas. This was by no means merely a question of conservatism or of local pride. Amid the economic, political, and social crises of the late 1920's and 1930's, a dominant strain of social and esthetic thought appeared which rejected the atonal and experimental avant-gardism of the earlier part of the century in favor of a kind of musical populism, of simplicity and accessibility expressed through the use of tonal forms as well as popular and folk materials.

EASTERN EUROPE: BARTÓK

The most important figure to come out of Eastern Europe was Béla Bartók (1881–1945). Hungary, although an intensely musical country, had long been under the political and artistic hegemony of Vienna and Central Europe; Bartók was thoroughly trained in the traditional manner, and his early works are strongly resonant of Brahms and Richard Strauss. The liberating influences were Debussy and Magyar folk song. With Zoltán Kodály, Bartók went out into the Hungarian countryside and made the first definitive collections of Eastern European folk music. He transcribed this music in a manner virtually free of the nineteenth-century prejudices which had squeezed the highly distinctive character of folk art into the Procrustean bed of traditional tonality and which had confused genuine Hungarian folk expression with the popularized "Gypsy" music of the cafés. Bartók was not only able to establish the distinctive character of the true Magyar style; he was also able to record and distinguish other Eastern folk music of differing and equally distinct character. None of this music adheres to the conventions of Central European tonal thinking. Much of it is heterophonic in nature; a drone or rhythmic accompaniment underlays a single-line melody which often appears in different versions, sometimes simultaneous and often highly embellished.

In Bartók's earliest published works, his *Rhapsody*, Op. 1 (1904), and his *Suites* for orchestra, Op. 3 and 4 (1905, 1907), the setting of the Hungarian material already seems to owe something to Debussy; a certain special kind of impressionist color and form can be found in works like *Bluebeard's Castle* (1911) and the many characteristic "night music" movements of the later instrumental works. In his *Two Portraits* of 1907–1908 and, especially, in his *Bagatelles* for piano of 1908, Bartók moved quickly and with assurance into a mature and original phase—a phase quite equal and parallel to other developments elsewhere. The *Bagatelles*, besides being technical studies in new rhythmic, melodic, and harmonic devices, also suggest the way in which Bartók stylized melodic and rhythmic ideas and extracted from them their

Béla Bartók, drawn in 1944, one year before his death, by Alexander Dolbin. Meyer Collection, Paris. Reproduction forbidden.

characteristic sound qualities, now transformed into harmonies, counter-lines, and colors. In his String Quartet No. 1, of 1908, Bartók reverts to a big contrapuntal, Central European style with a wandering kind of tonal chromaticism that is not always persuasive. But in the piano music of 1909–1911 (especially the well-known *Allegro barbaro*), in the *Two Pictures* for orchestra of 1910, in the two big theater works of 1911 and 1914–1917 (*Bluebeard's Castle* and the ballet *The Wooden Prince*), and in the Piano Suite, Op. 14, of 1916, Bartók develops a broad and colorful speech of great force and vitality. There is little if any actual folk material in the music, but the Hungarian character is omnipresent. The harmonic structure is still basically triadic; or, at least, the triad represents the main point of departure and return. The basic structures are tonal, although of course not in the old sense. Bartók's tonal writing and his structural sense are not completely consistent; rather he proceeds from point to point with the modal character of the melodic invention sustained by rhythmic vitality, changing meters, Debussyan color, and parallel harmonic motion. Softer ninth- and eleventh-chord sounds, punctuated by sharp harmonic dissonance, open out at key points of articulation into triads.

At about this time Bartók must have become acquainted with recent developments in Vienna and Paris: his String Quartet No. 2 of 1917 and *The Miraculous Mandarin*, a ballet of 1919, show, respectively, strong influences from Schoenberg and Stravinsky. These two impressive works present a remarkable contrast: the former contrapuntal, highly developed, and intensely expressive in an introspective way; the latter big and violent in the manner of the sophisticated primitivism of *Le Sacre du printemps*. It is almost as if Bartók had to recapitulate for himself the revolutionary experiences of a few years earlier in order to gain mastery of the rhythmic freedom, harmonic dissonance, color range, block-form, and additive structures of a Stravinsky and the intense, crowded, contrapuntal, expressive chromaticism and orga-nizational control of a Schoenberg. Afterwards, Bartók was able to create his own imaginative world in which all these techniques and materials—folk song, tonal harmonies built in thirds, ultra-chromaticism and dissonant "atonality," contrapuntal, serial construction, percussive color-rhythm—could function (often side by side) as expressive and structural ideas compatible with the special qualities of his own invention.

The 1920's were a decade of chamber composition for Bartók: the "difficult" violin and piano sonatas of 1921–1922, the Piano Sonata and *Out of Doors* suite of 1926 and the Third and Fourth String Quartets of 1927–1928 are works of great intensity in which Bartók for the first time extended his own personal style into utterances of considerable size and shape. (The construction of the theater works, although extended, had been essentially an accumulation of localized events.) The string quartets No. 3, with its extended one-movement construction, and No. 4, with its tightly organized transformations and returns, sustain unified lines of thought over long expressive periods through a rather subtle manipulation of material that is imaginative in shape (if limited in content) and of broad and striking implications. (See Appendix; Example 8-1.)

These chamber works are built on a rhythmic and phrase character that is often strongly suggestive of folk ideas and dependent on a kind of assertive tonality-in-the-small, but they are organized in their large structure according to other principles. The typical method is one in which entire movements are permeated with a particular kind of sound (characteristic harmonic, melodic and rhythmic shapes, timbres, and/or articulations), a method that is about halfway between certain Stravinskyan tonal techniques and the more highly ordered serial construction of Schoenberg.

By contrast, Bartók's relatively few orchestral works of this period— orchestrations of folk-song sets originally written for piano, the *Dance Suite* of 1923, the Piano Concerto No. 1 of 1926, and the two *Rhapsodies* for violin and orchestra of 1928—are written in a more accessible tonal vein, and the use of Hungarian material is broader and somewhat more popular in nature. Beginning with the *Cantata Profana* of 1930 and the Piano Concerto No. 2 of the following year, Bartók showed a strong tendency to synthesize these aspects of his work. The Fifth String Quartet of 1934 is dissonant, lean, rhythmic, and hard-driving; but its tonal construction is clearer than that of the Third or Fourth. The Sixth String Quartet of 1939 is built on a clear triadic tonality derived from contrapuntal movement and intervallic structures based principally on thirds and fifths. In sound, the Sixth Quartet seems to be a reversion to an earlier, clearer tonal idiom. But the triadic construction, although clearly tonal in nature, is an extension of the intervallic principle which, in the earlier quartets, had been worked out of intervals like minor seconds and major sevenths but are replaced in the Sixth Quartet by thirds and fifths. Similarly, Bartók's earlier cyclical treatment of form is extended here, in that an introduction to the first movement expands, as it recurs before the other movements, until it constitutes the whole of the last movement. A transition between chromatic and diatonic, triadic-tonal styles is actually accomplished within certain individual compositions, notably the *Music for Strings, Percussion, and Celesta* of 1936. (See Appendix: Example 8-2.) The range of Bartókan techniques can also be studied in the remarkable series of studies which constitute the *Mikrokosmos* (1926–1939), a "Gradus ad Parnassum" not only for the piano student but also for the student of compositional ideas. Many later works of Bartók show some kind of creative synthesis: the Sonata for Two Pianos and Percussion (1937), the Violin Concerto (1937–1938), *Contrasts* for clarinet, violin, and piano (1938), the *Divertimento for Strings* (1939), the Concerto for Orchestra (1942–1943), the Third Piano Concerto (1945), and the Viola Concerto (1945; completed by Tibor Serly). A variety of clear, open, expressive elements, synthesized in large, tonal forms, has made these works some of Bartók's most popular—one of the few examples of a twentieth-century composer's later output achieving wider currency than his earlier and, artistically, more influential work. Bartók's style, which for a brief time was extremely influential among younger composers, was ultimately too personal to maintain a direct and continuous impact on the course of creative development, but the nature of his synthesis and the inclusive character of his composing techniques are perhaps of greater importance than has yet been recognized. There are universal qualities in Bartók's work which transcend the appealing and personal but surface character of his music; as time passes, they will emerge with greater clarity.

EASTERN EUROPE: HUNGARY AND CZECHOSLOVAKIA

The most important Hungarian composer besides Bartók was Zoltán Kodály (1882–1967), Bartók's close colleague and collaborator in collecting East European folk music. Kodály's best-known music is in the suite derived from the musical play *Háry János*, but its amusing if somewhat trivial adaptations of popular and folk styles are not necessarily representative of his serious work. Kodály's music is, in any case, more tonally and triadically oriented than Bartók's. There is a considerable body of chamber music; especially notable are a sonata for solo cello (1915), a *Serenade* for two violins and viola (1919–1920), and two string quartets (1908–1909, 1916–1918) which, while without Bartók's special qualities of intensity, originality, and reflective thought, are strong, lyric essays of convincing shape. Kodály's style, with its open, triadic sound and its derivation from a lyric, Hungarian melos, is eminently suited to—even derived from—the human voice. Kodály established in Hungary the principle that singing should be the basis of music education and he introduced a series of reforms and innovations in the organization and teaching of sight-singing which have had a wide influence. He wanted every child to participate in choral singing, and a great many of his own choral works are intended for performance by children, amateurs, and students. The core of Kodály's art is to be found in his songs, his choruses, and in big chorus-and-orchestra compositions like his *Psalmus Hungaricus* (1923).

A striking example of the liberation of the creative imagination of an Eastern European composer through the assimilation of new ideas is provided by the Czech composer, Leoš Janáček (1854–1928), ten years older than Strauss and hardly more than a decade younger than Dvořák. For years Janáček was a provincial music teacher in a little-known corner of what was to become Czechoslovakia, and his music was that of a provincial Dvořák. Suddenly, just at the turn of the century, his style and his creative powers broadened with the remarkable opera *Jenůfa* (1894–1903). Even so, it was more than ten years before *Jenůfa* was produced in Prague and Vienna (in 1916), and it was only in the last years of his life that Janáček produced the remarkable series of original and powerful works on which his reputation now rests: *The Diary of One Who Vanished* (1917–1919), *Káťa Kabanová* (from Ostrovsky; 1919–1921), *The Cunning Little Vixen* (1921–1923), *The Makropulos Affair* (text by Čapek; 1923–1925), *From the House of the Dead* (after Dostoyevsky; 1927–1928); the *Slavonic Mass* (1907–1908), the *Sinfonietta* of 1926, and several chamber works. Like Kodály, Janáček combined a folk melos with a basically triadic style, but the character of Janáček's music is utterly unlike that of his younger contemporaries in Hungary—and not only because of the differences between Czech and Hungarian folk music. Janáček never quoted actual folk material, but he derived his melodic speech from the prose-poetry character of Slavic folk music with its typical intervals and scales, its close identification with language, and the insistent, repeated character of its melodic lines. An almost obsessive concern with repetition is very characteristic, with small figures of an insistent, prosaic character repeated over and over in block-like sections; the larger sections are built up in layers through the juxtaposition and contrast of these very grand and simple building-blocks. The technique is at work in the single successful large symphonic piece—the *Sinfonietta*—but it is most basic to Janáček's dramatic works; he was, above all, a man of the theater with an intense, intuitive understanding of the role of simplicity and the impact of repetition and striking contrast in dramatic construction. The ironic pessimism of these works—strongly in the Slavic tradition—is expressed through the rather affirmative and sophisticated naïveté of the music, and this itself produces some of the great dramatic tensions. Janáček's mature style was almost certainly achieved through his contact with the main currents of Western musical thought after World War I—Stravinsky may have been an influence—but these currents (not easily recognizable at all except in the character of lean, even angular, poetic simplicity on the surface and the "additive" construction underneath) are transformed into a style of expressive precision and dramatic originality.

Dvořák's principal pupil and successor, Josef Suk (1874–1935), began as a kind of polyphonic Dvořák, whose harmonic horizons later expanded to include a range of modern techniques. In turn, Suk's best-known pupil was Bohuslav Martinů (1890–1959) who studied also with Roussel in Paris and mixed the Czech tradition with strong doses of French style (Ravel, d'Indy, Roussel), eventually turning to a rather international manner with a strong tonal and neo-classic bent.

EASTERN EUROPE: RUSSIA

Strong currents both of ultra-traditional conservatism and radical innovation co-existed in Russia from the late nineteenth century until the Stalinist anti-modern campaigns of the 1930's. The older Romantic tradition can be represented by Sergei Rachmaninoff (1873–1943), who, although he left Russia permanently in 1917 and lived for twenty-six more years, had already composed all but two or three of his best-known works before World War I. On the other hand, the strong personality of Skriabin attracted the attention of mystically inclined younger Russian musicians, who also began to show remarkable tendencies to strike out on their own. It is difficult to say what exactly are the sources of Prokofiev's early music—partly Skriabin, perhaps, but in any event not Stravinsky. Prokofiev composed his First Piano Concerto in 1911–1912, his early piano works between 1907 and 1913, and his First Violin Concerto in 1916–1917, before he could have known much about Stravinsky's development; and even the *Scythian Suite* of 1915, for all its obvious Stravinskyisms, is really a parallel to *Le Sacre* rather than clearly derived from it. The *Scythian Suite* marks the beginning of a distinct period in Prokofiev's life, a development only briefly interrupted by the composer's lively re-interpretation of tradition in his "Classical" Symphony (1916–1917). Such works as *Sarcasms* (1912–1914) and *Visions fugitives* (1915–1917) for piano, the Third and Fourth Piano Sonatas (1917), the ballet *Chout* (1915; revised 1920), the opera *The Gambler* (1915–1917; after Dostoyevsky), and *Sept, ils sont sept* for tenor, chorus, and orchestra (1917–1918) are built on highly dissonant textures often coupled with great motoric drive. Prokofiev's music at this period had the widest range of means, and within a few years between 1919 and 1923 he produced the masterpieces of his early period, *The Love for Three Oranges* and *The Flaming Angel*, utterly contrasting works, the former satirical and ironic, written with great wit and flair, the latter intensely dramatic, expressionistic, a curious and effective combination of the ironic and the visionary.

Prokofiev left Russia in 1918 and went to the United States and later to Paris, where he worked throughout the 1920's, composing two ballets for Diaghilev (*Le Pas d'acier*, 1925–1926; *L'Enfant prodigue*, 1928–1929), his symphonies Nos. 2, 3, and 4 (1924–1925; 1928; 1929–1930) and his piano concertos Nos. 3, 4, and 5 (1917–1921; 1931; 1931–1932). After *The Flaming Angel* and the remarkable symphony derived from it (No. 3), the music of Prokofiev's Paris period is brilliant, hard-driving, and powerful but, with one or two exceptions, not on a level with his earlier works. It is possible that he found it difficult to work in Paris and away from Russia; at any rate, in 1936 he went back and almost immediately plunged into a whole series

of "practical" projects which included the scores for the films *Lieutenant
Kije* and Eisenstein's *Alexander Nevsky* (both unpublished as film scores),
the ballets *Romeo and Juliet* (1935–1936) and *Cinderella* (1940–1944), the
propagandistic operas *Semyon Kotko* (1939) and *A Tale of a Real Man* (1947–
1948), an operatic setting of Tolstoy's *War and Peace* (1941–1943), the admi-
rable children's tale *Peter and the Wolf* (1936), and cantatas and other vocal
works with patriotic or propagandistic texts. Several chamber works, his
Sixth, Seventh, and Eighth piano sonatas (1939–1944), his Violin Concerto
No. 2 (1935), and his last three symphonies (1944; 1945–1947; 1951–
1952; including the popular Fifth) are also products of his Soviet period.
Most of this music is characterized by a drastic simplification of style; in line
with the political pressures of Soviet life and some of the prevailing esthetic
ideas of the period, there is a strong revival of tonal procedures. This stylistic
evolution took the form, not so much of any kind of conscious Russian
nationalism or populism, as of a very distinctive, accessible neo-Classicism.
Eighteenth-century ideals are invoked in the use of "sonata form"—at least
its external shell—in triadic harmonic structure, in the use of simple accompaniment figures of the "Alberti bass" type, in simple rhythmic and phrase
structures, and in the character of the cadences. The classical cadence is
very important to Prokofiev's style; he uses it as a point of reference, as a
local articulation, to clarify a constant series of sideslips into distant keys.
These cycles of keys, often very loosely related and only briefly touched
upon, give Prokofiev's music its characteristic sound—diatonic but constantly "modulating."

In spite of the composer's modification of his style in the direction
of clarity and simplicity, his music remained under frequent attack in the
Soviet Union for reasons which remain obscure to Western observers; perhaps its lack of overtly nationalist character was a factor. Nevertheless, there
are many points of correspondence between Prokofiev's development and
that of Stravinsky—not to mention younger Russian emigré composers like
Alexander Tcherepnin (1899–1977) and Nicolas Nabokov (1903–1978)—
and it seems reasonable to speak of a Russian tradition of "neo-Classicism"
of which Prokofiev's music forms a distinctive part. As with Stravinsky,
Prokofiev's artistic choices were careful and conscious; unlike Stravinsky, he
never succeeded in finding new and organic forms for either his new or his
neo-Classical ideas and ideals; the attraction of his work ultimately lies in
qualities like the lyrical character of the invention and, in his earlier compositions, the strong motoric character of the musical motion.

Prokofiev's musical personality was largely formed before the Revolution of 1917. Of the younger composers whose careers coincide with the
advent of the Communist regime, only three have more than a local significance: the Armenian, Aram Khatchaturian (1903–1978), Dmitri Kabalevsky
(b. 1904), and Dmitri Shostakovich. The first two have upheld the ideals of

a musical populism superficially based on folk materials but amplified in a big, colorful, late-Romantic, bourgeois, symphonic manner. Shostakovich is, however, a far more original and distinctive musical personality, whose career and development were closely identified with the political and esthetic vicissitudes of Soviet life for more than forty years.

Shostakovich's orientation was, from the first, "neo-Classic" and tonal, with a primary bias towards a simple, symphonic idiom. As with many of the later works of Prokofiev, the classical starting point for Shostakovich is Beethoven (from the viewpoint of Soviet Marxist criticism, Beethoven was the first "socialist realist" composer). But Shostakovich's individuality grows out of the contrast between an extended, almost sentimental lyricism and a vigorous, grotesque, dissonant wit—stylistic characteristics which have apparently not always resulted in music consonant with the dictates of official taste. (To the extent that Shostakovich's genius runs to parody and grotesquerie, the conflict is clearer from a Western point of view than the similar controversy over Prokofiev's music.) Shostakovich's First Symphony (1924–1925), the work that first brought him to world-wide attention and still possibly his most remarkable composition, is a lean, hard piece of music full of mordant wit; it is like a caricature of the Classical symphony (unlike Prokofiev's similar early work, which is executed with respect and affection for the traditional form). At this time, the Russian modernists were closely in touch with developments in Western music, and there is no doubt that Shostakovich was acquainted with and influenced by German and French art. His opera, *The Nose*, based on Gogol (1927–1928), *The Golden Age* ballet of 1927–1930, and the famous *Lady Macbeth of the Mtsensk District* of 1930–1932 are brilliant works of the most intense, satiric sort. Even in the composer's Second Symphony of 1927, dedicated to the October Revolution, there are the strong, intense, biting chromaticism, hard rhythmic edges, and lean, brittle orchestral sound with which Shostakovich made his mark and which brought him so many difficulties.

A visit by Stalin to *Lady Macbeth* marked the beginning of trouble. Shostakovich was bitterly attacked in the press; both the opera and the Fourth Symphony (1935–1936), then in rehearsal, were withdrawn. A ballet about a collectivist farm was not good enough; the manner was still too lean, too stylized. Only with the Fifth Symphony of 1937 did Shostakovich redeem himself, and for a while he devoted himself in his major works largely to a new synthetic, heroic style. The influence of Mahler, already present in compositions like the withdrawn Fourth Symphony, is basic to a whole series of long, ambitious symphonic works of substantial length and weight: the Seventh ("Leningrad"; 1941); the gigantic Eighth (1943); the Twelfth (1961), also dedicated to the Revolution; and others.

In addition to the usual patriotic cantatas, Shostakovich composed a great deal of incidental music for the theater and films. He also wrote con-

certos for piano and for two pianos—clattering, breezy, ironic, jaunty works—
and a quantity of solo piano and chamber music of simple, almost elementary
musical qualities. The classicism and directness of his chamber music, particularly the fifteen string quartets, have commanded admiration in some
quarters, but Shostakovich remains primarily a symphonist and secondarily
a dramatist. (*Lady Macbeth* was produced again in 1963 under the title
Katerina Ismaylova, and *The Nose* has had much success in Europe.) His
large structures, built on long, simple tonal planes, endless repetition, rhythmic
and harmonic insistence, and big dramatic contrasts spaced out on a Mahlerian time scale, are not profound though they generally affect the appearance
of profundity. Nevertheless, they do achieve, almost by sheer force of will,
a certain scope and grandeur.[1]

NORTHERN EUROPE: SCANDINAVIA

Leaving aside the late-Romantic Danish composer, Carl Nielsen (1865–
1931), who was touched by neo-Classicism in his later work, the only important Scandinavian composer considered here is Jean Sibelius (1865–1957).
Sibelius's position in twentieth-century music is an odd one; he is a rare
example of a composer of this century who evolved a notably original style
out of nineteenth-century methods and conceptions. He began at the end
of the 1800's as a composer of salon music, fashionable tone poems, and a
First Symphony of a strongly Tchaikovskyan cast. In a large number of songs
and piano and solo string works, Sibelius remained essentially—like Tchaikovsky in his smaller works—a salon composer of trivial taste. Only in a few
of these compositions and, particularly, in choruses, where something of a
folk character predominates, does the music take on a little more profile—
even if the profile sometimes resembles Grieg.[2] The tone poems, too, in
spite of their dark and impressive color and unmistakably personal style, are
works of limited means, with the grand gestures of German and Slavic
Romanticism doing service for Finnish national and folk themes.

Aside from a string quartet (*Voces Intimae* of 1909) and the Violin
Concerto (1903; revised 1905), Sibelius's significant development must be
traced in his seven symphonies, written over a period of twenty-five years,
between 1899 and 1924. The Second Symphony of 1901–1902 and, to a
lesser extent, the Third of 1907 show a strong handling of traditional mate-

---

[1] As more of Shostakovich's chamber music and, in particular, his late work became
known in the West, a more introspective side to his musical personality emerged. It has been
suggested that this introspection, his use of Jewish themes, and the treatment of certain literary
subjects represented the composer's "silent" protest against Stalinism and its legacy.

[2] There are, however, among the songs a few works of a spare and striking character
in a class with the best of Sibelius's symphonic music.

rials; but the most original of the series is the Fourth, written in 1911—the period of the great musical upheavals on the continent. The personal crisis in Sibelius's music was also, in part, a tonal crisis. The Fourth Symphony centers on the ambiguous interval of the augmented fourth, and from its opening measures until some point near its conclusion the tonal resolution of the piece is in doubt. The remarkable thing about this work, aside from its moody and dissonant character, is its strong conception of form generated organically out of the musical ideas. The ideas come in fragments, and the formal process—almost the reverse of traditional development concepts— is one of gradual cohesion; the fragments merge and develop into coherent tonal structures of considerable power. None of Sibelius's later symphonies—the Fifth of 1914–1915 (revised in 1916 and 1919) and the last two dating from the 1920's—shows anything like the harmonic, melodic, and orchestral originality of the Fourth; Sibelius even returned to firmer tonal ground in these later works. But they share his typical halting, expressive, tortured kind of musical speech; and they retain—and even expand—this remarkable "synthetic" technique, preserving a sense of organic, tonal symphonic form which, in the traditional sense, had otherwise vanished.

NORTHERN EUROPE: ENGLAND

England, like the countries of Eastern and Northern Europe, was a cultural dependency of Central Europe, and finally established a measure of musical independence and national idiom through folk style. Sir Edward Elgar (1857–1934) was a late and somewhat provincial representative of the great symphonic tradition, and both Gustav Holst (1874–1934) and Delius— two of the most important creative musicians in the development of English musical life in the early part of the century—had Central European parental and musical antecedents. Delius, as previously noted, was attracted by the new French style with its floating, suspended sense of tonality and its exaltation of timbre as a basic expressive and formal means of musical expression. His "impressionism" has individuality, but the first composer to use these techniques in a distinctly English manner was Ralph Vaughan Williams (1872–1958).[3] Like Delius, Vaughan Williams was brought up in the Clas-

---

[3] The combination of folk-song and early-music revival, with or without some kind of "impressionist" treatment, characterizes a number of highly individualistic English composers in the early part of the century. Cyril Scott (1879–1970) and Philip Heseltine (Peter Warlock; 1894–1930) are not very highly regarded any more, but time may well reverse some of those judgments. Such a reversal has already begun in the case of Percy Grainger (Australian-born, active in England and America; 1882–1961). Grainger, an eccentric and highly original figure, created a folk-based style using traditional English, Keltic, and Norse sources. The sound of his music is often deceptively light and popular; like Ives, he closely identified himself with the vernacular but also transformed and transcended the merely folkloric.

sical-Romantic central European tradition, both in England where it was dominant and in Germany where he studied with Max Bruch. Later, like Bartók, he began to collect folk songs; still later, he studied with Maurice Ravel. These facts are not unconnected. Vaughan Williams was never an "impressionist" in any meaningful sense, but impulses from old English music—including Tudor art music, also pre-tonal in its bases—in combination with "impressionist" harmonic and coloristic techniques formed a personal and indisputably English style. Aside from the early vocal works and fantasies on folk and Tudor themes, actual quotation of old English music is not prominent in Vaughan Williams's music. As in the case of Bartók, the double experience of pre- and post-tonal music made possible the formation of a distinctive style, anchored in some kind of modal-tonality, but free of the traditional tonal way of thinking. Vaughan Williams's later work is characterized by an expansion and consolidation of technique and style in an attempt to create a large-scale English symphonic manner, with new tonal techniques enclosed in adaptations of traditional forms. This big symphonic style, characteristic of English twentieth-century music particularly in the 1930's—for instance, that of Arnold Bax (1883–1953), Arthur Bliss (1891–1975), or William Walton (1902–1983)—is closely related to parallel Russian and Scandinavian developments, and it is significant that composers like Shostakovich, Sibelius, and Nielsen have always been notably well received in England.

The modern English symphony is essentially a neo-Romantic form, but there was a strong form of neo-Classicism in England as well. The initial impulses came from France—from the Paris of Stravinsky and "Les Six"; indeed, the piano music and ballet scores of Lord Berners (1883–1950) were written for and produced in the French capital. The most important English production of the type was Walton's *Façade* (1921–1922; revised 1942), a setting of Edith Sitwell poems declaimed (originally by Miss Sitwell herself) to the witty, agile commentary of a chamber orchestra. Walton later abandoned the free, lean, dissonant, chamber style of this work in favor of a more accessible, neo-Romantic, "English" symphonic style. (Significantly, he later romanticized *Façade* in a ballet version scored for large orchestra.)

The most important and original English neo-tonal composer was Benjamin Britten (1913–1976). Britten developed under the influence of the art of Stravinsky and the French, but he was able to strike a distinctive and original note. His fundamental idiom was based on a synthetic tonal technique elucidated with great simplicity, naturalness, and skillful clarity growing out of a kind of melodic thinking which is often vocal in origin. He also responded to English tradition—the tradition of Purcell and of English choral music, rather than that of the folk song or Elizabethan madrigal. Nevertheless, any specifically English qualities which can be ascribed to his music are more the result of its force of character than of any easily isolated musical features. Britten never hesitated to use—and often with conspicuous success—a wide range of musical techniques integrated by means of simple, artful, new tonal forms. His forms are nearly always, in spite of appearances, highly constructed; a problem is that they are not always organic. The music is typically put together in freely diatonic melodic-vocal phrases, often set into a simple contrapuntal web and punctuated by clipped, highly colored, triadic harmonies. The basic long-range motion, the big structure, and even ultimately the sense of convincing tonal organization depend, however, on a careful inner manipulation of relationships functioning at another and far less simple level than the attractive and easily apprehended exterior. This odd, double construction is not difficult to detect in works like the opera *The Turn of the Screw* (1953–1954)—based on a twelve-tone "row" which is simply a cycle of fourths—or the *War Requiem* (1961), where the opposition of levels and the transformation of intellectual and musical materials actually operate as a kind of intellectual drama beneath the more obvious Stravinsky-Verdi dramatic surface.

Any list of Britten's major compositions will serve to indicate the importance of the human voice in his work. Big choral-orchestral works like the *Spring Symphony* (1949) and the *War Requiem* and smaller conceptions like *Les Illuminations* (1939; Rimbaud settings for soprano or tenor and strings), the *Serenade* for tenor, horn, and strings (1943), *Rejoice in the Lamb* (1943; to a text by Christopher Smart), and *A Ceremony of Carols* (1942) are among his most successful pieces. Finally, his stage works (see pp. 104–5) are strongly oriented towards lyric-intellectual as well as purely dramatic expressions. Except for an "occasional" work like *Noye's Fludde* (1957), with its children's orchestra of carillonneurs and recorder players, and the later *Curlew River* (1964), they are within the framework of conventional operatic gesture and plan; nevertheless, they represent the first important English opera since Purcell, and, containing as they do some of Britten's best music, they serve to confirm the vocal basis of his art.

The special form of English classicism found in Britten's music has another representative in Michael Tippett (b. 1905), regarded by some as Britten's equal at the very least but less well known outside of England. Classicism continues to have a hold on the conservative English public, but, as nearly everywhere else, Classicism and neo-tonality were turned aside by or absorbed into chromatic style for a while. Even Britten cautiously expanded his own techniques to utilize ideas from serial and post-serial music.

SOUTHERN EUROPE: ITALY AND SPAIN

In spite of the great role that Italy played in the early establishment of the Classical tradition, there was a complete break in the tradition in every field except opera. After 1900, Italian instrumental and even vocal music had to renew itself in a manner not so different from that of East Europe, Scandinavia, and England. The difference—and it is an important one—is that the Italians did not strike out anew from folk music but rather from their Renaissance and Baroque backgrounds.

Two Italians with strong musical roots in the nineteenth century were touched by new ideas. One, Ferruccio Busoni, actually anticipated many important contemporary ideas in his remarkable writings about music, although as a composer he participated in the century's revolutions only to a limited degree; in any case, his work belongs largely to Central European musical life and had only small influence in his native country. The other, Giacomo Puccini (1858–1924), is an extraordinary case of a brilliant and successful composer in a conservative tradition who consciously enriched his own means of expression with new ideas: from the parallel fifths in *La Bohème* (1896) to the Debussyisms of *Il Tabarro* (1918) and the striking dissonances of *Turandot* (1924; completed by Franco Alfano), his operatic style continually assimilated techniques which had originated outside the conventional operatic apparatus. Puccini's tonal-vocal style is contemporary in this essential respect, and its influence is still great in the theater and in popular music.

A definitive break with the operatic tradition and the establishment of a new Italian symphonic-tonal—and, later, also vocal-operatic—style were accomplished by a younger group of composers including Casella (already discussed above in connection with neo-Classicism), Ottorino Respighi (1879–1936), Ildebrando Pizzetti (1880–1968), and Gian Francesco Malipiero (1882–1973). Respighi, a kind of modern Italian Rimsky-Korsakov (with whom he actually studied), was a sensualist who synthesized a variety of ingredients from Gregorian chant to Debussy, all in a brilliant, popular manner. Respighi's popularity rests on a small group of orchestral works, although the bulk of his output is to be found in more than a dozen operatic compositions, all failures. With the exception of Casella, these composers made extensive attempts to revive and renovate Italian opera with a new and modern tonal technique based on free and wide-ranging diatonic elements, essentially unrelated to prior Italian operatic tradition but nonetheless distinctively Italian in its particular adaptation of contemporary ideas. The bulk of Pizzetti's work, outside of his songs, belongs in this category; the results, whatever their intrinsic musical merit, have not been notably successful.

Of this group of composers, undoubtedly the most important is Malipiero, whose long list of compositions includes a number of stage pieces (including an attractive and occasionally performed Goldoni triptych written in 1920–1922) and an even more extensive catalogue of instrumental and orchestral works. Malipiero's free diatonic technique, strongly imbued with a kind of vocally derived counterpoint, a mild use of dissonance, and rather improvisatory lyric-dramatic forms, contains scarcely a trace of anything that could be described as local color; the basic wandering modal character of the "tonal" writing has nothing to do with folk music. However, Malipiero strikes a distinctively Italian note due in part to his derivations from pretonal Italian music, particularly the great vocal tradition up through Monteverdi.

In contrast to the rather reserved, simple, but almost aristocratic ideals of the new Italian art music (of the group after Puccini which attempted to renovate vocal ideals and synthesize them with a new instrumental music, only Respighi developed a really popular idiom), the revival of Spanish music, in large part the creation of the composer Felipe Pedrell (1841–1922), was consciously and thoroughly based on traditional music. The familiar elements of this tradition, derived largely from an aural performance style,[4] consist principally of some fairly complex rhythmic patterns within a steady and obsessive metrical frame, and a rich and highly ornamented melos based on a few characteristic modal patterns—of obviously Eastern origin— to which have been added or adapted a few simple Western harmonies. The extensive transformation of this material into "art" music is almost entirely due to the harmonic developments in French music at the end of the nineteenth and the beginning of the twentieth centuries. Some of the most important use of Spanish material occurs in the work of Debussy and Ravel, and composers like Isaac Albéniz (1860–1909) and Enrique Granados (1867–1916) were closely influenced by the "impressionists" (also by d'Indy, Fauré, and Dukas). Debussy, Ravel, and later, Stravinskyan "neo-Classicism" were also starting points for Manuel de Falla (1876–1946), not merely because Falla had no native precedents on which to base a new, Spanish style but also because the new materials of French music could give form to other characteristic ideas without wrenching them into the conventions of the old tonal system. Two of Falla's best-known pieces are concerted works: *Nights in the Gardens of Spain* for piano and orchestra (1911–1915) and the Concerto for harpsichord and chamber ensemble (1923–1926), the latter the most obviously "neo-Classical" of his works. There are also piano pieces and vocal works including the *Seven Spanish Popular Songs* (1914–1915), one of the surprisingly rare examples of the actual use of Spanish folk material in Falla's music. Falla's most important work, however, was for the theater; it ranges from the colorful, florid Spanish style of the opera *La Vida breve* (1904–1905) and the ballet *El Amor brujo* (1914–1915) to the drier, wittier neo-classicism of *El Retablo de Maese Pedro* (1919–1922), a scenic play with puppets, adapted from an episode in *Don Quixote*, and the attempted synthesis of the large *Atlántida* (unfinished; completed and orchestrated in 1961 by Ernesto Halffter).

The range of Falla's activity framed nearly all of the work produced in Spain for many years, from Ernesto Halffter (b. 1905), the most Stravin-

---

[4] Partly Gypsy and partly Spanish-Arabic in origin.

skyan of the Spaniards, to local-color composers like Joaquín Turina (1882–1949), Joaquín Nin (1879–1949), Joaquin Rodrigo (b. 1901), and others. Only recently and with great reluctance have Spanish composers begun to abandon Spanish tradition as a primary source of musical ideas and forms, and although the younger composers in Spain—as everywhere else—are now committed to modernist and even "post-modern" ideas, one can still find attempts to synthesize new with traditional materials à la Bartók or even shotgun marriages of *cante hondo* and serialism à la Boulez.

LATIN AMERICA

The impulse which produced the remarkable Mexican pictorial school of the 1920's also generated a new Mexican music of significance. Like the painting, this music was liberated by the new techniques and new freedoms produced in Europe at the beginning of the century, but it developed (up to a point) in a highly distinctive way.

Carlos Chávez (1899–1978) benefited, like many of his colleagues in the United States at the time, from the opportunity to develop an intense original musicality at a long distance from the old tradition. Chávez's early works are his radical ones: in his free use of percussion; in the intense, linear, chromatic, expressive angularity and dissonance of a work like the ballet *Antígona* (1932); in the remarkable use of percussion in works like the *Sinfonía India* (1935–1936), and the *Toccata* for percussion (1942); in the driving power of works like the ballet *HP* (i.e., horsepower; 1926–1927), Chávez established a musical line of expression which was both contemporary and national without being narrowly folkloristic. Nevertheless, in spite of the composer's awareness of the limitations of mere folklorism, Chávez was inevitably involved—as were his painter contemporaries—in social consciousness and social expression. For Diego Rivera and José Orozco, this meant a focus on subject matter and interpretation of the social situation; for Chávez it meant clarified tonal techniques and direct communicativeness without or (preferably) with folklore. From this point, Chávez later turned to big symphonic and Classical-Romantic tonal form.

The most curious figure of the Mexican musical renaissance was Silvestre Revueltas (1899–1940), who, in the brief span of forty-one years, produced an *oeuvre* in which an actual or imagined Indian-Mexican music of primitive intensity was put together with a kind of obsessive *Sacre du printemps* technique. Revueltas's music is, like much other experimental music of the period, not quite fully realized. The Cuban composer Amadeo Roldán (1900–1939) is a similar case; like Revueltas he was a talented extremist, and his *Rítmicas* V and VI (1930) are possibly the first works written for an all-percussion ensemble (they precede Varèse's *Ionisation*). Like Revueltas, Roldán died young, before his talents were fully realized. In any case, the output of these composers, very much part of an important New World creative flowering, ought to be better known.

The North American tradition of experimentalism did not extend to South America, although the southern continent's one really important composer of the period, Heitor Villa-Lobos (1887–1959), showed a remarkable affinity for and distance from European tradition in his temperament and style. Villa-Lobos, a Brazilian, had a penchant for modern French music dating from his friendship with Milhaud, who was the French cultural attaché in Brazil from 1917 to 1919. Any rough description of Villa-Lobos's music would have to contend with "Les Six," Brazilian-Portuguese-African folk and popular style, "impressionism" (especially in the instrumental usage), a bit of Indian music, and a touch of jazz. Villa-Lobos began his musical career playing in café orchestras; essentially self-taught as a composer, he was one of the most prolific—and uncritical—musicians who ever lived. The result is an enormous mass of music, tossed off with great ease and freedom, often utterly charming, very often trivial, sometimes utterly confused and inconsistent, sometimes impressive. Tonality was as natural a technique to Villa-Lobos as it was to the street musicians who provided the model for the ditties he loved so well; but his tonality is often clouded by huge masses of rich sound-color applied liberally with the palette knife and without much care. Perhaps the best—or at least the most characteristic—of Villa-Lobos's music is to be found in the various works titled *Chôros* and *Bachianas Brasileiras* written over a period of more than twenty-five years.

Among other South Americans, only the Argentinian Alberto Ginastera (1916–1983) produced important work in a national-tonal tradition. His ballets, *Panambí* (1934–1936) and *Estancia* (1941), have the now-classical Indian-Latin-*Rite-of-Spring* mixture, but his later music is atonal-serial in the post-war mode.

THE UNITED STATES

In another volume of this series,[5] twentieth-century music in the United States is discussed in the context of the American past and of American tradition. Here—and elsewhere in this volume—we will discuss the position of music in the United States vis-à-vis the international development of contemporary style. Certainly the first attempts to establish a new tonal,

[5] H. Wiley Hitchcock, *Music in the United States: A Historical Introduction*, 3rd ed. (Englewood Cliffs, N.J.; Prentice-Hall, Inc., 1988).

"national" style completely outside the tradition of functional tonality must be ascribed—along with so many other things—to Charles Ives (1874–1954), but Ives is perhaps more fruitfully considered along with the great American experimental and avant-garde movements discussed below. In several important and individual ways, the vast changes in European music during the first part of the century were paralleled—sometimes anticipated, sometimes followed—in the United States. Similarly, the development of new tonal styles and the new musical nationalisms in the 1920's, 1930's, and 1940's were paralleled—and, because of the war, often developed and continued—in this country. The new preoccupations with the relationship of the composer to the musical community, the public, and society; the brave attempt to re-integrate the creative artist into his society through musical populism, music for use, school music, workers' music, and songs for the masses; the preoccupation with the use of recordings, radio, theater, and films as a means for reaching a mass audience; the phenomenal success of Kurt Weill (1900–1950) and the interest in music as a vehicle for social commentary; the mystique of purposefulness and utilitarianism; the search for a national music combined with the revived interest in national, popular, and folk expression—all had a profound effect on this side of the Atlantic. Ironically, at the very moment when the United States had to assume most of the burden of international contemporary musical life, its composers were looking inward and backward trying to find a specifically American musical identity.

The initial impulses for this new American tonal music came from Stravinsky and the French, to a lesser extent from Hindemith, and, in the theater, from Kurt Weill. Stravinsky's neo-Classic "idea" appeared as a stylistic vessel which could carry many different kinds of contents: jazz as well as Bach, a folk tune as well as a neo-Mozartian melody. Roger Sessions's First Symphony (1927), Aaron Copland's "Jazz" Concerto for piano and orchestra (1926), and a whole host of works by lesser composers—nearly all of whom studied how to make first-class neo-tonality with Nadia Boulanger in Paris—Americanized these techniques with skill and ease. Virgil Thomson (b. 1896), with his attitudes of elegance and artful simplicity, reduced such ideas to their absolute essentials: disassociated scales and triads treated exactly like the disassociated words and phrases in the texts of Gertrude Stein which he set.

The center of this activity in the 1930's and early 1940's was the theater and related media. After a period of working with chromatic and even serial techniques, Copland (b. 1900) developed his popular style in a well-known series of ballets (*Billy the Kid*, 1938; *Rodeo*, 1942; *Appalachian Spring*, 1943–1944). George Gershwin (1898–1937; the first actual arrival from the world of popular music); Marc Blitzstein (1905–1964; an intellectual convert from highbrow music); Thomson; the quickly Americanized Kurt

Weill; and others scored real theatrical successes. Copland, George Antheil (1900–1959), Louis Gruenberg (1884–1964), and Paul Bowles (b. 1910) wrote movie music; and there was considerable activity on the four radio networks, which sponsored a great deal of new music of the more popular sort. This was also the period of innumerable symphonic "Hoedowns" and "Square Dances" as well as of the growth of a broad, serious, symphonic style, strongly tonal (generally in a Stravinskyan or modal sort of way), based on traditional patterns often rather awkwardly arranged to fit the new local-color material; influenced as well by Hindemith and the Soviet composers but—in one way or another—definably American. The idea was, more or less, to adapt the great tradition to a New World style for the large, new American public— in short, to write "The Great American Symphony." Copland himself produced important music in this vein, notably his Third Symphony (1944–1946) and his more ascetic Piano Sonata (1939–1941), but the best and most consistent representative of the style was perhaps Roy Harris (1898–1979). Harris's works—even his notable Third Symphony (1937) and Piano Quintet (1936)—seem to have lost ground in recent years, but in their day they were considered models of serious style and form combined with clear, handsome, and accessible ideas that were identifiably American. The "American" character of these works—and many others on the same model—is only partly due to the actual use of folk or folk-popular material. Certain types of stylized, expressive melody, popular in origin but much transformed—a simple, halting motion, in scale steps within a small diatonic compass or in wide leaps of fourths and fifths, with metrical changes based on alternating threes and twos, and with a certain amount of syncopation—became hallmarks. So did wide, open harmonies built on major seconds, fourths, and fifths and a flat, colorful, open orchestration. The three- and four-movement forms were— except in the dance and theater pieces—almost invariably and rather uncomfortably borrowed from traditional patterns.

By no means all of the American symphonic music of this type was restricted to this model; it was just that the model was the most typical, distinctive, and obviously American. Conservative composers like Howard Hanson (1896–1981) and Samuel Barber (1910–1981) remained closer or returned to European prototypes, particularly those derived from Romantic symphonic literature. On the other hand, William Schuman (b. 1910) was involved in a much wider range of materials in his development of a big symphonic style based on chromatic ideas, a rich, dissonant harmonic material, high-powered rhythmic impulse and orchestration, and structures which come out of these materials. The music of Walter Piston (1894–1976) belongs somewhere in between; highly polished, basically diatonic in its orientation, and strongly dependent on classical models, it remains poised between ideals of serious, classical workmanship and high degrees of tension and articulation.

The generation of composers whose work became known in the 1930's and 1940's can be divided—a little too neatly perhaps—between those who attempted to carry forward some kind of development of the "American School" popular-symphonic idea—like David Diamond (b. 1915), Peter Mennin (1923–1983), William Flanagan (1923–1969)—and those who were working towards a lively American "neo-classical" style full of elegance, wit, and resonance—Arthur Berger (b. 1912), Irving Fine (1914–1962), Elliott Carter (b. 1908), and Lukas Foss (b. 1922). The former style has remained rather constant in the new works of older composers (occasionally showing twelve-tone influence) and it is essentially without influence on the younger generation; the latter has evolved into or been completely superseded by serial or other avant-garde developments.

There remains one composer, Ernest Bloch (1860–1959), who must be considered here—partly for want of a better place and partly because he spent most of his creative life in the United States. In spite of the fact that Bloch wrote an "epic rhapsody" for chorus and orchestra, *America* (1926), employing American folk songs, hymns, and even jazz, he can hardly be considered an American composer, and indeed, in spite of his well-known works on Hebrew motifs, he cannot be accurately or meaningfully classified as a Jewish composer. Bloch was born in Switzerland, studied in Belgium, lived in Paris and—after 1916—in the United States. He was a composer rooted in the Central European late-Romantic tradition; in spite of some important vocal works, he was oriented towards a symphonic style covered with literary and poetic trappings. His early style is an amalgam of Debussy, Richard Strauss, and Mahler, to which he later adapted the expanded vocabulary of early twentieth-century modernism and even—in the mode of Honegger or Kodály—a certain amount of neo-Classicism. Bloch was certainly not without influence on the development of American music, but he was a strong eclectic with an extremely various and uneven production that remains difficult to pigeon hole.

BIBLIOGRAPHICAL NOTES

The literature on local style is enormous and spread out in a multitude of languages. Two studies devoted to twentieth-century composers by country are *Music in the Modern Age*, ed. F. W. Sternfeld (Praeger History of Western Music, V, New York, 1973) and *Twentieth-Century Composers*, eds. A. Kallin and N. Nabokov (four volumes are out presently: Virgil Thomson's *American Music Since 1910*, H. H. Stuckenschmidt's *Germany and Central Europe*, Humphrey Searle and Robert Layton's *Britain, Scandinavia, and The Netherlands*, and Frederick Goldbeck's *France, Italy, and Spain*; London, 1970–).

The often-cited Bartók biography by Halsey Stevens (2nd ed., New York, 1965) contains musical analyses that are now dated. József Ujfalussy's *Béla Bartók* (Corvina, Budapest, 1971; English trans. Ruth Pataki, Boston, 1972) gives only cursory discussions of the music but includes a detailed presentation of Hungarian and central-European conditions during Bartók's lifetime. Paul Griffiths's *Bartók* (London, 1984) is short but contains some interesting comments on the music. Two outstanding examinations of Bartók's music are Elliott Antokoletz's *The Music of Béla Bartók: A Study of Tonality and Progression in Twentieth-Century Music* (Berkeley, CA, 1984) and Ernő Lendvai's *The Workshop of Bartók and Kodály* (Budapest, 1983). The latter book draws on much of the material found in Lendvai's earlier study, *Béla Bartók: An Analysis of His Music* (revised reprint, London, 1979). A collection of articles on Bartók's musical and personal relationships with other musicians has been compiled by Todd Crow (*Bartók Studies*, Detroit, 1976); Benjamin Suchoff has published a volume of *Essays* by Bartók (London, 1976) and János Demény a collection of his letters (New York, 1971).

Two biographies that appear in English on Janáček are those of Jaroslav Vogel (London, 1962, 1981; the more exhaustive) and Ian Horsbrugh (London and New York, 1981). Studies of Janáček's operas have been written by Erik Chisholm (Oxford and New York, 1971), using a Tovey-derived analysis; Michael Ewans (London, 1977); and John Tyrell, on *Kát'a Kabanová* (Cambridge, England, 1982). Brian Large's biography of Martinů (London, 1975) places the composer's *oeuvre* "against the background and times in which they were written."

For Russian and Soviet composers, see Gerald Abraham's *Eight Soviet Composers* (London, 1948), Stanley D. Krebs's *Soviet Composers and the Development of Soviet Music* (New York, 1970), and Boris Schwarz's *Music and Musical Life in Soviet Russia, 1917–1981* (enlarged ed., New York, 1983). Sergei Bertensson and Jay Leyda's biography of Rachmaninoff (New York, 1956) has not yet been superseded; Robert Palmieri's *Sergei Vasil'evich Rachmaninoff: A Guide to Research* (New York and London, 1985) is an annotated bibliography of primary and secondary sources. Israel Nest'yev's *Prokofiev* (trans. Florence Jonas, Stanford, CA, 1960) is distorted by its "Soviet"—not to say Stalinist—point of view; a useful corrective would be *La Musique russe*, ed. Pierre Souvtchinsky (2 vols., Paris, 1953). Victor Seroff's *Sergei Prokofiev: A Soviet Tragedy* (New York, 1968) takes the opposite point of view from Nest'yev. While there is no definitive biography of Shostakovich, there is a study of his symphonies by Roy Blokker and Robert Dearling (London, 1979) and a collection of essays on the composer and his music, edited by Christopher Norris (London, 1982). Two monographs are devoted to the writings and ruminations of the composer: *Dmitri Shostakovich: About Himself and His Times*, ed., by L. Grigoryev (trans. Angus and Neilian Roxburgh, Moscow, 1981) and the controversial *Testimony: The Memoirs of Dmitri Shostakovich* (as related to and edited by Solomon Volkov; trans. Antonina W. Bouis, New York, 1979).

For Sibelius, two recent volumes are noteworthy: Erik Tawaststjerna's *Sibelius*

I: *1865–1905* (trans. Robert Layton, Berkeley, CA, 1976), the first of a projected two-volume study; and Burnett James's *The Music of Jean Sibelius*
(Rutherford and London, 1983), mainly about the composer's symphonies.

For English composers see Peter J. Pirie's *The English Musical Renaissance*
(London, 1979). On Vaughan Williams, see *R.V.W.: A Biography of Ralph
Vaughan Williams* by Ursula Vaughan Williams (London and New York, 1964);
Michael Kennedy's study of his works (London and New York, 1964); and
Kennedy's more recent annotated bibliography (rev. ed., London, 1982). Wil-
liam Walton can be represented here by Frank Howes's *The Music of William
Walton* (2nd ed., London, 1974) and Neil Tierney's *William Walton: His Life
and Music* (London, 1984). On Britten and Tippett the English recently have
put out a series of important studies: Peter Evans's *The Music of Benjamin
Britten* (London, 1979); Michael Kennedy's *Britten* (London, 1981); *The Brit-
ten Companion*, ed. Christopher Palmer (London, 1984), a collection of essays
by scholars assessing Britten's importance in twentieth-century music; Arnold
Whittal's *The Music of Britten and Tippett: Studies in Themes and Techniques*
(Cambridge, England, 1982); and Ian Kemp's *Tippett: The Composer and His
Music* (London, 1984).

For Spanish and Latin American composers, see Burnett James's *Manuel de
Falla and the Spanish Musical Renaissance* (London, 1979) and Robert L.
Parker's *Carlos Chávez: Mexico's Modern-Day Orpheus* (Boston, 1983). For
Chávez, see the composer's own *Musical Thought*, the Charles Eliot Norton
Lectures of 1958–1959 (Cambridge, MA, 1961). The only book of note on
Villa-Lobos is in German: Lisa M. Peppercorn's *Heitor Villa-Lobos: Leben
und Werk des brasilianischen Komponisten* (Zurich, 1972).

For American composers see Wilfred Mellers's *Music in a New Found Land*
(1964; reprinted New York, 1975), H. Wiley Hitchcock's *Music in the United
States: A Historical Introduction* in this Prentice-Hall History of Music Series,
Charles Hamm's *Music in the New World* (New York, 1983), Daniel Kingman's
American Music: A Panorama (New York, 1979), and Alan H. Levy's *Musical
Nationalism: American Composers' Search for Identity* (Westport, CT, 1983).
For Aaron Copland, see the first volume of his autobiography (Copland and
Vivian Perlis, *Copland: 1900–1942*; New York, 1984), and JoAnn Skowronski's
Aaron Copland: A Bio-Bibliography (Westport, CT, 1985), which includes the
dates of performances of his works, a discography, and bibliography of writings
by and about Copland. Arthur Berger's biography of Copland (New York,
1953), which surveys the composer's life and works through 1952, has not been
updated or supplanted.

For comments on the development of neo-Classic and neo-tonal styles in
American music, see the author's own article "Modern Music in Retrospect"
(*Perspectives of New Music* [Spring/Summer 1964]) as well as Arthur Berger's
article "Stravinsky and the Younger American Composers" (*The Score and
I.M.A. Magazine* [June 1955]). There exist biographies of Roy Harris and
Ernest Bloch: Dan Stehman's *Roy Harris: An American Musical Pioneer* (Bos-
ton, 1984) and Robert Strassburg's *Ernest Bloch: Voice in the Wilderness: A
Biographical Study* (Los Angeles, 1977).

NINE

MUSICAL THEATER

Musical theater ought not to be considered apart from the general development of musical creativity, but unfortunately it must be so treated in any discussion of the music of the first two-thirds of this century. For the first time since the origins of opera, about 1600, the theater ceased to be a primary generating or creative force in musical evolution. Opera, long at the leading edge of musical development, became an ultra-conservative institution, resistant to change and highly dependent on routine. By contrast, the dance has been closely identified with new musical developments; however, this success was achieved in part by weaning dance away from theater in the direction of lyric or intellectual—in short, abstract—forms.

It is only in the last few years that this situation has changed; the new electronic media and non-operatic theater have become central in the evolution of new music, and music has become an important creative force in new theater. These important developments are discussed in the final section of the book; this chapter will attempt to survey the state of opera and musical theater in the earlier part of the century.

PUCCINI AND VERISMO

The operas of Giacomo Puccini scarcely seem to fall within the scope of this study at all, but *Turandot*—completed by Franco Alfano after the composer's death in 1924—is the last opera to enter the international repertory and one of the few in that repertory to employ twentieth-century melodic, harmonic, and orchestral techniques. French "impressionism" produced comparatively little for the stage, although assuredly three masterpieces in Debussy's *Pelléas et Mélisande* and Ravel's charming one-act operas *L'Heure espagnole* and *L'Enfant et les sortilèges*. As early as *La Bohème* Puccini began to come under the influence of Debussyan harmonic ideas. In spite of its origins in the Italian tradition, Puccini's melodic technique, with its "modal" turns of phrase, is essentially twentieth-century in conception, and his harmonic-melodic ideas are often quite surprisingly free—in implication at least—of traditional functional-tonal prejudices. The series of unrelated triads at the beginning of *Tosca*, the parallel fifths that open the third act of *La Bohème*, the tonal irresolution of the end of *Madama Butterfly*, the dabs of detached harmonic and orchestral color at the beginning of *Il Tabarro*, and the sequences of parallel seventh and ninth chords that appear in the later works are by no means isolated usages. Puccini's rather flexible diatonic melodic style (often curiously modal or pentatonic, even in the non-oriental operas) combines with a rich and free harmonic style based on piled-up thirds, parallel motion, and dramatic harmonic and tonal shifts to form a consistent musical style distinct from traditional practice, closely interwoven with the dramatic conceptions, and distinctly twentieth-century in character. Puccini's greatest influence was on the development of popular musical theater, film music, and—to a lesser degree—on certain related, lighter forms of pop music. Parallel sequences of ninth and eleventh chords, first extensively employed by Puccini as a way of enriching the support of a simple modal or diatonic melodic line, have become clichés of popular-song harmonization. In theatrical idea and form, Puccini was not an innovator, although his type of musical theater—as well as his musical style—has been much imitated. In general, the late operas of Verdi provide the models: set numbers of the classical type alternate with narrative or dialogue scenes, the whole framed in a continuous and prominent orchestral texture; indeed the orchestra often carries the entire musical motion and significance, with the vocal parts reduced to a simple, word-conveying *parlando*, sometimes the mere repetition of one or two tones. Puccini's contemporaries, Leoncavallo and Mascagni, introduced a popular or local subject matter in their operas, which thus pass under the name of *verismo*. Puccini's material, however, is far more wide-ranging—often exotic in a kind of *fin-de-siècle* way and always reflecting the theatrical taste of his period: *Tosca* (1899), *Madama Butterfly* (1904), and *The Girl of the Golden West* (1910) were based on popular plays of the time; *La Bohème* and *Il Tabarro* derive from scenes of contemporary life. Only in *Turandot*, a curious fantasty-comedy by the eighteenth-century Italian, Gozzi, did Puccini venture to treat a dramatic concept essentially removed from the missing-fourth-wall realistic theater concept. *Turandot* is a mythic, symbolic theater of masks, and its music—highly colored, full of dissonant accent, often tonally ambiguous— is equally far from tonal "realism."

Nearly all of Puccini's contemporaries—Umberto Giordano (1867– 1948), Pietro Mascagni (1863–1945), Ruggiero Leoncavallo (1857–1919)— bogged down in the almost impossible task of creating a significant operatic parallel to the literary realism of Sardou or Verga. The remarkable success of *Cavalleria rusticana* (1890) and *Pagliacci* (1892) and the exceptional ability of Puccini to overcome the inherent contradictions in the so-called realistic opera (which even Puccini deserted at the end of his life) misled a great many composers into thinking that a popular post-Puccini style was possible; it was not. Outside of the world of musical comedy, Puccini's operatic style has had dozens of imitators, but few consequents of note. George Gershwin's *Porgy and Bess* (1935) stands apart; Gershwin called it a "folk opera," but it is actually a full-scale grand opera, strongly influenced by Puccini, *verismo*, and other modern-opera trends. Recent full-scale productions of the work— it had previously always been cut and adapted for theater singers—have revealed the traditionally operatic scope and power of the piece. The Puccini- ism of Gian-Carlo Menotti (b. 1911) is not merely musical: Menotti thinks of musical theater in terms of function, space, dramatic incident, and struc- ture in much the same way that Puccini did, even when his subjects are most divergent. Menotti's theater is not always "realistic," but it is contem- porary in its subject matter and its concerns; his particular musical talent enables him to create orchestral and vocal parts which heighten the dramatic context in such works as *The Consul* (1949); *Amahl and the Night Visitors* (1951); *The Saint of Blecker Street* (1954); and *The Unicorn, The Gorgon, and the Manticore* (1956); among others.

THE WAGNERIAN TRADITION AND EXPRESSIONIST OPERA

For all the significance of "The Music of the Future" at the end of the nineteenth and the beginning of the twentieth century, the essentials of the Wagnerian theatrical concept remained more or less the exclusive property of Wagner. A great many "Wagnerian" operas were written in Wagner's day and afterwards; only a few—notably Humperdinck's *Hansel und Gretel* (1893) and Busoni's *Doktor Faustus* (1916–1924; completed by Jarnach)—have held on at the edge of the repertory or have had successful revivals, and the possibilities of a development in the operatic theater out of the direct inheritance of Wagnerian style are represented—indeed exhausted—in the work of a single composer, Richard Strauss. As we have seen, Strauss extended Wagnerian contrapuntal chromaticism to the edge of atonality in *Salome* and *Elektra* and then backed away. The rich orchestral and vocal web of the later *Der Rosenkavalier* is Wagnerian in technique but Classical and tonal in subject matter and style. From a certain point of view, *Ariadne auf Naxos* is actually a long dialogue—a conjunction of oppositions—concerning expressive freedom and Classical form. Strauss's later operas are often concerned with this kind of opposition, an aspect which enhances their contemporary intellectual interest but which weakens them in the theater. His later musical style coalesces around an expanded contrapuntal tonality, diatonic and even functional in the old way, but freely moving with shifting triads and seventh chords sliding through the entire chromatic range; it is a kind of super-enharmonic diatonicism in which all the implications of chromaticism are present, not necessarily in detail at all, but on a grand scale.

The later operas of Strauss, whatever their final value may be, stand apart from the mainstreams of twentieth-century development; *Salome* and *Elektra*, on the other hand, are key works. Aside from the huge apparatus of post-Wagnerian technique, these dramas are remarkable for their concentration of means and materials and their penetrating psychological subject matter. The two aspects—which are not unrelated—mark a fundamental departure from the Wagnerian esthetic, which is slow, developmental, and narrative in plan, schematic and mythic in subject matter. Where Wagner may use 136 measures to unfold and explicate an idea as simple as a tonic triad (in the prelude to *Das Rheingold*), Strauss concentrates a whole mass of conflicting motives, a dense, contrasting harmonic motion, and elaborate rhythmic and orchestral textures into a relatively few minutes; what happens in Wagner as a sequence of events occurs in Strauss as simultaneities or as a quick dialogue of opposites. From this point of view, *Salome* and, especially, *Elektra* are difficult works to hear; they seem to be full of unsorted detail, of half-phrases, antecedents without consequents, of tensions and energies never fully released. In a sense, the big shape of these works is neither a musical form nor, in the conventional sense, a dramatic one; the structure of both (excluding the rather disconnected and banal "Dance of the Seven Veils" in *Salome*) is psychological. Such a concentrated psychological form with its word-for-word setting, its constant opposition of conflicting

Richard Strauss as John the Baptist. Caricature by George Villa. Meyer Collection, Paris. Reproduction forbidden.

elements, and its rapid, intense pulse does not really exist in Wagner, although its strictly musical techniques may seem at first to be superficially Wagnerian; Wagner approached it perhaps only in isolated sections such as Tristan's monologue at the beginning of the last act of *Tristan und Isolde.* It exists in a limited way in late Verdi, and the clearest nineteenth-century prototypes are to be found in Mussorgsky. But with Strauss the form is essentially new and, one would be tempted to say, as valid in twentieth-century—one would almost say Freudian—terms as the psychological novel. Yet Strauss quickly abandoned the genre and, in the theater at least, the idea seems to have had only one direct and significant consequent: Schoenberg's *Erwartung*, with its single character and its intense, free, associative, atonal form.

All musical form is, of course, in some sense psychological, but music resists literal verbal-psychological interpretations; the very specific psychological, asymmetrical "free-association" form of *Erwartung* made it impossible to duplicate or use as a model. Nevertheless, the experience of this kind of form and expression—musical structure whose impulses and tensions reflect, parallel, or suggest by analogy psychological states and conflicts—had a profound effect on the music of Schoenberg and, particularly, of Alban Berg. These elements are apparent in Schoenberg's later operas *Die Glückliche Hand* (1913), *Von Heute auf Morgen* (1928), and even *Moses und Aron* (2 acts completed 1932; unfinished); they play essential roles in Berg's *Wozzeck* (1914–1922) and *Lulu* (1928–1935), both of which are thus transformed from mere social and symbolic documents to intense studies of the human condition. The classical forms of *Wozzeck*—the sonatas, variations, and passacaglias into which the individual scenes are molded—are not at all arbitrary but form the tight, tense frames which push against and hold in place the inner developing form of the detail. In the same way, the massive, cyclical structure of the complete *Lulu* parallels the mythic and symbolic content of the work and surrounds—in a sense, realizes on another plane—the intense, personal, gruesome, scabrous, or comic detail of the work.

A post-Wagnerian, post-Bergian style has more or less followed the diffusion of twelve-tone music (discussed in Chapter 11). This line of operatic development generally employs subjects of contemporary interest, a nontonal or freely tonal style with chromatic or twelve-tone techniques, and long chromatic vocal lines alternating with angular lines and *Sprechstimme.* The musical motion is generally continuous, in the tradition of Wagnerian "endless melody," but more condensed, more "expressionist," more psychologically oriented; in the manner of Berg, symphonic or other traditional forms underlie the structure. Many of these works are highly symbolic and, in one way or another, comment on modern life or the human condition.

Ernst Krenek's (b. 1900) *Karl V* (1930–1933) was the first major twelve-tone opera to be produced outside the original Schoenberg circle. *Il*

Prigioniero (1944–1948) of Luigi Dallapiccola (1904–1975) was one of the earliest outside of the German-speaking world. But the most important younger theater composer in this vein is Hans Werner Henze (b. 1926). *Boulevard Solitude* (1951; a modern version of the Manon story), *König Hirsch* (1952–1955 and revised 1962; based on Gozzi), *Der Prinz von Hamburg* (1958; based on a play by Kleist), *Elegy for Young Lovers* (1959–1961; text by W. H. Auden and Chester Kallman), *Der junge Lord* (1964; text by Backmann after W. Hanff), and the *Bassarids* (1965; text by Auden and Kallman) tend to merge the twelve-tone inheritance of Schoenberg and Berg with Stravinskyan formal and rhythmic structure as well as Stravinskyan-Audenesque detachment.

There is a fair body of Central European works in this tradition, including operas by Wolfgang Fortner (b. 1907; *Blood Wedding*, 1957); Rolf Liebermann (b. 1910; *School for Wives*, 1955); and Gottfried von Einem (b. 1918; *Dantons Tod*, 1944–1946; *Der Prozess*, 1950–1952). Boris Blacher (1903–1975; *Romeo und Julia*, 1943; *Abstrakte Oper No. 1*, 1953), Werner Egk (*Der Revisor*, 1957), and Nicolas Nabokov (*The Holy Devil*, 1958) are more distantly related. Two important American composers whose work ranks with such European efforts are Roger Sessions (1896–1985; *The Trial of Lucullus, Montezuma*) and Hugo Weisgall (b. 1912; *The Tenor*, 1948–1950; *The Stronger*, 1952; *Six Characters in Search of an Author*, 1953–1956; *Athalia*, 1960–1963). The Argentinian Alberto Ginastera developed an operatic style of considerable effectiveness by combining a post-Bergian twelve-tone and serial style with highly melodramatic stage material in the Verdian tradition: *Don Rodrigo* (1963–1964), *Bomarzo* (1966–1967), and *Beatrix Cenci* (1971).

In addition to the works that are directly heir to the Central European tradition, a number of important theater pieces composed between the wars fall under an extended definition of the term "expressionism." In these pieces, intense, internal psychological conflicts are represented externally by certain violent, striking, artistic materials whose shape grows out of conflict, paradox, contradiction, and psychological conflict. Bartók's *Bluebeard's Castle* and his ballet-pantomime *The Miraculous Mandarin* belong here; one might also include a number of works which relate to expressionist theater— Prokofiev's *The Gambler* and *The Flaming Angel* (1919–1923), Shostakovich's *Lady Macbeth of Mtsensk*, Hindemith's *Cardillac* and *Mathis der Maler*, Krenek's *Jonny spielt auf* (1925–1926), Milhaud's *Le Pauvre matelot*, *La Création du monde*, and *Christophe Colomb*, even Louis Gruenberg's *The Emperor Jones* (1932). All these share, at the very least, the use of anti-realistic, "expressionist" techniques to represent and communicate some kind of symbolic, social, moral, or philosophical meaning. None of these works is psychologically oriented in a profound way, just as none of them is atonal or involved in the psychological significance of new materials and new forms. They are all operatic in the traditional sense and they all deal with essentially contemporary problems with means that—however tonal—are certainly of the twentieth century; nevertheless, they have all remained essentially isolated expressions.

THE MIXED GENRE AND CHAMBER OPERA

The history of opera has often been described as a continuous struggle between the dominance of language and the dominance of music. Even more significantly, the problem of musical theater has always been the problem of form. Every composer who writes for the theater faces the problem of resolving his or her ideas in dramatic forms or self-contained musical ones. The solutions need not be mutually exclusive: Verdi's and Mozart's forms are musical but they are hardly undramatic. Nevertheless, the tendency of post-Wagnerian opera—well into the twentieth century—was towards dramatic, "expressive" structures, and this seemed, even for a composer like Schoenberg, an open road leading to the development of new forms for new ideas. Stravinsky, on the other hand, closed his forms, eliminated psychological development, and created the prototype of the one really new and successful music-theater form of the first part of the century.

The fact that so many of Stravinsky's major works were written for the theater is often overlooked. The ballet, of course, occupies the first place: the famous Diaghilev ballets—including *Pulcinella*—and later the "classical" ballets and the collaboration with Balanchine culminating in the remarkable *Agon* of 1957. The Stravinskyan ballet—or, one should say, the Stravinsky-Balanchine ballet—is characterized by the development of equal, abstract closed forms of movement and sound which in no way intersect or "express" each other but remain independent if parallel.

In addition to his ballets, however, Stravinsky also created a unique and important music theater built on closed forms and on abstraction—one would almost say ritualization—of content. Interestingly enough, while the forms remain closed, the materials are open and various. Thus, *Renard* uses an on-stage chamber orchestra, motionless singers, and actor-mimes; *L'Histoire du soldat* replaces the singing with narration and dialogue, and adds dance. *Les Noces* uses an orchestra of percussion and pianos with solo and choral singing and dance-mime. *Oedipus Rex*—designated an "opera-oratorio" and often staged today—uses a narrator, orchestra, chorus, and soloists and is realized scenically in a series of masked marmoreal stage tableaux. *Perséphone* and *The Flood* (1961–1962), originally created for television but also staged, similarly combine a variety of techniques. Stravinsky also wrote three operas that use scene, singing, and stage action in the more-or-less usual way: *Le Rossignol*, an early work in the Russian-French manner (begun in 1909 but finished only after *Le Sacre*), *Mavra*, a one-act burlesque not far removed in manner from *L'Histoire* and *Renard*, and *The Rake's Progress* (1948–1951), Stravinsky's farewell to opera and his final and most complete homage to Classical form. In all of these works—after *Le Rossignol* (completed 1914), at least—Stravinsky abstracted the essence of an experience and the essence of a form, and in this process of abstraction he created perhaps the only new and workable musico-dramatic form of the first half-century. The importance of the Stravinskyan mixed-genre theater has perhaps been underestimated; the mixing of means in the context of schematic, prototypical, neo-classical forms; the abstraction of classical themes—musical and literary-dramatic; and the treatment of theatrical experience as a kind of ritual embody conceptions of modern musical theater which remain vital.

Some of the more superficial aspects of Stravinsky's theatrical conceptions had an immediate and important effect: simplification of treatment and reprise of tonal techniques; use of limited and practical means; stylized treatment of popular subject matter; clear, closed forms. Exactly like *L'Histoire*, Honegger's *Le Roi David* was written in small, closed forms on a "popular" or folkish text originally for a small Swiss travelling theatrical company; only later was it amplified to its full orchestral form. Milhaud's *Les Chóephores* (1915), based on Aeschylus, and his tiny *opéras minutes* (*L'Enlèvement d'Europe, L'Abandon d'Ariane, La Délivrance de Thésée*) are highly stylized treatments of classical subjects. Poulenc's operas—the farce *Les Mamelles de Tirésias*, Cocteau's monodrama *La Voix humaine* (1958), and the rather grand and impressive *Dialogues des Carmélites*—use clear, fastidious tonal techniques in contexts of great simplicity and directness. The clearest representative of Stravinskyan techniques on the modern stage, however, is Carl Orff, whose musico-theatrical style is based on tonal simplicity and directness. Works like *Carmina Burana* (1937; a Stravinskyan type of scenic-dance oratorio) and its companions *Catulli Carmina* (1943) and *Il Trionfo di Afrodite* (1953) are vast expansions of one small part of the Stravinskyan esthetic—stylistic abstractions from *Les Noces* expanded to fill up an entire musical *Weltanschauung*. Other operatic works, such as *Der Mond* (1939), *Die Kluge* (1943), and *Antigonae* (1949), are conceived more completely in terms of dramatic planes and juxtapositions. In *Antigonae* a huge percussion apparatus punctuates music of chant and intonation. Ostinato and rhythmic outburst are set against simple melodic curves, the whole structured in immobile blocks and layers. The operas of Philip Glass owe something to Orff.

The sheer size of the physical apparatus of nineteenth-century opera inevitably provoked a reaction in the twentieth century; the new simplicity and concision of form and expression were accompanied by an enormous reduction of means and scope. Strauss, surprisingly, was an important pioneer here, although his *Ariadne auf Naxos*, scored for an orchestra of twenty-three musicians, now generally appears in the context of "grand opera." Works like *L'Histoire*, *Mavra*, and *Renard* actually established a new genre of short chamber opera that was both practical and appealing. Hindemith (who, in *Wir bauen eine Stadt* of 1930, wrote a tiny "opera" for performance by young children) composed several chamber operas in the late 1920's—notably *Neues vom Tage* and *Hin und Zurück*—with brief, lively, contemporary subjects and musical matter. Kurt Weill's early operas are similar—short, bustling, concise and small-scaled, freely diatonic and tonal in a serious, lively, contrapuntal way. Later, under the influence of Brecht, Weill definitively turned to popular forms. Like Stravinsky, Weill wanted to re-create the "number" opera concept, but in the context of a meaningful musical play filled with the popular music of the cabaret. With Weill, the divergent streams of popular musical theater and opera merge in a musical theater of social consciousness.

The flowering of new opera in Germany between the wars was a phenomenon of considerable scope. Subjects from contemporary life, often treated in an ironic or satiric manner, were common. The so-called *Zeit-oper*—the term might be translated as "up-to-date opera"—sometimes took the form of opera-house opera (e.g., Krenek's *Jonny spielt auf*) but much of it was chamber opera performed in smaller houses like the Kroll Opera in Berlin. Some of this work took the form of plays with music intended for the so-called legitimate theater—even the popular or commercial theater (e.g., *The Three-Penny Opera* of Brecht and Weill). Mass media, including radio and film, were also employed for the first time.

This kind of musical theater is so firmly associated with the work of Bertolt Brecht and his collaborator Kurt Weill that we call it Brechtian or refer to it as the Brecht-Weill theater. Brecht himself wrote or adapted music and often appeared as a music-hall singer. The work that formed the original Brecht *Mahagonny* had tunes provided by Brecht, and at least one of them was later adapted by Kurt Weill. Writers on Brechtian theater have long taken the position that it was Weill's encounter with the playwright which changed his basic style from a fairly advanced and difficult "modernism" to his later populism. But a closer look at Weill's evolution and his writings about the *Zeitoper* reveal an internal revolution that was quite independent and antecedent to his encounter with Brecht. *Der Protagonist*, based on a Georg Kaiser libretto, is a lively chamber opera which enjoyed a major success when it was first performed in 1926. *The Czar Has His Picture Taken (Der Zar lässt sich photographieren*; 1927) is an absurdist farce about an assassination attempt; its "hit" song, a tango played on a phonograph record in the show, was actually released as a single with considerable success.

The first Brecht-Weill collaboration dates from 1927, when Weill set the *Mahagonny* poems and Brecht staged them (in a boxing ring) for a modern-music festival at Donaueschingen. Although the style of these settings is quite acidic and dissonant (and the settings are surrounded by modern-music interludes quite in the style of Weill's earlier work), the popular style of the melodies—bitter, brilliant, deadpan, soaring, low-life—as well as the subject (a city founded in America by crooks, pimps, whores, and gangsters) and its unorthodox staging provoked intense controversy. The *Three-Penny Opera* (1928; adapted from Gay's *The Beggar's Opera*) was more specifically a play for actors with songs and other numbers separated by dialogue. It was a huge success and made Brecht-Weill as familiar a collaboration as Gilbert and Sullivan.

This famous and influential collaboration did not last long. An extended operatic version (or versions, for there were several) of *Mahagonny* enjoyed some success; *Happy End* (1929), on the other hand, was almost a complete failure. A *Lehrstuck*, or instructional piece, based on a Japanese Noh play, *Der Jasager* (1930), a radio work based on the story of Lindberg (*Der Lindberghflug*, 1929), some other non-theatrical settings, and a curious music-dance work written in exile in Paris (*The Seven Deadly Sins*; 1933) complete the list.

In spite of the brevity of the collaboration, these works have had—and continue to have—an enormous influence. At a distance of half a century or more, it is easy to see and hear how they belong to their time. And yet the break with the conventions of opera, theater, and music (even in their most modernistic forms) was very great. Brecht and Weill seemed to be taking an anti-art position; their work was popular, vulgar, and not esthetic. We can now see that Brecht and Weill were not anti-art, only anti-Romantic—that is, against the conventions of Romanticism as they had been adopted wholesale into modern art. Brecht and Weill were anti-realist as well. There is never a pretense that the theater is merely a room with the fourth wall removed; we are constantly reminded that we are in the theater watching a musical play. And they were anti-expressionist. Expressionism is a style that brings deep inner feelings to the surface; it is cathartic, and Brecht and Weill were not interested in catharsis; their aim was to "stir" people, not so much to move them to an emotional experience in the theater as to send them outside ready to act.

Weill's music is full of paradoxes. It has a low-life side: bitter, ironic, intentionally awkward, and even brutal in its rhythmic and instrumental style. The popular influence is everywhere; it is never joyous, but always gripping, often witty and intense. Where Brecht is detached and even cruel, Weill is melodic and emotional. Weill's melodies, inspired by popular, cabaret, and jazz styles of the age but very much his own, caught the popular imagination—and still do. The music contradicts the text very often; the quality of the musico-dramatic moments actually seem to grow out of these contradictions. We are in the theater being amused but are also sur-rounded—as the actors wittily and bitterly inform us dramatically and musically—by the cruelties of real life outside.

Weill resumed his collaborations with other writers (e.g., *Silbersee* with Georg Kaiser; 1932–1933) even before he and Brecht had to leave Germany; with the exception noted above, the Brecht-Weill collaboration never resumed. After World War II, Brecht went back to Germany—the Eastern part—where he worked with the composers Hanns Eisler (1898–1962) and Paul Dessau (1894–1979). Weill, on the other hand, became a very successful composer in the American musical theater, collaborating with many of the leading playwrights, poets, and lyricists of the day: Maxwell Anderson, Ogden Nash, Ira Gershwin, Elmer Rice, Langston Hughes, and Alan Jay Lerner, among others. Works like *Knickerbocker Holiday* (1938), *Lady in the Dark* (1940), *One Touch of Venus* (1943), *Love Life* (1947), *Street Scene* (1946), *Down in the Valley* (1945–1948), and *Lost in the Stars* (1949) had a major influence on the course of American musical theater. The concept of a serious popular theater built on contemporary themes of social signifi-cance, using popular, accessible musical and theatrical means, was much discussed in the 1930's and 1940's, and there is a direct line that connects Kurt Weill with Marc Blitzstein (1905–1964) (*The Cradle Will Rock*, 1936–1937; *No For An Answer*, 1938–1940; *Regina*, 1946–1948); Leonard Bern-stein (b. 1918; *Wonderful Town*, 1952; *Candide*, 1955–1956; *West Side Story*, 1957); and Steven Sondheim (the lyricist for *West Side Story*, which is an easily recognizable descendant of *Street Scene*). There has been a major revival of Weill and Brecht-Weill in recent years, and these works have been an important influence on recent music theater (see Chapter 21).

OPERA IN ENGLISH

The lack of success of opera in English is a complex phenomenon having nothing to do with the supposed lack of suitability of the language. Opera as a social institution has always been an exotic in both England and America; the native forms are ballad opera, operetta, and the musical. The only English-language composers to achieve any extended success in the opera house are Benjamin Britten and Gian-Carlo Menotti. Britten's *Peter Grimes* (1944–1945), *A Midsummer Night's Dream* (1960), *The Rape of Lucretia* (1946), and *The Turn of the Screw* (1954) (the last two chamber operas often adapted to larger operatic stages) renovate tradition in contem-porary English-language terms. The starting point is the ongoing music

drama, but Britten—like Berg but with a more tonal, neo-Classical orientation—has imposed on it forms of classical severity. In addition to works
of the grand and chamber opera type, Britten has also experimented with
medieval and Eastern forms, in *Noye's Fludde*, based on a miracle play, and
Curlew River, based on a Japanese Noh play.

Verismo opera, which had no important continuation in Europe, was
kept alive in America by Menotti and a few of his American followers. Most
of these works are suffocated by the past and by their dominant themes of
nostalgia and regret. A few, like Carlisle Floyd's (b. 1926) *Susannah* (1955),
have had some success in integrating *verismo* with American themes and
musical matter, but there has been no long-range development in this direction. More in the vein is the "folk opera" tradition—really derived from
Broadway and pop music—apparently inaugurated by Gershwin and continued by Kurt Weill in his American works. Douglas Moore's (1893–1969)
The Ballad of Baby Doe (1956) is a successful latter-day example. The Virgil
Thomson and Gertrude Stein collaborations—*Four Saints in Three Acts*
(1927–28) and *The Mother of Us All* (1947)—mix folk and popular ideas, a
syntactical treatment of verbal and musical elements, a kind of popular
surrealism, and what can only be described as an anticipation of minimalism
(see Chapter 19) to produce unique results.

The Broadway musical itself seems to have come through its golden
age with the works of Kern, the Gershwins, Rodgers and Hart, Rodgers and
Hammerstein, Cole Porter, Weill, Lerner and Loewe, and others. More
recently it seems to have passed its prime, often drawing heavily on its own
past and emphasizing spectacle. The problems of Broadway turned out to
be similar to the problems of the opera house; rising costs, the old-fashioned
institutions, and the traditional ways of doing things all seemed to preclude
the development of important new work. Change was clearly in the offing.
The appearance of the so-called "rock opera," the large-scale importation of
spectacular works from England, the innovations of Stephen Sondheim, the
revival of the song-play in the Brecht-Weill tradition, the intensely musical
character of much off-off-Broadway and other innovative theater, the influence of media and multimedia, and the extensive experimentation with non-
traditional performance art forms all heralded major changes in musical
theater (see Chapter 21).

BIBLIOGRAPHICAL NOTES

George Martin's *The Opera Companion to Twentieth-Century Opera* (New
York, 1979) is an excellent reference work; lengthy chapters are devoted to
discussions of twentieth-century opera—Janáček, Puccini, Stravinsky, Pro-

kofiev, the *commedia dell'arte*, and rock opera. Probably the best biography of Puccini in English is Mosco Carner's (2nd ed., London, 1974). On Puccini's operas there is William Ashbrook's study (New York, 1968) and Mosco Carner's *Tosca* (Cambridge Opera Handbooks series, Cambridge, England, 1985). Norman Del Mar's multi-volume Strauss biography was cited on page 15; to it may be added Willi Schuh's *Richard Strauss: A Critical Study of the Operas* (London, 1964), Donald G. Daviau and George J. Buelow's *The "Ariadne auf Naxos" of Hugo von Hofmannsthal and Richard Strauss* (Chapel Hill, NC, 1975), and Alan Jefferson's *Richard Strauss: Der Rosenkavalier* (Cambridge, England, 1985). The October–November 1952 issue of *Musical Opinion* (London) was devoted to "Britten, Strauss, and the Future of Opera." Joseph Kerman's *Opera as Drama* (New York, 1956) is a general essay which includes contemporary problems.

Until now, there has been surprisingly little material of note on opera and musical theater as popular forms—on Menotti and neo-*verismo*, Blitzstein and Bernstein, the Broadway musical, or the off-Broadway Brechtian show. The few notable exceptions to this include Gerald Bordman's *American Musical Theatre: A Chronicle* (New York, 1978) and the many recent volumes on Weill: Kim H. Kowalke's *Kurt Weill in Europe* (Ann Arbor, 1979), which draws on many manuscripts in the private possession of Lotte Lenya, the late composer's wife, and covers his music up to his departure for the United States in 1935; the same author's *A New Orpheus: Essays on Kurt Weill* (New Haven and London, 1986); Ronald Sanders's *The Days Grow Short: The Life and Music of Kurt Weill* (New York, 1980), an "unofficial" biography; and Douglas Jarman's *Kurt Weill: An Illustrated Biography* (Bloomington, IN, 1982). To these may be added Charles Schwartz's *Gershwin: His Life and Music* (Indianapolis and New York, 1973). The only musical publication to cover musical theater in all of its aspects over a period of years was the magazine *Modern Music* in the years of its existence, 1924–1946.

There is a collection of essays on *Stravinsky and the Theatre* (ed. Minna Lederman, New York, 1949; repr. 1975) as well as Paul Griffiths's study on Stravinsky's *The Rake's Progress* (part of the Cambridge Opera Handbooks series, Cambridge, England, 1982); this small volume contains essays by Stravinsky ("The Composer's View"), Robert Craft ("A Note on the Sketches and the Two Versions of the Libretto"), and Gabriel Josipovici ("Some Thoughts on the Libretto").

The program of the 1964 Maggio Musicale Fiorentino, which was devoted to "expressionism," contains a number of studies (in Italian) on "expressionist theater." Two separate studies in English exist on Schoenberg's operas: Ena Steiner's *"The 'Happy' Hand*: Genesis and Interpretation of Schoenberg's *Monumentalkunstwerk" (Music Review* 41/3 [1980], 207–22) and Pamela C. White's *Schoenberg and the God-idea: The Opera "Moses und Aron"* (Ann Arbor, 1985), which focuses on Schoenberg's deep involvement with religious and philosophical thinking as expressed in this opera. George Perle's two books on the Berg operas, *Wozzeck* (Berkeley, 1980) and *Lulu* (1985), cover both historical and musical aspects; his *Wozzeck* is essentially a reprint of earlier articles that appeared in some of the major journals. Janet Schmalfeldt's study of *Wozzeck* (New Haven, 1983) is more of a technical investigation of the music, using pitch-class set theory. On Krenek's operas, see Wolfgang Rogge's *Ernst Kreneks Opern: Spiegel der zwanziger Jahre* (Wolfenbüttel and Zurich, 1970) and Claudia Maurer Zenck's article "The Ship Loaded with Faith and Hope: Krenek's *Karl V* and the Viennese Politics of the Thirties" (*Musical Quarterly* 71/2 [1985], 116–34).

To the literature on Britten cited on page 92, the following studies devoted to his operas should be added: Eric Walter White's *Benjamin Britten: His Life and Operas* (2nd ed., London and Boston, 1983); *Benjamin Britten: "Peter Grimes,"* a collection of essays compiled by Philip Brett (Cambridge Opera Handbook series, Cambridge, England, 1983); and *The Operas of Benjamin Britten*, ed. David Herbert (New York, 1979), which, in addition to essays written by a number of people who worked with Britten, contains the complete librettos.

Brecht's still-pertinent ideas on music and theater along with discussions of his ideas about "epic theater," "alienations," and "gest" appear in *Brecht on Theater*, a collection of essays and notes edited and translated by John Willett (New York, 1964). Brecht's collaborations with Hindemith, Weill, Eisler, and Dessau are referred to in this volume.

part four

Atonality and Twelve-tone Music

TEN

THE VIENNESE SCHOOL

SCHOENBERG AND THE TWELVE-TONE IDEA

After *Pierrot lunaire*, Op. 21, and the *Four Orchestral Songs*, Op. 22, both written on the eve of World War I, no new work of Schoenberg appeared for almost ten years, although for part of that time he worked on a large oratorio, *Die Jacobsleiter*. All of the composers who participated in the revolutions of the first twelve or fifteen years of the century moved afterwards toward some kind of artistic, expressive, and/or intellectual synthesis of the new materials in new but clear and comprehensive forms. Schoenberg, whose atonal works of 1910–1915 represent the most thoroughgoing renovation and extension of the musical material, proposed the most radical and thorough consolidation. In *Die Jacobsleiter* he worked his way towards a systematic exploitation of the complete gamut of tempered chromatic sounds. The oratorio was never completed—perhaps because Schoenberg discovered the basic conception only as he was composing, and each step forward seemed to imply a recasting of what had come before. But the Piano Pieces, Op. 23, and the *Serenade*, Op. 24 (both 1920–1923) contain twelve-tone music; and the Piano Suite, Op. 25 (1921–1923), and Wind Quintet, Op. 26 (1923–1924), are complete twelve-tone conceptions.[1]

Schoenberg's twelve-tone procedure is a synthesis of two formal ideas which are actually separable and which have in fact been used independently; both ideas appear in embryo—not necessarily connected, and more or less informally—in the "atonal" music of Schoenberg himself, and of Berg and Webern. The first is the continuous use of patterns which contain all of the twelve pitches; the second is the organization of pitch materials according to a consistent order principle. Thus in Schoenberg's "classical" formulation of the technique, each piece is based on a given ordering of the twelve tempered pitches—abstracted (without regard for octave or register) as the twelve-tone series or row[2]—and the work itself is an exposition or realization of this order structure. Schoenberg thought of musical space as multi-dimensional and as having essential unity. Thus any given pattern of notes—and, specifically, a series of twelve different pitches—can appear unbroken and without internal change (like a physical object being rotated in space) in four forms: forward, backward, upside-down, and upside-down backward (see Appendix, Example 10-1).

The question of the repetition of tones in twelve-tone music is much misunderstood. Clearly, in the underlying ordering, each class of pitches (regardless of octave) can appear once and only once if all twelve pitches are to be always "rotated." In the actual compositional realization, however, small repetitions of notes or groups of notes often appear without disrupting the larger cycles of twelve notes. Furthermore, since the twelve-note groupings may appear as purely melodic voices in counterpoint (each line made up of constantly revolving cycles of the basic row), or as blocks of chords (e.g., three chords of four notes each or four chords of three notes), or as some combination of the above, certain duplications may appear between parts; this, however, can also be avoided by distributing the twelve notes between the melodic and harmonic parts or by conceiving the music in aggregates of sound in such a way that the complete twelve-note groupings constantly succeed each other in small time segments. All of these questions are, in the end, compositional matters; they do not necessarily disturb the basic "twelve-toneness" of the conception.

---

[1] Apparently Schoenberg had formulated his twelve-tone ideas in precise form by 1921, while he was working on the last piece of Op. 23 and the first of Op. 25.

[2] The terms "series" and "row" (hence "serial" and "row" music) are used interchangeably. Milton Babbitt has proposed the mathematical term "set." Twelve-tone (or "twelve-note") music is sometimes called dodecaphony, the adjectival form of which is "dodecaphonic."

Portrait of Arnold Schoenberg by Oskar Kokoschka. Reproduced by permission of Annie Knize.

Schoenberg's first tendency was to use the row melodically and contrapuntally, a technique which produces a kind of ongoing variational form. The variation principle, perhaps the oldest and most basic formal device in music, is not particularly associated with functional tonality (it was used long before tonality), and it remains a basic technique in many forms of popular and non-Western music. Oddly enough, it did not play an important role in early twentieth-century music but reappears in various forms in the new syntheses of the 1920's and 1930's; it is not without significance that some important works or movements of Stravinsky, Schoenberg, Berg, and Webern are explicit variations, and the technique appears in other guises throughout the period (see Appendix; Example 10-2).

Schoenberg also attempted to integrate the harmonic elements of his music through chordal groups fashioned from the row; and this, in turn, helped produce new melodic elements derived from but not restricted to the exact sequence of the original row (see Appendix; Example 10-3).

The mere counting of the notes of the row in a twelve-tone work is in itself meaningless without a clear understanding of the way in which the sound of the resulting harmonic and melodic combinations penetrates the entire piece; the way in which the parts intersect and relate forward (motion, energy) and backward (recall, association); the role of repetition, of changing register, of accent, and of dynamic in defining the phrase-structure, which itself is intimately related to the twelve-tone process; the way in which the piece moves from one type of structure and organization to another, i.e., from a static idea to a developmental one and then back again. The twelve-tone technique is not a form imposed from the outside, it *is* the piece; that is, it is the way the ideas of the piece take shape in time—at once, the content and the form.

A great deal of discussion has centered on the precise definition of the role that the twelve-tone idea should and does play in musical compo-sition. Schoenberg himself rejected the term "system"; he preferred the word "method," in the sense of procedure, although in his actual composition it probably functioned more as a mode of musical thinking analogous in certain ways to tonality. The twelve-tone principle was, for him, a way of organizing musical thought that is coherent, that controls every aspect of every piece but is uniquely established anew by each piece, and that can generate appropriate and organic forms by relating every aspect of a piece to an overall and underlying conception. The mere arrangements of the row in a piece do not constitute the whole piece anymore than the E♭ tonality of Beethoven's Third Symphony equals the whole "Eroica"; but the twelve-tone conception in a Schoenberg piece—like the tonal conception in Bee-thoven—pervades the whole, gives it its characteristic sonorous and intellectual qualities, and permits the composer to express his ideas through a big, coherent, and organic form. To say that is to say a great deal. Schoenberg was perhaps the true Classicist among contemporary composers because he understood the underlying principles of Classical form and discovered a viable equivalent in modern terms.

Schoenberg set about establishing the universality and scope of his new art immediately. With the exception of the choruses of Op. 27 and 28 (both 1925), all of the early twelve-tone compositions are pieces of consid-erable size which evoke their Classical equivalents not simply by references or parallels in texture, rhythm, or form but because they also embody a unity of thought and expression in terms of large-scale statement, process, and resolution. Thus in a multi-movement work like the Piano Suite, Op. 25, or the Septet, Op. 29 (1925–1926), the basic material is realized in a series of different guises, each revealing aspects of the underlying idea, each with its own possibilities of discovery, elucidation, and expression. In the Wind Quintet, Op. 26, and the Third String Quartet, Op. 30 (1927), the twelve-tone ideas become subjects for development. The row—or significant segments from it—generates very specific shapes which, in turn, develop and interrelate over wide time-spans to make long and expressive structures formed, for the most part, at the very outer limits of performer and listener capabilities. The row itself does not really function as a theme nor, certainly, as a scale or mode (as it does sometimes in Berg's music), but as a set of materials, a complex of relationships, offering enormous possibilities to the ordered imagination that can master them. Schoenberg was able to redis-cover organic large form—classical by analogy only, and not necessarily "neo-Classical" at all; in Schoenberg's mature, large-scaled works, the big form is an essential and inevitable result of the working-out of the impli-cations of a rich basic material.

At the end of the 1920's and specifically with the *Variations for Orchestra*, Op. 31, of 1928, Schoenberg centered his concern on the direct derivation of a form out of the implications of the basic material. Although the general plan of the *Variations* is traditional (introduction, theme, vari-ations, coda), the conception of these variations is both universal and yet specific and unique to the work. The variations themselves grow out of the conflict between the generality of the basic material (the intervals and rela-tionships which appear in the introduction in fragmented, unordered form) and its very specific realization as a row-based theme. The two very different conceptions of the row—on the one hand, as generative material far beneath the surface (functioning, as Schoenberg believed, in a manner somewhat analogous to tonality and not necessarily consciously perceived) and on the other, as thematic material—are here very deliberately juxtaposed; this is, so to speak, the dialectic of the piece. With each new variation-transfor-mation, the thematic character of the row becomes again more and more generalized until, in the long and remarkable finale, virtually a new formal level is reached; in this finale, the idea of transformation has been taken up into an ongoing twelve-tone structure. The theme, as it were, is absorbed into the row idea which generated it in the first place. Thus the work moves from the specific towards the universal, from musical idea towards structure, from "inspiration" towards intellectual resolution.

In *Von Heute auf Morgen*, Schoenberg's Op. 32 (1928–1929), and in the opera *Moses und Aron*, the completed portion of which was written in 1930–1932, the twelve-tone method was applied, apparently for the first time, to music for the theater. *Von Heute auf Morgen* treats a light, contemporary subject. *Moses und Aron* has a rather lofty philosophical text by Schoenberg himself, full of intellectual oppositions and dualisms which are reflected in the music itself. One curious thing about *Moses und Aron* is that although only two acts were set—the brief third act remains only in text—the existing music is complete in thought and structure; the work is a unity which generates a richness and diversity of ideas and means: huge divided singing-and-*Sprechstimme* choruses; the solo voice of Aron and the spoken part of Moses; a large and masterfully handled orchestra with a wide range of colors. The opposition between rich, even sensual variety and color on the one hand and a complex intellectual unity on the other[3] is a direct image of the philosophical issues which animate the text.

The forms of the *Accompaniment to a Film Scene*, Op. 34 (1929–1930), are also presumably dramatic, but this *Begleitmusik* was written for an imaginary cinema; the events of the scene are purely internal musical events, and the "dramatic" form is nothing but an expressive function of the ideas and the material.

In 1933, after the advent of Hitler, Schoenberg was forced to leave Germany. In the same year, he came to the United States, where he remained for the rest of his life—principally in California, where he taught at the University of California at Los Angeles. A number of his American works show a marked or partial return to a tonal idiom: a Suite for string orchestra (1934), a *Theme and Variations* for band, Op. 43 (1943), and the *Variations on a Recitative* for organ, Op. 40 (1941), are practical pieces, almost *Gebrauchsmusik*; and works like the *Ode to Napoleon* of 1942 and *A Survivor from Warsaw* of 1947 use tonal references in tension with twelve-tone techniques. On the other hand, the Fourth String Quartet (1936) and the Violin and Piano Concertos (1935–1936 and 1942) are large-scale, thematic, wholly twelve-tone structures in which the technique becomes fluent and pliable, focused in a way that parallels the role played by tonality in similar Classical forms.

Schoenberg's attitude towards this material in no way implies a return from or a renunciation of his early ideas; quite the contrary, it suggests rather a widening of the possibilities of the technique. In certain early works of Schoenberg and other twelve-tone composers there is a conscious attempt to avoid any combination of tones which might suggest a tonal reference or center. Later on, this rather arbitrary rule of thumb was superseded or bypassed. (The reasons for banning, say, a major triad in a twelve-tone piece are, presumably, psychological rather than musical, and, in fact, there are some very successful twelve-tone pieces built largely on triads, e.g., the

---

[3] Musically resolved in the existing two acts; hence the impossibility of music for the third, which was to demonstrate the triumph of the latter over the former.

Webern String Quartet.) Schoenberg expanded his conception of the possibilities of twelve-tone technique enormously in the later part of his life, and very late works like the String Trio, Op. 45 (1946), and the *Phantasy* for violin and piano, Op. 47 (1949), evolve distinctive forms out of new material. Schoenberg came to think of the row material not as a specifically linear ordering but as a series of groupings of pitches and intervals whose potentialities would be revealed by the process of the piece (see Appendix; Example 10-4). These techniques, which bind harmonic and linear ideas closely together with timbre, dynamic, rhythmic, and phrase provide a sense of continuity and even inevitability within a musical material which is constantly changing, constantly in motion, yet always basically the same. This linking technique—a kind of continuous development—suggests the possibilities of strict forms which are nevertheless open at the far end, forms in which everything is intertwined and in which the motion from one sound to another, from one end of the piece to the other, seems inevitable yet remains, until it is actually realized, unforeseen.

Schoenberg's music, unlike that of his pupils Berg and Webern, has never been popular and it probably never will be. All his life Schoenberg faced obstinate incomprehension on the part of musicians and the public, but probably the deepest and most ironic challenge has come from the post–World War II generation who posthumously charged him with having failed to realize the consequences of his own revolution, with having remained a Classicist all his life, faithful to the traditional notions of what constitutes a piece of music, and with having failed to extend the concept of serial technique beyond the organization of the twelve tempered chromatic pitches. There is more than a grain of truth in the charge; Schoenberg was, in a deep sense, a Classicist, and of all the early twentieth-century masters, the one most involved in re-discovering the deep and universal significance of the great tradition. But the charge that he was not sensitive to the implications of what he was doing is not just. It is true that Schoenberg's music was composed out of the traditional ideals of music making and that it proposed no new context for musical communication; but that is equally true of most twentieth-century music. It is also true that Schoenberg wrote cause-and-effect music and that John Cage, Karlheinz Stockhausen, and even Steve Reich do not. But Einstein's physics is hardly that of Newton, and cause and effect in Schoenberg is scarcely what it was in Rameau or Brahms.

Just as Schoenberg was the first to discover and explore a rich and complex new sonorous universe, he was the first to discover valid laws which operate in that universe. The parallel with scientific inquiry would have pleased Schoenberg, although he himself came out of the rather more dubiously scientific tradition of Hegel and historical determinism: he thought of himself as having, like Hegel or Marx, discovered immutable laws about the process of history which made his conquest of total chromaticism and his twelve-tone procedure a historical necessity. But it is not necessary to accept the analogy between the process of inquiry and discovery on the one hand and that of creation on the other (although the analogy has, interestingly enough, been recognized in many recent studies of the philosophy and psychology of scientific inquiry). Schoenberg's early music is the fruit of what we might call analytic inquiry: the refusal to accept traditional hypotheses; the discovery of a whole new set of realities; the creative exploration of the artistic, intellectual, and psychological significance of these new realities, "tested" in creative terms in a series of works of art. His later music is, in the best sense, synthetic—the statement of new unifying hypotheses which relate these realities in terms of a creative synthesis to underlying artistic, psychological, and intellectual truths. As we shall see, these processes have been recapitulated in avant-garde thought since World War II.

BERG AND WEBERN

Schoenberg's influence on Berg was, in one sense, decisive, yet Berg never took from Schoenberg any more than he needed to realize his own ideas. Thus, although Berg's later work is impossible to imagine without the influence of the twelve-tone idea, he never wrote a really thoroughgoing twelve-tone work. His *Chamber Concerto* for violin and piano with thirteen instruments (1923–1925) is not twelve-tone at all; it is, to be sure, full of complicated numerical patterns, but these are of a type characteristic of Berg, not of Schoenberg. The influence of Schoenberg is discernible in the complex and rich web of structural relationships derived from the initial statement of the material—not a twelve-tone row but a three-part subject based on those letters in the names "Schoenberg," "Berg," and "Webern" which have musical equivalents. Out of this unpromising and arbitrary material, Berg creates a big three-movement structure: a concerto movement with piano solo, one for violin solo, and a finale for both soloists. Like many of Berg's works, the *Concerto* tries to be inclusive; it is long and full of a great variety of ideas, materials, and techniques. The big shape of the piece emerges—not without problems which present formidable obstacles to the performers—from the free, disassociated character of Berg's imagination and the conscious restraints of form and technique that he imposed on himself with an almost mystical fervor.

The *Lyric Suite* for string quartet (1925–1926) is, in its individual movements at least, less ambitious, but by turning his imaginative enterprise to a series of shorter, characteristic movements Berg was able to create expressive structures that grow naturally out of the ideas themselves. These ideas are not only themes in the traditional sense but also colors and expressive shapes, an aspect which Berg emphasizes by qualifying the tempo indications with strong, associative "color" words: *Allegretto gioviale, Largo desolato, Presto delirando, Trio estatico,* and so forth. Two of the movements are twelve-tone; however, Berg uses the technique not so much as a structural principle but as a way to "color" the music from the inside. Thus the famous *Allegro misterioso* is the most elaborately twelve-tone movement Berg ever wrote, but all the careful, precise manipulations on the printed page are no more (and, to be sure, no less) than a great whispering, rustling, rushing murmur.

The concert aria *Der Wein*, after poetry by Baudelaire (1929), is Berg's first and only attempt at writing a large concert work completely unified in row technique, but even here the function of the row is special and peculiarly Bergian. The series, which begins with an ascending D-minor scale, works not so much as a theme nor, on the other hand, as underpinning but much more simply: as a kind of mode in the old, original meaning of that term. The ancient modes—or, for example, the Indian *raga*—are not "scales" or "tonalities" in the modern sense but repertoires of melodic formulas, often associated with specific kinds of rhythmic ideas, embellishments, and tone colors. Thus an Indian *raga* is not a theme, and there may be no definitive, meaningful way of writing it down as a "scale"; but a piece is instantly recognizable as being "in" a certain *raga* by its characteristic turns of phrase. Berg used the twelve-tone row in just this way (so did Schoenberg, but secondarily). In the opera *Lulu* this becomes the basis of a rich and complex technique of dramatic and psychological identification.

The text of *Lulu* was drawn by Berg himself from two plays of Frank Wedekind; the opera was finished in short-score form, but part of the orchestration of the last act was left incomplete by the composer and the work has only recently emerged in its full three-act form. *Lulu* was planned as a symmetrical form, with the third act providing a dramatic climax, psychological realization, a good deal of the intellectual meaning, and a musical recapitulation and resolution. Lulu is a kind of archetypical character, part whore, part earth mother; as an incarnation of female sexuality she moves with the inevitability and indifference of nature through a series of love adventures that are in turn macabre, tragic, comic, grotesque, and sublime. Berg's music is at once specific (it defines the characters by their rows, by the ways they sing, even by the orchestral sounds that dog their footsteps) and general (in the way it universalizes an ironic, expressionist theater bordering on the grotesque into a grand "comi-tragedy").

Berg's last completed work was his Violin Concerto (1935), commissioned by the American violinist Louis Krasner; the work, dedicated to the memory of Manon Gropius (the daughter of the architect and Alma Mahler, who was also Berg's patron), became Berg's own monument. The row consists of major and minor triads with a bit of whole-tone scale at the end; thus within the framework of this basic material Berg can make use of the open-string "tuning-up" sounds of the violin, some tonal progressions, Viennese waltz motifs, an Austrian folk song, and a Bach chorale (see Appendix; Example 10-5).

The intensity and diversity of Berg's ideas come close to shattering their structure; it is almost as if he wanted to charge his music with more expressive weight than it could bear. But the very range of expression, combined with the carefully defined freedom of technique, makes Berg much less of a traditionalist than he has sometimes been made out to be. Berg's obvious references to the past are no more a model for a new music than his specific musical personality is a good subject for imitation; but his work remains meaningful because he was able to communicate precise, prede-termined, expressive forms that somehow seem to grow out of the wide scope of his creative imagination.[4]

During and after World War I, Webern was occupied with a series of eight consecutive vocal sets, mostly for solo voice and instruments; among these are the songs of Op. 17 (1924–1925), Webern's first twelve-tone works. Webern accepted Schoenberg's ideas neither casually nor quickly; but with the String Trio, Op. 20, of 1926–1927, the Symphony, Op. 21, of the fol-lowing year, the Quartet, Op. 22, of 1930, for violin, clarinet, tenor saxophone, and piano, and the Concerto, Op. 24 (1931–1934), he embraced the strictest kind of twelve-tone procedure and fully incorporated this into his own esthetic (see Appendix; Example 10-6).

From one point of view, Webern's solutions are Classical; Classical tonal music also had a one-to-one relationship between all aspects of the musical material—or, at any rate, between pitch, rhythm, and the dynamic shape of the phrase—and Webern's musical periods are of the traditional type. The first movement of the Symphony is a rather closely worked (and somewhat arbitrary) sonata form with a repeated exposition, "development," and a careful recapitulation. Many of Webern's later works are sets of var-iations based on a kind of "song-form" phrase-structure with real antecedent and consequent phrases. A classical sense of balance, symmetry, and stability is present throughout his work.

Webern's tendency to transform and re-create certain aspects of clas-sical tradition is particularly evident in his twelve-tone instrumental works, which are in many ways much less far-reaching and more classically abstract than his earlier "atonal" pieces. To the works mentioned above can be added the Variations for piano, Op. 27 (1935–1936), the String Quartet, Op. 28 (1936–1938), and the Variations for orchestra, Op. 30 (1940). On the other hand, in the later vocal works, and most particularly in *Das Augenlicht*, Op.

---

[4] Berg's music continues to be influential, especially on the so-called "neo-expres-sionists" (see Chapter 19).

26 (1935), and the two cantatas, Op. 29 and 31 (1938–1939, 1941–43), the verbal material and the relationships between solo, choral, and instrumental sound suggest a whole new set of problems and solutions. The conceptions of line and of the relationships between line and harmonic structure are new and generate new ideas of organizing expressive musical thoughts; indeed, the very obliteration of the Classical distinction between line and harmony (and, to some extent, between pitch, duration, timbre, and intensity), characteristic of the early works of Webern and Schoenberg and later schematized by Webern in his earlier twelve-tone works, is taken up again in these later vocal compositions.

Webern extended serial principles into many musical domains and in such a way as to make his miniature forms a function of the ideas themselves. One superficial influence of Webern on later music was an esthetic of silence and brevity; more profound ones grew out of the organic qualities of his thinking, the sense of a delicately balanced web rather than a linear or dramatic process, and the totality of a work implied from the start yet unforeseen in its unfolding. In spite of the complex implications of Webern's music, its most immediate qualities are clarity and transparency of idea realized within tiny, schematic, and crystalline forms. These qualities are also, in spite of appearances, personal and inimitable. The long-range significance of Webern's work may turn out to be not so much the isolation of the single musical event—the bit of glowing sound set in a starry void—or the consistency and purity of the ideas as the richness of the reconstruction of form. Webern reduced the experience of sound to its essentials; he also demonstrated the possibility of an organic reintegration which evolved from universal prototypes into new and meaningful expressive structures.

BIBLIOGRAPHICAL NOTES

The founding fathers of dodecaphony produced surprisingly little in the way of written formulations of the twelve-tone idea. The most important are Schoenberg's lecture "Composition with Twelve Tones" printed in *Style and Idea* (cited on page 15) and transcriptions of some of Webern's lectures published in translation as *The Path to the New Music* (cited on page 44). There has been, however, no shortage of texts from the later generations: Ernest Krenek, *Studies in Counterpoint* (New York, 1940); Herbert Eimert, *Lehrbuch der Zwölftontechnik* (Wiesbaden, 1950; also translated into Italian); Josef Rufer, *Composition with Twelve Notes* (New York, 1954); Leopold Spinner, *A Short Introduction to the Technique of Twelve-Tone Composition* (London, 1960); Reginald Smith Brindle, *Serial Composition* (London, 1966), and Charles Wuorinen, *Simple Composition* (New York and London, 1979). Most of these are prescriptive teaching abstractions which seldom reflect the reality (and sometimes actually violate the substance) of the music of the Viennese.

On the history of twelve-tone ideas and of the "school," see Luigi Rognoni's *The Second Vienna School: Expressionism and Dodecaphony* (trans. from the Italian by Robert W. Mann, London, 1977); the first volume of Martin Vogel's more extensive study is now out, but is available only in German (*Schönberg und die Folgen: Die Irrwege der Neuen Musik*, I: *Schönberg*, Bonn, 1984). It is now generally agreed that Josef Matthias Hauer's *Zwölftontechnik* (published Vienna, 1926, but developed earlier) and certain early compositions of Nicolay Roslavetz antedated Schoenberg's arrival at a twelve-tone formulation. The origins of twelve-tone ideas have been discussed by Eimert, by Willi Reich in *Alte und neue Musik* (Zurich, 1952), and by Egon Wellesz in *The Origins of Schoenberg's Twelve-Tone System* (Washington, 1958). The best general discussion of the techniques can be found in Perle's *Serial Composition and Atonality* (5th ed., 1982).

Schoenberg's writings have been cited on p. 15; they can be supplemented by Rufer's catalogue of Schoenberg's works (London, 1962, from the German original of 1959), which contains many excerpts from unpublished writings of the composer. Jan Maegaard's *Studien zur Entwicklung des dodekaphonen Sätzes bei Arnold Schönberg* (Copenhagen, 1972) is the best source for dates of composition. The most satisfactory critical assessment of Schoenberg in print is Charles Rosen's small volume, cited in the bibliographical notes for Chapter 4. (See also the other sources cited there, most of which cover the Viennese composers' twelve-tone works as well as their earlier atonal works.) Mention should be made of Martha Hyde's work on Schoenberg's sketches: *Schoenberg's Twelve-Tone Harmony: The Suite Op. 29 and the Compositional Sketches* (Ann Arbor, 1982) and "The Format and Function of Schoenberg's Twelve-Tone Sketches" (*Journal of the American Musicological Society* 36/3 [Fall 1983], 453–80), as well as the many articles and analyses of the music of all three of the Viennese which can be found in many issues of *Perspectives of New Music, Journal of Music Theory, The Score,* and *Melos.*

ELEVEN

THE DIFFUSION
OF TWELVE-TONE MUSIC

Between the two World Wars modern music was often considered to be divided into two major opposing camps: the "neo-Classicists" and the "dodecaphonists," Stravinskyans and Schoenberg followers. But after World War II and Schoenberg's death, even Stravinsky became a twelve-tone composer, and an immense number of other, younger composers adopted the method.

The reasons for this shift—which marked the end of an old era as much as the beginning of a new one—are complex. It is not necessary to accept any mystical superiority of twelve-tone music or even any particular notion of historical necessity to recognize that certain ideas have enough innate power and richness to gain, sooner or later, widespread acceptance. One important point is that the twelve-tone idea—in contrast to "neo-Classicism"—does not presuppose any particular style. "Neo-Classicism," in spite of its superficial ability to absorb many different kinds of contents, appeared as a dead end because it was a style or a specific set of styles located in a particular moment of history. So, indeed, were the "styles" of Schoenberg, Berg, and Webern; but the twelve-tone *conception* by no means required the manner or even the forms employed by its originators.[1] Total chromaticism and the whole range of associated rhythmic, dynamic, and color material offered a rich source of ideas, and the twelve-tone notion of Schoenberg—or some modification of it—suggested a way of handling this material without necessarily adopting a specific idiom. Furthermore—and in spite of Webern's success with small forms—it offered a way of re-creating large forms, which was hardly possible with most of the neo-tonal, non-functional diatonic idioms. Historically, the creation of the large form was precisely coincidental with the growth of functional tonality with its potential for incorporating significant small-range motion and detail into a network of long-range relationships, created out of the tensions and interconnection of horizontal and vertical events and of structural contrasts, extensions, and resolutions. Many of these big formal tensions were inevitably lost in a non-functional tonal style which tended to build on repetition, juxtaposition, and rhythmic articulation. The rather arbitrary imposition of the skeleton of classical "sonata form" on neo-Classic works was a stopgap solution at best. Indeed, some of the most successful neo-tonal structures—works like Stravinsky's *Symphony of Psalms* that go far beyond a mere motion from one tonal area to another—come surprisingly close to serialism. What Schoenberg had found was a new way of articulating long-range structures through a rich and suggestive range of musical ideas; and the impact of this was far-reaching. As the characteristic diatonicism of the 1930's began to wane, and as the associated esthetic notions of a new simplicity, a new "practicality," and of musical nationalism and populism began to be played out, an increasing number of composers began to concern themselves with chromaticism, with chromatic line and harmony more and more detached from tonal processes. Thére is a discernible psychological-historical pattern in the gradual aural acceptance of chromatic ideas and processes as "natural"; the pattern is reflected in the cycle of acceptance and influence of this century's major composers, which ran chronologically about like this: Stravinsky and Hindemith, Bartók, Berg, Schoenberg, Webern.

CENTRAL EUROPE

Schoenberg had many pupils besides Berg and Webern but none of comparable stature. The first important composer outside of the Schoenberg circle to adopt the twelve-tone technique was Ernst Krenek. Krenek was

---

[1] Boulez's famous polemical article "Schoenberg est mort" was a rejection of the assumption that expressionism and "neo-Classic" post-expressionism are necessary concomitants of twelve-tone technique; it was not merely an attack on Schoenberg's music.

not a Schoenberg pupil and had made his mark earlier with the opera *Jonny spielt auf*, a lively, dissonant, but tonal work touched by jazz. In the 1930's, Krenek began using twelve-tone technique—notably in his big opera, *Karl V*—and, for a number of years, he alternated or intermingled tonal and twelve-tone ideas. After the war, Krenek's music became more and more strictly twelve-tone and more and more concerned with numerological method. A musician of great natural fluency, Krenek long personified a link between the Hindemith tradition and that of Schoenberg and Webern; the latest of his long list of compositions similarly link the Schoenberg-Webern tradition with more recent techniques of serialism.

The accession to power of the Nazis in 1933 and the Austrian *Anschluss* in 1935 forced Schoenberg to leave Central Europe and abruptly put an end to the teaching and performance of twelve-tone music. The Nazis demanded a simple art with a popular base of support; the new simplicity of composers like Orff and Egk was a powerful anti-twelve-tone force in German-speaking countries. Nevertheless, after the war, a number of middle-generation composers—Wolfgang Fortner, Rolf Liebermann, Boris Blacher—cautiously adopted some form of dodecaphonic writing. The French-Swiss composer, Frank Martin (1890–1974), should also be included with this group since a great deal of his work and activity has been associated with Central Europe; his gradual infusion of twelve-tone techniques into a basically tonal style— mainly for structural strength and a broadening of scope—is typical.

The break between the older and younger generations in Germany is very marked. Most of the younger composers—Karlheinz Stockhausen (b. 1928) is the best-known and most important—actually started their musical careers as ultra-twelve-tone composers à la Webern and developed from that point. Some of the younger German composers who have become known since the war have continued to develop a twelve-tone idiom in a fairly direct line of descent from the Viennese; the best-known of these is Henze, whose work remains closely identified with expressionist techniques: chromatic and twelve-tone in a dissonant-melodic style worked up into large-scale theatrical and symphonic works. Henze's music represents a conscious attempt to create a free-flowing, serious, popular-practical twelve-tone style—a latter-day chromatic Hindemith, as it were. Significantly, Henze's turn towards political radicalism has widened his creative approach and led him into new areas of social concern and theatrical experimentalism, but in terms of a kind of post-expressionist *Gebrauchsmusik*.

ELSEWHERE IN EUROPE

Schoenberg had a number of foreign pupils—the Greek Nikos Skalkottas (1904–1949), the Norwegian Farten Valen (1887–1952), the American

Adolph Weiss (1891–1971), the Spanish-British composer Roberto Gerhard (1896–1970), and others—who introduced twelve-tone ideas outside of Central Europe, but most of these composers worked in an obscurity only partially dispelled by recent revivals of interest in their work. The first Latin composer to use twelve-tone materials in a distinctive and personal way was Luigi Dallapiccola, an Italian whose only direct relationship with the Viennese was through a brief contact with Webern. Dallapiccola began to write twelve-tone music in the late 1930's under the combined influences of Webern, early Italian lyric tradition, and the so-called "hermetic" movement in contemporary Italian poetry. Later Dallapiccola moved briefly towards a more highly charged, complex style (the opera *Il Prigioniero* of 1944–1948 was influenced by Berg and Schoenberg), but in general his music represents a distinctive development and extension out of the Webern esthetic—always remembering Webern's strong orientation towards vocal and lyric style. Dallapiccola's twelve-tone technique is generally orthodox and in itself not very complex, but there is a special interest in the way the material is manipulated, much in the manner of a strict counterpoint constructed on given schematic principles or plans: groups of triads, elaborate canonic part-writing, twelve-tone ideas arranged in conjunction with numerical or schematic patterns often of literary or symbolic significance. Dallapiccola was always oriented towards vocal music and, to a lesser extent, towards the theater; literary and philosophical notions—derived from Italian "hermetic" poetry and a commitment to the theme of personal and intellectual freedom—formed an important part of his esthetic. Dallapiccola approached twelve-tone technique through the increasing use of chromatic contrapuntal methods based on small serial nuclei in *Tre laudi* of 1936–1937 and in *Canti di prigionia* for chorus and percussion orchestra of 1938–1941, one of the composer's most important works and one of his first to break definitively with "neo-Classic" tonality. A major turning point is apparent in the wartime settings of Greek poetry (*Liriche greche*; translations by Ungaretti) for voice and instruments; quiet, intense, and persuasive, these small lyric works form simple, clear, twelve-tone structures, found in later works such as the *Quaderno musicale di Annalibera* for piano (1952; see Appendix; Example 11-1). The large post-war theater works, *Il Prigioniero*, and the ballet *Job* (1950) based largely on a single series, although are a deep plunge into the world of expressionism—undoubtedly facilitated by far greater contact with the music of the Viennese. Both these works are effective and powerful theatrical and human statements which gain strength, not from Dallapiccola's typical allusive lyricism (here much subordinated) but from a brilliant adaptation of twelve-tone ideas set forth in broad, theatrical strokes. With the partial exception of the large-scale *Canti di liberazione* of 1951–1955 (again a work with a "freedom" subject treated in terms of a simple, broad twelve-tone music for chorus and orchestra), the later works return to a lyric-elliptical style arising not from the theme of awakening conscious-ness of early antiquity, as in *Liriche greche*, but from the nature mysticism of medieval Italian religious poetry and the German Romantic lyric. Many of these aspects of Dallapiccola's work are synthesized in a major work on Greek mythology, the opera *Ulisse*, first performed in 1968.

A number of the younger and middle-generation Italian composers with a basically diatonic and neo-Classical outlook have introduced twelve-tone materials in their work. Goffredo Petrassi, whose earlier work was strictly neo-tonal in a Stravinskyan sense, has been using twelve-tone and serial material, first in a loose manner and without breaking the tonal bonds, later as a dominating factor. Petrassi's recent music abandons direct tonal techniques and approaches avant-garde serialism—which in Italy, as else-where, had its point of departure in twelve-tone technique.

Both the musical style and the direct techniques of the Viennese school have had a relatively small overt influence in France. The conductor and composer René Leibowitz (1913–1972) was one of the first non-German composers to begin using twelve-tone ideas, and his book *Schoenberg et son école* (1947; in English, 1949; reprint ed., New York, 1975), one of the first on the subject in a non-German language, was influential; however, his position in French music has been one of extreme isolation. Olivier Messiaen (b. 1908) has used twelve-tone technique to his own purposes, abstracting serial ideas without the style or esthetic of the Viennese, and this approach has proved to be more fruitful. Pierre Boulez (b. 1925), who studied with both Leibowitz and Messiaen, began using twelve-tone techniques in the 1940's, and his early works—the first two Piano Sonatas, the *Sonatine* for flute and piano, *Livre* for string quartet, *Le visage nuptial* for voice and orchestra, and others—show the transition from post-expressionist influence to serialism.

The transfer of Schoenberg's pupils Roberto Gerhard and Egon Wel-lesz (1885–1974) to England, the work of the Hungarian-British composer Mátyás Seiber (1905–1960), and the teaching and writing of the theoretician Hans Keller (b. 1919) had an influence on the development of English music somewhat analogous to that of the European composers who came to the United States during the war. The first British composers to use twelve-tone technique were Elisabeth Lutyens (1906–1973) and Humphrey Searle (1915–1982), the latter a pupil of Webern although stylistically much closer to Berg. Other important twelve-tone composers in Great Britian include the Scottish composer Iain Hamilton (b. 1922), Alexander Goehr (b. 1932), and Peter Maxwell Davies (b. 1934). Davies evolved a very personal, lyrical twelve-tone style based on medieval and early English music; some of his works are specifically intended for vocal and instrumental performance by children and are thus among the rare examples of twelve-tone music not necessarily intended for professional performance. More recently Davies has incorporated pop and theatrical elements in a striking expansion of stylistic outlook.

Twelve-tone ideas have permeated every corner of Europe. The Swedish composer Karl-Birger Blomdahl (1916–1968), originally a neo-Classicist, developed a twelve-tone line of thought in a series of instrumental works of note. His best-known work, the "space-ship opera" *Aniara* (1957–1958), combines twelve-tone, pop, and electronic elements. Even Eastern Europe, long closed to non-tonal, highly chromatic, or experimental music, has accepted twelve-tone ideas. The first break with an effective censorship took place in Poland where, from 1958, all forms of modern technique received wide acceptance. After an initial impact of Bartók and Hindemith, the introduction of twelve-tone ideas materially changed the entire course of Polish contemporary music. A key work in this development was the *Funeral Music* (1958) of Witold Lutoslawski (b. 1913), dedicated to the memory of Bartók and one of the first Polish works to make use of twelve-tone technique. Lutoslawski's music has developed through a chromatic, twelve-tone symphonic phase into a freer kind of avant-garde style laid out in broad rhythmic and color planes and blocked out in levels of intensity and timbre. Most of the younger Polish composers as well as Lutoslawski himself have moved well out of the area of closely controlled twelve-tone style and idea, but the block-like manipulation of large instrumental and orchestral intensities and timbres laid out in broad bands or blocks of sound and set into dramatic juxtapositions has remained characteristic of recent Polish music. The direct techniques of twelve-tone music remain influential in the music of the older generation and in the work of a few of the next generation: notably Tadeusz Baird (1928–1981), whose derivation from the Viennese was quite direct, and Kazimierz Serocki (1922–1981), who turned towards and then away from a rather static, dramatic-theatrical style towards a music of a developmental symphonic character often employing open or flexible materials but characterized by control.

Outside of Poland, the most important modern music center in Eastern Europe has been Yugoslavia, where a number of younger composers have been using contemporary ideas for several years; the best-known of these is Milko Kelemen (b. 1924), who has worked through the typical stylistic evolution from Bartók to Boulez with twelve-tone technique as a turning-point in between.

The situation all over Eastern Europe, however, has changed dramatically and, with the exception of Albania, there is no country in that part of the world where the impact of rapid change has not been felt. Within a period that could almost be measured in months, avant-garde techniques— even extreme ones—were taken up in nearly all of the major Eastern European centers. Twelve-tone technique has been adopted by composers even of the older generation in Czechoslovakia, Hungary, Rumania, and elsewhere. The Soviet Union has remained more isolated, but similar changes (at a more evolutionary pace, perhaps) have taken place there. Over a period of years a number of Soviet composers have been working with twelve-tone and other contemporary materials, but this music has remained little known and little performed in or out of Russia. Among the best-known are Andrey Volkonsky (b. 1933 in the West, but later moved to Moscow) and the Kiev composers Edison Denisov (b. 1929) and Valentin Sil'vestrov (b. 1937), whose twelve-tone chromatic styles suggest roots in Skriabin as well as Schoenberg and Berg. Among the younger generation are the Moscow composer Alfred Shnitke (b. 1934), who has been influenced by Boulez, and a Latvian group including Arvo Pärt (b. 1935), who has created static color structures of considerable effectiveness. As elsewhere, twelve-tone music has become commonplace, has even penetrated "official" musical life, and has been challenged by a more radical avant-gardism and even by post-modern tonality and modality.

THE UNITED STATES

The strongest line of continuity between the Viennese and latter-day twelve-tone composition is to be found in the United States, where Schoenberg settled in 1933 and remained as a teacher until his death in 1951. He taught composers as disparate as Leon Kirchner and John Cage; and indirectly, through the teaching and influence of a composer-teacher like Roger Sessions (1896–1985), twelve-tone ideas became a dominant part of American music. In the 1920's Sessions had developed a distinctive, rich, and contrapuntal neo-Classical style, which he modified in the 1930's and 1940's into a characteristic, dense chromaticism of an expressive and individual character. This style, a personal way of speaking which—in works like the Violin Concerto (1935), the Symphony No. 2 (1946), and the opera *The Trial of Lucullus* (1947)—can be easily differentiated from Viennese chromaticism, gradually absorbed constructive elements of row technique. Later works—particularly the Sonata for violin solo (1953), the Piano Concerto (1956), the *Idyll of Theocritus* for voice and orchestra (1954), the Symphony No. 4 (1958), and the opera *Montezuma* (1941–1963)—are dominated by row material which adds constructive strength and solidity while actually reinforcing the sense of stylistic identity and individuality. The primary impulse of Sessions's music is contrapuntal, and in this he resembles Schoenberg; a characteristic web of long, shaped lines gives a typical sound to the music. But Sessions's line is also concrete in conception, vocal in shape, and dependent on a complex sense of phrase accent and motion which gives a dynamic impulse to the music remarkably parallel to the way in which Classical harmonic progressions performed the same function.

This type of linear chromaticism dominates the work of a large group of American composers, many of whom studied with Sessions; Andrew Imbrie (b. 1921), Seymour Shifrin (1926–1979), and Leon Kirchner (b. 1919) are outstanding examples. Composers like Ben Weber (1916–1979) and George Rochberg (b. 1918) have worked on essentially independent but parallel lines.[2] Chromatic idioms (mainly but not exclusively twelve-tone) based on a "narrative," ongoing phrase structure and some kind of contrapuntal, developmental form succeeded "neo-Classicism" as the mainstream of American concert music—equivalent, in effect, to the abstract expressionism that dominated American painting.

These large-scale directional-developmental or narrative forms which replaced the old functional tonality by some kind of row thinking stand in contrast to a number of important recent works which interpret twelve-tone ideas in terms of static, suspended structures which interlock in various cyclical patterns; these have, in fact, a relationship with certain "neo-Classic" structural (as opposed to stylistic) notions, now newly propounded in terms of the chromatic material. The late music of Stravinsky belongs here, along with a number of parallel (and, in some cases, earlier) twelve-tone pieces by American composers whose work has been identified with his, notably Aaron Copland and Arthur Berger. Copland's involvement with chromatic techniques goes back to the 1920's; his *Piano Variations* of 1930 employ very closely worked and effective serial techniques based on a four-note row that is, in type, not at all unlike certain ideas used by Webern. Copland returned to this kind of serial, chromatic material in 1950 with his Piano Quartet and again with the *Piano Fantasy* of 1952–1957 and the *Connotations for Orchestra* of 1962. They are strongly twelve-tone in sound and method but express characteristic Copland techniques of layers and planes, angles, and juxtapositions; these conceptual principles even carry over into a non-twelve-tone work like the *Nonet for Strings* of 1960. Berger, whose earlier music was strongly "neo-Classic," developed a technique for projecting long-range linear motion—chromatic and contrapuntal—in terms of big blocked-out static structures which themselves interlock through internal twelve-tone relationships. In his first works of this kind (e.g., the *Chamber Music for 13 Instruments* of 1956) these techniques are specifically adapted to neo-Classic rhythmic and phrase structures. Later (in the String Quartet of 1958, for example), this "neo-Classicism" disappears or is absorbed into larger patterns; the detail is chromatic, highly inventive and serial-twelve-tone; the big forms remain sectional and additive in the neo-Classic sense but are made organic by being interpenetrated by the row and the row-sound.

---

[2] Rochberg's more recent work, however, uses quotation-collage techniques (see Chapter 18).

Stravinsky's original involvement with row technique was with the serial-order principle; the tenor solo in the *Cantata* (1951–1952), the Septet (1952–1953), the Shakespeare songs (1953), and *In Memoriam Dylan Thomas* (1954) are based on rows, but they are not twelve-tone. Only later and through his specific interest in a technical-structural idea—not altogether unrelated to quasi-serial techniques he had earlier developed for detail patterns and even (as in the *Symphony of Psalms*, 1930) for longer-range relationships—did Stravinsky begin to work with the full chromatic material. The score for the ballet *Agon* actually sums up the process as part of its own developing form: it begins diatonically, becomes chromatic and twelve-tone, and eventually returns to the diatonicism of the opening. A similar and even more wide-ranging process takes place in *Canticum Sacrum* (1955), a work which moves from Gregorian intonation to dodecaphony. After 1958, however, Stravinsky's music was strictly twelve-tone although, to be sure, always in a very distinctly Stravinskyan way. *Threni* (1957–1958), a large-scale work for soloists, chorus, and orchestra, is completely organized in twelve-tone fashion not only in matters of detail but in the way the larger plan relates to that detail; for example, points of major articulation are often as clearly organized with respect to one another as are the smaller events in between. The result—particularly in the choral and vocal writing—has the effect of a series of unyielding statements (big choral declarations, *a cappella* solo voices in canon, etc.) with a sparse ornamental detail which, in effect, represent a transformation into twelve-tone thinking of Stravinsky's characteristic underlying formal and esthetic sense. Stravinsky's dodecaphonic music is neo-twelve-tone in the same sense that his earlier works are neo-tonal— "neo-Classic" or "neo-Baroque." *Movements* for piano and orchestra (1958–1959) stands in the same relationship to the music of Anton Webern as the *Dumbarton Oaks Concerto* and *The Rake's Progress* do to the music of Bach and Mozart. Neither in the latter nor the former case is there any question of a model but rather of the materials of a discourse whose actual forms— propositions and conclusions—are, as always, quite personal and original.

After *Movements* Stravinsky again turned to vocal and vocal-dramatic materials in a series of spare, aphoristic works—*A Sermon, A Narrative, and a Prayer* (1960–1961); *The Dove Descending Breaks the Air* (1962), an anthem for *a cappella* chorus; the *Elegy for J.F.K.* (1964); the television dance-drama *The Flood* (1961–1962); *Abraham and Isaac* (1962–1963), a Biblical setting in Hebrew for baritone and orchestra; the *Requiem Canticles* (1965–1966). Virtually all of these unite a special permutational twelve-tone technique, a pointed thinness and brevity, a kind of abstracted religious mysticism expressed in a contemporary twelve-tone stylization. Stravinsky's unexpected turn towards the twelve-tone idea, treated in his own personal manner, was a remarkable demonstration of the essential unity underlying apparently dissimilar and contradictory twentieth-century art.

BIBLIOGRAPHICAL NOTES

An extensive bibliography of writings on twelve-tone, serial, and electronic music by Ann Basart was published by the University of California Press in 1962. See also Effie B. Carlson's *A Bio-Bibliographical Dictionary of Twelve-Tone and Serial Composers* (Metuchen, NJ, 1970). Roman Vlad's *Storia della dodecafonia* (Milan, 1958) is one of the few general sources to discuss the diffusion of twelve-tone ideas; however, it contains nothing about American music and is not translated. Boulez's "Schoenberg is Dead" and other early essays on the impact of twelve-tone music and ideas are contained in his *Relevés d'apprenti* (Paris, 1966; English transl. as *Notes of an Apprenticeship*, New York, 1968). The best sources of information on the diffusion of twelve-tone music after World War II are various music journals, notably *Melos* (Germany), *The Score* (English), and the American *Perspectives of New Music*.

A number of studies on individual composers have come out only in the past ten years; some are not yet available in English translation: Claudia Maurer Zenck's *Ernst Krenek—Ein Komponist im Exil* (Vienna, 1980) probes the psychology of exiled (Austrian- or German-American) composers in general, and Krenek in particular; Bruno Zanolini's *Luigi Dallapiccola: La Conquesta di un linguaggio (1928–1941)* (Padua, 1974) covers this composer's works through his *Canti di prigionia* of 1938–1941; *Luigi Dallapiccola: Saggi, testimonianze, carteggio, biografia e bibliografia*, ed. Fiamma Nicolodi (Milan, 1975) is a compilation of articles written mostly by Italian composers; it includes a short biography and a useful bibliography of works about Dallapiccola. One study in English on Dallapiccola's music is by Rosemary Brown: "Dallapiccola's Use of Symbolic Self-Quotation" (*Studi Musicali* 4 [1975], 277–304). In English also there are studies by Steven Stucky on *Lutoslawsky and His Music* (Cambridge, England, 1981) and Andrea Olmstead on *Roger Sessions and His Music* (Ann Arbor, 1985), as well as a volume edited by Edward Cone, *Roger Sessions on Music: Collected Essays* (Princeton, 1979).

part five

The Avant-garde

TWELVE

INTRODUCTION: BEFORE WORLD WAR II

The cycle that began after World War II, although in part a continuation of earlier motifs, in part parallel to the first half-century, is far from a recapitulation of earlier events. An "avant-garde revolution," the second of the century, began well within the traditional Romantic conventions of alienation, individuality, originality, progress, and avant-gardism, but in the past few years has evolved into something genuinely new—a "post-modern" art of the late twentieth century.

What distinguishes the second from the first half of the century is, above all, the intrusion of technology. With the development of magnetic tape, the long-playing (and, later, stereo) record, and FM radio as well as inexpensive, high-quality recording and playback equipment, the burden of musical communication shifted from live performance to recording. No aspect of musical life, from the study of traditional music to the dissemination of new musical ideas and the impact of mass media and pop culture, has remained unaffected by these changes. Technology has not only provided important new tools; it has changed the nature and the experience of musical life. In effect, technology has made the entire experience of mankind available as raw material and—potentially and, increasingly, in actuality—part of the common shared experience.

This remarkable situation, in conjunction with the larger movements of social change, has provided the background against which artistic innovation has taken place. In some ways, the changes have been more striking in Europe, where classicism, populism, political events, and World War II effectively ended the old avant-gardism, marked off an era, and compelled new beginnings. European post-war avant-gardism has been accepted as part of the mainstream of European culture. The American situation is quite different and more complex. Experimental music in the New World has had a long and quite continuous history and a more erratic and individualistic record of achievement; it has provided new music with some of its most important creative energies and has offered genuinely new possibilities for cultural renewal. It has existed side by side with a popular vernacular which has had its own rich and artistic development and with which it has continued to interact. And it has, in recent years, partly moved out of the restricted arena of the avant-garde to play a new and wider role for a much broader public.

The development of new musical ideas since World War II has, in spite of great diversity, taken certain characteristic forms: the isolation of the individual acoustic event; the extension of the sound material to include the entire possible range of aural sensation; the absolutely equal esthetic (though not necessarily equal artistic, psychological, or psycho-acoustical) validity of all possible material in all possible relationships (duration or loudness, for example, being potentially equal in significance to fixed pitch). Every level of control is possible, from total pre-determination to improvisation to randomness or indeterminacy, and choices within these may be determined at any level, at any time before or during (if not after!) the performance; all relationships (including none) are possible.

The first years after the war were marked by these discoveries, rationalized through some form of serialism or intentionally de-rationalized through the introduction of non-predictable or performer-option elements. These apparently contradictory approaches—sequential in European music but simultaneous in America—were reconciled or synthesized in the 1960's, largely through the intervention of media and technology. The re-evaluation of communications media, live performance, and the social role of music again raised the old questions of context and content. Everything is possible but nothing can be meaningful in and of itself. There were two significant reactions to this situation: minimalism, where each single experience is extended to occupy an entire universe, and its natural converse, maximalism—multi-level form, happenings, multi-media, music theater—where ranges of experience are in and of themselves subject matter, and where meaning and context again become issues, social context and concern again become relevant to the development of new forms of expression.

If certain cyclical patterns seem to repeat themselves, the turn of the wheel also takes us further down the road. Before examining the development of what is new and distinctive about post-war music, it is worthwhile to sketch the relationships with the past and to discuss here those earlier composers whose work seems to be linked most closely with recent developments.

SOURCES

As already suggested, post-war music was in part the continuation of motifs begun early in the century and interrupted by the achievement of closed, settled forms in between-the-wars European music. The freely atonal and "expressionist" works of the Viennese and Stravinsky's pre-World War I work not only led to the development of new, non-tonal materials but also to organic, non-developmental forms on the static, additive Stravinskyan model or to the associative ongoing form, created by Debussy, Strauss, and Schoenberg. The tendency towards miniaturism exemplified by Webern has been especially significant not only for brevity and concision of form but also for the way individual events can be broken down and isolated into clear, differentiated packets of sound with identifiable characteristics. This suggested the possibility of restocking and rebuilding the entire process of creative thought from its basic elements. The order principle of twelve-tone music, extended to articulate all levels of musical thought, was decisive in a great deal of post-war musical thinking.

There were other antecedents. The Futurists gave concerts of noises before World War I and the painter Russolo built a noise machine. The Dadaists gave performances which included musical and sound manifestations of various kinds; Marcel Duchamp's *Erratum musical* of 1913 consists of random isolated pitches without any indicated durations. Literary and intellectual movements from the French symbolists down to surrealism and Brechtian theater have had a long and continuing impact. The tradition of abstraction and individualism, derived from Romantic views about the artist and society, was a potent influence until recently. The brief but notable challenge of *Gebrauchsmusik* and the social involvement of the 1930's—a strong reaction against the isolated and alienated position of the artist—put only a dent in the generally accepted view of art music in Western culture and produced only a relatively limited group of works of importance; nevertheless, they anticipated a later turn of the wheel.

In addition to these connections with European modernist culture, there are still more direct connections with the American experimental tradition. American music has always been essentially syncretic, tracking and merging a whole variety of cultural source material; technological development, non-Western ideas, ethnic sub-cultures, folk and pop culture have all helped form a distinctive American experience which has had continuing significance for new music. The global impact of American commercial culture may be a reflection of American economic power, but the development of alternatives or antidotes—beyond a mere retreat into traditionalism—has had a significant testing ground in the New World. Even the young anti-American European radical is, in part, "American" in his culture. This is really a way of saying that, increasingly, we all live in a single super-culture and that we all face common problems.[1]

IVES

Charles Ives was the first important Western composer to stand essentially outside the mainstream of European culture, and he was the first to propose—with no direct influence of technology—the totality and unity of the human experience as a subject matter for art. Ives could do this because, although he was brought up on New *and* Old World culture, he kept an essential distance from received tradition and its dominant professional activities. This is the essence of Ives's "amateurism" and the source of his originality and unique position.

Ives worked far from the European centers and, in many cases, years ahead of his European contemporaries. He composed proto-serial and proto-aleatory music; he invented block forms and free forms; he used tone clusters and structural densities; he wrote in poly-meters and poly-tempi; he composed spatial music and music that could be realized in a multiplicity of ways; he anticipated recent improvisatory works-in-progress, assemblages, and "pop-art" ideals—in short, just about every important development of the last sixty years and some of the most notable of post-World War II avant-gardism. Yet Ives was also aware of the past, and he used aspects of American and European tradition throughout his creative years. In one sense, he stood so far outside of these traditions (although he understood them perfectly well) that—unlike Schoenberg and Stravinsky—he did not have to overthrow them and then labor mightily to rebuild. He knew and used what he needed in just the same casual, determined way he used any idea or material that was appropriate or relevant to what he had to say. Ives felt no "historical

---

[1] But see discussion about the revival of localism in Chapter 17 and in the final section of the book.

compulsion" to abandon tonality (or anything else); his music turns away from narrative and process in the conventional sense; its tendency is inclusive; it absorbs or even revels in contradictions. Like Whitman, Ives could contradict himself, he could contain multitudes.

Nothing in human experience was alien to Ives, but that does not mean that he was a "primitive." This is a myth which depicts him as an untutored pioneer in the New England wilderness; a visionary but a kind of musical Grandma Moses; a rugged individualist working in complete isolation, utterly lacking in technical skill and sophistication but totally original in a rough and ready way; a kind of inspired *naïf*; a phenomenon of nature. In actual fact, Ives's father was a well-known bandmaster who did many experiments in acoustics and temperament. Ives studied with his father in his hometown of Danbury, and later at Yale with the distinguished Horatio Parker. He had extensive practical experience with his father's band, arranging for it and playing with theater orchestras and on church organs in New Haven and New York. All of Ives's mature life and most of his composing years were spent, not in the wilderness, but in New York where he embarked on a double career as an extremely successful insurance broker and a composer. Most of his music was actually written between his arrival in New York in 1898 and the early 1920's; he spent the later years of life arranging, putting in order, and preparing for performance works from the enormous mass of material he had produced earlier.

None of this is meant to detract from Ives's stature as an innovator or as an individualist; quite the contrary, it should emphasize his real achievement by taking it out of the realm of nature mythology and emphasizing its origins in conscious decision and choice. For example, Ives was always able to use tradition—classical tonality, say—in exactly the same way he used his own new tonalities, poly-tonalities and non-tonalities, as a kind of special case, as it were, of his total experience of meaningful sound. It was this range of activity, this totality of experience that interested Ives, and it was out of this totality of experience—out of simplicity and complexity, coherence and contradiction—that he made his pieces. One of his best-known pieces, *The Unanswered Question* (1906), shows his technique of deriving a completely new form out of simple, contradictory elements. A small group of strings—it can be merely a string quartet—is seated off-stage or away from the other instruments; it provides an obsessive, endless rotation of a simple "chorale" sequence of triadic harmonies. On another level, entirely detached from the strings and without any specific rhythmic co-ordination, a trumpet reiterates a questioning phrase. Opposite, flutes (possibly mixed with an oboe and a clarinet) respond to the trumpet question, toss it around, and eventually get into a terrible tangle. There is, in the end, no answer, no resolution; only the question unchanged and the distant string "harmony of the spheres" fading out to infinity.

This tiny conception is full of prophetic Ivesisms: the literary idea which generates a form; the unification of seemingly contradictory material through the very exploitation of the fact of contradiction; the easily perceptible external references; the spatial arrangement of the instruments; the projection of distinct layers of sound with informal vertical arrangements. What is not so obvious is just how all these elements come together to make an expressive form which communicates on a subtler level by no means equivalent to the verbal descriptions (see Appendix; Example 12-1).

The Ivesian view of art and life has to do with the value of a poetic idea realized as a human action or activity. In spite of all his presumed impracticality (but many of the old difficulties of performance, of notation, and of general comprehensibility have vanished over the years), Ives thought of his music as a kind of non-passive, performance activity, primarily something to do, to be actively involved with and only secondarily to be listened to. He seems to have had the idea that audiences might, at some point, sing along or that someone might jump up with a flute or a harmonica and join in. Ives wanted to transform even the passive state of reception into positive involvement, which accounts in part for the intentional use of familiar and popular music to produce a shock of surprise or amused recognition. During his creative years, he poured out a continuous stream of musical expression—works for chorus and organ, five symphonies, four sonatas for violin and piano, two string quartets, many piano works including the massive "Concord" Sonata (1911–1915), a large number of songs, and extremely important works for chamber orchestra or chamber ensemble: the sets of *Tone Roads* (1911–1919), *Three Places in New England* (1908–1914), *Central Park in the Dark* (1906), *Over the Pavements* (1906–1913). There is no question that Ives knew what he wanted in these works—he claimed to have tried many of his ideas out in practice during his theater orchestra and organist days and, by accounts, he could show what he wanted on the piano. On the other hand, what he wanted was often intentionally unclear or imprecise, and he himself changed the way he played his music over the years. His idea was to involve the performer in the activity of creating the music, and the works themselves from a kind of continuous stream of musical expression, portions of which have coalesced—indeed all are still coalescing—into individual scores. This is more than just composing unusual music; it is a change in the meaning of the act of composing itself.

Ives disliked and distrusted the conventionalized rituals of public music making; he wanted to get back to some underlying realities about human activity, about the physical reality of human beings communicating immediate and almost tangible experiences—even experiences of complexity, contradiction, and incoherence. He wanted a speaking kind of music, a music that could be jotted down to convey fresh impressions and thoughts, that could flow with the naturalness of plain speech; a music that could somehow get across that impenetrable barrier between art and life, not to "express" nature but to flow along as part of it. On the one hand, he wrote music that was and is difficult, every part a separate and individual activity; on the other, he wrote things that are easy and banal. He was wildly visionary; one music runs exaltedly or humorously into the next, and in some cases only with the greatest difficulty have performable pieces been separated out into a practical, usable state. Yet there is nothing abstract about any of Ives's work; all of it is conceived, not as paper music, but as matter for action. He wanted performers to decipher illegible and complex new notations, but he also wanted them to understand his ideas and ideals and act freely within them. He wanted to speak to those who understood, yet he also thought that anyone could understand and he wanted everyone to participate. He was not himself a "phenomenon of nature," but he wanted to think of his music that way. He wanted to break down the distinctions between man and nature, between art and life, and to integrate them into some all-embracing experience. His last piece was to be a "Universe" Symphony to be played and sung in the fields and mountains by thousands—indeed, by all of humanity.

Ives's music has had a direct and continuing influence and can be linked quite directly with certain recent avant-garde ideas. But Ives was also a kind of traditionalist—if one realizes that Ives and his father were the only important musical representatives of that tradition! The tradition was a literary and philosophical one: that of Whitman, of Thoreau, Emerson, and the New England transcendentalists; Ives set himself the job of creating, single-handed, a musical equivalent. This had to be something that was at once personal, free, and spontaneous, close to "natural" expression. Ives's range runs from hymn tunes and ragtime to complex, atonal polyphonies. He had to take the raw material and invent the music of an entire tradition from one end to the other. His vision was of the totality of human experience within a personal utterance; it was an evocation of some Golden Age in which art and life were—or would be—naturally and inextricably woven together.

OTHER INNOVATORS: VARÈSE

The period of the 1920's was one of extensive exploration in American music, and the intensity and importance of the activity have scarcely any parallel in the European music of the time (a similar kind of activity seems to have existed in the young Soviet Union, but years of Stalinism all but obliterated even the very names of pioneers such as Roslavetz). The creation and assimilation of new ideas was a primary aim, and the strong musical voices were recognizably those dealing most directly with new materials and new ways of organizing sound: Edgard Varèse (1883–1965), Henry Cowell (1897–1965), Carl Ruggles (1876–1971), George Antheil, and, of course, Ives. The works of Wallingford Riegger (1885–1961) and Adolph Weiss, Leo Ornstein (b. 1892; a Russian-born American who specialized in thick cluster dissonance and static accentual forms), John J. Becker (1886–1961) and Ruth Crawford Seeger (1901–1953; her husband, Charles Seeger [1886–1979] was an important theorist of new resources and Mrs. Seeger's remarkable String Quartet of 1931 is, as an example, full of proto-serialism) extend and diffuse the experimental tradition well into the 1930's and 1940's. Copland's music of the 1920's and early 1930's was strongly influenced by the current avant-garde ideas. It is curious to realize that the position of Roger Sessions was, with respect to the American modernist movements of the day, quite conservative. Ideas such as tone clusters, new scale and rhythmic formations, new instruments, and, especially, new technological means were very much in the air. In an entire issue devoted to new "mechanical" and electric means, the journal *Modern Music* clearly anticipated the idea of *musique concrète* ("Recorded Noises—Tomorrow's Instrumentation") as well as electronic synthesis ("electrical musical instruments" or "eminos").

Some of these pioneers have remained essentially isolated figures without—until now at least—significant influence. Antheil made an international reputation as a wild man and was sponsored by no less a personage than Ezra Pound, but his sensational *Ballet mécanique* (1923–1925) for percussion, player pianos, and airplane motors now seems mildly attractive, overlong, and rather tame in a manner obviously derived from Stravinsky's *Les Noces*; its importance has been eclipsed by much more remarkable percussion works such as Varèse's *Ionisation*. Antheil's later music, much of it written for Hollywood, was tonal, conservative, and unimpressive. By contrast, Ruggles remained the classic type of American rugged individualist; late-developing, uncompromising. His rare, dense, personal, chromatic music forms a distinct kind of American expressionism. Unlike the European expressionist, whose approach is psychological and often suggests anxiety and alienation, Ruggles was a visionary who strove for the sublime, always remembering that the path upwards is not a little rough and torturous. His titles themselves suggest the intense character of the vision: *Angels* (1920), *Men and Mountains* (1924), *Portals* (1925), *Sun-Treader* (1926–1931), *Evocations* (1935–1943), *Organum* (1944–1947).

This tradition of American individualism continued in the personalities of composers like Henry Brant (b. 1913) and Harry Partch (1901–1976). Brant, Canadian-born and active as a jazz arranger in his early years, anticipated many recent ideas with his open rhythmic structures ("polychronic," that is, using independent, multiple meters and tempos) set into large, freely co-ordinated spatial counterpoints which derive ultimately from Ives. Brant creates out of the character of the instruments, their physical disposition, and the acoustical properties of the space in which they are enclosed; typically, he distributes instruments around a hall, with various groups working individually on flexible material in a free, even, unco-ordinated stereophony. He has also proposed a kind of collective performance-practice ideal and has suggested a method of teaching music through creative activity.

Partch can be, to some degree, associated with the West Coast percussion movement of the 1930's and 1940's discussed later in this chapter. And his major importance undoubtedly lies in his remarkable, ritualistic music-theater works: *The Bewitched* (1955), *Revelation in Courthouse Square* (1962), *Delusion of the Fury* (1963–1969). But it is impossible to put Partch in any of the standardized modern-music categories; he has little to do with any of them. Essentially self-taught, he lived for years as a wanderer and a recluse. Later he built a studio in an abandoned shipyard in the San Francisco area where he constructed instruments of his own devising. Then, after a period at the University of Illinois, he settled in Southern California where he was able to work with younger people, training them to play his instruments and act out his theater rituals in a kind of communitarian performance ideal. Partch, not Ives, is Rousseau's "natural man" among American composers. He had to construct or reconstruct everything for himself. His instruments bear picturesque names such as Cry-Chord, Mazda Marimba (made of light bulbs), Cloud Chamber Bowls, The Harmonic Canon, and Spoils of War; they are striking both to hear and to look at. At the same time, he created new tunings and scale patterns based on microtonal divisions of the octave but using mainly the small-number ratios of just intonation. He also developed techniques of repetitive, ongoing polyrhythm, wide ranging, chant-derived vocal style, appropriate new notations as well as significant new music and theater forms. Partch's work has practically nothing to do with the main currents of Western modern music. It has distant points of origin in Greek mythology as well as in folk and non-Western music, but it is uniquely his own, a kind of composed ethnic music created not by a whole culture but out of individual creative need.

Partch's use of microtonalism (the division of the octave into more than the conventional twelve tempered chromatic steps) is connected with his theories about "natural" tunings, with his "ethnic" style and his instrumental creations. An interest in microtones—generally connected with very different ideals—appeared earlier in the century; it seemed the logical next step after the exploitation of the total chromatic. Among the composers who worked with microtones in more than a passing way are the Czech Alois Hába (1893–1973), the Mexican Julian Carrillo (1875–1965), and the Russian Ivan Vishnegradsky (1893–1979).[2] More recently, problems of tuning and

---

[2] Bartók, Bloch, and others used "quarter-tones" but only as special inflections of the traditional half-steps.

microtones have attracted the attention of several youngers composers including
Ben Johnston (b. 1926) at the University of Illinois (where Partch was formerly in residence), John Eaton (b. 1935), who has used them in conjunction
with live-electronic performance, Easley Blackwood (b. 1933), who has written pieces based on a variety of equal-tempered tunings, and Joel Mandelbaum
(b. 1932), who basically writes in an expanded tonal idiom. Microtonal materials and techniques have been most extensively used in electronic music.
In instrumental and, especially, vocal music they require greater refinement
on the part of performers and audiences than has been generally forthcoming;
the new spectrum of electronic possibilities seems to offer more promise for
microtonalism.

The most direct connections between the American avant-garde scene
of the 1920's and the recent post-war period can be found in the work,
personality, and ideas of Edgard Varèse. Varèse was born and educated in
France, worked briefly in Germany, and came to New York in 1915 with a
vision of artistic new worlds already amazingly fully formed. He was perhaps
the first composer to conceive of sounds as objects with sculptural, spatial
configurations held together by rhythmic energy. The traditional idea of
developmental process and variation plays virtually no role in his music,
which is composed of planes and volumes. His starting points perhaps included
the experiments of the Futurists and certain "cubist" aspects of *Le Sacre du
printemps.* But Varèse's esthetic position was vastly different from that of
his contemporaries, and he stands apart as one of the most original figures
of twentieth-century music.

The development of new resources based on technology—an ideal
perhaps derived in part from his contact with Busoni in Berlin before World
War I—was part of Varèse's vision from the very beginning. However, his
first mature works in the new style—*Amériques* (1917–1921), *Hyperprism*
(1922–1923), *Octandre* (1923), *Intégrales* (1924–1925), *Arcana* (1925–1927)—
are compositions for chamber or large orchestra which make striking use of
winds and brass along with large percussion sections. The "melodic," fixed-
pitch content is reduced to small, insistent groupings of single notes or two
or three cells strikingly articulated by rhythm and accent. The vertical,
"harmonic" element consists of highly dissonant, static structures filling out
various segments of the total chromatic, usually symmetrical around one or
more pivot notes, and framed by the expanded use of percussion. Melody,
harmony, and timbre (the terms are hardly valid in the traditional sense)
are assimilated to rhythm and accent, and the fixed, invented musical shapes
are thus built up in a highly unified manner. These powerful, static building-
blocks, held together by rhythm—percussive energy—are piled up in great,
spatial juxtapositions which define Varèse's new conceptual musical space.
Enormous amounts of energy are created by these works, but the tensions
are internal. There is no sense of motion in the conventional sense at all but

rather a play of kinetic and potential energies which give the impression of holding together complex, unyielding physical sound objects set, as it were, into a dynamic musical space.

If timbre and accent and rhythm are aspects of melody and harmony in traditional music, the situation is reversed here. Indeed, there is often a kind of continuum with fixed pitch at one extreme and pure rhythm and accent on the other; but there is constant interaction and even flow between these fixed extremes. Pitch is no longer the ongoing, developmental, all-powerful generator of form but it is by no means abandoned, even in an all-percussion piece like the famous *Ionisation* of 1929–1931. Thus the sirens represent the use of pitch on a continuum, and the entrance of piano clusters and bells near the end are structurally essential in a work which puts color, rhythmic form, and accent in the first plane (see Appendix; Example 12-2). Only a few years later Varèse wrote a wholly successful work based on a single, pitched instrumental line, the well-known *Density 21.5* (1936) for solo flute.

During the 1920's Varèse was a major figure on the American scene, organizing and directing an important series of new-music concerts which introduced new European and American works in New York. The International Composers' Guild and its successor, the Pan-American Association of Composers were associated with the work of Varèse, Ruggles, Ives, Cowell, and others. Concerts directed by Leopold Stokowski, Nicolas Slonimsky, and others, were presented in New York, California, Havana, and several European cities. However, this intense activity subsided in the 1930's when, under the influence of populist ideologies, avant-garde ideas and forms were set aside.

During this period, Varèse expended most of his energies in the fruitless attempt to spur the development of a creative sound technology for the realization of large-scale musico-dramatic concepts. A science-fiction opera dealing with attempts to contact extra-terrestrial intelligence was turned over to the playwright Antonin Artaud; a libretto is extant but little or no music survives. Of a projected "Symphony of the Masses" with André Malraux—one of its forms was to involve simultaneous performance in various parts of the world connected by radio communications—nothing remains but a fragmentary piece for chorus. One completed work of the early 1930's, *Equatorial*, was scored for the Theremin and later revised for Ondes Martenot—both early attempts at electronic musical synthesis. Significantly, however, both *Equatorial* and the large-scale unfinished *Nocturnal* (completed after the composer's death by his pupil Chou Wen-chung) make important use of the human voice in conjunction with large instrumental forces. These works bring to the foreground an aspect of Varèse's work not often discussed; his exploration of very deep-seated and elemental areas of the human psyche. Varèse's work, which looks forward in so many respects, also looks "backward"—not into the historical past, but to unexplored recesses of the human mind and very basic, elemental forms of human expression.

Varèse's music is non-linear, non-process, non-narrative in form; its creation of sound objects and musical space are quite distinct from most of the music of his contemporaries but is fundamental to much of the music of recent decades. Varèse specifically and conceptually anticipated the new percussion music as well as the basic form of tape and electronic music. After World War II, with the widespread diffusion of magnetic tape and the development of tape and electronic equipment and studios in Europe and America (see Chapter 13), Varèse himself was finally able to realize some of the visionary concepts he had conceived so many years before. Fittingly, he provided the *musique concrète* movement with its first masterpieces: *Déserts* (1954) for tape, winds, brass, and percussion, and *Poème électronique*, commissioned for the 400-odd loudspeakers that sent sound spinning around the inside of Le Corbusier's Philips Pavilion at the 1958 Brussels Worlds Fair. These powerful montages—Varèse's own preferred term was "organized sound"—are worked out of recorded sound images, altered, rhythmicized, juxtaposed, overlaid and intercut, the whole built up into new spatial structures of great originality, breadth, and scope. *Poème*, although designed for a continuous 360° sound space, is overwhelming even in its stereophonic form, realized by the composer for the purposes of recording. The spatial concept is not merely a matter of the physical arrangement of the sound sources; it is actually built into the juxtapositions of aural images, slowly turning and colliding in cataclysmic spatial encounters.

With Varèse the notion of a continuous musical space, proposed intellectually by Busoni in 1907 and, in another sense, by Ives at the same time, becomes a reality. Varèse's work not only anticipates but actually merges with a new post-war music.

COWELL: NON-WESTERN INFLUENCES

Henry Cowell was the most direct representative of the Ives "tradition" in the 1920's, the most important link between Ives and the latter-day avant-garde, and himself one of the most prolific innovators of the century. Cowell's work is a vast accumulation of new materials and ideas. The most famous of these, the "tone cluster," is simply an agglomeration of adjacent fixed frequencies in which, however, the overall impression is that of a texture rather than of a chordal sonority consisting of separable fixed-pitch elements. The "cluster" occupies an intermediate ground between fixed pitch and noise; it is made up of fixed frequencies, but the confused interaction of the upper partials of these frequencies produces an indeterminate effect closely related to noise. Cowell's *Mosaic* (1935) for string quartet and *26 Simultaneous Mosaics* (1964) for five players are remarkable examples of open form. He also did extensive and important creative investigation in the field of rhythm and was perhaps the first person to propose—and realize in a piece of music—the concept of deriving rhythmic–durational relationships from the ratios of harmonic vibrations (2:1, 3:2, 4:3, etc.). Cowell also developed a great number of new instrumental resources—most notably, a great variety of timbres plucked, scraped, strummed, and scratched out of the insides of the piano—and he pioneered in new notational techniques appropriate to his new resources (see Appendix; Example 12-3). His later work was largely concerned with materials drawn from folk, "ethnic," and non-Western sources treated in terms of Western instrumental and musical organizations—again an anticipation of contemporary concerns and an illustration of the developing notion of ranges of experience.

Cowell's work provides an immediate connection between the experimental activities of the 1920's and the rather special, quiet, East-oriented American movements of the 1930's and 1940's. These developments, centered in Cowell's home state of California, had two closely related aspects. One was the absorption of strong influences from the East; the other, related to new Cuban and Mexican music, was the extensive use of percussion instruments and ensembles. The most important composers associated with these developments were Cowell, Partch, Colin McPhee (1901–1964), Alan Hovhaness (b. 1911), Lou Harrison (b. 1917), and John Cage (b. 1912). Cage and Harrison actually collaborated on *Double Music* (1941), a percussion work with a notable Eastern influence. Harrison's work, after encounters with the influence of Ives and Ruggles, has taken him back to this area; his recent work involves Eastern instruments, adaptations of Eastern instrumental and vocal styles, and the use of non-tempered tuning. Cage's early involvement with this movement, his experiments with rhythmic serialism and recording technology, and his involvement with Eastern philosophy led him to challenge the traditional Western supremacy of pitch organization. He went on to challenge the relationship between one sound event and another and, ultimately, even the need for conscious determination and control of such events.

BIBLIOGRAPHICAL NOTES

Duchamp's *Erratum musical* is given in Robert Lebel's *Marcel Duchamp*, trans. G. H. Hamilton (New York, 1959).

For Ives, see his own *Essays Before a Sonata and Other Writings*, ed. Howard Boatwright (New York, 1962), and *Charles E. Ives: Memos*, ed. John Kirkpatrick (New York, 1972); Vivian Perlis's *Charles Ives Remembered: An Oral History* (New Haven, 1974) is a collection of interviews done by Perlis with Ives's friends, acquaintances, business associates, and fellow musicians. Four recent volumes on Ives delve into the composer's esthetic and background: Rosalie Sandra Perry's *Charles Ives and the American Mind* (Kent, OH, 1974); David Wooldridge's *From the Steeples and Mountains* (New York, 1974); Frank R. Rossiter's *Charles Ives and His America* (New York, 1975); and J. Peter Burkholder's *Charles Ives: The Ideas Behind the Music* (New Haven, 1985; a projected second volume will cover Ives's music). Henry and Sidney Cowell's *Charles Ives and His Music* (New York, 1955; reprinted with additions, 1969) is an early study by two of Ives's near-contemporaries; H. Wiley Hitchcock's *Ives: A Survey of the Music* (Brooklyn, 1983; originally published in 1977 under a slightly different title as part of the Oxford Studies of Composers series) covers Ives's musical output by genre. Some important papers, covering both musical and cultural aspects, are contained in the volume *An Ives Celebration: Papers and Panels of the Charles Ives Centennial Festival-Conference*, ed. H. Wiley Hitchcock and Vivian Perlis (Urbana, IL, 1977).

There is surprisingly little material in English on Varèse. Fernand Ouellette's *Edgard Varèse* (New York, 1968) and Louise Varèse's memoirs *A Looking-Glass Diary* (New York, 1972) are biographical; Chou Wen-chung's article in *The Musical Quarterly* (52 [April 1966], 151–70) and the volume edited by Sherman Van Solkema, *The New Worlds of Edgard Varèse: A Symposium* (Brooklyn, 1979) deal with his music. See also Robert P. Morgan's "Rewriting Music History: Second Thoughts on Ives and Varèse" (*Musical Newsletter* 3/1 and 2 [Jan. and April 1973], 3–12; 15–23). The Spring 1974 issue of *Soundings* is devoted to articles on Ives, Ruggles, and Varèse, written by many composers active today. For Ruggles, see the author's article in the September 1966 issue of *Stereo Review*.

There is as yet no major publication on Cowell's musical compositions nor his life; however, William Lichtenwanger's *The Music of Henry Cowell* (Brooklyn, 1987) is a comprehensive descriptive catalogue, and two useful bibliographies exist: Martha L. Manion's *Writings About Henry Cowell* (Brooklyn, 1982) and Bruce Saylor's *The Writings of Henry Cowell* (Brooklyn, 1977). On Henry Cowell's *New Music*, see Rita Mead's *Henry Cowell's New Music 1925–1936: The Society, the Music Editions, and the Recordings* (Ann Arbor, 1981).

Cowell's *New Musical Resources* (New York, 1930; repr., New York, 1969) and the essays he edited under the title *American Composers on American Music* (1933; repr., New York, 1962) are basic documents for the American 1920's and 1930's. Other material on or from this period would include Virgil Thomson's writings, notably *The State of Music* (rev. ed., New York, 1962) and *American Music Since 1910* (New York, Chicago, San Francisco, 1970–1971), Paul Rosenfeld's *Musical Impressions*, ed. Herbert A. Leibowitz (New York, 1969), Aaron Copland's *Copland on Music* (London, 1960), and the issues of *Modern Music* during its existence. See also Chou Wen-chung's "Asian Concepts and Twentieth-Century Composers" (*Musical Quarterly* [April 1971],

211–19) for a discussion of Asian traits in the music of Cowell, Hovhaness, Harrison, McPhee, Cage, Varèse, and others, and Peter Yate's *Twentieth-Century Music* (New York, 1967) for its treatment of the American pioneers.

For Antheil, see Linda Whitesitt's recent study *The Life and Music of George Antheil, 1900–1959* (Ann Arbor, 1983). Pound's *Antheil and the Treatise on Harmony*, originally printed in 1927, has been reissued (New York, 1968); Antheil's own *Bad Boy of Music* (New York, 1945) is an anecdotal autobiography. On Riegger there is Stephen Spackman's *Wallingford Riegger: Two Essays in Musical Biography* (Brooklyn, 1982). Partch's *Genesis of a Music* (Madison, WI, 1949) exists also in a second, enlarged edition (New York, 1974).

THIRTEEN

TECHNOLOGICAL CULTURE AND ELECTRONIC MUSIC

The expansion of audio technology, the creation of *musique concrète*, the concept of a totally rationalized music, and the introduction of indeterminate elements into performance were almost simultaneous events. Suddenly composers seemed to turn back to that exploration of materials, techniques, and new perceptive forms which had marked the early years of the century. The movements of the late 1940's and 1950's returned to the discovery of new kinds of experience and new ways of experiencing, all propounded in rigorous forms—serial or indeterminate—pushed to their logical and physical extremes, much in the manner of controlled experimentation.

There are many parallels with the pre-World War I situation, but there are also many differences, notably the tremendous development of electronic technology. Among the tools and media that became widely available after World War II were magnetic tape, the long-playing record, improved recording technology including multi-track recording, two- and four-channel playback, FM radio, various signal generation and modification equipment, and component sound reproduction. The availability of a variety of new means for creation and dissemination of new music has had a tremendous cultural impact. Technology has created a remarkable extension of common shared experience, an availability of (admittedly transformed) sound events, and the means for the quick dissemination and dispersal of new ideas. Attention is turned towards and then away from the minutiae of musical experience. As a result, the meaning of notation and the role of live performance have been drastically re-evaluated. The availability of new sounds, although significant, is nevertheless the least important result of the introduction of electronic technology. Total control, infinite repeatability, the widening of experience to include all possible sound and music, and the development of new modes of communication—these have been more important, particularly in suggesting strikingly new ways of dealing with the old questions of creation and communication.

THE BACKGROUND

The initial aim of technology was to transmit, store, and reproduce the live experience of sound; towards this aim the essential recording and playback devices were developed. Sound was coded for amplification, long-range transmission, or storage as electrical energy. But this energy could also be created with generators and used to drive loudspeakers directly; the result was sounds whose only existence was in the form of emission from a loudspeaker. The early work in this field was directed towards the invention of performance instruments such as the Hammond organ, the Theremin, and the Ondes Martenot, all developed before World War II. The earliest sound experiments of Cage, Pierre Schaeffer (b. 1910), and Pierre Henry (b. 1927) were with disc recordings; however, it was the invention and availability of magnetic tape that made the electronic-music movement a reality. Tape is a faithful, pliable storage device which itself can be edited and manipulated in a variety of ways. Improved recording techniques as well as various generators and sound modification devices offered the means for shaping sound much as a sculptor shapes his material. For the first time in music history, the composer was enabled to work directly in his medium without the necessary aid of performing interpreters. So-called "pure" electronic music is based on the fact that a loudspeaker can be driven to produce sound by electromagnetic impulses derived (with or without the use of tape storage) from electronic generators. These generators produce impulses ranging from the simple pulse of a sine wave (producing a "pure" sinusoidal tone) to the complex, random oscillation of all the audible frequencies (producing "white noise"). By contrast—although as we shall see the distinction has been rendered obsolete in practice—the use of recorded "real" sounds, no matter how manipulated, falls into the category of *musique concrète*.

Most tape/loudspeaker music shares certain basic techniques: the superimposition of layers of sound through simultaneous recording and over-laying, and the alteration of sound characteristics through the use of electronic filters, reverberation, tape loops (providing endless pattern-repetition), con-trol of intensity, change of tape speed (producing transposition up or down to the limits of equipment response). Tape can be chopped or spliced in limitless combinations and juxtapositions, affecting the character of single sounds or whole structures. Sound transformations involving the finest dis-tinctions or the most gradual rates of change may be juxtaposed with the most violent contrasts, and the extremes can be mediated by every possible gradation in between.

These early, basic techniques were considerably modified by the development of electronic music synthesizers built especially for sound pro-duction (or "synthesis") and modification. The R.C.A. Synthesizer, developed for commercial purposes and later installed at the Columbia-Princeton Elec-tronic Music Center in New York, was the first. Synthesizers were originally designed for studio work with the results recorded, edited, and mixed on magnetic tape. These have largely been replaced by performance synthe-sizers, which have become widespread in every area of music. They have also become more sophisticated and complex; electronic pieces which took months to realize because of formidable technical hurdles can now be pro-duced or reproduced in a few hours or even minutes.

The vast expansion of the use of synthesizers has been largely due to their wide use in popular music, both live and recorded. The development of multi-track recording has similar origins. Two-track recording became the norm in the 1950's; four- and eight-track equipment became available in the 1960's. Modern sixteen-, twenty-four-, and thirty-two-track recording, com-bined with noise-reduction systems, permits the building up of musical matter in a kind of electronic "score" that can be realized from its parts with perfect rhythmic precision, supplanting the multiple tape-recorder mixing of the early studios.

The synthesis of loudspeaker sound through the use of computers was the logical next step. Computer synthesis may involve anything from a relatively simple synthesis of sounds—there is no theoretical reason why any loudspeaker sound cannot be synthesized—to the creation of programs for actual computer composition. Simple computer technology has entered the marketplace in the form of digital recording and sound reproduction, and digital synthesizers, which can be programmed in a variety of ways, have dramatically increased the quality and sophistication of relatively inexpensive sound technologies. In digital systems, the information is broken down into milliseconds and stored in the form of binary numbers. An extremely large amount of information is required to store even fairly simple sounds this way, but modern computer technology is quite able to deal with this volume of information even in small home systems. Only wanted information is stored, so there is almost no noise or distortion inherent in the process. Also, existing sounds can be analyzed, broken down, stored in this form, and easily retrieved. The characteristic sound patterns of instruments and voices can be reproduced, extended beyond their normal ranges and, if desired, altered in almost any way.

PRINCIPAL CENTERS

Although esthetics based on technology have played and continue to play a role in the history of recent music, tape and electronic music cannot be considered as a movement. It is a paradox that the single most widely influential medium of post-war musical life has produced no single "style" or "school"; the influence has been rather cultural, conceptual, and technical. In a real sense, technology is a set of tools as well as a cultural condition and, therefore, its relationship to the culture that produced it is one of continual feedback.

The closest approach to a tape-and-electronic movement is *musique concrète*, first realized in 1949 at the studios of the French national radio by Pierre Schaeffer and Pierre Henry. A number of important composers have worked at these studios including Varèse, Yannis Xenakis and, among younger French composers, Luc Ferrari (b. 1929). Although the long-range value of the work produced in Paris has been challenged, the *musique concrète* ideal—images of the external world juxtaposed, overlaid, fragmented, enlarged, dissected—remains important.

The Columbia University Studio, founded by professors Otto Luening (b. 1900) and Vladimir Ussachevsky (b. 1911) in 1952, tended from the very first to use live-recorded sound in conjunction with tape techniques. Luening and Ussachevsky were the first, after Varèse, to explore the important area of tape and live sound. In 1959, with the acquisition of the RCA Synthesizer and the participation of Milton Babbitt of Princeton University, the studio became the Columbia-Princeton Electronic Music Center; it remains the principal center for tape and electronic music in the United States. Composers who have worked there include Varèse, Ussachevsky, Luening, Babbitt, Luciano Berio, Charles Wuorinen (b. 1938), Jacob Druckman (b. 1928), Alcides Lanza (b. 1929), Wendy (Walter) Carlos (b. 1939), the author (b. 1933), and others. Two composers closely associated with the studio are Mario Davidovsky (b. 1934), an Argentinian now living in New York and known for his adroit live-tape combinations, and Bülent Arel (b. 1918), who has founded electronic studios at Yale University and the State University of New York at Stony Brook, Long Island. Electronic music studios are now common in universities and colleges across the country.

The first and most important of the European electronic music studios was founded in Cologne, Germany, in 1951 by Herbert Eimert (1897–1972) with an emphasis on the purely electronic production of sound. This studio was closely associated with the work of Karlheinz Stockhausen. The most important of the numerous and often ephemeral studios that sprang up in these years—in Stockholm, Amsterdam, Warsaw, Tokyo, and elsewhere— was the Studio di Fonologia at the Milan radio station in north Italy. The studio was directed by Luciano Berio (b. 1924) and Bruno Maderna (1920– 1973). The electronic work of Berio and Maderna—and also that of the Belgian Henri Pousseur (b. 1929)—although originally identified with the serial style of their instrumental music, was characterized by a close, empirical experimentation with new material. With a few exceptions, most of the works to come out of Milan have the character of exploratory essays in the discovery and transformation of materials, which was fairly typical of much of the early work in the medium.

Many composers became interested in electronic music as a source of new sounds; others were looking for control. What they discovered was the continuum, the range of experience available in every domain. The unexpected result for some was a turn away from the tempered scale and a turn away from a simple twelve-tone approach—an expansion or even rejection of serialism. Nearly every serial composer who worked with electronics returned to live music with some modification of his or her approach. Some abandoned predetermined, fixed, and closed forms as not being suited to live performance; tape could do it better. Most enriched their approach to performance in some way; nearly all combined live or recorded performed elements with the purely electronic textures. It is striking that the most significant tape and electronic pieces of the 1950's and early 1960's used the human voice—on tape or live with tape—as an essential part of the conception: Stockhausen's *Gesang der Jünglinge*, Berio's *Omaggio a Joyce* (1958) and *Visage* (1961), Babbitt's *Vision and Prayer* and *Philomel*.

After the mid-1970's, the importance of the old electronic music studio dwindled considerably and the electronic-music esthetic tended to split in several directions. Work with computers assumed particular importance, notably at Stanford University in California, at the newly established IRCAM center in Paris, and in the work of a few individual composers specialized in this area.

At another extreme, the pure, fixed forms of electronic music were dissolved in a kind of noise/junk esthetic pioneered by John Cage and highly influential in this country and abroad, notably in the work of Stockhausen. It was also Cage, with his associates David Tudor (b. 1926) and Gordon

Mumma (b. 1935), who first began working with electronic extensions of live sound, a common idea in pop music but curiously slow to penetrate avant-garde music. These ideas, first used independently by the Cage group, later by the author, and by Stockhausen and Boulez in the mid-1970's, provided the basis for a new kind of live-performance ensemble specializing in the electronic production and projection of sound. Examples of such groups include the ensembles founded by John Eaton and William O. Smith (b. 1926) in Rome, the Musica Elettronica Viva, also originally founded in Italy, the Sonic Arts Group, and others (see Chapter 18).

In the late 1970's and 1980's, the availability of relatively inexpensive, high-quality equipment has made the use of electronic instruments in live performance commonplace. Composers like Steve Reich and Philip Glass have toured extensively with their own ensembles, which have strong electronic and amplified components. Rock and jazz ensembles with strong experimental or artistic points of view have come almost invariably to depend on synthesizers and on techniques of electronic sound modification such as distortion and echo. Live electronic performance of one sort or another has come to dominate a great deal of new music in America in recent years and has achieved a good deal of importance in Europe as well. Electronic music is no longer a thing apart; it has been absorbed into the mainstream. Technology, which at one time was thought to replace live performance, has in fact ended by reinvigorating it.

BIBLIOGRAPHICAL NOTES

Electronic Music: A Listener's Guide by Elliott Schwartz (revised ed., New York, 1975) is a thoughtful, popular overview—if slightly outdated—by a composer with broad interests and a great deal of insight. A more recent study devoted to electronic music is Joel Naumann and James Wagoner's *Analog Electronic Music Techniques: In Tape, Electronic, and Voltage-Controlled Synthesizer Studios* (New York, 1985); it is essentially a textbook on tape, studio, and synthesizer techniques. Allen Strange's *Electronic Music: Systems, Techniques, and Controls* (2nd ed., Dubuque, 1983) is another. The special issue of the *Revue musicale*, No. 236 (for *musique concrète*), and *Die Reihe*, No. 1, are interesting from a historical point of view; see also Stockhausen's "The Origins of Electronic Music" (*The Musical Times* [July 1971]), which gives his view of the subject.

For volumes devoted to both electronic and computer music, see the anthology edited by Jon H. Appleton and Ronald C. Perera, *The Development and Practice of Electronic Music* (Englewood Cliffs, NJ, 1975), which includes chapters by Otto Luening (*Origins*), Wayne Slawson (*Sound, Electronics, and Hearing*), Gustav Ciamaga (*The Tape Studio*), Joel Chadabe (*The Voltage-*

Controlled Synthesizer), John E. Rogers (*The Uses of Digital Computers in Electronic Music Generation*), and Gordon Mumma (*Live-Electronic Music*), some of which are now dated due to the quick rate of change in this field; Peter Manning's *Electronic and Computer Music* (Oxford, 1985), a concise history with not too much technical discussion and including a discography covering both the United States and Europe; Herbert S. Howe's *Electronic Music Synthesis: Concepts, Facilities, Techniques* (New York, 1975), which, although slightly out of date, was written by one of the pioneer designers of computer-music programs; and Barry Schrader's *Introduction to Electro-Acoustic Music* (Englewood Cliffs, NJ, 1982), which discusses techniques used in many actual compositions.

The most important writings on computer music include Charles Dodge and Thomas Jerse's *Computer Music: Synthesis, Composition, Performance* (New York, 1985), a comprehensive practical guide with sections devoted to the theory of computer music as well as to actual practice of the theory of composition; *Foundations of Computer Music*, eds. Curtis Roads and John Strawn, (Cambridge, MA, 1985), a volume containing revised and updated articles from the *Computer Music Journal*; and *Computer Music Tutorial*, a companion volume to the Roads-Strawn volume, which provides the necessary foundation for the more advanced papers in that book.

Studies concerning the work of specific composers include Seppo Heikinheimo's *The Electronic Music of Karlheinz Stockhausen* (Helsinki, 1972); Friedrich Spangemacher's *Luigi Nono: Die elektronische Musik, historischer Kontext—Entwicklung—Kompositions-Technik* (Regensburg, 1983); and Otto Luening's *The Odyssey of an American Composer: The Autobiography of Otto Luening* (New York, 1980), which covers not only his involvement with electronic music but also much about the history of twentieth-century music in general.

FOURTEEN

ULTRA-RATIONALITY AND SERIALISM

With some validity, the history of Western composition since the Renaissance might be described as a continuing process of articulating the inarticulate. Gradually and increasingly, unorganized or purely conventional aspects of musical performance—phrasing, dynamics, articulation, timbre— were brought under notational control. The relationships between background and foreground, harmony and melody, in Classical-Romantic music are essential to the success of that music. Schoenberg's twelve-tone method, an attempt to organize the total chromatic material, is in part an extension of this control process. Schoenberg consciously attempted to make these relationships explicit with his twelve-tone idea; in his later music and, in particular, in the music of Webern, this process was extended to include the rhythmic, dynamic, and even timbral domains. What had long been the prerogative of the performer or lay within the domain of "tradition" now became part of the articulated compositional process. The notion of bringing all the elements or dimensions of musical discourse to the foreground and of rationalizing them seems to have occurred almost simultaneously in Europe and America.

BABBITT AND AMERICAN SERIALISM

The first works in which linear succession, harmonic simultaneity, duration (including rhythm and tempo), dynamics, articulation, register, and timbre are all strictly derived from a single, all-inclusive premise were written in 1948 by Milton Babbitt (b. 1916). Most of these techniques are worked out in his *Three Compositions* (1947) for piano; they are fully realized in his *Composition for Four Instruments* and *Composition for Twelve Instruments* of the next year. With Schoenberg and even Webern, the twelve-tone idea remained essentially a process or, to use Schoenberg's own term, a method. With Babbitt, it is most definitely and carefully a "system" in the strictest sense. The row not only becomes a "set" of pitches but also of values and relationships, absolutely and strictly defined in terms of structure as well as operational process. Thus the twelve-tone material represents the totality of possible relationships inherent in every aspect of the music, and the actual unfolding of each piece is a process of permutation within which all these potential relationships are revealed.

In the late 1950's, Babbitt began working at the newly re-organized Columbia-Princeton Electronic Music Center with the RCA Electronic Sound Synthesizer. With the Synthesizer, a sophisticated instrument specifically constructed for the production of electronic sound, every aspect of both pitched and non-pitched sound—duration, quality of attack and decay (dying away), intensity, tone color, and so forth—can be set out with precise definition, and any sound can be tested immediately and, if necessary, readjusted down to the finest possible gradations. Babbitt's interest in electronic techniques has not been so much in matters of new sounds as in the possibilities of control, and his electronic works—*Composition for Synthesizer* (1961), *Ensembles for Synthesizer* (1962–1964)—have been primarily concerned with new ways of organizing time and form perception.

As with some of his contemporaries, Babbitt's electronic experience seems to have affected the character of his "live" performed music, which has taken on a new vitality and color. Works like *All Set* (1957) for jazz ensemble, *Partitions* (1957) for piano, and *Sounds and Words* (1960) for soprano and piano combine his typical clarity and care with a new richness and lively virtuosity appropriate to the conditions of live performance. Babbitt has also combined live performance with tape in works for soprano and synthesized tape: a setting of Dylan Thomas's *Vision and Prayer* (1961; with a purely synthesized accompaniment) and *Philomel* (1964), to a specially written text by John Hollander using live voice, recorded and altered vocal material, and purely electronic sound. The Greek legend of Philomel—a woman who was raped, had her tongue torn out and then, through the pity of the Gods, was turned into the nightingale—is rich in metaphoric material, which is emphasized by the musical and structural qualities of Hollander's poem. Language becomes a kind of musical expression, while the music becomes articulate and precise, almost like language. Inarticulateness and the quality of musical experience are rationalized and, as in all of Babbitt's work but with the greatest force in this one, a certain range of perception, carefully planned and controlled, is used quite literally to "express" complex, non-verbal thought processes (see Appendix; Example 14-1).

Babbitt has had a strong influence as a teacher and theoretician, primarily in the United States. The most skillful of his pupils—Donald Martino, Henry Weinberg, Peter Westergaard (all born in 1931)—have developed individual means and styles of considerable originality within the premises of total rationalization and control, and Babbitt's influence can be seen also in the work of composers like Charles Wuorinen, Harvey Sollberger, and others connected with the Group for Contemporary Music in New York. In the end, Babbitt's influence seems most significant not so much in specific matters of method or style as in the more general diffusion of concepts of technique and intellectual responsibility.

EUROPEAN SERIALISM

The first "totally organized" piece of music to be written in Europe was the etude *Mode de valeurs et d'intensités*, one of a set of piano pieces written by Olivier Messiaen in 1949. Messiaen has a particular place in recent music both as the father of the European avant-garde and as a highly original figure in his own right. He is a professional organist in the tradition of Franck and Widor and a professed Christian mystic with strong pantheistic overtones to his thought. His position in European music has certain parallels to that of Varèse, who may have influenced his concepts of sonority and of static, spatial form. An influence of impressionism and even a touch of a rather (intentionally?) vulgar popular harmony is present in his earlier work. Later, he absorbed influences from some of the younger composers he himself had influenced. He developed a personal system of rhythmic modes derived from East Indian practice; other techniques, notably the use of plainsong, derive from European medieval music. He has also made extensive use of transcriptions of bird song in works like *Oiseaux éxotiques* (1955–1956) and *Catalogue d'oiseaux* (1956–1958). From the rather insistent religiosity of his early works, often bordering on banality without any trace of redeeming irony, and the completely inward, brooding, meditative quality of his *Quartet for the end of time*—written in 1940 in a German concentration camp—Messiaen's music has evolved into a distinct and unique amalgam of disparate elements. His studies in twelve-tone music, the serial innovations deriving from his work with rhythmic modes, and the influence of his pupil Boulez helped bring about this synthesis. *Chronochromie* (1960), *Couleurs de la cité céleste* (1963), *Turangalîla* (1946–1948), *Et exspecto resurrectionem mortuorum* (1964; written for the 700th anniversary of the Rheims cathedral), and his recent opera *St. Francis of Assisi* are works of great spiritual intensity and, like the later works of Varèse, fully belong with the new post-war music.

Messiaen's importance as a teacher and as an influence on the younger European composers has been very great. After the war, he was one of the few European musicians who taught twelve-tone technique, the first to relate pitch serialization with organized rhythm, and almost the only one who was entirely free not only of the prejudices of the tonal system but of the orthodoxies of the Schoenberg followers as well. He was the teacher of Pierre Boulez and Karlheinz Stockhausen and thus influenced directly the course of post-war European avant-garde music.

The most powerful impulse in the initial development of new ideas in post-World War II Europe was the re-appearance of twelve-tone technique. Whereas the development of twelve-tone ideas was fairly continuous in the United States, it was completely cut off in Europe by the crises of the 1930's and the war. The first task of the younger European composers— and, for that matter, many of the older ones—was the rediscovery of the one technique that seemed to offer a means of expressing new ideas in new ways; hence the great importance of a handful of teachers like Messiaen and of the newly created international school and festival at Darmstadt, where the long-suppressed music of Schoenberg and Webern could be heard and its techniques studied. Although the Schoenberg models were important, it was finally Webern who seemed to offer the way out of expressionism and the possibility of building a new music from the simplest and barest of premises: the younger European composers began as Webernites. Their initial premises were the individual, isolated sound event and the rational, organizing power of the serial principle; they did not hesitate to draw the most extreme conclusions from these simple propositions. The twelve-tone idea in pieces like Boulez's *Structures* for two pianos or Stockhausen's *Kontra-Punkte* (1952) is not a method (in Schoenberg's sense) nor a complex system (in Babbitt's sense) but rather a total generating principle through which a new and complete identity of materials, means, structure, and expression could, it was hoped, be achieved. The difficulty with this identity was always that it remained, even in the best works, a mere play of numbers arbitrarily translated into various musical facts, without a real organic base in perceptive experience. But it also gave rise to the characteristic European "serialism" with its idea of a fixed scale of values.

In serialism's simple early form, the twelve-tone arrangement of pitches was paralleled by an arrangement of twelve durations, a fixed grouping of twelve dynamic values, and so forth. All of the possible points of intersection of these values could then be plotted; the result was the piece.[1] The reign of this strict and narrow interpretation of serial technique was in fact rather brief, although literally dozens and even hundreds of totally organized, post-Webern serial pieces were written, nearly all for small combinations of instruments and nearly all based on a highly rationalized arrangement of isolated, "pointillist" events and textures, often surrounded by generous amounts of highly organized silence.

The initial impulses towards this refined, ultra-rational post-Webernism came from Messiaen and Boulez in Paris; a second group of composers in northern Italy—Luciano Berio, Bruno Maderna, Luigi Nono—came out of the Webern-Dallapiccola line partly under the influence and tutelage of the German conductor Hermann Scherchen (1891–1966), one of the few musical personalities whose activity links the Viennese School and the postwar avant-garde. But the most influential architect and theorist of European serialism was Karlheinz Stockhausen. Stockhausen's initial concerns were the complete isolation and definition of every aspect of musical sound and the extension of serial control into every domain. The latter point is important: Stockhausen envisaged the possibility of serializing and thus pre-controlling even such matters as the density of harmonic, vertical masses; the number of musical events occuring in given time segments; the size of intervals and the choice of register; the types of attacks and articulations employed; the rate of change of texture and tone color. Often the technique and the formal ideas far outrun the actual materials; in the *Klavierstücke I–IV* (1952–1953), for example, there are combinations and refined distinctions which cannot be meaningfully realized. Later, Stockhausen was to return to performed music with new ways of applying serial technique to the necessities of live performance; in the early 1950's, however, electronic music seemed to offer the solution to the serial dilemma.

The use of electronic media had a very specific importance in Stockhausen's work; it offered him the possibility of creating new forms out of transformation and rate of change. Stockhausen's earlier instrumental works use material based on values arranged in fixed steps—sometimes conceived in terms of arbitrary and unidiomatic distinctions. In his electronic music—in particular, in his *Gesang der Jünglinge* of 1955–1956—he could break away from the discreteness imposed by the use of individual instruments and by the tempered scale and literally break down conventional distinctions between noise and pitch, between clarity and complexity, between simple statement and transformed event, between pure electronic and recorded

---

[1] It is not quite accurate to say, as some commentators have, that this is music in which analysis precedes composition. The analysis is quite equivalent to the piece.

vocal sound, even between sound and silence. Later, partly under influences from the United States, Stockhausen was to discover a way of re-interpreting these principles in terms of "live," performed music; in a way, it was the electronic experience that was decisive. In 1959, Stockhausen wrote a tape piece, *Kontakte*, which is entirely structured on great continuous sliding transformations of every possible aspect—every dimension or parameter— of musical sound. *Kontakte* also exists in a version with two piano and percussion performers, in which even the gap between purely electronically produced and live sound is closed. Nearly all of Stockhausen's later work uses one form or another of electronic sound processing, and in works like *Mikrophonie, Mixtur*, and *Hymnen* electronic transformation is the essential aspect of the form.

BIBLIOGRAPHICAL NOTES

Ann Phillips Basart's *Serial Music: A Classified Bibliography of Writings on Twelve-tone and Electronic Music* (Berkeley, 1961) covers what might be called the classical period of the subject. See also Effie B. Carlson's bibliography on twelve-tone and serial composers (cited on page 130) as well as J. D. Vander Weg's "An Annotated Bibliography of Articles on Serialism 1955–1980" in *In Theory Only* (April 1979), which updates Basart. Milton Babbitt's formulation of twelve-tone structure as a system is scattered in several highly technical articles in *The Score, Perspectives of New Music, Journal of Music Theory*, and *The Musical Quarterly*. Perhaps the most accessible expositions are those in *The Score* (Dec. 1963; reprinted in *Twentieth-Century Views of Music History*, New York, 1972) and *The Musical Quarterly* (April 1960; entire issue reprinted in paperback form as *Problems of Modern Music*, New York, 1962).

For European serialism, see *Die Reihe*, especially Nos. 3 through 5; *Contemporary Music in Europe*, eds. Paul Henry Lang and Nathan Broder (New York, 1965; repr. 1967), and Ulrich Dibelius, *Moderne Musik 1945–1965* (Munich, 1966). Stockhausen's *Texte zur Musik* (4 vols., Cologne, 1963–1978) is essentially his commentary about musical currents over the past forty years, with extended discussions on serial as well as electronic music. Boulez's *Notes of an Apprenticeship* (New York, 1968) does the same on a much smaller scale.

On Messiaen, see his *The Technique of My Musical Language* (Paris, 1944; English trans. John Satterfield, Paris, 1956) and Claude Samuel's *Conversations with Olivier Messiaen* (trans. Felix Aprahamian, London, 1976), as well as the recent monographs on his life and music: Robert Sherlaw Johnson's *Messiaen* (Berkeley and Los Angeles, 1975), Max Forster's *Technik modaler Komposition bei Olivier Messiaen* (Neuhausen-Stuttgart, 1976), and Paul Griffiths's *Olivier Messiaen and the Music of Time* (London and Boston, 1985).

FIFTEEN

ANTI-RATIONALITY AND ALEATORY

CAGE AND HIS "SCHOOL"

The appearance of "totally organized," totally rational music and the systematic abandonment of conscious, pre-set composer control were precisely coincidental in time. John Cage came out of the Ives-Cowell line and his early music is, in some respects, the end rather than the beginning of a development; it is, like much of Cowell's work of the 1930's and 1940's, concerned with non-tempered sounds, with percussion, and with Oriental ideas. Cage's famous prepared piano is a kind of one-man percussion ensemble (often closely related in sound to the Indonesian gamelan). A more prophetic idea was the use of phonographic test records to produce a kind of proto-electronic music. Eventually Cage abandoned not only steady-state pitch phenomena but also rational control over many aspects of the musical

event. He threw dice,[1] used the *I Ching*, plotted star charts or the imper-
fections on a piece of paper—not to give the performers freedom, but to
de-control the conscious manipulation of sound. He produced a pair of tape-
collage pieces (among the earliest tape pieces anywhere) as well as his famous
Imaginary Landscape No. 4 (1951) for twelve radios, random noise assemblages whose subject matter is a fixed time span within which aural objects—
any aural objects (including other music) in any combination—may occur,
plucked from the real world by random, intentionally irrelevant methods
and put in random juxtaposition. Fixed time segments and some kind of
graphic, schematic, or diagrammatic notations—newly invented or plotted
for each piece—are characteristic of the live performed pieces. These notations are basically programs for activities, they renounce any specific control
of actual sound results but merely define the limits of choice and possible
field of activity, and quite explicitly show the impossibility of prediction.
Scores or parts may be played separately, together, or not at all. Instruments
are objects to be acted upon; sounds are a series of unpredictable disturb-
ances and interferences. The graphic representation becomes partly an end
in itself, a significant catalyst in an ongoing relationship between creator,
performer, and listener. (See Appendix: Example 15–1). Musical performance becomes a kind of existentialist activity in which the notions of "musical
composition," of "performance," of "communication," and of the "work of
art" itself are destroyed or drastically altered; in which the real, determined
world and the unreal, accidental world of "art" merge; in which the listener
becomes directly involved in an activity in which the old distinctions and
relationships are meaningless. Ultimately there need be no activity at all—
only an open piano and the contemplation of 4'33" of nothing at all. Cage's
famous silent work, the classic and pure piece of non-music (1952), may be
taken as a frame for the natural sounds of life, a segment of time isolated
and defined in order to trap, for a moment, the experience of the haphazard,
"real" world. Or it may be taken as the zero point of perception where total
randomness and aleatory meet total determinism and unity in the literal
experience of nothing.

Cage is not perhaps to be considered as a creator in the ordinary
sense—but then he has done a great deal to change that "ordinary sense."
He has been and remains one of the most influential figures in avant-garde
arts since the war, and aspects of his work have generated whole esthetics
of graphic notation; of performance as gesture; of chance, choice, and
changes; of "neo-realist" use of accidental or chosen sound objects from the

---

[1] *Alea*, Latin for dice, is the root of the word "aleatory," loosely used to describe
various kinds of music in which chance elements, randomness, and indeterminacy figure in
the "realization" in performance. Another adjectival form is "aleatoric"; this is decried by some
critics on the grounds that "aleatory" is already an adjective presumably derived from the
French *aléatoire* meaning "chancy" or "risky." As usual, usage outruns etymology.

exterior world. Electronic music suddenly seemed to make the whole question of perfect order and rationality in performed music irrelevant. It is in the nature of human activity that a precise action can never be repeated and that no event can ever recur; it seemed logical, particularly to the European dialectic mind, that irrationality and randomness should be built in as qualifications for the construction of a new instrumental and performed music. Actually, of course, irrationality and randomness are no more the essence of the human condition than is man's capacity to impose or conceptualize order in the external world. When a mathematician wants true randomness he turns to the machine and computer, and related techniques have been used, notably by Yannis Xenakis (b. 1922), to generate random statistical patterns—bunches of unpredictable events sprayed over a given field—which are subsequently translated into instrumental sound values.

An obvious corollary to the de-rationalization of composer control was the increased importance given to the performer's role in determining the details or the actual shape of a conception in performance. Already in the early 1950's, a number of composers—Earle Brown (b. 1926), Morton Feldman (b. 1926), Christian Wolff (b. 1934), comprising a New York school of "action music" close to but distinct from Cage—began to open up spaces within which multiple possibilities could be realized at the moment of execution. New notations were invented for these purposes, not only to indicate graphically the limitations of the space within which the performer could operate but also to re-engage the interpreter in a kind of dialectic vis-à-vis the score. The notations generally have exactly the opposite significance from the scientific, graphic indications which they often externally resemble. Scientific notations are ways of representing the precise course of observed events, generally on a continuum. Most of the musical graphics are, on the contrary, only generalized guides intended merely to outline or suggest to the performers the areas in which choice and chance are permitted to operate. Thus Feldman indicates, within a typically soft and spare range of sound events, general areas of attack, pitch, or register, the exact choice being left to the performer; the sound events are carefully isolated and disassociated from one another. Intentional disassociation—statement without relationship, evolution, or process—is a fundamental, underlying idea. (See Appendix: Example 15–2). Brown's *December 1952* is a series of horizontal and vertical black rectangles inked on a white sheet, indicating only some very general co-ordinates; within these, all choices are possible and equally valid. It is important not to confuse this music with improvisation; there is no question here of performance tradition or spontaneous invention within some given pattern but only controlled-choice situations in which any rational basis for decision has been intentionally removed or minimized.

These techniques of performer choice and of automatic chance mechanisms are also applied to the actual sequence of events in a performance and, thus, to larger "structure." By the application of an inexhaustible series of devices—shuffling pages, selecting fragments, performers interacting with one another, performers ignoring one another, live performance pitted against tape, and so forth—a conception is designed that will, on each reading, result in a new juxtaposition of the parts. In theory, there will be some constants from one performance to the next that will define the basic conception throughout all its transformations, but in some cases this constant would seem to be only the program for action itself.

Cage's earlier chance compositions tend to be fixed, principally in some kind of determined time span (details open, overall space closed); after Cowell, Brown seems to have been the first to propose open form (details fixed; sequence variable). Later on, Cage also adopted the notion of multi-directional structures, applying this to diagrammatic programs of action; a work like his *Piano Concert* (1957–1958) consists of a piano part, whose elements can be played in any order desired, and an orchestral part, to be realized by any number of players (including none) on any number of instruments, playing parts made up of pages of which any number may be played (including none), with or without other instruments. Beyond the free-will, existentialist music of chance and changes, Cage moved on into a vaster area of activity and gesture. He attached contact microphones to instruments and scratched record pick-ups and mike heads, clogging the lines of amplified communication with violent, random electronic "distortion"; he sent electronic feedback whirling through speaker systems and across the thresholds of perception and pain; he smoked cigarettes and swallowed water, contact mike at the throat, volume at full blast. Typically, he has left the exploration of complex and multiplying noise levels and indeterminacies to others and has moved logically onwards (he has always been more of a dialectician than his interest in Oriental ideas would lead one to believe) to a kind of ritual theater in which the act of performance becomes a way of drawing together meaningless and unordered bits of real life. *Indeterminacy: New Aspect of Form in Instrumental and Electronic Music* (1958) is, in spite of its grand title, a set of ninety funny stories—accompanied, interrupted, or blotted out by piano and electronic activities taken from the *Piano Concert*—slowly recited or gabbled through to make each story fit a one-minute space. His *Theater Piece* (1960) is a big amalgam of action and gesture indeterminately organized in a determinate time space.

HPSCHD (1967–1969) is a multi-media work realized with Lejaren Hiller, based on a musical dice game attributed to Mozart and including computer read-outs, chunks of traditional music, and various visual elements. *Roaratorio*, originally written for radio, is a large-scale performance work based on fragments from James Joyce's *Finnegans Wake*. From *4′33″*, the programmed absence of planned sound, Cage has come to programming excerpts from the totality of possible experience (give or take a possibility or two).

A good deal of this kind of activity is defined in a negative way by excluding certain ranges of possibility or, in some cases, by reversing the traditional premises. This is clearest in Morton Feldman's music where, instead of organizing sounds in relationship to one another, the elements are carefully disassociated. In traditional music (including earlier modern music) the essential character comes out of the way the music goes from one note to another. In Feldman's it is the isolated sounds themselves that are the essential experience, intentionally unrelated and disassociated from one another, thus creating a new time sense, previously unknown in Western music. In many Cageian and post-Cageian works, there is a set of activities regulated by a set of limitations, often with an intentional disassociation between the nature of the activity and its possible results in sound. Instead of being conceived as sound, performances may be based on visual definitions, programs of activity, ideas of non-sound or silence. Instead of defining time, the compositions are themselves defined by the random passage of time, extending to indeterminate or theoretically infinite length. Instead of a music of definable identity, we have conceptions whose essence is lack of identity.

In spite of their seeming opposition, serialism and indeterminacy have certain things in common. Both were, in their pure state, essential, relatively brief phases—a clearing of the ground, as it were, before reconstruction could begin. Both came out of philosophical attitudes about music and art—serialism contemplating the activity of the mind and its internal order, in Western determinist style; indeterminacy contemplating an Eastern-influenced philosophy of activity in the indifferent external world. In the end, Cage's use of chance or randomness was the least important aspect of his work; his conception of art as a human activity and his opening up of the external universe as subject matter for an art that had become almost entirely interiorized will stand as his major contributions.

The influence of Cage and his "school" (if one can use this terminology any more) has been very great in all the arts in the Americas, in Europe, and even in Asia.[2] This influence has ranged from the simple use of random noise techniques and chance procedures to various projects for a "neo-realist" theater of gesture and objects. Stockhausen used some kind of aleatory or open-form procedure in a whole series of works beginning with his *Klavierstücke XI* of 1956 (made of short piano segments which can be put together in different ways) and *Zyklus* of 1959 (a percussion piece written

---

[2] A curious return of a compliment, since Cage and the "New York School" have appropriated ideas from the Orient. Japanese (and also Korean) composers have participated actively in musical developments of recent years. The best known of the Japanese Cageians is Toshiro Ichiyanagi (b. 1933). Many of the other Japanese, the Matsudairas (father and son; Yoritsuné, b. 1907, Yori-aki, b. 1931), Toru Takemitsu (b. 1930), Toshiro Mayuzumi, and Kazuo Fukushima (b. 1930), as well as the Korean Isang Yun (b. 1917), have tended towards an adaptation of European serialism tempered by Oriental elements and chance, indeterminate, open-form, or even gestural materials derived from the "New York School."

in a graphic notation and open for various realizations on a simple ground plan). Virtually all European avant-garde music of the last few years has been affected in some way. Mauricio Kagel (b. 1931), an Argentinian now living in Germany, has been specifically involved with the character of performance as gesture and activity. Others, including a number of young Germans and an Italian group working in an area close to "pop art," have used actual pre-existing sound objects as well as sets of activities and gestures for the materials of paste-up neo-realist collages. Stockhausen himself has written a Cage-like (but structured) theater piece (*Originale*) and there have been a number of random gestural-theater ventures of one sort or another (see Chapter 21). In the United States, "action" activity groups like 'Fluxus' in New York and exponents of a kind of mobile, kinetic music like the 'Once' group in Michigan (active 1961–1969) have paved the way for a wide acceptance of the idea of activity—musical, meaningless or otherwise—as a way of life. Pop art, happenings, multi-media, minimalism, concept art, and contemporary music theater all owe something, or trace their origins, to Cage; the impact of his ideas is now so generalized that one can only describe them as having entered the mainstream of twentieth-century art.

BIBLIOGRAPHICAL NOTES

There is no clear line of distinction between Cage's writings and his musical works; see his collections *Silence* (1961), *A Year From Monday: New Lectures and Writings* (1969), *Writings '67–'72* (*M*, 1973), *Empty Words: Writings '73–'78* (1979), and *X* (1983), all published in Middletown, CT. See also his *For the Birds. John Cage in Conversation with Daniel Charles* (Boston, 1981). A full Cage bibliography would be immense; material on his work and ideas has appeared in many languages and in many kinds of publications dealing with contemporary culture. The major study on Cage is edited by Richard Kostelanetz (New York, 1970, with a very extensive bibliography); see also Paul Griffiths's short survey of his music (Oxford Studies of Composers, London, 1981) and the catalogue of his works put out by his publisher (C. F. Peters), which is, in the Cageian tradition, something more than a catalogue (New York, 1962). *Notations* (with Alison Knowles; New York, 1969) is a collection of manuscript pages by more than 250 composers together with a typographical arrangement of their comments about notation; it constitutes at once a documentation of an important subject and at the same time a typical Cage project. The recently published *A John Cage Reader: In Celebration of His 70th Birthday*, eds. Peter Gena and Jonathan Brent (New York, 1982), contains articles by many of the people associated with him. Michael Nyman's *Experimental Music: Cage and Beyond* (London, 1974) discusses Cage's music and philosophy as well as the later composers who were inspired by him; Peter Yates's *Twentieth-Century Music* (New York, 1967) is particularly valuable for its comments on the American individualist or experimental tradition and Cage's place in it.

On the Fluxus group and related phenomena, there are a number of collections of events, proposals, and other material; one anthology (called *An Anthology*) was put together by La Monte Young and George Brecht. The *Something Else Press Newsletter*, ed. Richard Higgins (New York and Vermont, 1966–1983), and other publications as well as various issues of *Source* magazine document this period and these ideas.

For the European view of aleatory, open-form, and related ideas, see later issues of *Die Reihe* and the *Darmstädter Beiträge*. Boulez's "Alea," originally presented as a paper at Darmstadt in 1957, is published in translation in *Perspectives of New Music* (3/1 [Fall–Winter 1964], 42–53); the Fall–Winter 1965 issue includes "Indeterminacy: some Considerations" by Roger Reynolds. "The Significance of Aleatoricism in Twentieth-Century Music" by Anthony Cross, originally published in *The Music Review* (London, 29/4[1968], 305–22), has been reprinted in *Twentieth-Century Views of Music History*, ed. William Hays (New York, 1972).

SIXTEEN

THE NEW PERFORMED MUSIC:
THE UNITED STATES

In a sense, it was possible to grasp the real impact of electronic music only when its limitations began to be understood. Anything can be reproduced or synthesized on tape except the act of performance itself. The result was that the experience of working in the studio led composers back to the performance situation with a new understanding of that medium. If total control was part of the genius of the electronic medium, then this was no longer a necessary goal for live performance. Since no two live performances can ever be identical anyway, it seemed to make sense to make variability and choice a part of the music. Since an essential element in the performance act is the personality and ability of the performer, performer choice, virtuosity, and freedom could be built in from the start; open form and graphic notations flourished. Other influences from the tape and electronic experience were equally important. The notion of working with the sound material on a continuum could be applied very well to the live situation. Tempered-scale restrictions need no longer be universally observed. New techniques, new sounds, new extremes of range and virtuosity could be explored by composers working closely together with a new breed of performers. The richness and virtuosity of instrumental and even vocal performance were sought out and developed to a remarkable degree with the performer—who was sometimes also a composer—as a collaborator in the realization.

Some of the conditions of this performance situation are the following: (1) control (the tension growing out of the necessity to put the right finger in the right place at the right time) interacting with freedom (the flexibility of actions whose precise value is determined only at the moment of performance); (2) interaction between composer and performer as well as between performers; (3) interaction between the musicians and the performing space and, possibly, between the live performance and electronic transformation through amplification, modification, and playback; (4) performer choice, improvisation, and controlled virtuosity set at the limits of performer possibility; (5) exploration of the limits of perception.

This "new virtuosity" was not mere embellishment but an organic part of the musical substance itself. A unified set of actions and gestures functions as a source of thematic ideas which form relationships—between performer and score; between real (i.e., clock) time and psychological time; between fixed units of measure and open cadenza; between control and complex precision on the one hand and the open play of color and virtuosity on the other; between the uniqueness of the individual performers (in character, in material, even in space) and the overall unity of the conception; between the requirements of what can be perceived and new ideas of concept, activity, and substance extended in every direction and dimension to the most extreme limits.

This is no longer a music of fixed goals but of transformations which take place in every dimension and throughout the range of perception. These transformations become ways of acting and experiencing, and relating action and experience, i.e., of knowing. In a sense, the aim is actually to alter, extend, and redefine the quality of our experience and the limits of our ability to perceive and understand.

In Europe, some change of direction could already be seen in the mid-1950's; Boulez's *Le Marteau sans maître* (1952–1954), in which a complex poetic and conceptual form replaces a "merely" serial one; Nono's *Il Canto sospeso* (1955–1956), with its use of *engagé* texts (letters from the partisan underground) set for large, multi-layered orchestral and vocal forces; Stockhausen's *Zeitmasse* (1956), with its alternation of controlled and flexible situations. Change is evident in Milton Babbitt's *All Set, Vision and Prayer,* and *Philomel,* works which, although they remain faithful to a vision of total rationality and control, also relate to the character of the live performance situation and the virtuosity of the performer. The appearance of a new generation of performers—Bethany Beardslee (b. 1927), Cathy Berberian

(1925–1983), David Tudor (b. 1926), Paul Jacobs (1930–1983), Severino
Gazzeloni (b. 1919), Paul Zukofsky (b. 1943), Siegfried Palm (b. 1927)—
skillful in the traditional ways but open to the extension of techniques and
ideas, was essential. The evolution of a new generation of conductors—the
composers Foss, Boulez, Maderna as well as Andrzej Markowski, Michael
Gielen (b. 1927), Michael Tilson Thomas (b. 1944), Dennis Russell Davies
(b. 1944), and others—completed the cycle.

THE NEW VIRTUOSITY

Not all of the composers involved in the new performance practice
were veterans of twelve-tone serialism, aleatory, or electronic music; the
presence of an active, younger generation of American performers, a certain
currency of ideas and personalities, and a more unbroken tradition of new-
musical and experimental activity and performance gave a certain distinct
"third stream" character (to use in a wider sense Gunther Schuller's term
for the jazz/non-jazz merger) to much new-musical activity in the United
States. In this respect, the work and influence of two older composers, Stefan
Wolpe (1902–1972) and Elliott Carter, and a number of younger Americans
must be considered here.

Wolpe, like Varèse, was born and trained in Europe where his early
work was connected with radical musical and political movements. After a
sojourn in Palestine in the late 1930's, he came to the United States where,
after World War II, he evolved a mature, radical, and highly influential
abstract expressionist style. In this sense Wolpe's work is parallel to that of
certain highly influential emigrés connected with New York School painting—Josef Albers, Hans Hoffman, and Willem de Kooning. Wolpe's
experimental work of the 1940's and early 1950's—*Battle Piece* for piano
(1943–1947), Quartet (1950) for trumpet, tenor saxophone, percussion and
piano, *Enactments* (1950–1953) for three pianos—is connected with jazz
and American performance practice on the one hand and with Cage, Tudor,
and the nascent New York action-painting, action-music avant-garde on the
other. His later work combines a striking individuality and assertiveness
with a development of organic form and a concept of ordered freedom which
is related to but quite distinct from either European or American serialism.
Works like *In Two Parts* (1960) for flute and piano, *In Two Parts* (1962) for
six players, and *Piece for Two Instrumental Units* (1962–1963) take shape
from the constant interplay of oppositions of clarity and complexity, simplicity and density, careful articulation and freedom. Wolpe's forms, like
Varèse's, accumulate as great static objects, but the ideas and the small-
range motion are packed with intense, revolving detail. Many of these works

are built on tiny, cell-like structures which retain their essential, immovable identity through every kind of registral, rhythmic, dynamic, and color shift; the larger result is an accumulation of potential energies which twist, turn, combine and recombine, destroy and reconstruct an apparently unyielding material. Nearly all of Wolpe's work is closely involved therefore with a complex use of the energies produced by the act of performance and, as much as anything else, it is this flow of form-making energy which gives his music its unique character.

Wolpe taught at the Third Street settlement in New York, at Black Mountain College in North Carolina, and privately. Most of the older American avant-gardists did little or no teaching; Wolpe was for many years one of the few who espoused new ideas. As a teacher, as a source of new ideas, and as a highly original composer, Wolpe exerted a major and not yet fully documented influence on the course of new music.

The concept of cumulative form, deriving from the work of Varèse and Wolpe, had two major influences. One, essentially East European, flows through the work of the sometime Varèse collaborator Yannis Xenakis, the Hungarian György Ligeti (b. 1923), and the new Polish school, notably Krzysztof Penderecki (b. 1933). The other stream is connected with the building-block structures of a number of American composers, most notably Ralph Shapey (b. 1921) and George Crumb (b. 1929). Shapey, perhaps one of the most underrated contemporary composers, can also be associated with New York School painting, although for a number of years he has been directing a contemporary music ensemble in Chicago. Like Boulez, Maderna, Foss, and Schuller, Shapey has been active as a conductor, and his music revels in the power of large ensemble sound. Shapey's work—*Discourse* for flute, clarinet, violin, and piano of 1961 can serve as a typical example—uses large, contrasting, block-like ideas set forth in broad planes and constantly turning and returning in great, overlapping, phased cycles. Shapey's ideas are highly charged patterns, melodically simple, often quite dissonant, and strikingly articulated with rhythmic energy and accent. Within a static structure of balanced, inflexible, and immobile units, there is a kind of internal play of energies resulting from the continuous redefinition of a fixed material which remains set in a constant state of tension. Occasionally these accumulated energies are let loose in an explosive manner: in *Rituals* (1959) for orchestra, this actually takes the form of improvisational elements; elsewhere, this release is expressed by a more controlled pile-up of instrumental and percussive energies.

Shapey's output is considerable and encompasses a variety of traditional and non-traditional instrumental and vocal/instrumental media. A number of his works, notably the Violin Concerto (1959), *Rituals*, and *Ontogeny* (1958) for orchestra, are organized into larger cycles. Shapey's music represents a major extension of the old idea of originality, individualism, personal expression, and a kind of visionary power as the artist's true domain. In a sense, all his work is a representation of a kind of personal willfulness and protest—the act of individual will imposing itself on a not always very receptive mass society. It is against this background that Shapey's startling decision to stop composing and withdraw his works must be understood, fortunately he has since rescinded the ban.

The music of George Crumb stands rather apart from that of his contemporaries in its special feeling for sonority, its exploitation of unusual, invented, or even familiar and referential gestures, its ritualistic and mystical qualities, its essential simplicity and intense poetic sensibility. Crumb's static forms and juxtapositions are derived from the Varèse tradition and relate to certain European music, mainly East European and French. His extreme sensitivity to timbre and isolated sound grows out of the most rarefied forms of post-Webernism; his simplicity, block form, and use of repetition suggest a Stravinskyite turned minimalist; and his sense of time is not unlike that of Morton Feldman. These points of reference may suggest influences, but in fact Crumb's independence and individuality make it difficult to categorize his work. Whereas, for example, Feldman tries to do away with the linear, developmental aspects of time to focus on the "it-ness" of the sound experience itself, Crumb is engaged in a larger and much more difficult task: the suspension of the sense of passing time in order to contemplate eternal things. This preoccupation with time is characteristic of Crumb's work from the several compositions titled *Madrigal* and *Night Music* (1963–1969) to instrumental works like *Eleven Echoes of Autumn* (1966), *Echoes of Time and the River* (1967), the vocal and instrumental *Night of the Four Moons* and *Ancient Voices of Children* (1970; see Appendix; Example 16–1), and the more recent ritualized chamber pieces utilizing masked performers and amplified instruments (e.g., *Black Angels* for electric string quartet, 1970). Many of these works use texts or fragments from Federico García Lorca, often spoken or whispered by the instrumentalists. All of them share the very special sense of ritual which is Crumb's particular contribution to the contemporary live performance idiom.

The other major, and older, American whose work must be considered here is Elliott Carter. Carter, who was born in New York in 1908, studied at Harvard and with Nadia Boulanger, and was one of the few composers of his day who was close to Ives. Although his earlier work reveals a rather complex American neo-Classicism, there are many musical and intellectual strands which connect him with Varèse, Ruggles, and the American experimental tradition. At the end of the 1940's and early in the 1950's Carter began to expand his vocabulary in the direction of a non-twelve-tone instrumental chromaticism. Works like the intense First String Quartet (1950–1951), based on long, contrapuntal lines, and the more decorative and elegant Sonata for flute, oboe, cello, and harpsichord (1952), with its new element of ornamental virtuosity, grow out of the interaction of complex parts; the *Eight Etudes and a Fantasy* for woodwind quartet (1950) constitute a set of close-up studies of simple and very precisely defined material; the most remarkable is a study on a single pitch. By the *Variations for Orchestra* of 1954–1955 and the Second String Quartet of 1959, Carter had achieved an identification of the material, the performing situation, and the individualization of the players through a form which is non-serial yet controlled, flexible and "invented" yet completely organic. In the Second String Quartet, the four players are separated in physical space and completely individualized in their musical way of speaking; the parts are related by a common virtuosity—a kind of highly ornamented fantasy style in which the "embellishments" and colors are not merely decorative but organic and essential—and yet each has distinct characteristics of pitch, rhythm, and dynamic. The totality of the piece is a confluence of divergent currents which retain their identity while remaining essential parts of the larger flow (see Appendix; Example 16–2). In the *Double Concerto* for piano and harpsichord of 1960–1961, the two solo instruments are set off against one another, each with its own small ensemble of winds and strings, plus a huge battery of percussion which literally frames the piece in highly articulated noise. The pitch content of the piece—essentially made up of two all-interval chords, one for each soloist/ensemble group—emerges from and eventually returns to a more undifferentiated state of percussion "noise," and these transitions are, so to speak, mediated by the soloists who perform on what are, in effect, pitched percussion instruments. The same integrated opposition that exists between pitch and noise on one level operates, on another plane, between interval pattern and rhythm; and these in turn generate a big structure of changing, "modulating" tempos. Again, as in the Second String Quartet, the parts are distinguished by complementary pitch and rhythmic content. The total impression becomes that of a sum of disparate elements—a sum of rhythms, for example, which generates a higher-level pulse which ultimately determines the overall motion. The rhythmic groupings and phrase articulations, taken through wide changes of register and timbre, carry out the association of pitch, texture, and rhythm; just as there is a sum of rhythms, there is a sum of textures, lines, and harmonic conglomerations which integrates highly differentiated material and derives a new and expressive form from them. These are difficult pieces to listen to; one gains an appreciation for them through their highly organized, methodically worked-out design. Later compositions, such as *A Mirror on Which to Dwell* (1974) and *Syringa* (1978), are more accessible; both show a renewed interest in expressive melody: both are set for voice, although the instrumental accompaniment sometimes shows the type of dense complexity characteristic of Carter's earlier compositions.

The "tradition" of Varèse, Wolpe, Carter, and Shapey forms a New York School of a distinct character, and their influences are carried forward in the work and activity of a group of composers associated with Columbia

University: Charles Wuorinen (b. 1938), Harvey Sollberger (b. 1938), and Chou Wen-chung (b. 1923 in China). Chou was one of Varèse's few formal pupils and is his musical executor; in 1973 he completed his teacher's last major uncompleted work, *Nocturnal*, from the surviving sketches. His own music represents a fusion of conceptual ideas derived from the East, Western serialism, and Varèse's idea of block or cumulative form. Serialism plays an important role in the music of Wuorinen, who, with the flutist and composer Sollberger, founded and directs the Group for Contemporary Music, which was active for a decade at Columbia and was then sponsored by the nearby Manhattan School of Music. Wuorinen, who is also a skilled pianist and conductor, is a prolific composer whose earlier work is closely connected with his own performing interests and abilities; his *Piano Variations* (1965) includes, besides fistfuls of notes articulated in the usual way, the brushing and slamming of the keys with fingers, palm, and fist; plunking, hitting, and scratching the strings directly inside the piano; and so forth. This earlier, wilder, more intuitive style has gradually been replaced by a more elaborated and studied approach that owes a great deal to Babbitt and twelve-tone serialism (thus somewhat reversing the evolutionary sequences found in European avant-garde music). This style, which can be heard in Wuorinen's Concerto for amplified violin and orchestra (1972), his music theater piece *The Politics of Harmony* (1968), based on Chinese legend, and many other chamber and symphonic works, develops a very highly controlled and intellectualized series of modes controlling extremes of density, register, virtuosity, forward thrust and immobility, violent energy and violent calm.[1] Sollberger's *Chamber Variations* (1964) similarly grows out of an extraordinary virtuoso instrumental technique characterized by a tension of contrasts and the unified opposition of extremes, tightly controlled at first, then ultimately decontrolled, in every dimension and with extreme precision.

Many of the American composers of the middle generation are expert instrumentalists or conductors. One can speak of a new performance practice involving the closest interaction between the creative and performance processes. Chicago and New York ensembles have already been mentioned. Other important composer-performance centers in the 1960's included a group at the University of Illinois—Kenneth Gaburo (b. 1926), Lejaren Hiller (b. 1924), Ben Johnston (b. 1926), and Salvatore Martirano (b. 1927)—working with a performance ensemble, a new-music chorus, an electronic studio, and a lively performance situation. Gaburo and Martirano both extended the idea of solo virtuosity into choral ensemble music. Martirano's *O, O, O,*

---

[1] Ironically, Wuorinen won the Pulitzer Prize for a purely electronic work, *Time's Encomium* (1968–1969), realized on the RCA Synthesizer at the Columbia-Princeton Center. However, Wuorinen, whose interest in the electronic medium stems from the total-control philosophy of Babbitt, is not primarily an electronic composer; the use of technology remains secondary in his work.

O, That Shakespeerian Rag (1959), a setting of Shakespeare for chorus and instruments, is built on a complex of singing, speaking, trilling, hissing, whispering, and shouting; the instrumental frame (informed by a virtuoso performing technique evolved to a point close to jazz) is at once contradictory and essential, equally free and planned, in a structure that is both controlled and dramatic. His *Ballad* for pop singer and ensemble, *Underworld* (1965, a theater piece), and *L's G A* for actor, film, and tape extend a virtuoso solo style in the direction of a wider consciousness, close to multi-media and music theater.

Gaburo, who founded and directed the new-music chorus at Illinois, has reconstituted this activity at the University of California at San Diego. California, now a major creative and performance center, has revived the performance-practice traditions of the 1930's: Partch spent his last years there, and the Cageian tradition is still very much alive. Robert Erickson (b. 1917), originally from the San Francisco area but currently active at San Diego, has been working out new performing situations which combine improvisation and written scores; he has also been active in the continuing development and construction of new instruments and instrumental types. Other composers who have or had links to Southern California performance practice include Larry Austin (b. 1930), Pauline Oliveros (b. 1932), and Morton Subotnick (b. 1933). Subotnick, one of the pioneers of multi-media character of the instruments and the skill and personality of the players. forms; similarly, the concept-art and theater work of Austin and Oliveros take us into new areas (see Chapter 21).

Perhaps the first and best-known ensemble for non-jazz improvisation was that of Lukas Foss, who founded the Improvisational Chamber Ensemble in Los Angeles in the late 1950's. Foss's idea was—in the absence of an improvisatory performing tradition in music other than jazz—to invent the conditions (basically the limitations) within which a new kind of improvisation could take place. The importance of the Ensemble was not so much its demonstration of the possibilities of spontaneity and "discovered form" as the corroboration of a new vitality in creative performance based on the character of the instruments and the skill and personality of the players. Significantly, Foss's own creative work—up until then closely identified with American neo-Classicism—underwent a striking evolution at this time. *Time Cycle* (1959–1960), a twelve-tone work for voice and instruments, has several versions, some of which can include actual improvisation. *Echoi* of 1961–1963 is directly involved with post-serialism and performer choice; indeed, it has the character of a set of free and exceptionally successful improvisations. The forms are in fact controlled, yet they give the impression of growing out of the character of the detail—which is, in turn, an outgrowth of a genial conception of the pleasures and possibilities of the live perform-ance situation.

After Foss's appointment as music director of the Buffalo Symphony, the activity of the Ensemble lapsed. But, with the collaboration of the State University and the Albright-Knox Gallery and the Symphony, Foss organized a major new-music center in Buffalo. This center, which emphasized close relationships between performer and composer, produced an ambitious and wide-ranging program of new-musical performance involving the entire spectrum of new ideas in Buffalo, in New York, and on tours. Foss's own work typically absorbed and synthesized most of these new trends. His *Baroque Variations* (1967) is a meditative or hallucinatory experience of eighteenth-century music far removed from "neo-Classicism." *Paradigm* (1968) re-introduces texts and repetition in a manner that owes something to the minimalists (see Chapter 19). *Geod* (1969) employs four orchestras disposed in a 360° area, each playing a different kind of material—in effect, an environmental work using traditional forces. All of Foss's recent music reveals his exceptional ingenuity and musical facility; his work is always conceived very close to the act of performance itself, and this gives it a concreteness, a sense of reality, and a sense of spontaneity and inventiveness that is never far from the improvisatory performance-practice ideal.

"THIRD STREAM"; THE NEW PERFORMANCE PRACTICE

It is impossible to talk about performance practice and new virtuosity without some mention of jazz, the most important surviving improvisational art in Western music. Jazz—like many other kinds of music—began as a popular or vernacular genre which evolved very rapidly into an art form. Modern jazz and its offshoots (see Chapter 20 for a brief survey) is a complex performance art with a wide harmonic and melodic range and special emphasis on instrumental virtuosity. Its impromptu, intuitive, and even ecstatic qualities have been enormously influential on almost every kind of new music.

Many thoughtful composers from Ives to Copland, Gershwin, and Weill have been influenced by popular and jazz traditions, but it is only relatively recently that musicians have emerged who have consciously advocated the breaking down of the categories—the so-called "third stream" of the 1960's, more recently revived under the term "crossover."

Gunther Schuller (b. 1925), who coined the term "third stream," has long been active as a performer, conductor, and educator (Tanglewood, New England Conservatory) working in several areas of music. Schuller's basic orientation is a kind of American twelve-tone expressionism informed by virtuosity and jazz tradition. He has explored various stylistic cross-cuts (*Seven Studies on Themes of Paul Klee* for orchestra, 1959), spatial polyphony

(*Spectra* for multiple orchestras, 1958) and a modern instrumental *Ge-brauchsmusik* (many chamber and ensemble pieces for standard and non-standard combinations). The pieces that incorporate jazz or improvisatory elements include *Abstraction* (1959, for jazz group and orchestra), *The Visitation* (1966, an opera based on Kafka's *The Trial* but set in the American south), and other works. Schuller has carried the third-stream idea even into his written-out music, which shows a spontaneous and idiomatic instrumental invention that often opens up to allow for the image, if not the actual substance, of improvisation.

In Schuller's own work—and also in his activity as an organizer, conductor, and impresario, during his stint as president of the New England Conservatory, and in his sponsorship of younger composers—he has strongly supported the third-stream ideal through collaboration with both jazz and non-jazz musicians. Although the third stream did not quite emerge as a movement—as Schuller and others expected—it nevertheless paved the way for the integration of non-classical musicians into the mainstream of artistic life, for the emergence of musicians skilled in several areas of music, and for the crossover developments of a more recent period. "Third stream" remains a useful concept. Music, like all the arts in a technological society, no longer flows in one or two main currents and—to give the argument a somewhat more dialectic cast—the merging of seemingly opposing streams or traditions continues to play a role in producing the new syntheses that have become increasingly important in twentieth-century art.

There is a connection between "third stream" and the performance-practice music of Earle Brown. Brown, who studied the Schillinger system[2] and was long active as a recording engineer, was one of the original Cage group about 1950; he produced some of the first work to use graphic notation, open form, and performer choice. Out of this he evolved a kind of "action music"; the analogy is with New York School of "action painting," with the important difference that the ultimate goal is the performance activity itself and not the production of an object. This music is not aleatory (chance plays little or no role in it), and it is not improvisational in the traditional way (which uses fixed or periodic forms with improvised details). The basic principle is that of controlled improvisatory freedom arrived at through the interaction of the musicians at the moment of performance. Works like *Available Forms 1* and *2* (1961–1962; for chamber and large orchestra respectively) are made up of fixed details which can be "improvised" into a form. The performers make their decisions by reacting, within a specified technique, to each other as well as to the flexible character of the materials. In

---

[2] Josef Schillinger (1895–1943) attempted to produce a mathematical synthesis of music and musical theory; ironically, his influence was much greater in the pop and jazz world than in other areas of new music.

Available Forms 2 a more or less standard symphony orchestra in a normal seating pattern is divided into intermeshed groups, each of which responds to the cues of an independent conductor; each conductor chooses material at the given moment by responding to the immediate situation and to the choices of his confrère. As with any improvisation, the results can be extremely variable depending on, among other things, the skill and sensitivity of the performers; when everything is working well, there is a sense of lively, organized spontaneity, a kind of controlled incoherence of great vitality, and, from time to time, a real impression of "discovered" form arising from the interaction of an effectively conceived musical action and gesture (see Appendix; Example 16–3).

Brown's approach to structure—best described as open or kinetic form and often compared to the mobiles of Alexander Calder—is a satisfactory meshing of the desire for control and need for performer flexibility and freedom; it has had a particularly notable impact on the course of European serialism. Brown has more recently returned to fixed, larger forms within which, however, graphic notation permits flexibility in detail. The composer-performer collaborative process is always important in his work.

One of the natural results of the new performance practice and the emphasis on composer-performer collaboration has been the formation of performance and improvisation ensembles. Besides the Foss group and other California activity already mentioned, there have been a number of collaborative or composer-directed ensembles formed in the United States and in Europe. The analogy with jazz and rock is clear (see Chapters 18 and 20).

Open form, the new performance practice, and improvisation were foci of certain kinds of new-music activity not very long ago, but they are no longer at center stage. This is not because these ideas are no longer "viable" but because, as with many important new ideas, they have passed into the new-music mainstream.

BIBLIOGRAPHICAL NOTES

The author's contribution to *The New American Arts* (ed. R. Kostelanetz; New York, 1964; paperback, 1967) is an amplification of the material found in this chapter. Various issues of *Perspectives of New Music* offer further information about the composers discussed here. Stefan Wolpe, in "On New (and Not-So-New) Music in America" (a lecture he delivered to the International Summer Course for New Music in Darmstadt in July 1956; transcribed by A. Clarkson in *Journal of Music Theory* 28/1 [1984], 1–45), discusses the music of Babbitt, Brown, Cage, Carter, Feldman, and others. See as well George Clarke's essay "The New Eclecticism" (Chapter 8 in *Essays on American Music*, Westport, CT, 1977) for a discussion of Cage, Crumb, and Rochberg, and John Rockwell's

All-American Music (New York, 1983) for individual chapters on Babbitt, Carter, Cage, and Shapey.

Flawed Words and Stubborn Sounds—A Conversation with Elliott Carter, by Allen Edwards (New York, 1971), and *The Writings of Elliott Carter: An American Composer Looks at Modern Music*, ed. Else and Kurt Stone (Bloomington, IN, 1977), contain many of Carter's ideas on music. David Schiff's *The Music of Elliott Carter* (New York, 1983) and Charles Rosen's *The Musical Languages of Elliott Carter* (Washington, D.C., 1984) are largely concerned with elements of his musical style; both studies, despite some excursions into "purple prose," provide many insights into his characteristic musical language.

For Robert Erickson, see his own *Sound Structures in Music* (Berkeley, CA, 1975). Among a number of treatises on new notation we might mention Kurt Stone's *Music Notation in the Twentieth Century: A Practical Guidebook* (New York, 1980). For new instrumental techniques, see (among others) Reginald Smith Brindle's *Contemporary Percussion* (London and New York, 1970), Thomas Howell's *The Avant-garde Flute* (Berkeley, 1974), Bertram Turetzsky's *The Contemporary Contrabass* (Berkeley, 1974), Phillip Rehfeldt's *New Directions for Clarinet* (Berkeley, 1977), and Gardner Read's *Contemporary Instrumental Techniques* (New York, 1976).

SEVENTEEN

POST-SERIALISM: THE NEW PERFORMANCE PRACTICE IN EUROPE

There are many good arguments against any continuing separation of European and American music—or, for that matter, of a separation of either of them from Asian music. Communications systems are now effectively global, and influences travel quickly. There should be, presumably, no reason for provincialism anymore; and avant-gardism has been an international, although distinctly Western, phenomenon. Nevertheless, the old social and economic structures continue to exist, and influences continue to radiate from the powerful economic centers; what we call internationalism sometimes turns out to be only a form of cultural imperialism. The inevitable reaction to this has now set in—and there is an important need for artists once again to work on the community level—and localism, barely banished, is back with us.

Even during avant-gardism's most international period, there were meaningful distinctions between the Old World and the New; in retrospect, it is not hard to hear clear differences between, say, Stockhausen, Boulez, and Berio—differences that certainly have something to do with national character. It is a moot point whether it is the connections or the differences which are more important; every successful work of art or artistic experience, even the most "advanced," partakes of both the particular and the universal.

STOCKHAUSEN

After the middle 1950's, the character of new European music began to change drastically. Totally controlled serialism, growing out of the identity of the isolated musical event, gave way to a new idiom based on transformations of densities, colors, and textures; on the "statistical" (i.e., controlled chance) arrangement of events; on multiple, open, or "chance" forms. The systematic development and application of such ideas in European music is largely due to Karlheinz Stockhausen. Stockhausen argued for the controlled use of multiple realization as a new conception of performed music, and he argued that such new techniques were in themselves new forms; a work like his *Momente* (1964) is conceived as a complete set of possible realizations for what he designates as the "moment" form—the scheme, so to speak, for an infinite number of possible actual realizations. In effect, the basis of these new forms—one to a piece, with Stockhausen—is an extension of the concept of serialization into every dimension of the musical conception; even the amount and quality of specific compositional control over the performers is arranged on a serial scale of values ranging from total notated control to extreme variability. Performer action may be designated by graphic notations that delimit fields of wide or limited choice, elaborate and loose densities of note-spattering or very closely unified sound structures with transformations through all possible values in between. Similarly, Stockhausen began to use a basic material which ranges away from pitch towards a complex use of "noise"—that is, patterns of unfixed or random frequency content—and away from all types of simple steady-states to complex superimpositions of oscillating patterns. He serialized density and complexity themselves; he serialized periodicity (that is, cyclical and repeated structures) and aperiodicity (or asymmetrical and non-repetitive structures); he serialized the concept of transformation and change, the disposition of sounds in physical space, and the perception of clarity and complexity, comprehensibility and confusion; he serialized ways of perceiving; and he serialized the construction of time and the ways of acting—of "performing"—in time. Out of all this, Stockhausen derived a characteristic notion of form: the unique set of propositions in each piece which relates these various kinds of serialized activity. Beginning in 1956 with *Zeitmasze* and continuing with *Klavierstück XI*, *Zyklus* (1959), *Refrain* (1959) for three keyboard-percussion players, the theater piece *Originale, Gruppen* (1955–1957) for three orchestras, *Momente* for chorus, keyboard, percussion and brass instruments, and *Carré* (1959–1960) for four choruses and four instrumental ensembles, each conception is a specific representation of very carefully defined formal, serial techniques, each developed uniquely for the particular conception. Thus *Momente* is based on an enormous range of performing activities including all kinds of playing, banging, singing, speaking, hand-clapping, foot-shuffling, whispering, and babbling, all arranged in varying degrees of control and randomness, clusters and isolated tones, densities and simplicities, clarities and confusions. Even the communication of the texts (which must be translated into the language of the local country) is serialized with regard to comprehensibility. All of this material is arranged into a series of events or "moments"— not isolated sounds but complex occurrences of a given duration—which, by an arbitrary arrangement of the pages of the scores and parts, may be placed in any order. Finally, even any given sequence of these events or "moments" is further complicated by a system of interpolations—insertions or "tropes," one might say—in which material from certain events may be anticipated or recalled during the performance of others. Many of these elements can be found on a much smaller scale in works like *Refrain* which show the influence of electronic music on live performance, the influence of Cage and aleatory, as well as the new notational devices designed to score some of these ideas. (See Appendix: Example 17–1).

In one sense, all of Stockhausen's work has been based on a series of propositions about sound material and ways of acting on this material— not so much about form as about ways of forming. Thus the microphone and amplification techniques in his work of the 1960's and 1970's are used, not, as in similar American works, to project a faithful or distorted image against live sound, but to extend and project the relatively fixed and discrete actions and events of a live performance onto a broader continuum in which every sound possibility is extendable and capable of being merged into any other sound possibility. *Mikrophonie I* (1964) is a work for a single tam-tam set in motion by four performers in every conceivable way; two of the players hold microphones which are brought towards and away from a vibrating gong or even actually put into contact with and rubbed against it; these amplified vibrations are further taken up by performer-technicians who transmit them to a pair of loudspeakers under all kinds of electronic-filter transformations. The piece is built—like all of Stockhausen's works—directly out of its techniques, out of its ways of forming and of acting on its materials. Stockhausen has synthesized and systematized—and occasionally created—technique with the ultimate aim of regulating all possible ways of acting on all possible materials. This total, anti-dualistic attempt at composing out the unity of experience approaches an almost mystical view of life and art.

The idea of a music based on transformation appears in Stockhausen's work in *Kontakte* (1959–1960) for percussion, piano, and electronic sounds. In the *Mikrophonie* pieces and the two versions of *Mixtur* (1964; 1967), acoustical and instrumental sounds are "modulated" (in the electronic rather than musical sense) by various devices. In *Telemusik* (1966), *Hymnen* (1966–1967), and *Prozession* (1967), Stockhausen uses folklore, national anthems, conversations and radio broadcasts, and even his own earlier music as the subjects for extended transformations on a Wagnerian time scale. In *Kurzwellen* (1968) the material is taken à la Cage, from whatever signals are picked up on shortwave radios; only the method of transposing is specified. In these works, Stockhausen approaches an "American" performance-practice style, but always elaborating and codifying rather than merely adopting the intuitive or "action" approach typical of his sources. In *Stimmung* (1968), a work for vocal ensemble based on a single chord, Stockhausen is elaborating an idea of La Monte Young, surrounding the elements of a sustained, finely tuned, evening-long pedal with all kinds of other verbal and vocal elements. These works approach a pure performance-practice style with little written music, like certain American works which have no score but only verbal instructions. As the same time, Stockhausen returned in *Mantra* (1969–1970) to a totally composed, almost traditionally serial work—without, however, giving up the principle of transformation.

There is in Stockhausen's work a kind of reverse pantheism which seeks to internalize all possible experience in a kind of endless present; the wholeness and simultaneity of the experience and the transformation suggest a kind of mysticism seemingly at variance with his own earlier ultra-rationality. More clearly than any of the other Europeans, Stockhausen has responded to technological innovation and the impact of new media and has sought the basis for a new music of size and scope growing out of the varieties of contemporary experience filtered through his extraordinary capacity to absorb and transform. This desire to engulf and recapitulate global experience and return it to the world transformed, "Stockhausenized," will be summed up in an immense, Wagnerian music-drama cycle, *Licht*, with one full-scale work for each day of the week. As of this writing, Thursday (*Donnerstag*) has appeared, the beginning of a gigantesque life-and-modern-music summation in an allegorical theater form.

Stockhausen was and remains the dominant figure in Central Europe as the source, transmitter, and codifier of new ideas. Composers who have worked in related areas include the Swede Bo Nilsson (b. 1937), one of the first to serialize open-form and chance techniques and one of the first Europeans to use amplification; the Italian Franco Evangelisti (1926–1980), who worked with graphic techniques and the consequences of certain systems of transformation and randomization and, more recently, with improvisation; and the Polish-Israeli-Austrian Roman Haubenstock-Ramati (b. 1919) and the Austrian Friedrich Cerha (b. 1926), with their clusters and densities of sound, twisting and turning in open, spatial arrangements. Two important, independent figures are the Belgian Henri Pousseur and Mauricio Kagel. Pousseur, like Stockhausen, has widened the notion of serialism to include the familiar as well as the unfamiliar, the periodic as well as the aperiodic. His major work, *Votre Faust* (1960–1967), is a theatrical collaboration with the French new-novelist Michel Butor. Pousseur's extensive critical and theoretical writings document the shift in new-musical thought from what we can call a "positivist" point of view—logical, internally consistent—to a "structural," linguistic and even anthropological approach.[1] Kagel, who lived and worked in West Germany for many years, is even more directly involved with a kind of gestural theater, with music as activity, with the elaboration of complex, invented acoustical phenomena, with an interaction between music and everyday or external phenomena. Pousseur represents a link between Central Europe and the Latin countries; Kagel, like Stockhausen, links Old and New World ideas.

BOULEZ

Surprisingly, the first important post-war European manifestations of twelve-tone and serial technique developed in countries that had previously been the most hostile to them: France and Italy. In a special and remarkable way, the twelve-tone idea had a very particular appeal for the kind of French rationalism which, rather than imposing a total vision of order on the world, German style, seeks to rationalize the relationship of man to his experience of the world. Pierre Boulez, a pupil of Messiaen, began as a theater composer, a twelve-tone *enfant terrible* and, for a brief moment, a totally organized, totally serial super-rationalist. His early twelve-tone works of the late 1940's— the Second Piano Sonata (1948), the *Sonatine* for flute and piano (1946), the *Livre* for string quartet (1948–1949)—find their rationale not only in the Viennese operations of an expressive twelve-tone method but also in the relationship of this method to a virtuoso content built on timbre, texture, dynamic accent, and an ongoing form. Later, with *Polyphonie X* for 18

---

[1] Philosophical positivism can be connected with determinism and certain aspects of serialism. Opposed to it is "structuralism," an important philosophical theory in analytic and cognitive psychology, linguistics, and anthropology connected with the names of Carl Jung, Wolfgang Kohler, Noam Chomsky, and Claude Lévi-Strauss. The structuralist attitude, reached independently in several fields and supported by recent work in neurobiology, is opposed to behaviorism in holding that certain knowledge is innate and that information reaches the mind only through the transformation of sensory data into patterns that match our mental structures. This point of view, which has importance for all contemporary arts, has influenced the ideas of Pousseur, Berio, and others. Ironically, Lévi-Strauss has attacked certain new-musical ideas, with Pousseur acting as the principal advocate for the defense.

instruments (1951) and the first book of *Structures* for two pianos (1951–1952), Boulez committed himself to a completely systematic and pre-determined conception of a total material. But these works raise more problems than they solve. *Structures I* is the classical monument of totally organized serial technique in the European avant-garde music of the early 1950's, but its method of making relationships is at once too easy, too numerological, and too irrelevant to the real issues of organic form to be convincing. (A second book, written in 1956–1961, is an intentional antithesis to the closed, classical, unidirectional rationality of the first.) In general, the authority *Structures I* possesses seems to stem from Boulez's own considerable personal authority as a pianist and performing musician.

Le Marteau sans maître (1952–1954; revised 1957) is, by contrast, one of the first avant-garde European works to escape the narrow confines of a strictly interpreted serialism. In some ways a continuation of Boulez's earlier twelve-tone music, it also marked a development of ideas descended from the "new" music of the first decades of the century, now informed by a generalized serial technique and a newly rationalized conception of form whose aim was the effective control of fluctuating masses, colors, densities, and intensities of sound (see Appendix; Example 17–2). After *Le Marteau*, Boulez extended this conception in still other directions—notably in the use of performer choice and multi-directional forms. But *Le Marteau*, a group of vocal settings surrounded by instrumental "commentaries," already contains the basic patterns and many of the modes of thought which became dominant in his middle-period works: the Third Piano Sonata (1955–1957), *Pli selon pli (Portrait de Mallarmé)* (1958; 1962) for voice and orchestra, and *Doubles* (1958) for orchestra. These works are by no means the free, improvisatory, post-serial fantasies they have sometimes been made out to be. They all contain related but free-standing sections or movements, each based on independent and preconceived forms or formal plans of action. The sections were written and often performed separately as a series of steps in a "work-in-progress" conception: even the present form of *Le Marteau* is a revision dating from 1957; several sections of *Pli selon pli* were rewritten after being composed and performed separately; *Doubles*, already reworked, is a movement from a projected larger work. *Répons*, Boulez's latest work in progress, is an hour-and-a-half-long work of which half is written to date; it uses a conventional chamber ensemble surrounded by an audience, surrounded by an ensemble of mallet instruments (including pianos and cimbalon) and harp with electronic extensions; three-dimensional space is an integral part of the piece. The intentionally ambiguous, open relationship of the parts to the total scheme is built into the conception of these pieces; the whole might be compared to a system of planetary bodies discovered, one by one, to be moving around a center of gravity according to fixed relationships, yet in a multitude of different actual juxtapositions. The forms themselves originate in a special conception of the relationship of the composer to his material, to the world of experience, and to the act of creative communication. These modes of creative thought, often constructed on very specific literary, poetic, or psychological premises, are conceived as ways of acting on a vast and pliable material which is poetic, even in a sense discursive, but never really narrative or directional in character. After *Le Marteau* (which is still a series of closed and fixed shapes), Boulez developed ideas of embellishing and of moving on, around, and through a chosen material as revealed in the act of performance. Actually, the compositional process seems to be exactly the reverse: that of imagining a concrete and idiomatic material which will function as the poetic realization in time of a preconceived plan of action.

Unlike most of the European avant-garde composers, Boulez was involved with pure electronic music only very briefly, and he has always been engaged—as a pianist and, particularly, as a conductor—with music as a performing art. An involvement with the physical, tangible, even sensuous qualities of the musical material and with the poetic and psychological significance of the activity of producing it has, aside from his brief encounter with strict serialism, given Boulez's music a distinct character within the general flow of new ideas in Europe. His forms are preconceived and rationalized, but they never uniquely generate or predetermine the character of the material; rather, they seek to reveal themselves through the quality, fantasy, and imaginative rightness of the ideas. Hence the impulse—rare among avant-garde composers—to revise and rewrite, to seek the clearest, the richest, the most meaningful realization of the conception. The forms may be open and flexible, but they do not rest on the operations of a chance, a statistical, or even an improvisatory method; instead, they seek to reveal the multiple possibilities—the poetic facets, so to speak—of the creative imagination. Boulez is very much involved with the significance and impact of personal statement, with the performance situation as a mode arising out of an invented and seemingly open and flexible material which is, however, realizing and revealing a hard strategy underneath—a ground plan, a path, a map that is in itself a rational, poetic realization of the relationship between the acts of creating and performing, as well as experiencing, a work of art.

Boulez's antecedents are Debussy and Messiaen; he is a composer of distinctly French style and thought, often close to the clarity and fluidity of the French language itself. Nevertheless, his outlook is essentially cosmopolitan, and, until recently, he chose to live and work outside of France. Now, after an international conducting career, he has returned to France, founding and directing IRCAM, an important center for research, development, and performance of new music in Paris. His influence, very widely diffused, is hard to pinpoint except in France itself, where a group of younger composers may fairly be called *Boulezistes*. Of these, the most important and independent are André Boucourechliev (b. 1925) and Gilbert Amy (b.

1936). A number of other French composers—notably Luc Ferrari and the *musique concrète* group as well as Michel Philippot (b. 1925) and Jean-Louis Barraqué (1928–1973)—have produced work of individuality outside of the direct Boulez influence.

XENAKIS AND EASTERN EUROPE

Yannis Xenakis, born in Rumania of Greek parents and long resident in Paris, studied music with Messiaen and architecture with Le Corbusier; he worked with Le Corbusier and Varèse on the Philips Pavilion at the 1958 Brussels World's Fair. With *Métastasis* of 1953–1954 he began to apply mathematical probability theory to the composition of music. In essence, *Métastasis* and, in varying ways, *Pithoprakta* of 1955–1956 and *Achoripsis* of 1956–1957 are orchestral ensemble works built on sliding, shifting masses and densities whose definition is derived by a "statistical" probability method. Later works—*ST/10-1,080262* of 1956, *Eonta* for piano and brass of 1963–1964, *Stratégy* for two orchestras of 1959–1962—extend this conception of the rationalization of the irrational in all domains through the use of electronic computers. With Xenakis, the use of these techniques has to do, not with any kind of "automatization" of the creative process, but rather with the search for new materials and new forms. Esthetically, the music is big in scale, violent in density and intensity of character, and strongly involved in an idea of the re-creation of the meaning of the act of performance. *Stratégy* is a piece for two orchestras and two conductors who literally compete with one another in an attempt to realize a given set of preconditions. Xenakis always defines his conditions precompositionally and in the strictest terms, even when he is dealing with so-called irrationalities. (If Cage's is "music of the absurd," this is "music of the surd.") For better or for worse, the ultimate reality of the music (even when miscalculated from a psychological point of view) is to be found in the solution—the engagement with the performing material—as realized on real instruments in real time.

Xenakis inherited from Varèse a concern with volumes and densities of sound and, in effect, helped create a kind of subdivision of European music devoted to changing color and density. This style is also associated with György Ligeti, a Hungarian expatriate working in Vienna, and with the new Polish school, notably Krzysztof Penderecki. New ideas have, by now, appeared in the work of composers in all the Eastern European countries, including the Soviet Union, but Yugoslavia and Poland have led the way. The turning point was the bloodless Polish "revolution" of 1956 and the remarkable declaration, by the Polish intelligentsia, of cultural independence from the prevailing policies of artistic and intellectual direction in Eastern Europe. Since that time, Poland has quickly developed what is undoubtedly the most remarkable modern-music life in all of Europe and an important and individual creative production as well. The most striking fact of musical life in Poland in recent years has been the amount of contemporary music performed—in festivals and in concert—and the size and involvement of its public. Virtually all modern and avant-garde ideas from the West have been well represented in Poland, and Polish composers have available to them an immense variety of resources including a well-equipped electronic studio; well-trained, experienced orchestras; ensembles and soloists with ample rehearsal time at their disposal; and a sympathetic and involved audience. These facts are important in understanding the new Polish music in its variety, its extensive use of resources, and its strong, direct character. Older Polish composers, notably Witold Lutoslawski, Kazimierz Serocki, and Tadeusz Baird, have moved from the development of twelve-tone and serial ideas towards a rich, intense, thoughtful kind of expression, informed by latter-day avant-garde ideas. The younger group—Penderecki, Boguslaw Schäffer (b. 1929), Henry K. Górecki (b. 1933), Wojciech Kilar (b. 1932), and Wlodzimierz Kotoński (b. 1925)—can be characterized by their direct engagement with the *matière sonore*, virtually stripped of everything but its immediate impact as sound. Works like Penderecki's *Threnody: to the Victims of Hiroshima* (1960) and his *St. Luke Passion* (1963–1965) create intense, dramatic effects with their use of tone clusters, free choral babbling, Gregorian motifs, striking contrasts, and even major triads. Their weakness is that the entire effect lies on the surface—but it is a surface of great, intense effect.[2]

The range of new Polish music is large, and composers like Schäffer, involved in an experimental work of Cageian and post-Cageian dimensions— extreme ideas carried to extreme conclusions (one piano work lasts indefinitely until the last member of the audience leaves)—really belong in the final section of this book. On the other hand, the music of Górecki and Kilar, born of the remarkable richness of the percussive-white-noise Polish language, are mainstream European avant-garde; they achieve a significant and expressive identity between means and materials that deserves to be better known in the West.

ITALY

A close involvement with a new and wide-ranging material and an interest in psychological, linguistic, or dramatic form arising out of the character of musical performance and communication are typical of recent Italian

---

[2] There are connections between the earlier music of Penderecki, Carl Orff, and the minimalists. Penderecki's recent music is strongly triadic and "neo-Romantic" (see Chapter 19).

composers, notably Nono, Maderna, and Berio. All three were identified with the Central European serial group of the early 1950's, and all worked with electronic means at the Milan studio and elsewhere; but all of them later become closely involved in the projection of poetic, dramatic, or even specifically philosophical-verbal ideas through the medium of a new-performed music. In the case of Luigi Nono (b. 1924), these ideas have a specifically social orientation. Nono is an artist with a strong commitment to relate artistic revolution to social revolution. The opera *Intoleranza* (1960) is a curious hodgepodge of contradictory notions; *La Fabbrica illuminata* (1964), a kind of Orwellian anti-capitalist, anti-Stalinist sound-study of the factory of the future, gains strength from its dramatic, impressive tape babble of voices but is nearly destroyed by its climactic, agonized cry, "factory as concentration camp." The problem is crucial for Nono, and not only because of this view about the social value and impact of avant-garde ideas. Nono's instrumental works, although possessing a certain importance, lack the imaginative, concrete, and personal push, the impulse toward expressive form, that one finds in his vocal and vocal-dramatic works from *Il Canto sospeso* (1955–1956), a relatively early serial setting of letters by condemned anti-Fascist resistance partisans, to the more recent dramatic and semi-dramatic works for voices, instruments, and tape.

The commitment of Maderna and Berio has been not only to a view of the social value of art but also to the quality of the new material and the significance of the act of producing it. In addition to being active at Darmstadt, both composers were identified with the pioneering electronic studio at the Milan national radio station. The electronic experience everywhere profoundly altered attitudes towards serialism and the role of performed music; in Milan, the studio became a kind of escape hatch for composers who felt compelled to adopt serial controls but were anxious to find a new, substantial musical matter. The electronic realizations of Maderna and Berio in particular have the character of improvisations arising out of a direct and fresh experience of the materials. Both composers came back to vocal and instrumental music with something of this attitude, to which was added an intense faith in the expressive and dramatic power of action and gesture as well as the musical form-building potential of word and language.

Maderna's opera *Hyperion* (1964), though defective as an overall conception, illustrates these musical and philosophical tendencies very well: the "protagonist" is a flutist who spends the first ten minutes of the work quietly unpacking piccolo, flute, alto flute, and bass flute; when he finally gets around to the actual act of performance, the sound that gushes forth is in fact an enormously amplified percussive fortissimo (on tape). The piece has a complex choral part—also on tape—with a babbling-of-tongues text made out of isolated words taken from many different languages. There is an instrumental ensemble part and, finally, a long and sensuous—almost Bergian—

solo soprano song at the end. In a work for solo flute by Maderna, the flutist must perform against the pre-recorded image of his own playing.

Berio's work is notable for its involvement with language and linguistic structure as well as its important development of music theater and social-gestural content. This is true even of his instrumental works, but it is obviously more evident in his vocal and dramatic works. *Omaggio a Joyce* (1958) is a tape piece made entirely out of the sounds of a James Joyce fragment. *Visage* (1961) combines electronic sound with a structure of highly emotive vocal sounds, images, and gestures. *Circles* (1960) is a live setting, for voice and percussion, of poems by e. e. cummings in which the physical movements of the performers become part of the acoustic and visual space of the piece. *Passaggio* (1961–1962), commissioned by La Scala, and *Opera* (1969–1970), written for Santa Fe, are anti-opera operas dealing with the very function of art and theater in our culture. *Laborintus II* (1965), on a poem of Edoardo Sanguineti, was written for the 700th anniversary of Dante and is, in effect, a culture-shock piece. *Sinfonia* (1968–1969), written for members of the Swingle Singers with orchestra, has one movement made out of the sounds of the syllables of the name "Martin Luther King" and another which contains a symphonic movement by Mahler embedded in a context of quotes, references, and original remarks. The need for dramatic context and form and the concern with verbal and language problems—sound as language, language as sound, the relationship of meaning to sound, of linguistic to musical structure, of content to sound—are strikingly illustrated in Berio's work. The involvement with significance and gesture has important antecedents not only in new music but also in linguistic and anthropological structuralism and in the tradition of Brechtian epic theater. Berio's organic and dramatic forms, his concern with content and context and his integration of sound, language, and conceptual structure are a continuing source of influence and ideas and—except for his use of traditional media—carry us beyond modern music.

BIBLIOGRAPHICAL NOTES

The best sources for information on European serialism and post-serialism are those cited on pages 130 and 158, as well as the series of volumes published by the Institut für neue Musik und Musikerziehung in Mainz; see especially *Die Musik der sechziger Jahre* (Vol. 12, 1972) and *Über Musik und Sprache* (Vol. 14, 1974). Extensive material on Stockhausen has been published in German, notably the *Texte zur Musik* in the DuMont Dokumente series (Cologne, 1963–1978) and Vol. 6 of the Kontrapunkte series (Rodenkirchen, 1961). Karl H. Wörner's *Stockhausen: Life and Work* (trans. and ed. Bill Hopkins, Berkeley and Los Angeles, 1973) is now somewhat out of date, but includes the only extensive biography available. On the music, see Jonathan Harvey's *The Music of Stockhausen: An Introduction* (Berkeley and Los Angeles, 1975) and Robin Maconie's *The Works of Karlheinz Stockhausen* (London, 1976). Herbert Henck's *Karlheinz Stockhausen's Klavierstuck X: A Contribution Toward Understanding Serial Technique: History, Theory, Analysis, Practice, Documentation* (trans. Deborah Richards, Cologne, 1980) is of use to performers especially, although the translation is somewhat choppy; Henck had access to Stockhausen's sketches for this study. He has written another, on *Klavierstuck IX* (Bonn, 1978), but this is not available in translation. Jonathan Cott's *Stockhausen: Conversations with the Composer* (New York, 1973) conveys the composer's increasing concerns with perception, communication, and anti-dualistic views of the unity of human experience right up to and including its outer fringes. Stockhausen remains the key figure in European music for the transmission of ideas, and a great deal of his recent thought is contained in this volume.

For Boulez, see the composer's *Pensez la musique aujourd'hui* (Mainz, 1963), translated as *Boulez on Music Today* (Cambridge, 1971), and *Conversations with Célestin Deliège* (London, 1975). There are two biographies of Boulez, by Paul Griffiths (London, 1979) and by Joan Peyser (New York, 1976), the latter of which attempts to be a psycho-biography. Ulrich Siegele's *Zwei Kommentäre zum "Marteau sans maître" von Pierre Boulez* (Neuhausen-Stuttgart, 1979) contains detailed analyses of the piece's form and of Boulez's compositional technique.

Pousseur has published two important volumes, *Fragments théoriques I sur la musique expérimentale* (Brussels, 1970) and the difficult *Musique, sémantique, société* (Tournai, 1972). Xenakis has written about his ideas and theories in *Musiques formelles*, translated as *Formalized Music* (Bloomington, IN, 1972); the translation is even more difficult than Pousseur's original. Essays attempting to clarify and assess Xenakis's philosophies and esthetic can be found in *Regards sur Iannis Xenakis*, ed. Hugues Gerhards (Paris, 1981). Nouritza Matossian has written a biography of Xenakis (Paris, 1981) which concentrates more on his philosophy and connection to mathematics and morphology than on his music. The crisis of serialism can be surveyed in a series of articles, with contributions from both the Old World and the New, in the French review *Preuves* over a period of several months from Fall 1965 to Spring 1966.

In English there is a short monograph on Ligeti by Paul Griffiths (Contemporary Composers series, London, 1983) and *A Study of the Penderecki St. Luke Passion* by Ray Robinson and Allen Winold (Celle, Germany and Totowa, NJ, 1983). Other notable studies on the Polish and Italian composers of the 1960's are not in English: they include Wolfram Schwinger's *Penderecki: Begegnungen, Lebensdaten, Werkkommentare* (Stuttgart, 1979); Ernst Flammer's *Politisch engagierte Musik als kompositorisches Problem*, focusing on certain compositions by Nono as well as by Henze (Baden-Baden, 1981); and Norbert Dressen's *Sprache und Musik bei Luciano Berio: Untersuchungen zu seinen Vokalkompositionen* (Regensburg, 1982). Nono's own writings (translated into

German) can be found in *Texte. Studien zu seiner Musik* (Zurich, 1975), which also contains transcriptions of interviews with him and a good selection of writings on him and his music. The "Double numéro spécial" 265–266 of the *Revue musicale* (Paris, 1969) is devoted to articles on Berio and Xenakis as well as Varèse and Pierre Henry.

part six

Post-modernism

EIGHTEEN

BEYOND MODERN MUSIC

The experimentalism of the early twentieth century was followed by the syntheses, retrenchments, and tonal returns of the second quarter-century: twelve-tone music, neo-Classicism, the folk revival, and the *Zeitoper*. In exactly the same way, and on a very similar timetable, the serial, aleatory, and other "modernist" movements after World War II were followed by the returns and syntheses of post-modernism.

"Post-modernism," a term already used in earlier editions of this book, has been popularized by recent art criticism to refer to the use of historical forms in art: figuration in painting, decorative structures in architecture. In music it means, above all, a revival or renewal of tonality—usually in close association with metricality, repetition, and recollection as structural elements.

Is post-modernism and the new tonality a return to the past or a forward evolution? The question is difficult to answer; the terms of the argument have perhaps changed. If we look at the period from the mid-

1920's to World War II from a late twentieth-century perspective, we can find many paradoxes. Schoenberg regarded his invention of twelve-tone music as a way to maintain the continuity of the great tradition while carrying it forward into the future; from our perspective it looks like a form of neo-Classicism. On the other hand, Stravinskyan neo-Classicism, once criticized as backward-looking, now seems as firm and essential a part of the evolution of twentieth-century art as the work of T. S. Eliot or Picasso (with which it has many parallels).

Similarly, much new concert music has been categorized as "neo-Romantic," a label that suggests a strong vein of conservatism. Perhaps this is an inevitable development in music created for the traditional music-making organizations, which came into their prime during the nineteenth century and were shaped by and for Romantic music in the first place. But other forms of new music have arisen out of other situations. The development of new media, and of new performance venues outside traditional music-world locales, have helped to generate very different kinds of post-modernism: minimalism, a re-evaluation of pop as culture, the revival of pop forms in art music, various crossovers between popular and art music, and a vast expansion of inter-art and music-theater forms. These developments are hardly conservative; in some ways they suggest a major break with nineteenth-century Romanticism, a break that modernism—even in its most extreme avant-garde forms—rarely achieved.

Post-modernism is widespread. In a larger sense it may be said to include neo-Romanticism, minimalism, art rock, disco, so-called new-age music, media, multi-media, performance art, and new music theater. All of these phenomena share the new or revived interest in tonality as well as in repetition and recollection; and they all represent some kind of new *engagement* with the culture and a larger public. But within themselves they also represent radically differing points of view—from conservative to progressive, from "uptown" to "downtown," from traditional to experimental.

THE SETTING FOR POST-MODERNISM

Something should be said about the changes in new-music life and their effect on the music itself. It is true that in the context of traditional music making there has been a push for greater acceptance of new music. Special concert series and festivals, such as Boulez's Prospective Encounters (1971–1976) and the more recent Horizons festivals (1983–1987) at the New York Philharmonic; the annual New Music America festivals in various cities (1979–   ); commissioning and composer-in-residence programs at major orchestras; the proliferation of chamber ensembles specializing in new music (Speculum Musicae, Continuum, the American Composers Orchestra, and many others)—these are all well-grounded efforts to expand or alter what has been called the "museum" function of traditional concert institutions. But by far the greatest changes have been associated with new media and non-traditional performance contexts. These have included new collaborations of musicians in theater, dance, and performance art; the incorporation of pop, rock, jazz, and non-Western music into the new-music spectrum; and a continuing expansion of electronic media (compact-disc and cassette audio, video, public radio), not only as tools for new music but also as important, sometimes primary, vehicles. All this has happened in artists' studios and lofts, galleries and museums, clubs, other places and spaces especially developed for new-music events and closely related forms of visual, media, and performance art.

Some of these developments are clearly continuations of earlier motifs. Others are new or so increased in intensity as to be qualitatively different. All have consequences. Most obviously, there has occurred a redefinition—in many cases an erosion—of the traditionally recognized boundaries between music, dance, theater, visual arts, and media—and, in a parallel way, between the so-called classical and popular arts. These crossovers have more than mere structural or esthetic interest because they have led new and diverse audiences to a wider involvement with new music. And the growth of such audiences has, inevitably, influenced the arts that created them.

These changes and expansions of mode and venue have also accelerated the process by which new electronic instruments and media have invaded the creative field; traditional—one might say European—instrumental ensembles are no longer standard in any area of new music outside the orchestra hall and the opera house. The tape- and electronic-music studios of the post-World War II period were influential, but the pop-music recording studio and the rock concert are the major sources of recent technological developments. The crossovers from pop/rock/jazz have brought rhythm sections, guitars, and synthesizers into the mainstream of new music. Microphone amplification and sound-modification equipment are now standard in live concert performances. The new generation of synthesizers—in particular the modern digital instruments capable of reproducing acoustic instrumental sound and constructing new ones—is as important today in art music as in rock. Unconventional acoustic instruments—many adapted from folk or non-Western cultures, others recently developed—have also become popular. Styles taken from early music, pop and jazz, and non-Western music are used. Vocal ideals have changed, and newly extended vocal techniques, ranging from speech to unusual types of singing to "natural sound" (animal sounds, non-verbal sounds, vocal noise, etc.) have become major subject matter for creative exploration.

There have been, in short, major changes in the relationship between composers, their work, and the public. The serial and chance musics that defined the avant-garde of the 1950's and 1960's were deductive, experimental in a literal sense. The premises were simple and limited but the deductions thorough, extreme, encompassing, complex. Each piece establishes its own unique premises; everything that happens has to be defined within the work or the performance. Instead of a piece of music being an instance of its class, each work created its own class, of which it might be the only member. Art of this kind functions as a kind of "research" activity and must be well subsidized. It is purist, difficult, abstract, heroic, hermetic, intentionally isolated. It was, for a time, the only viable alternative to commercial mass culture, and for this reason some critics—particularly in Europe—believed that it had a social and even political impact. But for the most part it was a retreat inward to a world of pure vision or pure form and, as such, it played largely to a specialized audience of adepts, connoisseurs, critics, and scholars.

Post-modern art has sought to change all this. While the key to modernist avant-garde music must be found—often with difficulty—within the works themselves, post-modern music looks outside to the culture. Context becomes an essential part of the work and the act of performance. The language of tonality, and the associated uses of rhythmic and phrase repetition as well as recollection, come out of or relate to a broadly shared, culturally determined, and commonly understood basic vocabulary. For the first time since the 1930's, the composer is in the position of reaching a larger public—and of being influenced by the presence and common culture of that public.

HAPPENINGS, CONCEPT ART, THE NEW ENSEMBLES

The open microphone, like the open camera, creates not so much a frame as a window, an opening out to the world. The class of which an individual work is an instance becomes everything that can be recorded. Any experience is therefore potentially available; its significance can only depend on its use. The totality of experience is not merely a new or larger fund of materials and processes but the actual context out of which each new work grows. The "global village"—the electronic network connecting ideas and experiences in an ongoing and continuous exchange of information—is now close to universal. The totality of forms and perceptions is available and, increasingly, shared. This has inevitably influenced the way we think about the world and about art. A quantitative change has become a qualitative one.

In the 1960's, a number of things occurred—not necessarily only in the narrow world of music—that reflected the changing nature of the culture. One was the rise and fall of "happenings" and the associated inter-art and noise/junk-music experiments. Another was "pop" as an art movement. At moments of crisis, artists think about art; meditations on art and life sometimes turned into idea-pieces or concept art. In addition—partly under the influence of pop, jazz, and non-Western music—composers turned away from highly elaborated notation and back to performance practice: improvisation, performer choice, and the development of non-notated works with composer/directors functioning like choreographers or avant-garde theater directors.

The first happening is usually said to have taken place in 1952 at Black Mountain College in North Carolina as a collaboration between the composer John Cage, pianist David Tudor, dancer/choreographer Merce Cunningham, painter Robert Rauschenberg, and others. Cage's influence at Black Mountain and at the New School in New York, as the chief composer for the Merce Cunningham Dance Company and as a musical activist/Zen philosopher was enormously influential and extended far beyond the confines of the musical world. Allan Kaprow, sometimes described as the inventor of happenings, was a Cage student and disciple, as were many poets, dancers, and visual artists. Many of the composers (and near-composers) at the edge of cross-cultural activities in the 1960's—George Brecht (b. 1925), La Monte Young, Jackson Mac Low (b. 1922), Richard Higgins (b. 1938), Philip Corner (b. 1933), Alison Knowles (b. 1933), Yoko Ono, and others of the group or movement called Fluxus—were "performance artists" (as we would now say) functioning almost entirely outside of the established music world.

Although Cage can be explained historically, his philosophy is anti-historical, non-contextual. When there is no longer any common practice or context, all art becomes, willy-nilly, "concept" art. But the conceptual art of Cage and his followers is specifically devoted to the art work as an idea about art or about life or, even more radically, the idea as art. Instead of a historical or social context there is a set of ideas or concepts which generates the art experience—or *is* the art experience. The work or the performance is only the carrying-through of an idea. Some activities by La Monte Young consist of directions like "Hold [such-and-such] for a long time" (from *Composition 1960—#7*) or "Draw a straight line and follow it" (from *Composition—1961*). There are works and events in this vein which direct performers to sit on the stage and look at the audience, to burn musical instruments, or to sit in their cars in a parking lot, blowing the horns and flashing the lights.

Related to happenings—and also generated directly by the work of Cage and his associates—was a kind of performance-practice music which mixed live and electronic media in free, noisy, spatial terms. Performers *acted* on their instruments rather than performing on them in the usual way.

There was no conventional score, but the nature and limits of the activity were quite clearly defined. Every possibility was carried to its extreme—mixed, transformed, distorted to the very limits of perception. Besides Cage and Tudor, practitioners of this style included some composers who came out of the Once group in Michigan, including Gordon Mumma (who worked with Cage), Robert Ashley, and Roger Reynolds (b. 1934), and certain San Francisco and San Diego musicians including Pauline Oliveros, Ramon Sender (b. 1934), and Larry Austin. Mumma and Ashley formed the Sonic Arts group (active 1966–1976) with Alvin Lucier (b. 1931) and David Behrman (b. 1937). The Musica Elettronica Viva group, formed in Rome in 1967, included several expatriate Americans including Frederic Rzewski (b. 1938), Alvin Curran (b. 1938), and Richard Teitelbaum (b. 1939). The Cageian philosophical inheritance and the communitarian political ideas of the period suggested the subordination of an individual ego in favor of a collective approach. This performance music was characterized by randomness and chance, a noise esthetic, and collective electronic exploration and improvisation.

Closely related European work of the 1960's includes a series of pieces by Stockhausen (from *Mixtur* of 1964 through *Telemusik* and *Hymnen* to *Aus den sieben Tagen* of 1968); some of Mauricio Kagel's non-theater compositions (such as *Acustica* [1968–1970], for invented instruments or sound sources); and various works by Dieter Schnebel (b. 1930), Hans Otte (b. 1926), and Michael von Biel (b. 1937) in Germany, Luc Ferrari (b. 1929) and the GERM group in France, and, from Eastern Europe, the Pole Boguslaw Schäffer and Petr Kotik (b. 1942), originally from Prague.

We might characterize much of this as "junk music"—equivalent to junk sculpture—in which useless and discarded bits and scraps from the aural junk heap of industrial civilization were arranged, re-arranged, and de-ranged. The noise esthetic was often pitched at some outer edge—harsh and ugly, sometimes vulgar, banal, or even pornographic, intense but never passionate, extended in time, environmental in effect, curiously objective and detached but close to (and sometimes beyond) the threshold of bearability and even pain.

Conceptual art is a strategy in which art—the actual experiential results—may be unimportant; how a piece of conceptual music actually sounds may not matter, and in fact that may be the point. There is often ambiguity as to where the center of interest actually lies—in the idea, the activity, the philosophical conceit, or the sensual experience. John Lennon (1940–1980) and Yoko Ono (b. 1933) invented a work (or activity) in which fans blow open the pages of a Beethoven symphony score and instrumentalists are directed to play whatever happens to fall under their eyes. In *Vespers* (1968) by Alvin Lucier, a group of blindfolded performers, equipped with a kind of sonar, attempt to orient themselves by producing a clicking sound—in the manner of oilbirds or bats. (Kagel has produced a somewhat similar work, *Pas de cinq* [1956], in which blindfolded actors tap their canes rhythmically to find their way around a stage.) Lucier's *Music for Solo Performer* (1965) consists of the amplification of the electrical energy emitted by the brain as the performer goes (or attempts to go) into a state of alpha sleep; *Portable Gold and Philosophers' Stones* (1972) by David Rosenboom (b. 1947) is based on the same idea. These activities all involve sound, or produce sound as an end result—but the extent to which the sound can be predicted or controlled is variable and may not even be important.

The work of the percussionist and composer Max Neuhaus (b. 1939) is set nearer the "real" world. Some of his "public access" works (*Public Supply*, 1966; *Radio Net*, 1977) connect the listener with the performance via radio or telephone, and the audience reaction is not only incorporated into the result but influences its course. Some of the "game pieces" put together by Morton Subotnick and the visual artist Anthony Martin in the mid-1960's are even more specifically audience-involving: the piece is the playing of the game. Out of these and similar ideas an entire genre of environmental works, sound sculptures, and sound installations has grown up—perhaps inevitable in a situation in which art galleries and museums are major patrons of new music and performance art. Such works are exhibited rather than performed. They are often reactive: the sound appears, changes, and disappears according to the activity of the viewer and/or the environmental conditions that prevail. The connections between the work, its performance, the audience, and the event as a whole may be realized through random or unpredictable feedback technology.

Large-scale environmental or participatory events may or may not have a technological component. The philosophy of Ives and Cage is important here, as are communal and egalitarian ideals. Some of the solstice events coordinated by Charlie Morrow (b. 1942) during the 1970's involve simple performance activities, often by non-musicians; but he has also used the technology of satellite radio transmission to link simultaneous events in different parts of the world. Many theater, dance, and music-theater activities have had participatory and collaborative elements, often aimed at or designed for non-musicians, including those of Quog Music Theater, the Natural Sound Workshop, and other such organizations (see Chapter 21). Wendy Chambers (b. 1953) has organized a number of public activities— usually in connection with some holiday or celebration—with large numbers of people participating (*Street Music*, 1978; *Music for Choreographed Rowboats*, 1979; *One World Percussion*, 1981). Some of the biggest events of this kind have been created and realized—in both the United States and Europe—by Robert Moran (b. 1937); he has actually attempted to orchestrate whole communities into collective, participatory action (*Hallelujah* [1971], requiring various musical forces and, in theory, the entire city of Bethlehem, Pennsylvania).

Technological change, which has continued unabated, has had a steady interaction with new music of all kinds. The most important recent developments include the advance of digital and computer technology. In computerized digital recording and sound-synthesis, information is coded and stored in the digital language of computers; this permits an enormous amount of information to be created, stored, manipulated, and endlessly replicated without the introduction of distortion or noise. Charles Dodge (b. 1942), now at Brooklyn College, John Chowning (b. 1934) and others at the Stanford Center for Computer Research in Music and Acoustics, Roger Reynolds at the University of California at San Diego, Paul Lansky (b. 1944) at Princeton University, Barry Vercoe (b. 1937) at the Massachusetts Institute of Technology, William Buxton at the University of Toronto's Structured Sound Synthesis Project, and a number of composers at the IRCAM center in Paris have been involved in the development of computer music, largely as a studio-based enterprise involving the creation and shaping of complex sound structures through complex programs. Many of the difficult and time-consuming procedures used in the earlier electronic- and computer-music centers have been superseded by the development of pre-programmed digital synthesizers, capable of real-time performance. This extraordinary growth of live-performance electronic instruments has had a major influence on the composition and production of contemporary music, and "synthesist" is now a recognized category of instrumental performer.

As the traditional institutional base for new music has eroded, the specialized new-music ensemble has come into its own. Collaborative notions, the idea of a new performance practice, the use of alternative venues, and the new technology have led naturally to the development of ensembles devoted to new instrumentation and directed at new audiences. Ensembles based on synthesizers are now widespread in new music and in rock and jazz-rock as well. The more traditional chamber ensembles specializing in new music are generally oriented towards new music of the "modernist" type but sometimes branch out into post-modernism. Certain groups, beginning with Lukas Foss's Improvisation Chamber Ensemble in the 1960's, were born out of a desire to explore collective creativity, new ideas about the nature of performance, or new forms of improvisation. A third type of ensemble is that formed by a composer for the realization of his or her own work, thus recombining the creative act and the activity of performance. The music is often developed and set on a particular group of performers, a way of working that is the norm in rock and jazz as well as in modern dance, where most of the companies have been formed by and for the creative vision of the choreographer/director.

The developments in amplification and electronics have played an important role in the formation of all these ensembles. Among other things, the new technologies permit an exploration of new sounds, a new balance and détente between heterogeneous performance forces and sonic ideas;

they permit a small ensemble to sound like a large one, not only in loudness but also in variety of tone color. Examples of groups that mix amplified voices and acoustic instruments with electronic instruments are the Philip Glass Ensemble, Steve Reich and Musicians, the Vocal Ensemble of Meredith Monk (b. 1943), and the Love of Life Orchestra founded in 1977 by Peter Gordon (b. 1951) with David Van Tieghem (b. 1955).

SOUND AS IMAGE: MUSIC AND LANGUAGE

Abstraction, atonality, non-linearity, athematicism, and ametricality once seemed revolutionary; now we can understand them as extensions of nineteenth-century ideals. The Romantic tradition of high-art, dominated by the creative individual and the notions of originality, individualism, abstraction, purity, and formalism are prime characteristics of modernism in all the arts. The Cageian view is quite different. It replaces the Romantic concept of art with activity and awareness. It tells us that art is only what we think it is—sunset awareness perhaps, or, as Cage once said, listening to the sound of spores falling off a mushroom. Accepting the electronic network and opening up art to random experience allows the real world back inside the sanctuary.

Schoenberg kept tonal reference out of his twelve-tone music, and serialism long held onto the ideal of purity. Tonality, like all familiar forms and images, is "impure" because it resonates with cultural meanings that can be very powerful and disruptive and which cannot be completely controlled by the composer. Ironically, these "uncontrolled" qualities are essential in Cage's work and they have interested many post-Cageians—not only because of the randomness of such meanings (which approaches the experience of the "real" world) but also because of a renewed interest in the social contract. Tonality, musical imagery, and a reevaluation of language and music (even language *as* music) re-entered contemporary music in the form of concept art, but they quickly opened up old issues concerning new music and the larger culture.

Musical imagery can take the form either of quotations from existing music or imitation of sounds from the natural or man-made world. Quotations of pre-existent, and often familiar, music in new work is fairly common in earlier Western art music: examples can be found in the cantus firmus and parody masses of the Renaissance, in the ubiquitous sets of variations on popular melodies from many historical periods, and in a variety of musico-dramatic contexts. Imitation, a much discussed and vexed subject in early esthetic discussions, that is really only obvious to us in such examples as the bird calls in the slow movement of Beethoven's Pastoral Symphony. In the early twentieth century, quotation and imitation gained strength, i.e., Mahler's cowbells and folk-song quotes; Ives's hymn tunes, stylistic references, and musical pictures (i.e., brass bands passing each other in a parade playing different tunes in different keys and tempos). Respighi used a recording of a nightingale with an orchestra; Messiaen quoted chant and imitated bird songs. Composers of *musique concrète* by definition incorporated recorded noise and natural sound (not always in easily recognizable form). But the use of musical references in certain recent work represents a kind of super-realism in which familiarity and association, strictly ruled out of serialism and most forms of aleatory music, reappear and are essential to the esthetic. The juxtaposition of sound objects previously unassociated, the experiencing of the familiar along with the unfamiliar, the shock of recognition, and the recognition of transformation produce new meanings and forms. Analogies in other fields can be found: structuralism in anthropology and linguistics, deconstructionism in criticism, the new figurative painting, the return of decorative detail and historical allusion in architecture, and, especially, neo-realism or super-realism in film.

One of the first contemporary composers to make extended use of musical quotation was George Rochberg, in such works as *Contra mortem et tempus* (1965), *Music for a Magic Theater* (1965), and *Nach Bach* (1966); this represented a very sharp and conscious break with serialism in his work (see Appendix: Example 18–1). Lukas Foss's *Baroque Variations* (1967) are an extensive series of transformation wrought on musical material by Bach, Handel, and Scarlatti. The Pousseur/Butor *Votre Faust* contains, among other things, musical and literary palimpsests of earlier versions of the Faust legend. Stockhausen based *Adieu* (1966) on a classical cadence, and *Hymnen* (1966–1967) uses various national anthems, all subject to the composer's characteristic transformational activities. Stockhausen's *Kurzwellen mit Beethoven* (1969) and Kagel's *Ludwig van* (1970) are "tributes" to Beethoven for the bicentennial of his birth. Berio's *Sinfonia* contains an entire movement of Mahler's Second Symphony surrounded by an ongoing musical commentary layered in by the composer. William Bolcom's *Session IV* and *Black Host* (both 1967), Michael Sahl's *String Quartet* (1969), *Special Trash* (1971), and *Cocktail Wanderings* (1982), as well as the author's *Foxes and Hedgehogs* (1963–1967), *The Nude Paper Sermon* (1969), and *Ecolog* (1971), use stylistical reminiscence rather than literal quotation, but the purpose is similar. The solo vocal line ("for amplified night club singer") in Salvatore Martirano's *Ballad* (1966), the use of popular song in Stephen Albert's *Voices Within* (1975), and the variations for violin on the "The Last Rose of Summer" in Sahl's *A Mitzvah for the Dead* (1966) are like musical double entendres: they are the thing itself and, at the same time, the transformed image of it.

There are close ties between the use of musical imagery, the influence of pop, and new forms of interaction between music and language; many of the same composers have been involved in all three. The traditional relationships between text and music can now be seen as a special case of a much wider field of relationships between words, language, sound, and music. Verbal meaning and structure—from phoneme to word formation to narrative to non-linear verbal complexes—may interact with sound and music on many levels: meaning and sound quality, clarity and confusion, linearity and non-linearity, comprehensibility and incomprehensibility. The newly broadened attitude towards language is reflected in a number of Stockhausen's works from *Momente* (1961–1964) to *Stimmung* (1968), in Foss's *Fragments of Archilochos* (1965) and *Paradigm* (1968), in the work of composers like Dieter Schnebel and Hans G. Helms (b. 1932) in Germany as well as Alvin Lucier, Robert Ashley, and others in the United States; it is essential in many of Berio's vocal and theater pieces from *Laborintus II* (1965) to *A-Ronne* (1974–1975), and in the author's larger pieces for voices and instruments.

Extended use of the sonic or musical qualities of language—with a whole range of attitudes about reference and meaning—is characterized by a large area of new work known as *concrète* poetry or, in more recent terminology, "text-sound." Cage's writings and lectures, which are put together by the same methods and with the same philosophy as his music, are often included in text-sound performances or anthologies, as is the work of many of the people he influenced in the 1950's and 1960's, i.e., Jackson Mac Low (see Appendix; Example 18–2). Many of the leading text-sound poets are also composers—for example, the San Francisco composer Charles Amirkhanian (b. 1945). (See Example 18–3.) Richard Kostelanetz (b. 1940) is a literary and music critic who has done extensive visual, *concrète*, and text-sound poetry. Others have crossed over into a no man's land between the printed page, the spoken word, noise, environmental sound, *musique concrète*, and musical tone; the German term *Hörspiel* (which literally translated means "earplay," but refers to experimental sound work in the medium of radio) is sometimes used in this connection. The West German radio has established a *Hörspiel* department that regularly broadcasts and commissions text-sound works. The recent popularity of "rap" (rhythmic speaking over a rock or soul beat) has given a new impetus to language/music settings over rhythmic styles inspired by minimalism and pop. Laurie Anderson's "songs" are examples of this; Paul Dresher (b. 1951) makes extensive use of such techniques in his theater piece *Slow Fire* (1985–1986).

Magnetic tape provides almost limitless opportunities for neo-realistic imagery and image transformation: of music, one can cite *Collage #1—(Blue Suede)* (1961) of James Tenney (b. 1934), based on a rockabilly song; of language, Berio's *Omaggio a Joyce*, Reich's *It's Gonna Rain* (1965) and *Come Out* (1966), and Ashley's *She Was a Visitor* (1967); or of noise, the author's *Queens Collage* (1967), based on the "found sound" of an urban college

campus and edited like the visual images of a film. Still further along this
line are certain "documentary" works of the 1970's in which the artist intrudes
only to frame or define a certain sound environment: Alvin Curran's *A Day
in the Country*, Luc Ferrari's *Presque rien* pieces (No. 1 [1970]; No. 2 [1973]),
the "listening exercises" of Philip Corner (*I Can Walk Though the World
as Music*, a "listening walk"; *Soundaround*, standing in one place and listening to the environment; *Ear Here*, putting one's ear close to a sustained
sound), and the *Earth Music* series produced by the author for radio. In the
former group of works, what we hear is art because the source is transformed;
the "meaning" is in the recognizability of the image and its transformation.
In the latter group, what we hear is music simply because we experience it
that way (if we do).

Some of the activities, groups, composers, and music discussed in
this chapter survived the evolution from modernism to post-modernism, but
much of what has been described proved to be transitional. Happenings,
certain forms of media, noise/junk art, conceptual art, the new improvisation,
quotation, text-sound, neo-realism—these and other experimental developments of the recent past have not entirely disappeared, but their heyday
was brief and their constituencies are widely scattered; many of the composers have gone on to other things. As in the Dada period more than half
a century earlier, the artistic—and certainly the musical—pickings were
slim but the legacy is great. If we except a few live-performance albums—
all but impossible to listen to—much of this activity seems to have fallen
by the wayside. And yet out of all the ferment has come, somehow or other,
the late twentieth-century phenomenon that we call post-modernism.

BIBLIOGRAPHICAL NOTES

The writings and anthologies of Richard Kostelanetz cover the upheavals of
the 1960's in music and the other arts; the most notable is *Metamorphosis in
the Arts: A Critical History of the 1960's* (Brooklyn, 1980), but see also his
*The Theatre of Mixed Means: An Introduction to Happenings, Kinetic Envi-
ronments, and Other Mixed-Means Performances* (New York, 1968), which
includes interviews with many of the artists discussed in this chapter, and
Esthetics Contemporary (Buffalo, 1978), which gathers together essays by these
artists and others. Adrian Henri's *Total Art: Environments, Happenings, and
Performance* (New York, 1964) is a well-documented history of happenings,
with many excellent illustrations. The author's article "The Revolution in Music"
in *The New American Review* 6 (New York, 1969; several times reprinted)
deals with music and technology of the 1950's and 1960's. The "Double numéro
spécial" 268–269 of *La Revue musicale* (Paris, 1971) contains the principal
papers delivered at the 1970 Stockholm UNESCO meeting on the subject of

"Musique et technologie." Leonard Meyer's *Music, the Arts and Ideas* (Chicago, 1967) is an extended consideration of the state of 1960's musical culture in English, and contains an extensive bibliography. On this subject see also Roger Reynolds's *Mind Models: New Forms of Musical Experience* (New York, 1975), which focuses on the philosophy, perception, and creation of music during the 1960's, and *Contiguous Lines: Issues and Ideas in the Music of the '60's and '70's*, ed. Thomas DeLio (New York, 1985), a collection of articles written by DeLio, Pozzi Escot, Robert Cogan, Alvin Lucier, and Christian Wolff, among others.

Source magazine, while it lasted, was a good point of reference for new developments in music. David Cope's *New Directions in Music* (4th ed., Dubuque, 1984) summarizes many of the prevalent musical trends and gives examples from composers' works. On some of the various experimental music groups, see Cornelius Cardew's *Stockhausen Serves Imperialism and Other Articles* (London, 1974), which contains Rod Eley's essay on the history of the Scratch Orchestra, and *Fluxus, the Most Radical and Experimental Art Movement of the Sixties*, ed. Harry Ruhe (Amsterdam, 1979).

On brainwave music, see the articles in *Biofeedback and the Arts: Results of Early Experiments*, ed. David Rosenboom (Vancouver, B.C., 1976). Rosenboom has also put out a record with some of the music created in this manner (A.R.C. Record #ST1002). Two important sources of information on text-sound texts and *Hörspiel* are available: the first is an anthology of text-sound texts, edited by Richard Kostelanetz, containing the work of a number of prominent figures including Amirkhanian, Cage, P. Corner, Charles Dodge, Jon Erickson, Kenneth Gaburo, Jon Gibson, Philip Glass, Dick Higgins, Tom Johnson, Kostelanetz, Alvin Lucier, Jackson Mac Low, Charles Morrow, R. Murray Schafer, Ned Sublette, and Robert Wilson (New York, 1980) as well as an introductory essay surveying text-sound art in North America; the second is Mark Ensign Cory's *The Emergence of an Acoustical Art Form: An Analysis of the German Experimental Hörspiel of the 1960s* (Lincoln, NB, 1974).

Three useful sources on the music of George Rochberg include Alexander Ringer's early study in the *Musical Quarterly* (October 1966, pp. 409–30); Rochberg's own *The Aesthetics of Survival: A Composer's View of Twentieth-Century Music* (ed. William Bolcom, Ann Arbor, 1984), a collection of Rochberg's articles written from 1959 to 1974; and George Clark's *Essays on American Music* (Westport, CN, 1977), which devotes a chapter to the "new eclecticism" of Rochberg, Cage, and Crumb, among others. Other sources which deal with musical quotation include Clemens Kühn's *Das Zitat in der Musik der Gegenwart* (Hamburg, 1972), which covers the music of Henze, Stockhausen, Kagel, Schnebel, Berio, Zimmerman, Diether de la Motte, and Hans Otte; David Osmond-Smith's *Playing on Words: A Guide to Berio's "Sinfonia"* (London, 1985); Diether Schnebel's *Mauricio Kagel: Musik, Theater, Film* (Dumont Dokument Series, Cologne, 1970), which covers his music to 1970; and Werner Klüppelholz's *Mauricio Kagel: 1970–1980* in the Dumont Dokument series (Cologne, 1981).

NINETEEN

BACK TO TONALITY

THE DARMSTADT CONTROVERSY

In the 1980's a crisis of modernism exploded at the Darmstadt International Summer Course for New Music in Germany. Darmstadt had nurtured the work of the young serialists in the 1950's and 1960's and had come to stand for the triumph of new music—in Europe and around the world. In the early 1980's Darmstadt was still dominated by serialists—a second generation whose work can be represented by the highly arcane and pythagorean music of the English composer Brian Ferneyhough (b. 1943). In 1982, however, Friedrich Hommel became the director and made a firm decision to open the 1984 Darmstadt course and festival to all tendencies and ideas. The result was an explosive confrontation between European serialism (complex, atonal, irregular, abstract) and American—or American-inspired—minimalism (simple, tonal, regular, gestural). Major works by Terry Riley,

Philip Glass, Alvin Curran, Robert Moran, John Cage, Morton Feldman, Tom Johnson (b. 1939), and Robert Erickson were performed, and many of them—particularly those by Moran, Johnson, Curran, Glass, and Riley—produced violent reactions, from opponents and supporters alike. In addition, five sessions were devoted to a symposium on tonality and modality in new music, and major European works were performed that exemplified neo-Romanticism, neo-expressionism, and a new interest in non-Western modal sources.

The Darmstadt controversy can be looked at in many ways. Europeans saw it as the latest eruption in a long history of Europe-vs.-America rivalry. Others thought the issue revolved around profundity (intellectual content) vs. hedonism (sensual pleasure)—but this was perhaps just another variant of the old-world/new-world debate. Many viewed the conflict as having not merely nationalistic but broader and deeper ideological overtones—notably those of progressivism vs. conservatism (although it was often hard to tell which side was which). American observers had a different view: they tended to see the controversy as an "uptown"-vs.-"downtown"[1] debate—i.e., establishment vs. avant-garde—but in a new context. According to this view, the old modernist music, once provocative and path-breaking, had become neo-conservative, state-supported, and academic; the new impulses, populist and grass-rooted, held the best promise for the future. Modernism and some forms of European post-modernism remained doggedly high-art, personal, and hermetic; American-style post-modernism—closely related to the energies of pop music, non-Western cultures, and an earlier, more heroic age of Western music—was held to be concrete, outgoing, communal, accessible, comprehensible. (This would suggest clear parallels with the old battles between early modernism and the populist movements of the late 1920's and 1930's.)

Is neo-tonality a retrograde or is it a forward-looking movement? The very terms of the question presuppose the language and world-view of modernism, so closely allied in its origins to the political and social views of liberalism and progress. An investment banker or land developer may cause radical change in small-town or rural society with the ensuing destruction of traditional values; yet he may be thought of as a conservative. On the other hand, a "radical" Green activist may be a staunch conservationist and espouse many traditional values. The same paradoxes apply in the arts today. Minimalist or new-theater tonality may be a kind of radical or populist conservationism, in the sense that certain traditional values and forms are

---

[1] These terms derive from the geography of New York musical life where the older and more established cultural institutions tend to be found north of the midtown area, while the newer and often more experimental activity spreads southward past Greenwich Village into the decaying industrial loft areas of SoHo, Tribeca, and the Lower East Side.

conserved or reinstated. Some forms of serialism, now quite mainstream, can no longer be thought of as avant-garde. And what is one to make of the European neo-tonalists—neo-Romantics mostly, but also some reviving modal usage—who have designed their compositional styles and practices according to the principles of serialism or very closely related theoretical ideas?

In the 1930's, Virgil Thomson proposed a connection between the way composers earn a living and the kind of music they write. Half a century later we might bring his thesis up to date as follows: modernist, uptown composers write for standard musical ensembles and earn their living from university positions and foundation grants (in North America) or from state-supported activities (in Europe). Post-modern, downtown composers have their own ensembles, perform in galleries and clubs, work in theater and film, and generally live and work in a free-lance style (although they too occasionally get grants). The driving esthetic force behind the music of the first group is idealism—derived from German Romantic philosophy. Most of the major writers on esthetics were Platonists and concerned with ideal form; they regard music as the purest and most ideal of the arts precisely because it is the most abstract and the most formful. This Romantic notion (made possible by the triumph of instrumental music) permeates twentieth-century modernism, which carried it to extremes. Modernist abstraction (or, more properly, non-objectivism) and the various forms of atonality (including athematicism, dodecaphony, non-metricality, and rhythmic asymmetry) represent the purest form of the Romantic ideal because they remove the art of music from its common shared and everyday usage. They reconstruct the art form from its own internal logic—a logic of the sound materials, a logic of thought-process and form, and a self-consistent world-view. Such music is bound to be highly internalized and personal—but also impersonal and objectified. It will be responsive either to pure order or pure randomness (the end results can be quite similar) but always faithful to its own internal vision. Each piece or performance strives to become its own artistic paradigm; each composer develops his or her own individual "system." In its most extreme forms, modernist music is about the "idea" of music rather than any incarnation in the real world. The score on the page, the notation itself, the computer tape, the impenetrable wall of noise or even silence may represent some pure and idealistic form; next to it, the reality of performers struggling to play notes or to improvise or to sing and act simultaneously may seem blatant, insufficient, or vulgar.

Post-modernism challenges the idealism of modernism. It is Aristotelian, not Platonic. It seeks to engage the real world of music making by dealing with creator-performer-public as a three-way interaction. The atonalities and asymmetries of modernism are personal, individual, recreated for and through each work. Tonality and metricality always imply something outside of and preceding the work; they imply a compact between creator and listener, or, to choose another metaphor, a canvas that is not blank but bears certain pre-existent patterns. These patterns (more like molds or templates perhaps than patterns on a canvas) are equivalent to the grammatical forms of language or the basic figurative structures (the horizon, the human figure) in the grammar of visual perception.

Not all post-modernists belong downtown. There are those—in the United States, in Europe, and elsewhere—who continue to write for traditional institutions, instruments, and ensembles. These are the composers who, by and large, have been labelled "neo-Romantic." The music of their downtown counterparts is likely to be simpler, leaner, less dependent on tradition, more obviously metrical and rhythmic, often pop-related, and generally based on patterns of repetition and rhythmic energy—in short, "minimalist." What the two groups share is a revived dialogue with the public and a new interest in repetition and recollection, metrical rhythm, and a return to some form of tonality.

NEO-ROMANTICISM

Neo-Romanticism and minimalism started out as something quite different from what they became; both grew out of ideas and techniques that first appeared as special cases of modernism. Collage and quotation were techniques for introducing familiar musical imagery into a non-tonal context; once admitted into the musical fabric, the tonal references tended to take over. In George Rochberg's *Music for a Magic Theater* (1965)—the evocative title comes from the German writer Hermann Hesse—music by Mahler, Varèse, and Stockhausen as well as Beethoven, Webern, and Rochberg himself is quoted, with a big chunk of a Mozart divertimento included virtually intact. In Rochberg's *Nach Bach* (1966), for harpsichord or piano, references to Bach and atonal distortions and overlays are played off against each other dramatically. This manner of quotation proved to be limiting and unstable; beginning with the String Quartet No. 3 of 1972 and continuing with the Violin Concerto (1974), the three "Concord" quartets (1977–1978), and the opera *The Confidence Man* (1982), Rochberg deliberately set out to use the Classic/Romantic style not just as a source of quotations and references but as his main subject matter. He has been quite explicit about the neo-conservative nature of his recent music and has talked about "a music of remembering" and "regaining contact with the tradition and means of the past." Although the tradition he is talking about reaches back as far as Mozart and Beethoven, his "remembering" goes back mainly to the early years of the century—to Mahler, early Schoenberg, early Bartók—before Schoenbergian atonality and *The Rite of Spring* changed the course of music.

Rochberg's work could not actually have been written by a late nineteenth-century composer—the lyric and dramatic late-Romantic gestures are often set against unresolved twentieth-century dissonance—but the underlying attempts to extend functional tonality, to resolve dissonance, and to recapture old-fashioned lyricism all represent a striking return to older ideals.

If Rochberg's music of the 1970's and 1980's harks back to Mahler, the music by David Del Tredici (b. 1937) often takes a Straussian turn. Del Tredici, like Rochberg, had a modernist background: he studied at Princeton and his early works belong to the atonal, serial wing of modernism. But expressivity rather than strict serialism was always dominant, and Del Tredici had an even shorter distance to travel back to Romanticism than did Rochberg. He is best known for a series of works based on Lewis Carroll's *Alice's Adventures in Wonderland* and *Through the Looking Glass* and their themes of lost innocence in a topsy-turvy world: starting with *Pop-Pourri* (1968; revised 1973) and *Lobster Quadrille* (1969) and including *An Alice Symphony* (1969–1976), *Adventures Underground* (1971; revised 1977), *Vintage Alice* (1972), *Final Alice* (1976), *Child Alice* (in two parts; 1977–1981), and *Haddock's Eyes* (1986). These works are typically scored for amplified voice (soprano), a "folk" group (mandolin, banjo, accordion, etc.) or a "rock" group (saxophones, electric guitars), and a chamber or large orchestra. The vocal parts include narration as well as operatic singing. The orchestrations are colorful and inventive, the harmonic sound is increasingly simple and triadic, and the vocal lines are increasingly lyric and motivic. The scale is Mahlerian: *Final Alice*, for instance, is an hour in length. The voice, with the help of amplification, soars above the huge orchestral sonorities in a manner that one immediately associates with the late German Romantics. A key element is the use of repetition—not the obsessive rhythmic repetition of the minimalists but extensive thematic repetition in a lushly tonal context in which orchestral fantasy, extreme beauty of sound, and a kind of pervasive nostalgic sadness prevail.

Rochberg and Del Tredici arrived at their neo-Romanticism through a conscious turning-away from modernism. Composers like John Corigliano (b. 1938) and Stephen Albert (b. 1944) have made less dramatic choices; their work is a continuation of an accessible post-Romantic modernism that has co-existed with more radical forms since the 1950's. Corigliano's best-known works are his Clarinet Concerto of 1977, which mixes tonality with tone-clusters and tone-rows, and his music for Ken Russell's film *Altered States* (1980; there is an orchestral suite drawn from it), with its strikingly theatrical use of the orchestra and dream-like distortions of an old hymn tune. Albert's *Voices Within* (1975) opposes a theater or pit band and an orchestra; its subject matter is based on the style and image of American popular tunes, but with no actual quotation or imitation. His *To Wake the Dead* (1977), for soprano and small ensemble, is a setting of excerpts from

Joyce's *Finnegans Wake* and uses a tune found in the book. *Symphony RiverRun* (1984–1985) is a large, intense orchestral work full of references to the Classic/Romantic tradition.

The impulse towards a revival of Romantic tonality is widespread and sometimes can be found in unexpected places. Frederic Rzewski, who was born in New England in 1938 and studied at Harvard and Princeton, has lived, taught, and worked in New York and in Europe. His early work, largely for piano, belongs with the most extreme and striking avant-gardism of the 1960's. In 1966 he helped organize Musica Elettronica Viva, and he became involved subsequently with live-electronic composition, collective improvisation, contemporary jazz, and New York minimalism, all informed with a strong political point of view. Rzewski's political ideas are displayed in his theories about improvisation, in his choice of texts (a letter from a convict written just before the Attica prison uprising was used in *Coming Together/Attica*, a work of 1972 for speaker and ensemble), in his increasing use of folk songs as the basis for extended compositions, in the influence of black jazz on his music, and in its increasing accessibility. *The People United Will Never Be Defeated!* (1975), based on a Chilean revolutionary song; *Four Pieces* for piano (1977), with a strong Latin-American melodic character; *Four North American Ballads* (1978–1979); and *A Long Time Man* for piano and orchestra (1979), based on a prison song—all are amalgams of Rzewski's political views with influences from improvisation and from jazz and folk sources, but put together with a European Romantic compositional technique.

Neo-Romanticism usually looks back to the turn of the century rather than to the heart of nineteenth-century Romanticism. It often suggests an attempt to pick up the thread of expressionist tonality just before it was overwhelmed by atonality, serialism, and neo-Classicism. In art criticism (and in European music criticism), the term "neo-expressionist" is often used for such an esthetic. Rochberg, Del Tredici, and some of their European counterparts (discussed below) seem to have wanted to return to a crossroads miles back, in order to choose a different path than the one previously taken. In so doing, they perhaps hope to create a new history from an old past, maintaining the viability of traditional musical institutions and forms while renewing the compact between the composer and the traditional musical public.

NEO-EXPRESSIONISM AND NEW TONALITY IN EUROPE

The first major modernist to return to tonality was Hans Werner Henze. We have commented on his earlier music-theater works as combining twelve-tone technique with Stravinskyan forms and a lyric style. From the middle 1960's on, he gradually introduced tonal, traditional, and popular elements in his music along with an extensive array of other technical features, all handled with great skill and imagination. Two features of his voluminous output are relevant here: his interest and success in the theater and his leftist political views. Besides the large-scale operas of the 1950's and early 1960's (see page 99), Henze composed in 1967 three "scenic cantatas" under the title *Moralities*, with texts by Auden after Aesop. Since then he has written a series of pieces for semi-theatrical, chamber-opera or music-theater situations, most of them with moral/political subjects and a more varied musical palette. These include *Das Floss der "Medusa"* ("The Raft of the Medusa"; 1968), *Versuch über Schweine* (1968), *El Cimarrón* (1969–1970), *Der langwierige Weg in die Wohnung der Natascha Ungeheuer* ("The Tedious Journey to the House of Natascha Frightful"; 1971), *La cubana, oder Ein Leben für die Kunst* ("The Cuban Woman, or A Life for Art"; 1973), *We Come to the River* ("actions for music"; a highly *provocateur* work of 1974–1976), *Pollicino, or, The New Adventures of Tom Thumb* (a "community opera"; 1980), and others.

Henze's use of lyric tonality, often set against the most harsh and non-tonal music, is part of his grand eclectic dialectic and is closely connected with his theatricality and politics. There is, in fact, a very romantic side to Henze's music and his ideas, but he is not so much a neo-Romantic as an artist who easily assimilates traditional elements (and, to a lesser degree, popular ones) into a basic wide-ranging modernism. Nevertheless, his importance cannot be overlooked, and the weight of his personality, ideas, and prolific output have had a considerable influence on the younger generation.

There are more clear-cut examples of a return to tradition in European music. One of the most striking is Penderecki, whose provocative use of dense tone-clusters, sculpted mass glissandi, and startling orchestral and choral strokes have already been discussed (see pp. 185-86). Penderecki has composed for the theater, but the influence of Catholicism, the expression of religious feeling in music, and the Polish liturgical tradition have been even more important. Beginning with a set of Psalms in 1958 and continuing with the *Stabat Mater* (1962), *St. Luke Passion, Dies irae* (1967), and *Utrenia* (a Slavonic Mass, 1970–1971), tonal elements gradually appeared in his music. The first usages provided dramatic contrasts: a unison set against a cluster, a bit of chant against choral babbles or shouts. By the time of the Violin Concerto (1976), the *Te Deum* (1979), and the *Polish Requiem* (1980–1984), these tonal elements—charged with the same kind of dramatic and emotional weight as his earlier dense atonal clusters—became increasingly important. "We can still use old forms to write new music," Penderecki said in 1977. This is very close to Rochberg's position, especially if the word "forms" is understood to mean not only structure but also the grammar of late Romanticism.[2]

The work of Hans Joachim Hespos (b. 1938) and Wolfgang Rihm (b. 1952) evokes not so much late Romantic form or tonality as the expressionist works of Schoenberg, Berg, and Bartók from the early years of the century. The emotional and musical climate of their music is extreme: blocks of loud, aggressive sound alternate with moments of quiet anguish; unisons are interrupted by chaotic heterophony, stasis with hysterical rushing movement. Not surprisingly, both composers have been involved with the theater. Rihm's opera *Jakob Lenz* (1978) is based on a novella by Georg Büchner (the author of *Woyzeck*), which is itself based on the life of a proto-expressionist playwright who went mad. The score lurches from lyricism to violent dissonance and highly distorted vocalism. Hespos's *Seiltanz* (1982) uses a much more unconventional concert/theater form with an actor, winds, double bass, and percussion. Everything is expressed in terms of extremes and violent oppositions. The players enter one by one, pushing themselves to their musical and technical limits. The conductor harangues the musicians. Hammering sounds emerge from a mysterious water tank on stage. The actor smashes a huge piece of wood to the floor, contorting his face and body. Someone— an actor? a percussionist?—cuts his way out of the water tank with a blowtorch and tries to reach the percussion instruments. The title *Seiltanz* means "tightrope walk," and the piece constantly skirts violence and danger.

The new-tonal and new-modal movements in Europe have developed out of social concerns, but with some of the same theoretical underpinnings as serialism. The work of the Dutch composers Peter Schat (b. 1935), Ton de Leeuw (b. 1926), and Louis Andriessen (b. 1939) illustrate aspects of this. All three collaborated (with a fourth composer, Jan van Vlijmen [b. 1935]) on *Reconstruction*, a strongly political music theater work of 1969. Schat, first known for large-scale multi-media and theatrical works with strong political implications, developed a system of tonality—or tonalities—which he calls the "Tone Clock"; in many ways this resembles medieval modal formulations or Eastern *raga* theory, as well as serialism. But Schat's later style—exemplified by such works as his Second Symphony (1983), a symphonic study for his opera-in-progress *Symposion* (to be premiered in 1988)— is neo-Romantic, lyric, and even programmatic. De Leeuw, who studied ethnomusicology with Jaap Kunst and has been influenced by both American and Eastern music (Indian, Indonesian, and Japanese), uses modal techniques, repetition, static cyclical forms as well as ideas about modal expression or feeling. Nevertheless, his music does not sound American or Eastern but

---

[2] Similar changes have taken place in the most recent music of György Ligeti (whose earlier work is also mentioned on pp. 185-86).

rather assimilates the musical modes as well as modes of thought into a European romantic style. Andriessen has written orchestral works under the title of *Anachronie* (I, 1968, dedicated to the memory of Charles Ives; II, 1969), several works for jazz ensemble (*Spectacle*, 1970; *On Jimmy Yancey*, 1973), *Workers Union*, a symphonic movement for loud instruments (1975), and a number of settings of social and political texts. Like many socially conscious European artists, Andriessen is politically anti-American but strongly influenced by American as well as traditional European culture—both high art and popular. *Hoketus* (1976–1977) for panpipes, electric and acoustic pianos, bass guitars, and congas combines American influences with medieval rhythmic technique.

Not surprisingly, ideas about modality have also returned with force in the work of certain Eastern European composers, notably the Romanian Anatol Vieru (b. 1926), who has written a book about the subject. The modal traditions of Eastern music and the ideas of process music—based on simple pulse, tonality, and slow, incremental change (see the following section, on minimalism)—clearly have something in common. Another related technique, which has antecedents in earlier Western modern music (e.g., the *Farben* or "Colors" movement of Schoenberg's Five Orchestral Pieces of 1909), is that of *Klangfarbenmelodie* or "coloristic melody," first proposed by Schoenberg and Webern but not highly developed by them. This was particularly important in the work of Eastern European composers after World War II, notably Ligeti and some of the Polish avant-gardists. It is a major element in the music of the Estonian Arvo Pärt, the youngest of a group of vanguard composers in the Soviet Union (see pp. 126–27). Pärt's earlier work, such as his *Collage on the Theme B-A-C-H* (1964) and *Pro et contra* (1966), is marked by strong contrasts. After *Tabula rasa* (1977), a kind of two-violin concerto in a minimalist style that evokes Vivaldi, he began to develop a very original style of *Klangfarbenmelodie* based on intense coloristic forms of great beauty which evolve from apparently steady states in slow patterns of change. The effect of Pärt's music is striking and hypnotic, but its meditative qualities are mystical and emotional rather than physical or nostalgic (as in much American music). The music sometimes actually seems to weep; its qualities of lyrical modality and sadness are strengthened by its coloristic and process form, and relate it very strongly to Eastern European tradition.

A very different sort of looking backward and forward can be found in the work of some Viennese composers who were among the first Europeans to introduce tonality in a modern-music context. Kurt Schwertsik (b. 1935) was a co-founder—with Friedrich Cerha, best-known for his completion of Berg's *Lulu*—of the ensemble Die Reihe. Like Rochberg and Sahl, Schwertsik began to introduce into his music, in collage fashion, fragments of familiar tonal material, much of it taken from Viennese Classicism as well as from light entertainment music. *Twilight Music* (1976) is subtitled "A Celtic Serenade for Octet." His ballets *Walzerträume* (1976) and *Tag- und Nachtweisen* (1978) are based, respectively, on Viennese waltzes and medieval music. *Starckdeutsche Lieder und Tänze* (1982) for baritone and orchestra, and the opera *Das Märchen von Fanferlieschen Schönefüsschen* (1983) suggest how Schwertsik's work has evolved from a commentary on social music making and the classical past into an artistic continuation of these traditions. Heinz Karl Gruber, who prefers to be called H. K. Gruber (b. 1943), began as a serial and electronic composer but moved stylistically to a witty Central European type of neo-tonality. His best-known work, *Frankenstein!!* (1976–1977), is designated as a "pandemonium" for narrative baritone voice with orchestra. Often narrated by the composer himself, it is in the actor-chansonnier tradition which had inspired Schoenberg's *Pierrot Lunaire* half a century earlier.

One of the characteristics of post-modernism is a return to localism and local traditions, and this in turn has changed the character of new-musical life. In the past, modern music was dominated by internationalism. Modernist work was brought out in a few international centers and travelled quickly around the world. Its constituency was a fairly small group of cosmopolitan critics, connoisseurs, and enthusiasts active in the major metropolises. The new post-modern musics tend to grow out of and relate more to local situations and traditions; one result has been the growth of many local centers with intense and, to some extent, popular activity. Works created for local situations and particular performers and ensembles often do not travel well; hence, the international diffusion of much of this music has been slow, and this has resulted in a split between European and American music which is only beginning to be modified.

This split is probably least marked in Holland and in England, which has close transatlantic ties with the United States (in both directions). In the 1960's, Peter Maxwell Davies, who studied at Princeton, began using popular and light music in his "serious" work, which had theretofore been quite austerely serialist. Beginning with *Eight Songs for a Mad King* (1969) and continuing with works like *Vesalii icones* (1969), *Miss Donnithorne's Maggot* (1974), and *The Lighthouse* (1979), Davies has explored music-theater forms outside of operatic conventions. These works include extended vocal techniques, non-narrative and non-proscenium theater forms, quotation and reference, a mixture of tonal and non-tonal elements, and non-traditional notation. (See Appendix: Example 19–1.) Davies was associated with the Pierrot Players and, more recently, The Fires of London, which has pioneered in new music-theater performance in England. Simon Bainbridge (b. 1952) has combined influences from Ligeti, Reich, and mainstream European modernism in his work. Oliver Knussen (b. 1952) has used tonal and non-tonal elements in striking mixtures from his earliest mature work. Two major projects based on the writings of Maurice Sendak—*Where the Wild Things Are* (various versions for concert and opera performance, 1979–1983) and *Higglety Pigglety Pop!* (1984–1985)—are children's fantasy-nightmares; their complex, collage-like scores include familiar and tonal elements together with more intense and expressionist passages, somewhat in the manner of Berio's *Laborintus II* or the author's *Foxes and Hedgehogs*. These pieces attempt to cross the boundaries between theatrical directness and the more complex musical demands of concert pieces—just as they cross the boundaries between tonal and atonal, and merge influences and ideas from popular, Romantic, and modernist art.

Davies and Knussen are, in American terms, uptown composers. Cornelius Cardew (1936–1981), Gavin Bryars (b. 1943), and Michael Nyman (b. 1944) are "downtowners" and, not coincidentally, they all have strong connections with related aspects of American music. Cardew studied in Germany and became Stockhausen's assistant in the late 1950's; he also studied in Rome, and later came under Cage's influence. Cardew's music in the 1960's was typically dependent on free performer reaction to graphic notation (as in his immense score of 1963–1967 called *Treatise*). In 1969 he founded the Scratch Orchestra, a defiantly anti-orchestral orchestra, and began to be interested in the social and political implications of new music and new-music making. Under the influence of Maoism, he turned away from modernism and began composing simple, violent, agitprop songs in the tradition of Hanns Eisler and other Central European musical ideologues.

Bryars and Nyman are both composers of a highly philosophical (rather than openly political) bent, and their recent work is closely allied to American minimalism. Bryars studied philosophy; his early musical activity was as a jazzman. In the 1960's he was influenced by European avant-gardism—but also by Cage, Reich (with whom he has performed), and Cardew (in particular, the Scratch Orchestra). Many of his pieces have theatrical qualities. *The Sinking of the Titanic* (1969) is supposedly based on the music being played by the *S.S. Titanic*'s deck orchestra while the ship was sinking; *Jesus' Blood Never Failed Me Yet* (1971), is based on a tape loop of a bum singing a sentimental religious song; and *Out of Zaleski's Gazebo* (1977–1978) evokes Victorian parlor music. Bryars collaborated on several recordings with the experimental rock musician and electronic composer Brian Eno (b. 1948), on an opera (*Medea*; 1983–1984) with Robert Wilson, and on a large-scale music-theater work in the Wilson vein (*The Last Days of Immanuel Kant*; 1986) with the writer Andrew Thomson.

One of Nyman's works is based on the "catalogue aria" of Leporello in Mozart's *Don Giovanni*, with the vocal line omitted and the accompaniment pattern turned into a kind of pulse music (*Re: Don Giovanni*, 1952). This suggests Nyman's connections with both American and European music.

Like the work of the Viennese group, Nyman's work of the early 1980's is more historically based than the comparable American music, and it makes a greater use of irony, quotation, and humor, with its obsessive twists on classical modes. His *A Handsome Smooth-Sweet-Smart-Clear Stroke* for orchestra refers to seventeenth-century England, as does the related music for the film *The Draughtsman's Contract* (1983), probably his best-known work. *The Man Who Mistook His Wife For a Hat* (1985–1986), based on a clinical study of neurological disorder by Dr. Oliver Sacks, evokes Schumann (the main character's favorite composer) and the memory of German Romanticism as part of a work whose themes are perception and memory. Nyman's neo-tonality, like much recent European music, has social and historical levels; the cultural context is essential.

MINIMALISM

Western music, like most Western art, has been traditionally dualistic, based on conflict and opposition. The idea of a non-dualistic music based on brief patterns and repetitions, regularity of pulse, economy of means, clear (if extended) structures, and transformation by slow incremental change is common enough in other musics of the world, but it has permeated Western music on a large scale only recently. The term "minimalism" was originally used in art criticism of the 1960's for simple, sculptural objects— so-called "primary structures." The term was later borrowed and applied to the process music of Glass, Reich, and others and, however misleading, the name has stuck. In spite of its many problems, it will be used here as a convenient label.

Musical minimalism can be defined in a number of ways. If it is regarded not as a style but as a formal way of thinking about music, it has precedents even in Western music. The simplicity and economy of Webern is based on the notion of one thing at a time; so is the otherwise very theatrical and dualistic music of Crumb. The notion of sound objects or clusters began with Varèse and continued in the density works of Xenakis, Ligeti, and several Poles. These use simple, non-dualistic structures in constant transformation; Xenakis's four-track tape piece *Bohor [I]* of 1962 is an example; so is the music of Arvo Pärt just discussed. Henry Cowell wrote cluster music and also music influenced by non-Western models; so did Partch (whose work often sounds like contemporary minimalism) and a number of Americans in the 1930's and 1940's (Cage, Harrison, Colin McPhee, Alan Hovhaness). Virgil Thomson's artful simplicity—especially his use of tonality and repetition in settings of texts by Stein—is minimalism *avant la lettre*. Cage's involvement with Zen Buddhism and his attempts, musical and philosophical, to accept the world "as it is" preclude (theoretically at least) conflict or dualism; if any and all experiences are equally valid, then each single experience is valid in and for its own sake. This is the philosophical— conceptual—underpinning of the music that evolved into process/pulse minimalism. Feldman's simple, isolated sounds, extended over increasingly longer periods of time, imply a strong rejection of conflict *and* process and put a premium on the essential "itness" of each sound; in older works and in recent pieces such as *Crippled Symmetry* of 1983 and *Coptic Light* of 1986 there are no levels, no meanings within meanings, no symbolism, only sound itself in a quintessential purity. The extended performance pieces of La Monte Young—a fifth, tuned and retuned (in *Composition 1960—#7*), a single electronic-and-vocal interval extended over vast lengths of time, changing only minutely—involve an enormous amount of energy focused on an absolute minimum of sensory experience.

Young's work is the result of a set of philosophical principles carried into the sound domain. Recent minimalism was, initially, a subset of concept art. The earlier works of Terry Riley and, in particular, of Steve Reich use patterns of overlapping repetition with gradual change occurring in small increments. This suggests an analogy to "op art," and in fact Young's performances have been accompanied by projections of works by Marian Zazeela (b. 1940), which are based on these principles in the visual domain. Minimalism has other roots, not only in non-Western music but also in rock, in improvisation (where repetition and small, incremental variation is a natural technique), and even in audio technology which facilitates mechanical repetition and variations as well as the projection of detail.

Ironically, minimalism, which rejects dualism or dialectic in its structure, arises out of a notable dialectic in the historical evolution of music. It is a reaction to information overload, to the buzzing, blooming confusion of a complex industrial society with its multiple and contradictory communications systems and messages. It reacts against the constant, shallow emission and exchange of information by seeking out a deep experience of limited, isolated events and by pushing the frontiers of perception inward. Minimalism had an early association with consciousness-altering drugs. Most practitioners today reject that association, preferring to emphasize the rational and structural aspects of their art. Nevertheless minimalism is hardly an intellectual exercise; concentration and involvement over long periods of time are essential, but it is not necessary to "figure things out." The simple repetitious tonality, the use of slow, incremental change as well as the pulsing, highly charged rhythmic patterns have immediate as well as long-range impact. Minimalism has attracted an educated young audience that was raised on the rock beat; it has the largest public of any form of twentieth-century art music.

In the early work of Terry Riley (b. 1935) we can hear the very quick transition from concept art to a full-blown and popular form of minimal neo-tonality. The Zen works of Cage and the aleatory pieces of Feldman are, in their individual ways, highly non-structural, non-tonal, and even non-composed. Riley's *In C* (1964), on the other hand, is (as its title suggests) all about tonality. It is a scheme for a performance in which 53 separate melodic phrases are repeated over a steady pulse in free, endless, overlapping sequence. The structural and philosophical aspects of the work tend to disappear under the overwhelming presence of the diatonic C, out of which everything is made and which nothing (except for a reinforcing F♯) is allowed to oppose or contradict. (See Appendix: Example 19–2.) In *Poppy Nogood and the Phantom Band* (1967; recorded in 1969), for soprano saxophone and electric organ, Riley himself is the only performer; his simple, modal phrases on the saxophone are extended, theoretically to infinity, by means of tape loops—creating an effect like the face-to-face mirrors in a barber shop. *A Rainbow in Curved Air* (1969) uses various electric instruments and a distinctively pop sound as its subject matter. The sensual (and cultural) effect of this material has taken over from the conceptual.

These early works of Riley were extraordinarily influential. Minimalism—largely conceived and developed outside of the musical establishment (and with the composer as performer)—spread quickly and widely. Riley, himself, having set a direction, did not pursue it. Like a number of composers of the time he turned to the study of Eastern music, working with a North Indian master musician and concentrating on vocal performance music. In the late 1970's, however, he returned to instrumental music with a series of works for the Kronos Quartet in California (*G Song*, 1973–1981; *Sunrise of the Planetary Dream Collector*, 1981; *Cadenza on the Night Plain*, 1984); the minimalism of these works was modified by Riley's experience of Indian music and by the influence of jazz performance style.

The composer who best represents the structural possibilities of minimalism and its potential for development is Steve Reich (b. 1936). Reich first became known for tape-loop pieces such as *It's Gonna Rain* (1965) and *Come Out* (1966). By changing the stereo synchronization and phasing of a short, spoken phrase of high profile and energy captured on tape (from a sermon of a black Pentecostal preacher for *It's Gonna Rain*, from testimony of a black youth involved in Harlem riots in the mid-1960's for *Come Out*), and by superimposing the changes on what had gone before, Reich produced large, cumulative, hallucinating effects. The result is not merely a hypnotic aural experience but a series of changing perceptual patterns and illusions. *Violin Phase* (1967) uses a live performer with taped patterns in a similar way. *Four Organs* and *Phase Patterns* (both 1970 and both for four electric organs with percussion) are live-performance pieces. At that time Reich established his own performing ensemble, studied with a master drummer in Ghana, and continued to develop his ideas in performance. One immediate result was the hour-and-a-half-long *Drumming* of 1971, scored for drums and mallet instruments with amplified voices integrated into the ensemble. In this work and in the slighter *Clapping* (1972) for two pairs of hands, Reich brought the idea of a music based on phase shifting—what he calls "process"—to its logical extreme.

In the middle 1970's Reich's music began to evolve in new directions. To the basic ensemble of percussion, keyboards, and amplified ensemble voices, he gradually added winds and strings, notably in *Music for 18 Musicians* (1974–1976), *Music for a Large Ensemble* (1978), *Octet* (1979)—Reich's first mature work for a conventional ensemble—and *Variations for Winds, Strings and Keyboard* (1979), which was also arranged for orchestra. Reich tempered his earlier obsession with phasing and process; a real sense of harmonic movement and larger phrase structure appeared for the first time in his music. He also gradually modified his instrumentation in the direction of classical chamber and orchestral combinations. These works established a large popular public for Reich's work at the same time that they made his music and his esthetic more acceptable to traditional musical institutions. (See Appendix: Example 19–3.)

Tehillim (1981) was commissioned by the Southwest German Radio and the Rothko Chapel in Houston, Texas. It was initially scored for voices and Reich's own ensemble; a larger version for chorus and orchestra was first performed by the New York Philharmonic in 1982. The use of texts (the biblical psalms in Hebrew) was new in Reich's music and it altered the character of his music. The voices are used to project the texts rather than, as in his earlier works, serving simply as instrument-like parts in the ensemble; the rhythm of the Hebrew and the meaning of the words profoundly influenced how they are set. As a result, Reich composed much longer lines and replaced his usual steady underlying pulse with more complex metrics. This evolution continued in *The Desert Music* (1982–1983), an hour-long work for chorus and orchestra using texts of William Carlos Williams. Like *Tehillim*, this is a multi-movement cycle of symphonic proportions and quality. Both the regularity of pulse and the short repeated phrases of Reich's earlier work appear, but also a more extended style of text setting, vocal line, and rhythm.

In his later music, Reich has moved away from pure repetition and slow change—from pure "process"—towards a much more developmental and symphonic form, without, however, losing the individual character of his own style. The evolution of an ongoing rhythmic tonality using cycles of harmonies and the expansion of the principle of repetition and rhythmic cycles have taken Reich's music from a decorative, hypnotic, and rather abstract form of minimalism towards an ongoing narrative form—with the character, however, not of dramatic conflict but of a lyric journey.

Reich has long (and unsuccessfully) attempted to designate his music as "structural" rather than "minimal." The former term has an important meaning outside of music in the work of anthropologists, semanticists, and psychologists concerned with problems of perception and culture. They hold that there are basic patterns in the brain—structures for visual and aural grammar as well as for language—against which new information is perceived, gathered in, and evaluated. According to this view, tonality, rhythmic pulse, and repetitive patterns correspond to structures in the brain—synapses or neural pathways—which are held to be common or universal in human beings; hence the use of regular, pulsating rhythm and tonal forms in much ethnic and popular music; hence also the strong impact that minimalism has had on popular audiences and the more adventurous pop and rock composers.

Along with Reich, Philip Glass (b. 1937) is the first American "classical" composer to command a mass public—due to both the nature of his music and the changing character of the audience. Glass studied at the Juilliard School and with Milhaud at Aspen; he began as an extremely prolific composer in traditional "modernist" idioms. In the mid-1960's he worked with Nadia Boulanger in Paris, but also for a time with Ravi Shankar and Alla Rakha. In 1967 he formed his own ensemble in New York and created a series of radically minimalist works, mostly for winds and electric keyboards: *Pieces in the Shape of a Square* (1967), *Music in Fifths* (1969), *Music with Changing Parts* (1970), *Music in Twelve Parts* (1971–1974), *Another Look at Harmony* (1975; the source of much of the music for *Einstein on the Beach*). Although most of Glass's earlier music was instrumental, he also worked in the theater in the mid-1970's, largely with Mabou Mines, founded in 1970 and one of the most fertile of the new theater ensembles. In 1976 he collaborated with the designer-director Robert Wilson on the monumental theater work *Einstein on the Beach*—first performed at the Avignon Festival in France, then across Europe, and finally at the Metropolitan Opera House (but not with the Metropolitan Opera Company) in New York. Wilson's stage style consists of a visual libretto—a series of stage images or tableaux grouped in non-narrative form around a subject (Albert Einstein and technological society in this case)—using slow-motion or repetitious movement in great cycles; the parallels with musical minimalism are obvious. There are spoken texts (also repeated). The singing is confined to a chorus in the pit; the sung texts are syllables and numbers, all delivered in a very ritualistic manner. The work is scored for an expanded version of Glass's ensemble, with amplified voices blended into the instrumental ensemble. The motoric impulses of the music—inspired by a railroad train and other images of technology which dominate the stage—provide energy and a ritualistic effect that evokes the ancient idea of music as magic. The work is a long meditation (more than four hours) in visual and aural form about rational and technological man that takes the form of a magical and incantatory ritual.

After *Einstein*, Glass embarked on a major career as a theater, opera, and film composer. *Dance* (1979), for the choreographer Lucinda Childs, uses film and dance. *Satyagraha* (1980), on the life of Gandhi and using texts drawn from the *Bhagavad Gita*, and *Akhnaten* (1984), on the life of the Egyptian pharaoh, are opera-house operas written for operatic voices, large stage forces, and the traditional orchestra. Glass also produced music for two films, *North Star* (1974) and *Koyaanisqatsi* (1982), as well as *A Madrigal Opera*, staged at one time as *The Panther* (1982), a theater piece for singers, actors, musicians, and panther. In *The Juniper Tree* (1985) Glass collaborated with another composer, Robert Moran, on a narrative story from the Brothers Grimm that combines motives of jealousy, murder, and redemption. The themes of music as ritual and magic are used to good effect. The contributions of the two composers are easily separable: Glass's music is more on the surface, evocative, magical, very much defining the fairy-tale climate of the work; Moran provides a more archetypal, dramatic, and even psychological note. The presence of the two styles actually translates the conflict—the good-evil dualism of the story—into musical terms.

In 1986 Glass made a recording called *Songs From Liquid Days*, working with some well-known, mostly popular songwriters as his lyricists (Laurie Anderson, Paul Simon, Suzanne Vega, David Byrne). This would seem to reinforce the common view that he deliberately created or imitated rock styles. In fact the opposite is true; he had a major influence on pop music in the late rock era—notably on the work of English experimental rockers and studio creators like Robert Fripp (b. 1946) and Brian Eno, but also on David Byrne (b. 1952) of Talking Heads (who also collaborated with Robert Wilson) and other younger musicians who regard rock as art and the rock song as an art form (see Chapter 20). Glass's song album merely reverses the direction of an already existing crossover; rather than trying to create a new public, it is an homage, very much on his own terms, to the popular audience already involved in his music.

Minimalism has strong West Coast roots: Terry Riley was born in California; both Young and Steve Reich did their first important work there. John Adams (b. 1947) and Paul Dresher represent two forms of California minimalism, one oriented towards symphonic work, the other towards music-theater. Adams's *Grand Pianola Music* (1981–1982) is scored for winds, brass, percussion, pianos, and voices used as part of the ensemble. His earlier *Harmonium* for chorus and orchestra (1980–1981) and his later *Harmonielehre* for large orchestra (1985) are more traditionally scored and, as the titles suggest, he makes a major effort—typical of much minimalist work—to regain and use tonal harmony in a fresh way. Like the neo-Romantics, Adams uses a more-or-less traditional orchestra, and his harmonic world often evokes the turn of the century—early Schoenberg, Berg, Mahler, even Ives or Debussy—but always in a distinctive and personal manner.

His opera *Nixon in China* (1986–1987) is a large-scale work of popular character in which the European opera form, American minimalist style, and a witty gloss on Eastern music crossover with presentational theater in the manner of Robert Wilson or the Mabou Mines troupe (see pp. 240–42).

Paul Dresher's work is more explicitly theatrical. His collaborations with George Coates (*The Way of How*, 1981; *areare*, 1983; *See/Hear*, 1984) are clever, illusionistic multi-media pieces that play visual and aural games. In *See/Hear* the set is white, the players, singers, and conductor wear white clothes, and there is a long sequence of projections which makes the performers seem to appear and disappear; the music has a similarly illusionistic and kaleidoscopic quality. *Slow Fire* (1985–1986) is a more dramatic music-theater piece with strong elements from rock and rap music.

The tendency towards steady-state minimalism has been very widespread—in the popular as well as high-culture arts. The brief rise and immense popularity of disco in the mid-1970's is as potent an illustration of this as are the more sophisticated works of Reich, Glass, and Adams. What started as a quirky and personal trend among conceptual artists—one among many—has come to dominate large areas of new music here and abroad. Tonality by assertion, cyclical repetition, slow and non-dialectical development, lengthy periods of formal time, and a return to tonal, metrical, and structural simplicity can now be considered as the mainstream of new music of all types—concert, theatrical, pop. This has helped to break down the old categories; the distance (or at least the perception of the distance) between the genres has never been narrower.

BIBLIOGRAPHICAL NOTES

For one report on the Darmstadt controversy, see Lisa Dominick's article "Darmstadt 1984" in *Perspectives of New Music* 23/2 (1985), 274–91. For information on many of the American composers discussed in this chapter, see John Rockwell's *All-American Music: Composition in the Late Twentieth Century* (New York, 1983) as well as Cole Gagne and Tracy Caras's *Soundpieces: Interviews with American Composers* (Metuchen, NJ, and London, 1982), which includes conversations with Robert Ashley, Milton Babbitt, Henry Brant, John Cage, George Crumb, Mario Davidovsky, Charles Dodge, Jacob Druckman, Morton Feldman, Ross Lee Finney, Lukas Foss, Philip Glass, Lejaren Hiller, Ben Johnston, Barbara Kolb, Conlon Nancarrow, Steve Reich, Roger Reynolds, George Rochberg, Roger Sessions, Ralph Shapey, and Charles Wuorinen.

For the European neo-expressionists, see especially Ernst H. Flammer's *Politisch engagierte Musik als kompositorisches Problem: dargestellt am Beispiel von Luigi Nono und Hans Werner Henze* (Baden-Baden, 1981) and Hans Werner Henze's *Music and Politics: Collected Writings, 1953–1981* (trans. Peter Labanyi; Ithaca, NY, 1982). Paul Griffiths's *New Sounds, New Personalities: British Composers of the 1980s* (London, 1985) includes interviews with Maxwell Davies, Knussen, Brian Ferneyhough, John Taverner, Gavin Bryars, and Harrison Birtwhistle, among others; his study of Maxwell Davies (Contemporary Composers Series, London, 1982) concerns mainly the music. For Maxwell Davies, see also the volume edited by Stephen Pruslin, *Peter Maxwell Davies: Studies from Two Decades* (Tempo Booklet #2, London, 1979).

Wim Mertens's *American Minimal Music: La Monte Young, Terry Riley, Steve Reich, Philip Glass* (trans. J. Hautekeit, preface by Michael Nyman, London and New York, 1983) attempts to trace the historical background of the minimalist idea through certain European compositions of the early and middle twentieth century; it also discusses the basic concepts in the work of the composers listed in the title. Nyman's *Experimental Music: Cage and Beyond*, cited in the bibliography for Chapter 1, contains an extended discussion of the minimalist idea in music, and gives examples from English composers as well. La Monte Young and Marian Zazeela's *Selected Writings* (Munich, 1969) and Steve Reich's *Writings about Music* (Halifax, Nova Scotia, 1974) explain the music from each composer's point of view; K. Robert Schwarz's "Steve Reich: Music as a Gradual Process," *Perspectives of New Music* (Fall/Winter 1980 and Spring/Summer 1981, pp. 373–92; Fall/Winter 1981 and Spring/Summer 1982, pp. 225–286) is a detailed survey of that composer's work through *Tehillim*. Schwarz's "Young American Composers: John Adams," *Music and Musicians* (March 1985, pp. 10–11) is one of a series of articles by him on young American composers.

TWENTY

POP AS CULTURE

There is a close bond between the social and musical forms of American popular music and the new tonalities of the 1970's and 1980's—just as there was in the 1930's, half a century earlier. For various reasons, a major survey of American popular music and its offshoots is not possible within the framework of this book; however, two closely related issues will be considered here. One is the revival of the view that popular culture *is* art and that American popular music and jazz constitute our major contribution to world culture. The other involves the crossing-over, the cross-fertilization of ideas and idioms, between high culture and the vernacular.

JAZZ AND ROCK

Scott Joplin (1868–1917), W. C. Handy (1873–1958), James Reese Europe (1881–1919), James P. Johnson (1894–1955), and many other early black ragtime, blues, and jazz musicians wanted to be taken seriously as artists. Joplin wrote two operas (*A Guest of Honor*, 1903; *Treemonisha*, 1911) and a ballet (*The Ragtime Dance*, 1906); Europe organized a black symphony orchestra before World War I (the Clef Club Symphony Orchestra); Handy and Johnson gave Carnegie Hall concerts (1928, 1938, 1944). Duke Ellington (1899–1974) composed in larger forms (*Black, Brown, and Beige*, 1933–1943; *New World a-Comin?*, 1945; *Harlem*, 1950); towards the end of his life he wrote or arranged works for symphony orchestra and left an unfinished "street opera" (*Queenie Pie*; completed and produced in 1986).

The contemporary view is that even the most untutored jazz musicians—Louis Armstrong (1900–1971), Fats Waller (1904–1943), Jelly Roll Morton (1890–1941), the great swing musicians of the 1930's—can be considered among the important creative artists of the century. With the advent of bop in the 1940's, jazz musicians began to think and create consciously as artists, and in fact their work has many connections with mainstream modernism. Charlie Parker (1920–1955), Dizzy Gillespie (b. 1917), Miles Davis (b. 1926), Bud Powell (1924–1966), Charles Mingus (1922–1979), and others were playing and improvising in highly personal and creative styles outside the mainstream of popular art; their music was dissonant, chromatic, full of complex and asymmetrical cross-rhythms—in short, virtuosic. Big bands of the time—particularly those of Woody Herman (b. 1913) and Stan Kenton (1912–1979)—and experimental originals like Thelonius Monk (1917–1982), Lennie Tristano (1919–1978), John Coltrane (1926–1967), Eric Dolphy (1928–1964), and (in a very different way) the Modern Jazz Quartet (active 1954–1974) brought jazz to a point where only a few elements—mainly instrumentation and the use of improvisation—separated it from its "classical" counterparts.

After 1960 many of these musicians almost completely cut their ties to tonality, chord changes, popular tunes, and metrical regularity. The so-called free jazz of Coltrane, Ornette Coleman (b. 1930), Sun Ra (b. 1914), Chick Corea (b. 1941), and Cecil Taylor (b. 1933) is expressed in a fully chromatic atonality that corresponds closely to the atonal modernism of composed, notated, European-derived music but with the freer energy of a performance-practice, improvised style. Much of the best jazz of the 1960s and 1970s—the music of men like Albert Ayler (1936–1970), Archie Shepp (b. 1937), Anthony Braxton (b. 1945), Leroy Jenkins (b. 1932), Leo Smith (b. 1941), and the Art Ensemble of Chicago (active 1968–)—was associated with the black-liberation movement and with firm convictions on the part of the musicians about their work as art. Many composers and critics associated with recent developments do not use the word "jazz" and have proposed the term "American classical music" as a substitute.

Like other forms of modern music, jazz also experienced a movement back to tonality—or in some cases modality. So-called modal jazz and various rock-jazz fusions have been espoused by a number of creative musicians; certain albums of Miles Davis (*Kind of Blue*, 1959; *In a Silent Way* and

Bitches Brew, both from 1969), and even of John Coltrane (*My Favorite Things*, 1960; *A Love Supreme*, 1964; *Ascension*, 1965) and Ornette Coleman (*The Shape of Jazz to Come*, 1959) have followed this path. Composer-performers such as Bill Evans (1929–1980), Keith Jarrett (b. 1945), and Anthony Davis (b. 1951) have crossed the lines between jazz and contemporary "classical" music with complete ease and skill. Davis, who was trained at the Yale School of Music, mixes written scores and improvisation. His opera *X (The Life and Times of Malcolm X)* (1984–1986) puts his group, Episteme, in the middle of an opera orchestra, and makes fully operatic demands on the singers. This is in no sense a "jazz opera" but a fully contemporary stage work that is informed by the black-music tradition and infused with the powerful energy of improvisation.

Traditional jazz was closely allied with popular song. It is ironic that, while progressive free jazz was severing its links with pop music, some striking developments were taking place in the popular song field. One was the recognition of the American popular song as an art form. Almost at the very moment when it seemed that rock had made Tin Pan Alley obsolete, the latter began to be taken seriously, and the pop songs and show tunes of Jerome Kern (1885–1945), Irving Berlin (1888–), Richard Rodgers (1902–1979), Cole Porter (1871–1964), and others began to be viewed as "classics."

The initial sources of American popular music were the operettas and revues—originally of European origin—and the Victorian salon and dance music that were extremely popular at the end of the last century. The particular genius of the American popular song in the 1920's was due in part to its incorporation of the rhythmic and melodic forms of black-American jazz—a development made possible by the fact that jazz had absorbed the tonality and harmonic progressions of Euro-American popular music.

The new popular song of the 1950's was very different. Rock-and-roll, derived from black rhythm-and-blues and dominated by a heavy beat, a few repeated changes, and strong sexual connotations, seemed an unlikely candidate for artistic development. But it proved immensely adaptable, merging with or incorporating elements from gospel and other black music, country-and-western, folk music, jazz, and even non-Western, minimalist, and electronic music. The lyrics of rock (the "-and-roll" part of the term was soon dropped) marked a departure—or, rather, series of departures—for popular music. The influence of, first, country music and later the politically conscious folk-song movement gave rock much greater breadth and enabled it to cross cultural, racial, and social lines.

The folk-song movement dated back at least to the 1930's, under the influence of ethnomusicologists like Alan Lomax and Charles Seeger (the father of the folk singer Pete Seeger and a notable "convert" from avant-gardism). The first great figure of the folk-song movement was Woody Guthrie (1912–1967), who perhaps more than anyone else established the idea that American folk song was not a dead art for scholars to study but a living form, close to the popular psyche and with a strong social and political agenda. There are direct connections between the earlier folk-song movement and the work of singer-writers like Bob Dylan (b. 1941). Dylan and his cohorts of the 1960's carried the new folk song from acoustic to electric instrumentation, from the coffee houses, college campuses, and political rallies into the center of the rock-music business, creating the genre known as folk-rock and reaching new audiences of millions. Instead of the limited vocabulary of private emotions (mostly dealing with love and sex) and the limited verse forms of the old Tin Pan Alley songs, rock lyrics started to cover a whole range of subject matter from the personal to the public; the songs themselves, much less conventionalized in form than the old pop AABA, used narrative and ballad forms derived from poetry. Dylan also continued the détente between rock and country music started by the Everly Brothers in the late 1950's and 1960's. The blues revival and the new mass appeal of country music launched a kind of neo-classical or revivalist movement which was quickly extended to include the resuscitation of ragtime, many forms of earlier jazz and pop, and early rock-and-roll.

The new folk-rock, the social upheavals of the 1960's, and the vogue for pop art and culture were simultaneous. In addition to folk-rock, the black music of Motown and the California styles of the Beach Boys and the San Francisco Bay area "acid rockers"—Jefferson Airplane (active 1965–1973), the Grateful Dead (active 1967–), Jimi Hendrix (1942–1970)—spread quickly and widely. Acid rock was, as its name suggests, strongly associated with drugs and drop-out culture and, later, with political protest. The electric sound—a fusion of rock and blues with electric guitars and a lot of outboard electronics—and the omnipresent light show moved rock music close to the conditions of electronic music and multi-media.

The cross-cultural nature of rock is best illustrated by a group of working-class English boys from Liverpool who learned their music from old rock-and-roll recordings. The Beatles (active 1962–1971), true children of the electronic age, ranged across the spectrum of popular music from English music hall to swing and various advanced forms of rock, mixing the whole with elements of classical music, from chamber to electronic. They used recording technology to merge these styles, taking what appealed to them (or what they needed) and making it their own. In their last recordings as a group (*Sgt. Pepper's Lonely Hearts Club Band*, 1967; *The Beatles*, 1968; *Abbey Road*, 1969), they appeared to be moving towards larger forms and concepts; these albums are not just collections of songs but have larger overall artistic and theatrical shape. Although The Beatles scored their initial successes as a live performing group (in Liverpool, in Germany, and then in the United States), the recording medium became, in effect, their real instrument, on which (with the help of producer George Martin) they played with much skill.

In all of this, the simple and characteristic beat of rock music was the single unifying factor (although even that was eventually to be expanded through the use of rhythmic and metrical overlays). Greater stylistic complexity was combined with a high level of melodic invention. The old Tin Pan Alley songwriter was replaced by a new breed of composer-author-performer. The new technologies were extensively and creatively incorporated into the music; the creative center was no longer live performance but the recording studio, where multi-track techniques and electric/electronic instrumentation elevated the studio recording to the status of high art. The Hit Parade or Top 40 mentality which had dominated pop music for decades was circumvented by using "classical" means of dissemination: the long-playing stereo record album, FM radio, live performance in untraditional locales, festivals, and college-circuit tours. The most popular songs eventually reached the larger public through the mass media, but even some of the more arcane, political, and experimental work achieved surprising success.

The evolution of cultural forms is often described as a cycle. A period of growth is followed by a stable, "classical" period when popularity and artistic quality are in balance. Diversity and break-up bring experimentation, fragmentation, shakedown, and breakdown. Eventually there may be a period or periods of revival and "neo-classicism." Such a cycle, which took place in European classical music over many centuries, lasted only three-quarters of a century in jazz and hardly twenty-five years in rock. In the course of this speeded-up evolution, both jazz and rock evolved from a vernacular music with roots in black culture to a popular art with wide (indeed worldwide) appeal; both became sophisticated art forms, with the possibility of interacting or crossing over with other sophisticated art forms.

The influence of rock has been so widespread and pervasive that it is difficult to assess. More than one generation has now grown up with this music, and it has become the natural means of expression or the basic listening repertory of many millions. Rock has black and populist roots, but it was disseminated in its present forms largely by middle-class artists who chose it—as a previous generation had chosen jazz—over more conventional forms. It has now fractured into specialized camps and styles, from the so-called middle-of-the-road to the most avant-garde. There are many paradoxes here. As a reaction to traditional and established musics, rock was long regarded as revolutionary in its message and appeal. But it is an essentially electronic/media music that is highly dependent on technology and, therefore, depends on marketplace economics and corporate policies for its ultimate diffusion.

As the inevitable popularization and commercialization of rock began to take place, experimental avant-garde reactions began appearing almost immediately. Beginning in the late 1960's, Frank Zappa (b. 1940) produced a pop-Dada mixture of rock, jazz, classical modernism (even atonal expressionism), camp and nostalgia, parody and protest, satire, and music theater, mixing them into a personal style that he later carried into the concert world. Zappa's music actually incorporates two distinct directions. One is jazz-rock fusion, which has been pursued from the rock side by groups like Chicago (originally Chicago Transit Authority; active 1968–) and Blood, Sweat and Tears (active 1967–) and from the jazz side by Miles Davis and Weather Report (active 1970–). The other is frankly experimental; it can be represented by the Velvet Underground, a group formed by Lou Reed (b. 1944) and John Cale (b. 1942), associated with Andy Warhol, and active in New York from 1966 to 1969. It was the first of a number of groups which bridged the gap between rock and the downtown avant-garde. In 1971 in England Brian Eno and Brian Ferry (b. 1945) founded the short-lived but influential Roxy Music; Eno produced many unusual experimental records that were ignored by the avant-garde modernists but had an important influence on rock. In both England and Germany there was an important development of new-music rock: Pink Floyd (active 1964–), King Crimson (active 1969–1974), Emerson, Lake and Palmer (active 1969–1979), and the German Tangerine Dream and Kraftwerk (both active since the late 1960's) were among the groups that pursued the experimental, idealistic, art-music side of rock throughout the 1970's. Punk rock, also an English phenomenon, was a short-lived form of protest music with working-class origins. Out of it came the so-called "new wave" groups of the late 1970's: The Clash (active 1976–), The Police (active 1977–), and Elvis Costello (b. 1955) in England; Patti Smith (b. 1946), The Cars (active 1976–), Devo (active 1972–), the B-52s (active 1976–), and, especially, Talking Heads (active 1976–) in the United States. American new-wave rock and its art-rock successors are very closely identified with the downtown New York scene—SoHo, Tribeca, and the Lower East Side—where the galleries, lofts, and clubs, and the art public that patronizes this kind of new rock are located. Very close relationships exist between such rock and visual and performance arts. David Byrne, Chris Frantz (b. 1951), and Tina Weymouth (b. 1950), who started the Talking Heads, were all art students at the Rhode Island School of Design; Byrne has worked independently as a composer for Robert Wilson and choreographer Twyla Tharp. Laurie Anderson (b. 1947) studied classical violin, but some of her work—notably *O Superman* (1980) from *United States*—has been released as pop songs. Her work is as much verbal, visual, and theatrical as it is musical (see page 239), and she is not easy to categorize in the traditional way.

These experimental tendencies demonstrate a conflict or tension between improvisational atonality and the persistence of traditional rock tonalities or—more accurately in the case of folk or ethnic-influenced music—modalities. The old-fashioned pop song is tonal in the traditional European sense, based on tension and release (the middle section or bridge is in fact often called the "release"). The typical rock song, on the other hand, like many folk songs, has no release; it is modal or very simply tonal with no moments of dramatic opposition or resolution. The form is cyclical or incremental rather than dramatic or dialectical. Disco is the *reductio ad absurdum* of these tendencies; one disco tune can be run right into another without a pause or transition. At another end of the spectrum is a Glass-like minimalism as transmitted by such experimental rock musicians as Robert Fripp and Brian Eno. Still a third extreme can be represented by the very aggressive tendencies of certain art rockers infatuated with loud noise and their popular counterparts, the so-called heavy-metal bands. These highly expressionist descendants of acid rock and certain forms of electronic music are characterized by rather nihilist—i.e., non-political—forms of protest and cultism.

Although popular music and rock itself have split up into a considerable number of categories, often with specialized publics, crossovers are common and there are increasing numbers of musicians and other creative artists whose work cannot easily be categorized as exclusively "pop" or "art." Among the younger musicians working in the area between minimalism, neo-expressionism, pop, and rock are Glenn Branca (b. 1948), Peter Gordon (b. 1951), Rhys Chatham (b. 1952), Todd Rundgren (b. 1948), and Scott Johnson (b. 1952). In the same way, the lines between the visual arts, poetry, theater, and other entertainment forms have become blurred. One speaks of new movement theater, the new vaudevillians, new music theater, new dance theater, or new performance art without any clarity as to where the lines between them are actually drawn—if they can be drawn at all. Art and entertainment move uneasily closer together. William Bolcom (b. 1938) has written a three-hour vocal-choral-symphonic setting of William Blake's *Songs of Innocence and Experience* (1956–1982) with rock interpolations; he also composes ragtime and performs old popular and cabaret songs with his wife, Joan Morris. The Kronos Quartet plays dance music for encores. The Tango Project, put together by composers (Michael Sahl and William Schimmel [b. 1946] with the author), revives the old palm court; both Sahl and Schimmel incorporate tangos into "serious" instrumental, vocal, and theatrical works. Robert Moran and Yvar Mikhashoff have organized sets of new waltzes and tangos that are half serious, half "new Kitsch." The lines between vernacular and high art, between art and entertainment, seem to blur or want to disappear.

NON-WESTERN CURRENTS AND NEW-AGE MUSIC

Post-modernism, like the comparable period between the world wars, is characterized by a major revival of interest in ethnic and folk styles. The new regionalism of the 1980's, like the national movements earlier in the century, involves more than parochialism; it is a natural (and not undesirable) result of composers cultivating their own backyards rather than creating for an international avant-garde that is widely but thinly spread across the global network. This new localism is inspired not by old-fashioned nationalism but by a resurgence of local traditions and a widely perceived need for artists to re-establish connections with their culture and public. At the same time (and somewhat paradoxically), there has been an international interest in and influence from non-Western styles.

In the earlier part of the century, Eastern Europeans led the way; there was also a considerable growth of interest in Anglo and Latino folk cultures and, to a degree, in Eastern arts as well. In recent times, this has extended more widely to the Asian, African, native-American, and other traditions loosely known as Third World. This has had a number of important consequences. It has turned composers from non-Western countries back towards native traditions (for instance, in the later work of the Japanese composer Toru Takemitsu [b. 1930]). It has brought composers and musicians from Third World countries increasingly into the international mainstream. And it has led to a wider Third World influence on both popular and art music everywhere.

The influence of "exotic" musics in the West goes back at least to Debussy, but its first major impact, in the 1930's and 1940's, was in the work of Cage, Harrison, Cowell, McPhee, Partch, and Hovhaness. World War II brought an invasion of non-Western cultures by Western pop music; nearly every major urban area in the world now has a popular music based on a mixture of local styles and Euro-American pop. Subsequently, genuine local rock styles have developed in many places; Africa, which gave so much to American music, has now absorbed Western jazz and rock and is in the process of developing new amalgams. In Japan, India, and Indonesia, new music for traditional, national forms and media is again being produced after a long period of stagnation or subordination to Western styles. In the West, interest in Third World musics—traditional and contemporary—has increased considerably; many avant-garde concert locales now regularly include non-Western music. Some of this new Third World music is traditional, but much of it reflects the cross-currents of international pop, traditional Western music, and even the avant-garde.

There are many lines of connection between new-tonal music, minimalism, and Third World music. Composers like Young, Riley, and Reich have worked with master musicians from non-Western cultures and have been stimulated or inspired by their divergent traditions. And in turn the popularity of modal rock and minimalism has helped make many forms of non-Western music accessible to Western audiences.

Not all of the non-traditional instruments found in recent new music are electronic. Many of the instruments invented by Partch were modeled on Eastern and African instruments. The Japanese shakuhachi, African mbira, the sitar and tabla from India, Peruvian panpipes, and others are now used with some regularity in Western music. Indonesian gamelan—instrumental ensembles of mostly percussion instruments—have been imported into Europe and America for many years; in recent years, new ones (not always conforming to the original Indonesian models) have been built. As many as 100 gamelan are reported to be in use in the United States and there are approximately 40 in Europe; among these are Gamelan Pacifica in Seattle, Gamelan Son of Lion in New York, the English Gamelan Orchestra, and a similar group in Amsterdam. New music is being written for gamelan—in the West and in Indonesia itself. Similarly, there have been crossovers between Indian music and jazz, and new repertoire for and by Indian musicians is being created again—even in India.

The influence of both Eastern music and minimalism is apparent in the phenomenon known as new-age music. An upsurge of interest in spiritualism, nature mysticism, Eastern religions and philosophy, meditation, and the occult has produced a whole genre of associated, meditative music. Ritualism and meditation in music are not new; they have in fact interested many contemporary composers, notably Stockhausen, in his later work (*Stimmung; Mantra*); La Monte Young, in his preoccupation with non-tempered tunings; and Pauline Oliveros, in a series of sonic meditations and ceremonial pieces. There are now a number of composers in Europe, Japan, and America who are barely recognized at all in the art-music world but have achieved considerable popularity through radio and recordings as writers, or producers, of so-called new-age or space music. One of the best known and most successful of these music-makers is the Swiss harpist and composer Andreas Vollenweider (b. 1953; *Behind the Gardens*, 1981; *Down to the Moon*, 1986); another is the American pianist George Winston (b. 1949; *Winter into Spring*, 1980; *Autumn* and *December*, 1982). Much of this music cannot be performed live but is media-produced, largely on synthesizers. The music of the Japanese composer Kitaro, the German Klaus Schulze, the Greek Vangelis, the French composers Maurice Jarre and his son Jean-Michel, and the American Steven Halpern are largely synthesized products of the electronic age which, unlike rock and other earlier electronic music, are meant to provide a soothing alternative to the heavier rhythms of contemporary urban life—the contemporary equivalent of the easy-listening music of an older generation.

BIBLIOGRAPHICAL NOTES

Many good sources for jazz have come out in the last few years. For the early period of jazz, see Gunther Schuller's *Early Jazz: Its Roots and Development* (New York, 1968), which goes up through the early works of Ellington (early

1930's). For the later period, see Joachim-Ernst Berendt's *The Jazz Book: From New Orleans to Rock and Fusion Jazz* (trans. Dan Morgenstern, New York, 1975). For the jazz giants, see Martin Williams's *The Jazz Tradition* (new and revised ed., Oxford, 1983), Mark C. Gridley's *Jazz Styles* (Englewood Cliffs, NJ, 1978), and Marshall W. Stearns's *The Story of Jazz* (New York, 1970). Leonard Feather's *Encyclopedia Yearbook of Jazz* (New York, 1956) and its two supplementary volumes (*The Encyclopedia of Jazz in the Sixties* [New York, 1966] and *The Encyclopedia of Jazz in the Seventies* [New York, 1976]) contain extended entries on the major and minor jazz figures; see also John Chilton's *Who's Who of Jazz: Storyville to Swing Street* (London, 1970). The *Journal of Jazz Studies* (founded in 1973) has been replaced by the *Annual Review of Jazz Studies*.

For Tin Pan Alley and other types of popular song in America, see Charles Hamm's *Yesterdays: Popular Song in America* (New York, 1979) and his *Music in the New World* (New York, 1983) as well as Alec Wilder's *American Popular Song: The Great Innovators 1900–1950* (New York, 1972) and H. Wiley Hitchcock's *Music in the United States* (3rd ed., Englewood Cliffs, NJ, 1988).

There has been a veritable explosion of writing on pop and rock music. See Arnold Shaw's *Honkers and Shouters* (New York, 1977) for the transition of jazz to rock-and-roll, Lillian Roxon's *Rock Encyclopedia* (New York, 1969), Irwin Stambler's *Encyclopedia of Pop, Rock, and Soul* (New York, 1974), and *The Age of Rock*, ed. Jonathan Eisen (New York, 1969), for the early period of rock; and *The Rolling Stone Encyclopedia of Rock and Roll*, ed. Jon Pareles and Patricia Romanowski (New York, 1983) for information on more recent rock music and musicians. See also Mark W. Booth's *American Popular Music: A Reference Guide* (Westport, CT, 1983) for an exhaustive coverage of literature on rock. Two periodicals, *Rolling Stone* (San Francisco, then New York, 1967–) and *Melody Maker* (London, 1926–), are good sources of information on both recent and not-so-recent rock.

On crossover musicians, see John Rockwell's *All American Music*, cited in the bibliography for Chapter 19, which has chapters on the Art Ensemble of Chicago, Keith Jarrett, Ornette Coleman, Eddie Palmieri, Neil Young, and the Talking Heads; Ronald Radano's Ph.D. dissertation, *Anthony Braxton and His Two Musical Traditions, The Meeting of Concert Music and Jazz* (U. of Michigan [UMI Microfilms], 1985; to be published by U. of Illinois Press); Thomas B. Holmes's *Electronic and Experimental Music* (New York, 1985), which contains a chapter on rock music and electronics as well as an electronic music record guide with many rock entries; *Breaking the Sound Barrier: A Critical Anthology of the New Music*, ed. Gregory Battcock (New York, 1981), a collection of articles by authors as diverse as Dick Higgins, Jonathan Kramer, Earle Brown, Brian Eno, Steve Reich, and Hubert Howe writing on many of the issues concerning post-modern music; and K. Robert Schwarz's short article on Anthony Davis in *Music and Musicians* (January 1986, pp. 12–13).

For a discussion of new-age music as well as other recent musical trends, including the crossover phenomenon, see John Schaefer's *New Sounds: A*

Listener's Guide to New Music (New York, 1987). Schaefer has a well-known program on WNYC, the New York public radio station, called "New Sounds" and dealing largely with new-age music. Another public radio program devoted exclusively to this genre, "Music From the Hearts of Space," originates in San Francisco but has been disseminated throughout the country.

TWENTY ONE

MEDIA AND THEATER

MEDIA AND MULTI-MEDIA

The revival of tonality, the crossover of musical styles, and the expansion of the new-music public are connected not only to the revival of concert music but also to the revitalization of music theater. As we have seen, the dominance of instrumental and concert music in this century—threatened only briefly by the chamber opera, *Lehrstuck*, and *Zeitoper* of the 1920's and 1930's—was closely bound up with ideals of purity and abstraction. Post-modernism, far less abstract and pure, quickly re-established the connections with theater that had been broken off earlier in the century. Since the opera house and the commercial theater were no longer in a position to cultivate contemporary work, the most important new impulses came from the electronic media, from experimental theater, and from developments in the other arts, notably modern dance and dance theater.

As was the case with instrumental and concert music, the development of new media—beginning with film and mechanical recording earlier in the century but accelerating with the huge expansion of electronic media after World War II—was a major force for change. The Latin word "medium"—pl. "media"—is used in its widest sense simply to designate the physical means employed by a work of art. Pen-and-ink is a medium in the visual arts; so is oil paint on canvas or a design etched into a plate that is to be used for multiple reproduction. The illuminated manuscript is a medium; so is the printed book. The proscenium theater, opera house, and concert hall are traditional live-performance media, each with its own character, technical requirements, and institutional history. Radio, television, and the various forms of audio and video recording began primarily as reproductive media but have gradually evolved original forms, style, and repertoire. Early films were essentially photographed plays; later, novels and plays were adapted for the medium, and only recently has the original film-play come into its own. Similarly, traditional recording attempted to reproduce the sound of live performance; it is only with the development of tape and electronic music, the multi-track rock recording, so-called video art, and the rock video that these reproductive forms have achieved independent creative life.

Experimental media work by artists began in the early years of the century and has continued with varying degrees of interest and intensity ever since. The biggest impact has come not from the world of art, however, but from the original feature film, the multi-track rock recording, and the rock video, all of which have undergone major development since the 1970's. In Europe—and to a lesser degree in North America—public broadcasting has played an important patronage role in the development of original works for media, and music intended for radio or television and uniquely realizable on recording or film has become common in all forms of new music.

Works created for the medium of the stereo recording include examples as diverse as the Beatles' *Sgt. Pepper* album, Berio's *Visage*, Subotnick's *Silver Apples of the Moon* (1967) and the author's *The Nude Paper Sermon* (both commissioned by a record company), the *musique concrète* of Pierre Henry and Pierre Schaeffer, as well as the work of Jon Appleton (b. 1939), Ilhan Mimaroğlu (b. 1926), and others whose main output consists of tape music existing only in recorded form. Stockhausen's *Telemusik* (1966), originally realized for Japanese television; Kagel's *Ludwig van* (1969), a film for German television; the author's *Ecolog* (1971) for New York public television; and recent videos by Laurie Anderson are examples of works expressly created for television. Cage's *Roaratorio: An Irish Circus on Finnegans Wake* (based on texts of Joyce), some of the *Hörspiele* of Richard Kostelanetz (including his *New York City*, 1983–1984), the author's *Voices* (1971), *Civilization and Its Discontents* (1978), and *Boxes* (1981)—the last two collaborations with Michael Sahl—the solstice events of Charlie Morrow, and some of the phone-in and feed-back projects of Max Neuhaus were created for radio. Sahl's *A Woman's Face* (1970–1972) is a kind of pop opera in the form of a feature film by Ed Emshwiller, just as *THX 1138* (1971) by Walter Murch (b. 1943) is a *musique concrète* or collage opera in the form of a film by George Lucas.

Video art, an experimental medium in the 1970's, has since become part of mainstream culture through the medium of tape. Relatively portable and inexpensive television equipment—cameras, mixers, cassette tapes, and playback—has led to a major expansion of television or video art; this field has developed in close relationship with new music. Among the media and multi-media artists who are primarily musicians, we might mention Nam June Paik (b. 1932), the Korean-American composer and video artist, well known for his collaborations with the cellist and intermedia entrepreneur Charlotte Moorman (b. 1933). The Kitchen, a well-known new-music performance center and the model for many such institutions across the country, was founded for both experimental music and video by Woody and Steina Vasulka, video artists with a strong interest in music. Experimental video has covered the range of possibilities from *verité* or documentary performance material to dramatic work, electronically generated images, complex editing, electronic manipulation, and even computers and video synthesizers—all closely corresponding to developments in electronic and tape music. The music-video or rock-video form was directly influenced by these experiments—a good example of new artistic forms taken over for popular or commercial consumption. As is often the case, things have come full circle and the music video is now influencing the art world.

In his famous analysis of media, the Canadian critic Marshall McLuhan coined the phrase "the medium is the message." This is an exaggerated form of two important ideas: that media forms, in and of themselves, have an enormous impact on the course of culture, and that it is essential to understand the nature—technical, sensory, social—of media in order to appreciate what they can do. Television, for example, has been described as a low-resolution medium with a visual picture that is smaller than life, not sharply defined, and accompanied by poor sound; it is watched not in a communal setting, but in the isolation of the home and is typically received with a low degree of concentration or focus. Viewing is often intermittent, and the rough, grainy sound may actually get more continuous attention than the visual imagery. Thus the rock video, with its simple, strong musical beat, its surrealistic non-linear visual form (easily sampled in bits and pieces), and its need for relatively short periods of visual attention grows directly out of the nature of the medium.

As the mechanical or electronic media have gained independence, taken on their own character, and developed their own repertory and audience, they have begun to influence traditional performance media. Live music, theater, and opera today tend to be more cinematic with fast pacing, shorter sections, and more emphasis on the visual rather than the literary. Concert music of all types has now a strong tendency to sound like recorded music. Amplification in live performance, the structure of new concert halls, theaters, and opera houses, and the use of tape and electronic modifications in live performance have all tended to break down the distinctions between acoustic and electronic sound. The incorporation of mechnical or electronic media as part of live performance has become widespread. The challenge and influence of media art has affected the character of the live performance situation and influenced its evolution.

The term "mixed media" was originally used in the art world to designate a hybrid work employing two or more graphic techniques. "Mixed media," "multi-media," and "intermedia" became the common terms for hybrid inter-art works which incorporated live performance with mechanical or electronic elements. These modern equivalents of the Wagnerian *Gesamtkunstwerk*, or "total theater work," were large-scale environmental productions without a fixed time frame. Instead of closed, dramatic forms, time and space were extended on a continuum into cyclic or open forms of indefinite duration; the public was permitted to come and go at will.

The earliest major exposition of media in live performance may have been the San Francisco Trips Festival of 1965, in which several composers participated, notably Morton Subotnick. Subotnick, who has worked extensively with combinations of live and electronic means, collaborated with the visual artist Anthony Martin, who is credited with the development of liquid projections, one of the stand-by techniques of the rock-concert light show. Subotnick and Martin later worked at the Electric Circus, a rock emporium in New York, and collaborated on a number of multi-media and participatory works. Another landmark event in this area was the "Nine Evenings" Theater and Engineering concerts of 1966; these events, staged at the 69th Regiment armory in New York City as a collaboration between artists and scientists, sparked a major movement towards the use of technology by artists. One direct outcome was the formation of Experiments in Art and Technology, an organization which sponsored performances and exhibitions of new work. This kind of activity has expanded greatly in recent years. New media and multi-media work takes place not only in rock clubs and armories but in lofts and art galleries, in specially created performance spaces, even in planetariums and science museums. The author's *Can Man Survive?* was commissioned for the centennial of the American Museum of Natural History and exhibited in 1969–1971. It used the cyclical forms of minimalism with the techniques and scale of multi-media to form an ongoing walk-through interior environment reflecting the exterior environmental crisis. *Feedback* (1968–1969), a collaboration with the late visual artist Stan Vanderbeek, is a structure for an environmental, participatory work on a large scale into which an infinitely expandable range of live performance and media elements can be plugged. Audience participation is built into such works; the auditor/spectator creates a new form of the work at every moment as he or she focuses, selects, concentrates, or simply moves through the environment. Multi-media is a collaborative and free-form art at every level. If serialism and aleatory were dialectical opposites, then multi-media is the dialectical antithesis to minimalism. The minimalist takes a certain narrow area of experience and examines it in depth. Multi-media art does the reverse; it takes the range of experience as subject matter and presents a slice of it—a cross-grain cut, so to speak. Multi-media works are "about" the quality and nature of heightened experience and perception; they are "about" artistic experience communicated through overload and extreme.

Many of the traditional verities are challenged here, most especially the image of the alienated artist "expressing" himself and the notion of personality and style as a starting point for (rather than a natural result of) the creation of works of art. The mixing of the media and the categories of musical style; the close interaction among creator, performer, technician, and public; the marriage of the vernacular with high culture; the creation of new and total performance spaces; the use of time and space on a continuum; the art work as total theater; the banishment of "style" in favor of a cross-range of experience; the art work as a complex "ecological" system made up of a balanced diversity of systems and processes; the relationship between the inner artistic environment and the outer social environment— all these suggest major changes in the very notion and function of art.

Multi-media in its original state was a big, expensive entertainment for which it has become increasingly difficult to find financial support. Overload for the sake of overload and the quick commercialization of its superficial aspects contributed to its waning popularity. But the influence of media art and multi-media has become so widespread that it is now apparent in popular, commercial, and high culture. And the more recent and more contained forms of performance art and music theater are its direct evolutionary descendants.

PERFORMANCE ART AND MUSIC THEATER

Performance art and music theater are crossover forms, hybrids descended from the experimental media and theater forms of modernism but incorporating traditional and popular elements within the framework of post-modernism. They renew the age-old compact between music and theater and point the way towards the development of contemporary musical theater forms.

Performance art is a simpler, more focused descendant of multi-media. It is less collaborative and more likely to be based on the work and personality of a creative performer or director. Just as the new tonalities return to closed, settled forms, performance art uses the concert platform, the proscenium arch, and dramatic, closed forms (although sometimes of considerable length). By far the best-known artist associated with this genre is Laurie Anderson. Although the underlying focus of her work is music, she is equally a visual and verbal artist. She has created and popularized a personal style based on spoken words over repetitive musical patterns, a minimalist rock-derived sound, simple, effective visual imagery, electronic extensions, and subject matter that seems to grow directly out of her performing personality: an urbane and witty but also threatened and vulnerable individual trapped in an incomprehensible technological society which, nevertheless, provides the materials of her art. Her major work in this genre, *United States* (1983), is an epic two-evening drama in which she speaks, chants, sings, and plays the violin, all extended electronically and surrounded by projected visual and sound images. One excerpt from this work, the "song" *O Superman (for Massenet)*, became a successful pop record (on the album called *Big Science*) and video as well.

Robert Ashley, mentioned earlier as a member of the Michigan Once group and Sonic Arts, has developed a kind of ritualistic theater based on the intonation of texts of his own devising. Ashley often collaborates with other musicians—notably the pianist and composer Robert Sheff (b. 1945; stage name "Blue" Gene Tyranny)—using improvisational musical accompaniments built out of repeated melodic and harmonic patterns that range from the simple to the complex, some of them prerecorded. His biggest project to date, *Perfect Lives (Private Parts)* (1978–1981), is a conceptual theater work which has had several incarnations as a live-performance and/or media work. Much of Ashley's theatrics depends on his own deadpan recitation—a kind of avant-garde counterpart to rap music—but his work has also been realized by others in differing speaking and singing styles.

Non-standard singing styles and extended vocal techniques have modified or replaced traditional European styles. The revival of early-music vocal techniques, folk, jazz, and popular traditions, non-Western singing, and even the Broadway musical have influenced the evolution of contemporary vocalism, which has also taken more extreme and experimental forms. Singers who pioneered vocal techniques include Cathy Berberian, working primarily with Luciano Berio, and Roy Hart, the original protagonist of Peter Maxwell Davies's *Eight Songs for a Mad King* (discussed on pp. 213 and 300, with Example 19–1), and founder of an experimental vocal ensemble in Paris. Other techniques have also been explored by American composers and composer/performers, including the author (with the Quog Music Theater), Kirk Nurock (b. 1948; with the Natural Sound Workshop, founded in 1971), and several major women creator/performers including Anderson, Joan La Barbara (b. 1947), Diamanda Galas (b. 1955), and the choreographer-composer-director Meredith Monk (b. 1943). The last-named, who performs with her own vocal ensemble in concerts and recording, has also created theatrical forms that include dance, mime, music, and theatrical imagery in non-linear narrative structures (*Education of the Girl Child*, 1972–1973; *Quarry*, 1976; *Turtle Dreams*, 1983).

Meredith Monk's work is closely related to an important new genre of theater and music-theater works created by directors with a strong visual (rather than literary or verbal) bent but usually working in close collaboration with a composer. These pieces treat recognizable historic figures and events which loom larger than life and assume mythic proportions. They use a non-narrative, presentational style organized as a series of tableaux or stage pictures. Texts—often taken from period sources—are treated almost as artifacts rather than as lyrics or dialogue in the usual sense. The works are conceived for the proscenium stage and, although the scale is sometimes huge, the works are closed in form. The music is usually in an accessible neo-tonal style, and formal repetition in all domains—musical, verbal, physical—is used to create a magical or ritualistic effect.

The best-known practitioner of this kind of theater is Robert Wilson and, although his early works were not musical, he characteristically described them as operas. His major collaboration with Philip Glass, *Einstein on the Beach*, firmly established this genre as a form of music theater (see page 219). Recently, Wilson has worked with Glass, David Byrne, Gavin Bryars and others in *the CIVIL warS: A Tree is Best Measured when it is Down* (1979–1984; a twelve-hour, multi-national, polyglot work yet to be produced in its entirety) and with Bryars in *Medea* (a re-working of Charpentier's *Médée*). A number of other directors (and composers) associated with this kind of music theater came out of the theater group Mabou Mines: these include Joanne Akalaitis (*The Photographer* with Philip Glass; *The Voyage of the Beagle* [1982–1986] with Jon Gibson), Lee Breuer (*The Gospel at Colonus* [1983] with Bob Telson [b. 1949]), Ruth Maleczech and Valeria Vasilevski (*Fireworks* [1986–] with Ned Sublette [b. 1951] and R.I.P. Hayman [b. 1951]). With *Satyagraha*, *Akhnaten*, and *The Juniper Tree* (the last-named with composer Robert Moran and writer Arthur Yorinks), Glass has carried this genre on into operatic form and style. John Adams's *Nixon in China* (with poet Alice Goodman and director Peter Sellars) and works by Peter Gordon (*Return of the Native*, 1982; *The Passion of Passion*, 1984–1985; *The Immigrant Road*, 1985–) are other examples of the tendency of this kind of music theater to move in operatic directions.

The musicalization of avant-garde theater is a process that goes back to the performing ensembles of the 1960's and 1970's: the Living Theater, the Open Theater, Daniel Nagrin's Work Group, Mabou Mines, Meredith

Monk's The House, Quog Music Theater, and a number of European and Latin-American ensembles. Quog Music Theater, which explored music-theater improvisation, also sponsored weekly open improvisation sessions for composers and composer/performers; regular participants included Frederic Rzewski, Philip Glass, Michael Sahl, Jon Gibson, and many others. Quog was founded by the author in 1970 for the study, creation, and performance of new media and music-theater works. The development of music theater in ensemble form involved group study, workshops, exercises, performance games, group interaction, and improvisation. Works done with Quog include *Ecolog* (originally created for television but also realized in a concert/theater version for the New York Philharmonic's Prospective Encounters), *Helix* (1971; originally realized for radio), *Voices* (1971), *Saying Something* (1972), *Lazarus* (1972), and *Biograffiti* (1972–1973). The tendency towards a simplification of style is evident in this progression and is a characteristic result of the encounter between a contemporary music style and the theater.

Improvisational encounters between composers, directors, musicians, and actor/singers have been the basis for a number of important music theater works since the mid-1960's. The collaborations between composer Elizabeth Swados (b. 1951) and director André Serban at the La Mama theater in New York—*Fragments of a Trilogy*, including *Medea* (1972), *Electra* (1973), and *The Trojan Women* (1974); *Agamemnon* (1977)—were enormously influential. Paul Dresher has used a collaborative, improvisational rehearsal process to create a series of multi-media or performance-art works with director George Coates (*The Way of How*; *See/Hear*) and singer-writer Rinde Eckert (*Slow Fire*). In these cases, the final result may be relatively fixed or even scored, but the work is created on and with the performers—something in the style of a modern-dance choreographer—rather than depending on a pre-existing script or score. Contemporary music theater of all types has moved strongly in the direction of a developmental process that may take place over a period of time through readings, workshops, rehearsals, and previews.

As new theater has become musicalized, the new music concert has been increasingly theatricalized and a whole range of intermediate situations have been explored. Many of Cage's concert performances have the character of "music as theater" and so do many rock performances, past and present. Cage realized his large-scale *Theater Piece*; so did Stockhausen shortly thereafter (*Originale*, 1961). Stockhausen's magnum opus, *Licht*, begun in 1977 and still in progress at this writing, is a seven-evening cycle of theater works, one for each day of the week. Mauricio Kagel's residence for several years at a German theater resulted in works such as *Pas de cinq* (for actors tapping out rhythms with canes and umbrellas) and *Sur scène* (1958–1960; a theater piece made out of a concert performance with lecture). Ligeti's *Aventures*

(1962) and *Nouvelles aventures* (1962–1965) were originally concert pieces; his *Le grand macabre* (1978) is however an opera-house opera. The majority of the works of Larry Austin, Carlos Alsina (b. 1941), and Pauline Oliveros as well as many works of Berio (*Laborintus II*, *Opera*, *Musical*, and *Recital I* [1972]), Sylvano Bussotti (b. 1931; *La passion selon Sade* [1965]; *Lorenzaccio* [1972]), Peter Maxwell Davies (*Eight Songs for a Mad King*, *The Lighthouse*), the author (*Foxes and Hedgehogs*), and Gruber (*Frankenstein!!*) are theatrical pieces in concert form, or theater works that occupy a middle ground between the stage and the concert platform. Theater and theatrical ideas play a major role in the work of European and American neo-Romantic and neo-expressionist composers as diverse as Henze, Crumb, Maxwell Davies, Del Tredici, Hespos, and Rihm, although of these, only Henze has written extensively for the traditional stage.

We have sketched two major lines of descent for new music theater—one from media and multi-media via performance art, the other descended from the European and American experimental tradition through the theatricalization of the concert. Another important type or genre is descended from Weill/Brecht via the Off- and Off-Off-Broadway theaters. The social play, parable, or fable with music need not relegate music to a secondary role; the theater-opera form picks up where some of the most promising music theater innovation of the 1930's left off (see pp. 100-104). The collaborations of William Bolcom and Arnold Weinstein (*Dynamite Tonight* [1960–1963], an anti-war, black-comedy "opera for actors," and *Casino* [1986–], a gangster opera-in-progress); some of the later musicals of Elizabeth Swados; the Stanley Silverman-Richard Foreman collaborations (*Elephant Steps*, 1968; *Dr. Sélavy's Magic Theatre*, 1972; *Hotel for Criminals*, 1974; *Africanis Instructus*, 1984–1985); the theater work of Richard Peaslee (b. 1930; *Marat/Sade* [1964] with Peter Brook, *Animal Farm* [1984] with Peter Hall, *The Garden of Earthly Delights* [1984] and *Vienna Lusthaus* [1986] with Martha Clarke); the author's collaborations with Michael Sahl (*The Conjuror*, 1974; *Stauf*, 1976, rev. 1987; *Civilization and Its Discontents*, 1977; *Noah*, 1977–1978; *The Passion of Simple Simon*, 1978–1979; *Boxes*, 1981–1982)—these works use social themes in a style influenced by the theatrical avant-garde, and they combine musical influences from the American musical theater and popular music with classical, even operatic elements, the old avant-garde and the new tonalism. The revival of tonality has influenced but also been strongly influenced by these developments in music theater.

Music theater of this kind wants to entertain but also instruct or provoke; the combination of artistic form and social subject matter with song and dance is highly characteristic. These serious comedies or "comi-tragedies" use closed forms and set numbers, but imbedded in a larger on-going or even architectural context. The themes and the treatment are non-realistic and non-psychological, and often play directly out to the audience in a so-called "presentational" style that leans on stylization and artifice but is also characterized by humor, conflict, and even shock. (See Appendix; Example 21–1).

The commercial theater has not been entirely immune to these winds of change. The longest-running Broadway hit of all time—still running at this writing—began as a collective workshop improvisation. Although the score for *A Chorus Line* (1975; by Marvin Hamlisch [b. 1944]) was added later, the work represents the transfer of stage ideas from the experimental theater into the popular arena. Many contemporary musicals—ranging from the "rock operas" of Andrew Lloyd Webber (b. 1948; *Jesus Christ Superstar*, 1971; *Evita*, 1979; *Phantom of the Opera*, 1986; among others) to *Les Misérables* (Parisian premiere in 1980; English premiere in 1985; music by Claude-Michel Schönberg, libretto by Alain Boublil, English version by Herbert Kretzmer) and works like *Dreamgirls* and *The Tap Dance Kid* (both composed by Henry Krieger)—incorporate extended musical treatments of dramatic scenes. Book scenes have become less important and dialogue is often spoken over extended musical "underscoring"; extensive sections and even entire works are through-composed. The musicalization of the popular theater is a major trend in the Broadway musical.

The most important and influential figure in this regard is Stephen Sondheim (b. 1930), undoubtedly the most original artist that Broadway has yet produced. Sondheim is hard to categorize. He was a protégé of Oscar Hammerstein II (1895–1960) and first made his mark as the lyricist of *West Side Story* (1957) and *Gypsy* (1959) and the composer of *A Funny Thing Happened on the Way to the Forum* (1962). But Sondheim also studied with Milton Babbitt and was influenced by contemporary literature and theater. *Company* (1970) contrasts the sophisticated outer and seething inner worlds of a group of modern urbanites. *Follies* (1971) takes place in an old music-hall theater as it is about to be demolished; its characters comprise the former denizens of that theater. *A Little Night Music* (1972), roughly based on Ingmar Bergman's *Smiles of a Summer Night*, is a take off of the Viennese waltz operetta from a contemporary point of view. *Pacific Overtures* (1976) deals with the "opening up" of Japan but told from the Japanese side (it even includes a Japanese orchestra on stage in addition to the pit band). *Sweeney Todd, the Demon Barber of Fleet Street* (1979) adapts a gruesome English tale in the manner of a folk opera or a social song-play—but one that is virtually through-composed. *Merrily We Roll Along* (1981), adapted from a George Kaufman play, follows the fortunes of the members of a high school class but in reverse chronological order. *Sunday in the Park with George* (1984) is an unconventional look at an artist (Georges Seurat); it is Sondheim's own meditation on the artistic temperament and what it means to be an artist today. The musical influences are extremely diverse; the Broadway tradition has been amplified by the Viennese operetta, Japanese music, Brecht/Weill, the English pantomime, music hall—even minimalism. But through all this diversity, there is a basic and easily recognizable Sondheim style. The rhythmic regularity and tonal clarity of American popular and show music have been modified (or expanded) by a more complex and ambiguous harmonic and rhythmic style closely related to and influenced by the classical Americana styles of Copland, Bernstein, and others. Sondheim's music is characterized by great economy of means. In its cellular patterns of repetition and build, it has something in common with Philip Glass and Steve Reich, but it is structured more in planes and levels which add contrast and conflict (See Appendix: Example 21–2). Sondheim chooses his subject matter and always writes his own brilliant and witty lyrics. He avoids the traditional emotional climate of Broadway, and his work is often said to be heartless. In fact, the material and the intensity with which it is treated inevitably arise from the artistic treatment of popular forms and from Sondheim's urbane and sophisticated ideas about music theater—somewhere between Weill and Stravinsky. This is not opera or operetta in disguise; nor, for all the innovation, is this experimental or avant-garde theater. It is, instead, an expansion of the idea of the American musical itself, carrying it—in a very personal and artistic way—into theatrical and musical areas previously not considered *a propos*. Sondheim's work has been enormously influential (any young theater composer who writes original-sounding show music will inevitably be called Sondheimish); but his work is also highly personal and grounded in his own sensibility and vision.

In spite of certain developments in the opera house and the commercial theater, new music theater has found its most receptive environment in the Off- and Off-Off-Broadway theater, in museums, galleries, and lofts and, increasingly, in the non-profit regional theater. The 1986 New York Philharmonic Horizons Festival was devoted to "music as theater" and several European festivals have begun to explore this area. The American Music Theater Festival, founded in 1983 in Philadelphia by the author with Marjorie Samoff, has provided a springboard for new music theater ranging from operas to musicals to experimental work. A similar festival is planned in Munich in 1988 under the direction of Hans Werner Henze.

The return to music theater is one of those turns of the wheel that has every aspect of inevitability about it. The separation of music and theater and the triumph of instrumental music were recent phenomena connected with the domination of new music by abstract ideas for more than half a century. Post-modernism challenges the old Germanic idealism and purity that dominated late Romantic music and modernism. Through its revival of tonality and rhythmicality, and because of its connections with popular and other common-language traditions, post-modernism has helped revive the old relationship between music and theater. But the influences also run the other way; the revival of music theater is helping to determine the course of post-modern music.

It is too soon to predict the direction of new music theater (if indeed there is to be any single direction). But, amidst the diversity, there are certain common elements: new or revived tonalities; the return of common practice and vocabulary; musical and scenic closure inside the proscenium arch; clear subject matter treated in stylized ways; the easy integration of technology in a live-theater context. Music theater reverses the purism of modern art. It is messy—like the real world. It is pragmatic; what succeeds is likely to be what works. It is a popular as well as an artistic form and is closely identified with mainstream culture. One must say what one means and, above all, say it simply and clearly.

However music theater evolves, it will ultimately reflect the synthesis that results from the creative conflict between art and entertainment, high-brow and lowbrow, classical structure and popular sentiment, vanguard innovation and common practice, storytelling and presentational stylization, through-composed and closed form, minimalist tonality and dramatic music, the desire to inform or provoke and the desire to entertain. Music theater has a message; music theater is fun.

As film takes over the functions of realistic storytelling in popular culture, theater inevitably moves towards the mythic, the stylized, the mag-ical—in short, towards the conditions of music theater. Abstract painting and modern—i.e., abstract—dance were the key arts of early modernism. It is rapidly becoming clear that music theater—in all of its various and even contradictory forms—is a seminal art of post-modernism in the final decades of our century.

THE NEW MUSICAL CULTURE

The era of exploration is over. All experience is available as raw material for art—through 360° and on a continuum. What matters is what happens to this raw experience. New ideas must be evaluated, not for their own sake but for how they happen and what they mean. The medium is not the message; context (the social setting) and content ("meaning" in a widened sense) are essential. The best new art concerns itself with the ordering of a particular universe of ideas and experience taken from the totality of pos-sibilities, the menu that technology offers us every day. We make choices; we must make choices. The range of experience and the act of communication are in themselves subject matter. Forms arise out of a dialectic of voice and instrument, live and electronic, strict and free, rational and irrational, writ-ten down and improvised, controlled and open, symmetrical and asymmetrical, periodic and aperiodic; a dialectic of extremes of pitch and noise, sound and silence, register and dynamic, motion and stasis, high and low tension, thinness and density, complexity and simplicity, clarity and confusion, the explicit and the implicit, the intelligible and the incomprehensible, expressive detail and large line, familiarity and abstraction, image and rhythm, words and music, association and invention.

Dramatic and musical forms arise naturally out of this dialectical process, in which opposition and conflict may lead to coherence and resolution or simply to dissonance, paradox, and contradiction. Structural forms based on opposition, or on resolution through a continuum which mediates extremes, provide a connecting link between musical form and development on the one hand and meaning, content, and context on the other.

As the era of modern music draws to a close, as the music and the social institutions that produced change are themselves replaced, we see that the music of the avant-garde is in fact a transition to something new. The categories turn out to be historical; the barriers are down, the categories irrelevant, the old battles over and done with. Any kind of statement is possible; all possible materials and relationships between creator, creation, performance, perceiver, and institution are possible (including none), but the significance of this is only to be found in the creative act itself. The raw material of every piece, even the most minimalistic, is the total possibility of experience. The subject of the discourse is the quality and the nature of experience, of perception, not in a vacuum but in a social context. Music, the most social of the arts, is always a metaphor for the society that produces it. The best new art will reflect, on the one hand, the cultural and social situation that produces it and, on the other, the structure of human perception and mind and, by extension, the biological history of the race and even some larger natural order. Music, in all cases, always tells its tales.

The best new music of the century has always proposed the most difficult, the most profound, as well as the most universal artistic problems, and has proceeded to resolve them anew. More than ever, the problems, materials, premises and forms, the context and content, the media, the expressive means and realizations, the psychological, artistic, esthetic, social, and human meaning of music are unique to each musical experience. But they must be related to some larger fund of experience and knowledge, established anew with each act of creation and realization, and yet full of wider resonance for our shared experience as human beings, as members of our own cultures and traditions and of the global, human culture as well.

BIBLIOGRAPHICAL NOTES

Marshall McLuhan's *The Gutenberg Galaxy* (Toronto, 1964) and *Understanding Media* (New York, 1971) are the classical statements of media impact on culture. Among the author's writings on music theater are articles in the *New*

York Times (Dec. 24, 1972), the *Musical Quarterly* ("Whither American Musical Theater?" 65/2 [April 1979], 230–44), and *Perspectives, Creating and Producing Contemporary Opera and Musical Theatre: A Series of Fifteen Monographs* (Washington, DC: Opera America, 1983). See also H. H. Stuckenschmidt's article "Total Theatre" in *World of Music* (9/1 [1967], 5-16), Richard Kostelanetz's *The Theatre of Mixed Means,* cited in the bibliography for Chapter 18, and *Music Theater in a Changing Society: The Influence of the Technical Media,* ed. Jack Bornoff (Paris, 1968).

For information on Diamanda Galas and other "downtown" composers, see K. Robert Schwarz's "Young American Composers: New York's 'Downtown' Music" in *Music and Musicians* (July 1985, pp. 10–11); for a lengthy discussion of Ligeti's *Nouvelles Aventures* as well as of Lutoslawski's *Trois poèmes d'Henri Michaud* and Berio's *Sequenza III,* see Istvan Anhalt's *Alternative Voices: Essays on Contemporary Vocal and Choral Composition* (Toronto, 1984); for Mauricio Kagel, see the studies by Diether Schnebel and Werner Klüppelholz cited in the bibliography for Chapter 18; and for Pauline Oliveros, see Heidi von Gunden's *The Music of Pauline Oliveros* (Metuchen, NJ, 1983) and Oliveros's *Software for People: Collected Writings; 1963–1980* (Baltimore, 1984).

MUSIC EXAMPLES

The musical examples and discussions of them below are meant to be illustrative only—"examples" in the literal sense. They are intended to suggest the variety of twentieth-century music as well as approaches to further study by the student. In such study, it should be remembered that musical notation, even in its most elaborate and artistic twentieth-century forms, is only an approximate if convenient representation of the music, and not by any means equivalent to the music itself.[1] The reader should always assume that he or she is being referred to the music. Most of the music exemplified below, and much that is discussed in this volume's narrative,

---

[1] This accounts for a relative lack of detailed, analyzed examples from the second half of the twentieth century. The extensive use of original and bizarre notations—sometimes for purely visual effect, often for quite practical reasons—only serves to re-emphasize the purely pragmatic significance of musical notation. It is no longer true that "the score" is the equivalent of the music itself, and, in many basic ways, recording has replaced printing as the means of "publishing" new music.

has been recorded; however, since discographies date quickly, one has not been included here.

The numbering of the examples below corresponds to the book's chapters, and references within chapters, e.g., Example 10-3 refers to the third example cited in Chapter 10.

EXAMPLE 3-1. Debussy. *Jeux.* Quoted by permission of Durand & Cie, Editeurs-proprietaires, Paris.

Examples of symmetrical structures which are tonally ambiguous.

a. Four-note chromatic group filling in minor third (meas. 1–2).

b. Whole-tone harmonies, moving by major thirds (meas. 5–6).

c. Major seconds in parallel motion; simultaneous, independent chromatic lines (meas. 25–30).

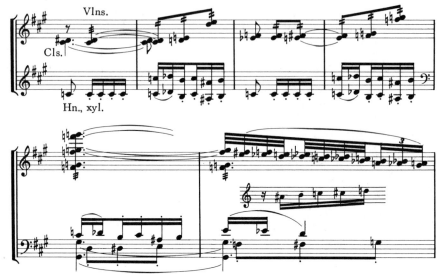

EXAMPLE 3-2. Stravinsky, *Le Sacre du printemps*. Copyright 1921 by Edition Russe de Musique. Copyright assigned to Boosey and Hawkes, Inc. Reprinted by permission.

Some uses of a basic block-chord structure.

a. The basic block-chord, in its first appearance.

b. At 14 . Articulated version.

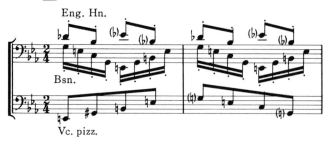

c. At 15 , a, and b (as above), with new elements superimposed.

d.

e.

EXAMPLE 4-1. Schoenberg, *Three Piano Pieces*, Op. 11, No. 1. Quoted by permission of Mrs. Gertrud Schoenberg and Universal Edition.

   Use of simple interval structures in early atonal Schoenberg. Closely related patterns—major third with adjacent half-step inside or outside (X), tritone with adjacent whole- or half-step (Y and Z)—generate the melodic as well as the harmonic material. Longer goals are also suggested; thus the opening melodic movement (X) outlines Z over the first three measures. Through the use of transposition and inversion (in the traditional sense, i.e., a minor second becomes a major seventh), all the intervallic material and almost all the chromatic steps are brought into play. These are all embryonic twelve-tone techniques, here used intuitively as a series of musical associations.

a.

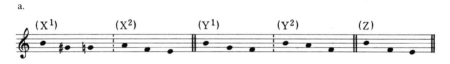

b. Opening measures.

EXAMPLE 4-2. Webern, *Five Pieces for Orchestra*, Op. 10, No. 4. Quoted by permission of Universal Edition.

A brief analysis of a brief movement from Webern's "expressionist" period.

The piece consists of slightly more than two revolutions of the total chromatic cycle with miniature phrases of six, four, two, and five notes set among brief chordal structures and repeated notes. The opening harp sonority—Gb, Db, F—is recapitulated in the fourth and fifth measures by the harp, clarinet, and celesta with the addition of another three harmonic elements, B, E, C (a re-arrangement and inverted transposition of a companion structure). This same figure also appears melodically in the mandolin (simultaneously with the harp chord) as the Ab, G, and Eb of the opening phrase. The mandolin phrase also contains secondary elements of great importance pivoted around the tritone (whole-step and tritone, tritone and half-step). The nine notes of the mandolin and harp fill the chromatic space between C and Ab. The next phrases, which begin by adding the missing Bb, A, and B, center on tritones with the attached whole- or half-step; i.e., the opening three notes of the trumpet's phrase are an arrangement and transposition of the opening mandolin notes; the final D of the trumpet phrase and the two notes of the trombone phrase are an arrangement of the second through fourth notes of the mandolin phrase. Similarly, the following F♯ in the harp and C–Db trill in the clarinet, as well as the subsequent E–F in the celesta and B in the mandolin (the same B–F relationship that began the trumpet phrase, now associated through timbre with the opening), are related figures. The final violin phrase, beginning with a major seventh (i.e., whole-step inverted) and a tritone, is a synthesis of all the basic elements of the opening.

a. Interval structures.

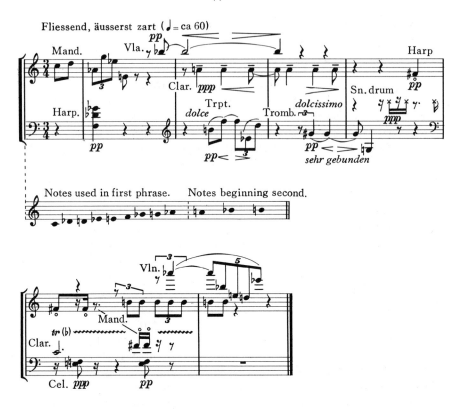

EXAMPLE 5-1. Stravinsky, *Symphony of Psalms.* Copyright 1931 by Russischer Musikverlag; renewed 1958. Copyright and renewal assigned 1947 to Boosey & Hawkes, Inc. Revised version copyright 1948 by Boosey & Hawkes, Inc. Reprinted by permission.

A specimen analysis of a "neo-tonal" work.

The *Symphony of Psalms*, scored for chorus and large orchestra without violins and violas, uses excerpts from the Vulgate Latin version of three Psalms; Stravinsky specifies that they must be sung in Latin. The work opens with an E-minor triad, spaced, scored, and articulated in a very characteristic manner (a). The short, isolated, mezzo-forte sound, which recurs half a dozen times in precisely the same form, strongly emphasizes the minor third between E and G, one of the pivotal relationships of the work. The figurations that follow are based on arpeggios and scales that refer to Eb and C, two of the principal tonal areas of the work, themselves separated by a minor third. The piece, as it turns out, is in a kind of super C, compounded out of the related keys and triads of C minor, Eb, E minor, and, to a much more limited degree, G. We might represent this tonality or polar center like this:

At the outset, E minor dominates, with a secondary tendency to move towards a G7 and through a flat area. At 4 the altos enter with a "thematic" idea—nothing more than E's and F's—over a version of the arpeggio figure now slowed up to eighth notes and including a new figure based on minor thirds a half-step apart (b). By 5 the impulse has carried the music to a G area (the omnipresent thirds are D and F in the soprano voice); the figuration remains stable although expanded. This impulse is checked by the ambiguous, compound harmony and instrumental melodic figuration at 6, and 7 is a return to point zero, but now more developed and intensified. By 9 the piece is heavily settled on the basic E and it remains so right up until the end of the movement, where the E to F melodic motion suddenly carries up to G while the bass struggles down through a B♭ and an A♭ to come to rest on its own G (c).

a. First movement, opening measures.

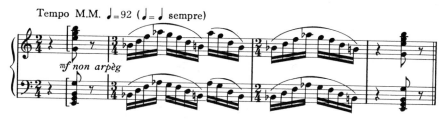

b. First movement, thematic idea.

c. First movement, closing measures.

      The second movement begins with a long woodwind fugue in C (minor) with a theme based on the pair of minor thirds a half-step apart already heard in the first movement (C–E♭; B–D) (d). The chorus enters in E♭ minor with its own fugue subject, which is developed over the continuation of the original woodwind subject (e). There is a brief *a cappella* stretto, a pause, a very intense compound of the main material, and then a very quiet final few measures in which repeated choral E♭'s hover over a harmonic and contrapuntal complex which ends the movement and implies the next (f).

d. Second movement, opening of instrumental fugue.

e. Second movement, opening of choral fugue.

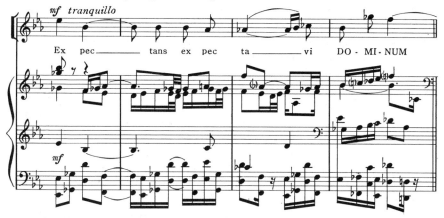

f. Second movement, closing measures.

The third movement opens in a modified C with a strong infusion of E♭'s (and B♭'s) (g); at the cadence, this E♭/B♭ turns to a clear, bright C.

The last time this C comes around, it does not shake off the Bb, which remains as part of a long pedal around which appear C major punctuation in the horns (with the familiar E – G at the bottom), a little half-step plucked figure centered on G, and a melodic line rising from G through Ab and Bb to C (h). The pedal sound pushes up to D and E, the bass picks up the G to C movement, then drops through the flats back to G and down to F at a big moment of climax. The climax is built on E and A triads with a bass that centers on F and G♯, eventually dropping through a long chain of thirds down to C. The E–G relationship of the opening movement is echoed by a C – Eb relationship here, while the half-step melodic figures of the opening are turned into whole-steps. With the rhythmic, repeated-note "Laudate dominum" at [8], the chorus returns to the pivotal E, and the continuation at [9] takes off from a very subtle extension of the basic E–G relationship, now clearly connected with the C-major seventh chord that is so characteristic of this movement. After the opening "Alleluia" recurs, the quick tempo returns with repeated Eb's and then a modified restatement of "Laudate Dominum" on the repeated E–G minor third and later another one on a Bb triad. At [20], the movement and tempo settle down briefly in G over an ostinato which at first consists of a G major triad but later turns into a big trio of fourths under a simple melodic ostinato based principally on the notes Eb–D–C at [22] (i). This Eb sound is the solid and static state of the piece until the very last measures, when only the Bb of the ostinato remains in the bass. The "Alleluia" returns — the top is suddenly discovered to come right out of the "Laudate" that came before — and the Eb – E♯ –G ambiguity is definitively dispelled in the final C with its E♯ on top.

g. Third movement, opening measures.

h. Third movement, orchestral interlude.

i. Third movement, at 22 .

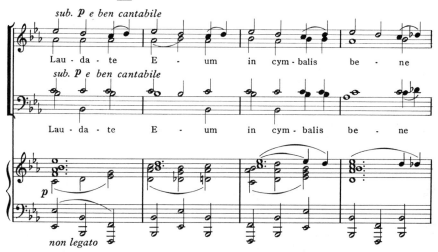

EXAMPLE 7-1. Hindemith, *Das Marienleben*, "O hast du dies gewollt"; 1922–1923 and 1948 versions. Texts by Rainer Maria Rilke. Quoted by permission of B. Schott's Söhne, Mainz.

The "softening" and regularizing of Hindemith's style illustrated by a comparison between the original and revised versions of *Das Marienleben*.

a. Comparison of opening measures.

b. Comparison of closing measures.

EXAMPLE 8-1. Bartók, String Quartet No. 4, First Movement. Copyright 1929 by Universal Edition; renewed 1956. Copyright assigned to Boosey & Hawkes Inc. for the U.S.A. Reprinted by permission of Boosey & Hawkes, Inc. and Universal Edition.

Intervallic structure in Bartók's music.

The basic intervallic content of this movement can be described as a half-step plus a whole-step. These elements, which have obvious parallels to traditional scale patterns, are used here in a very different way, to generate larger melodic units and harmonic relationships. Thus, a harmonic half-step plus a melodic whole-step (two melodic half-steps) creates a harmonic whole-step; half- and whole-step melodic sequences fill out and define minor thirds; similarly, a cluster of harmonic half-steps for the four instruments fills in a chromatic minor third. Adjacent whole-steps—melodic or harmonic—create and define major thirds. Thus intertwined melodic and harmonic steps and thirds (it is almost impossible to tell where "harmony" leaves off and "melody" begins) fill out defined segments of the chromatic spectrum—most significantly, the regions from C up to E♯ and, inversely, from C down to A♭. These intervals imbue the entire work with their characteristic sound and ultimately shape the entire harmonic and melodic invention. All of the elements are present in the figure in measure 7 as simply an extension of everything heard previously. The close of the movement (b) is a summation of the harmonic and melodic (and rhythmic) energies of the piece.

a. First movement, opening measures.

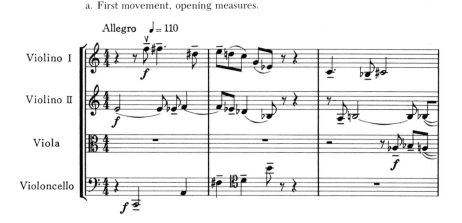

b. First movement, closing measures.

EXAMPLE 8-2. Bartók, *Music for Strings, Percussion and Celesta.* Copyright 1937 by Univeral Edition; renewed 1964. Copyright and renewal assigned to Boosey & Hawkes, Inc. for the U.S.A. Reprinted by permission.

Examples of the accommodation of intervallic chromaticism to modal/tonal music in Bartók's music.

The *Music for Strings, Percussion, and Celesta* begins with a rather dense chromatic fugue built on one of Bartók's most characteristic melodic types: a succession of ascending and descending half- and whole-steps contained within a very small compass (a). Locally this movement does not sound tonal at all, but its broad structure, which departs from and closes finally on A through harmonic and melodic cycles of fifths, suggests a chromatic interpretation of long-range tonal organizations.

a. First-movement theme.

The big A-major finale, based initially on a folkish theme (b), rounds off the entire work with a notable technique of re-interpreting the earlier chromatic sounds and types in diatonic and triadic-tonal terms (c, d, e).

b. Main theme of last movement.

c. Chromatic material in last movement.

d. Diatonic expansion (last movement).

e. Development of diatonic figures.

EXAMPLE 10-1. Row forms used in Schoenberg, Piano Piece, Op. 33a.

Note that the retrograde and retrograde inversion forms read from right to left. Together with the original and its inversion, these forms may be transposed to any of the other eleven degrees of the tempered chromatic scale (the inversion and retrograde inversion above are given at the transposition of a fifth—"I–5" and "RI–5"); the internal relationships—the intervals—remain constant and all twelve pitches appear once and only once.[2]

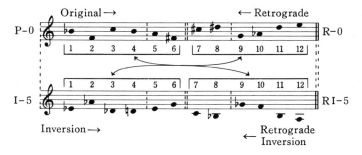

EXAMPLE 10-2. Schoenberg, Piano Suite, Op. 25. Quoted by permission of Mrs. Gertrud Schoenberg and Universal Edition.

Early use of row technique in Schoenberg's music.

a. The row, in all the forms used in the suite.

b. Präludium, beginning.

[2] Some commentators and analysts prefer to regard the first pitch as the zero point from which the series or row departs; thus the twelve notes are numbered from zero to 11. This has analogies to mathematical operations and presumably facilitates certain procedures. Nevertheless, the other common method—numbering from 1 to 12—may be clearer in an introductory description of the method. In any case, the spelling-out of the row and row-forms in analyses and discussions should be considered only a helpful abstraction, valid only as far as it is useful. Some of the technical problems associated with the development of twelve-tone and serial music now seem of greater historical than current technical interest.

c. Gavotte, beginning.

d. Musette, beginning.

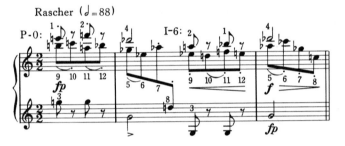

e. Intermezzo, beginning.

f. Menuett, beginning.

g. Gigue, beginning.

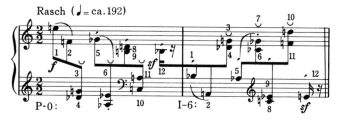

EXAMPLE 10-3. Schoenberg, Piano Piece, Op. 33a. Quoted by permission of Mrs. Gertrud Schoenberg and Universal Edition.

Brief analysis of Schoenberg's use of row material to generate harmonic and melodic elements of a piece.

Example 10-3 shows how the row material of Op. 33a (see Ex. 10-1) is used musically. The basic units are the three four-note chords at the beginning (a); they color the entire work.

a. First subject.

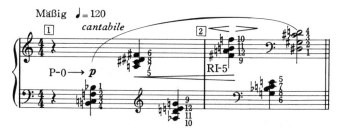

Only later, as the piece develops and unfolds, are lines extracted. Note the close relationship between the phrasing and structural articulation of the piece and the twelve-tone groupings; this kind of phrasing is particularly clear at the start and at the main points of articulation. The first three chords present a harmonic arrangement of the original form of the row; the second three, the retrograde inversion. In the next three measures, the arrangement takes the form of a succession of pitches with one form of the row (the retrograde inversion) in the upper register, and another (the retrograde) in the lower parts; measures 6 and 7, however, develop the pitch material of measures 1 and 2 in the original order. The following measures again present different forms of the material in "contrapuntal juxtapositions"; notice the important use of repetition as an extension device in measures 8 and 9 and in the new section beginning at measure 14. If the independent use of registers is kept in mind, it is not difficult to follow the twelve-tone thread through measure 20. In measure 20, however, the first "irregularity" occurs:

the final two notes of both the retrograde and the retrograde inversion do not appear; instead, the music seems to reverse its steps so that the return at measure 21 to the outline shape of measure 14 begins at the middle point of the rows.

b. Second subject.

It is clear that from measure 14 onwards (see b), the basic arrangement of the row material is no longer in three groups of fours but in two groups of sixes (subdivided into smaller units of threes). If the given rows are examined, it will be seen that the collection of the first six pitches of the original contains the same notes (although in a different order) as the first six pitches of the retrograde inversion; and, of course, the same is true of the last six pitches of each form. Thus if the original is presented simultaneously with its inversion (at the given transposition), the first and last six notes of each form combine to produce new, complete twelve-tone combinations; this remarkable fact, carefully calculated by Schoenberg, provides the structural basis for the music as its evolves from four-note chord sounds towards the arrangements in six-note groupings. Beginning at the end of measure 27, there is a kind of development section (continuing the development that began in measures 21 and 22) in which the pairs of three-note groupings began to appear transposed onto different levels (up a step and then down a fourth, first presented in complementary six-note groups and in complete transposed rows). The re-establishment of the original row material at the original levels after the *fermata* in measure 32, the return to the conditions of measure 14 in measure 35, the unified arrangement of complete rows in short descending and ascending phrases in measures 37 and 38, and the final re-interpretation of measures 1 and 2 at the end can be easily traced.[3]

---

[3] The attentive score-reader — perhaps even the alert listener — will find, in addition to the above-mentioned omissions at measure 20, a note taken from the lower register and substituted for a missing note in the upper in measure 22, exchanges of note order in measures 29 and 37, and a clear misprint in measure 35.

EXAMPLE 10-4. Schoenberg, String Trio, Op. 45. Quoted by permission of Mrs. Gertrud Schoenberg and Universal Edition.

Later evolution of row technique in Schoenberg's music.

This is the opening of the work, showing how the pitch groups of the row are revealed gradually. In measure 1, the total chromatic material is presented, divided into two groups of six notes, with the distinctive feature of a half-step trill. In the second measure, the pitch content of these groupings is established: B – C – G♯ – F♯ – G – F for one "hexachord"; the inversion (transposed) produces the other six notes. A primary order form of this material is revealed only in the fifth measure, first in groups of two notes divided between the violin and viola, then in a strictly linear form in the viola (accompanied by harmonies made up of complementary forms of the same material transposed to fill out the twelve-note groupings). In measures 6 and 7, the same material re-appears, now in four-note groupings. In measures 8 – 13, there is a systematic presentation of the material in three complete rows — taking off from the basic form of measure 4 — out of which the violin extracts a new line which in itself is a new grouping of twelve tones.[4]

[4] Later in the work, secondary row material is formed by permutations of note-order within the "hexachords"; the pitch content of the hexachords, however, remains constant.

EXAMPLE 10-5. Berg, Violin Concerto. Quoted by permission of Universal Edition.

Synthesis of row technique and tonality in Berg.

a. The row.

b. Solo violin, Introduction to First Movement.

c. Opening of Andante, First Movement.

d. "Viennese" themes, Allegretto, First Movement.

(♪ = 112)

(*rustico*)

(*scherzando*)

(*wienerisch*)

e. Carinthian Folksong, Allegretto, First Movement.

(♪ = 112)
(Solo Vln.)

(Hrn.)

f. Bach chorale, Adagio, Second Movement.

EXAMPLE 10-6. Webern, *Concerto for Nine Instruments*, Op. 24. Quoted by permission of Universal Edition.

Reduction and rationalization of row elements in Webern's twelve-tone music.

The twelve-tone row of the concerto is shown below (a). The basic intervallic units are the same as those of the *Bagatelle* mentioned in the text: major third and minor second. The row itself further breaks down into four groups of three notes, the last three of which are transpositions of the other forms of the original—retrograde inversion, retrograde, inversion; also the retrograde inversion of the whole row at the given transposition preserves the pitch identities of the three-note groups. Here are a few measures of the realization of this concept (b). The actual structure of the row is crucial; in the second movement, for instance (c), the groups of threes are formed by single tones in the "melodic" instruments complemented by two-note harmonic groupings in the piano. The solo line consists of the initial notes of each three-note group of the row, which themselves form other transpositions of the identical three-note group. The interlocking of these groupings is carried out systematically. Transpositions of this material are chosen which produce further relations and further identities. Certain pitches and certain groups of two and three notes re-appear in different forms and transpositions of the row material, and these relationships are exploited in terms of register, tone color, position in the phrase, and so forth; non-pitch aspects of the music are thus brought into close relationship with the twelve-tone pitch material.

a. The row.

b. First movement, meas. 1–5.

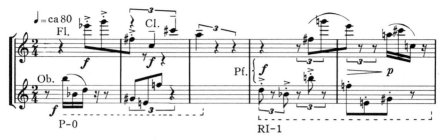

c. Second movement, meas. 1–18.

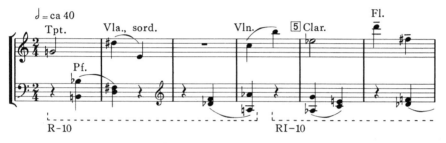

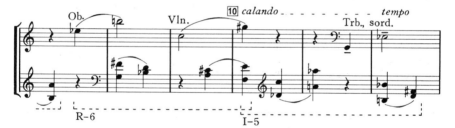

EXAMPLE 11-1. Dallapiccola, *Quaderno musicale di Annalibera*, No. 1, *Simbolo*. Copyright 1953 by S. A. Edizioni Suvini Zerboni. Reprinted by permission.

Triadic twelve-tone music from Italy.

    "The Musical Notebook of Annalibera" is a collection of simple piano pieces using straightforward twelve-tone technique in a strongly triadic style. The title, "Symbol," refers to the fact that the main motif of the piece is a transposition of the notes B♭ – A – C – B♮ — B – A – C – H in German musical nomenclature. The chords and accompaniment figures are arranged so that the four-note motif emerges in its original or inverted form (which in this case is identical with the retrograde). Note simple and regular phrasing which is closely allied to the feeling of triadic and even tonal harmonic movement.

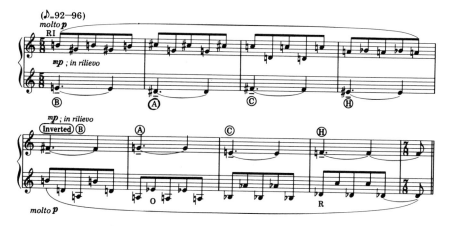

EXAMPLE 12-1. Ives, *The Unanswered Question.* Used by permission. Copyright 1953 by Southern Music Publishing Company.

Layering, juxtaposition of diverse elements, and symbolic reference in Ives.

This is an excerpt from the middle of the work showing the tonal string chorale, the questioning "expressionistic" phrase in the trumpet (or English horn or oboe or clarinet), and two of the dense, cluster-like wood-wind "answers."

EXAMPLE 12-2. Varèse, *Ionisation*, © 1934 by Edgard Varèse. By permission of Franco Colombo, Inc., Publisher.

New approaches to the use of rhythm, timbre, and frequency bands in an all-percussion work by Varèse.

This is an excerpt towards the end of the work, showing the structurally important entrance of piano and bells, the use of a low and high siren, and some of the important rhythmic motifs as well as the general variety and lay-out of percussion instruments. Note that the siren permits the use of pitched sound on a continuum, while the writing for piano and bells uses clusters and harmonic aggregates, creating a very distinct point of arrival in the piece.

EXAMPLE 12-3. Cowell, *Tiger*. Quoted by permission of Associated Music Publishers, Inc.

New keyboard techniques and notations: tone clusters and harmonics in Cowell's piano music.

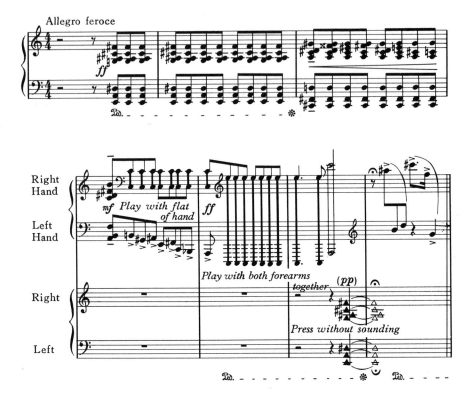

EXAMPLE 14-1. Babbitt, *Philomel*, excerpt. Quoted by permission of Associated Music Publishers, Inc.

Serialism with live performance and synthesized sound.

The score of Babbitt's *Philomel* shows the carefully notated solo voice part with a cue-score notation of the tape part, which is an amalgam of electronic music and electronically altered vocal sounds.

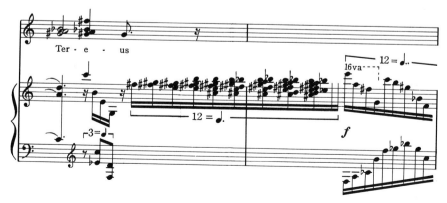

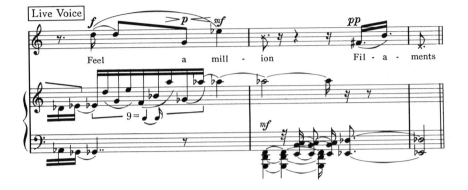

EXAMPLE 15-1. Cage, *Atlas Eclipticalis,* excerpts from instrumental parts. Copyright © 1962 by Henmar Press. Used by permission.

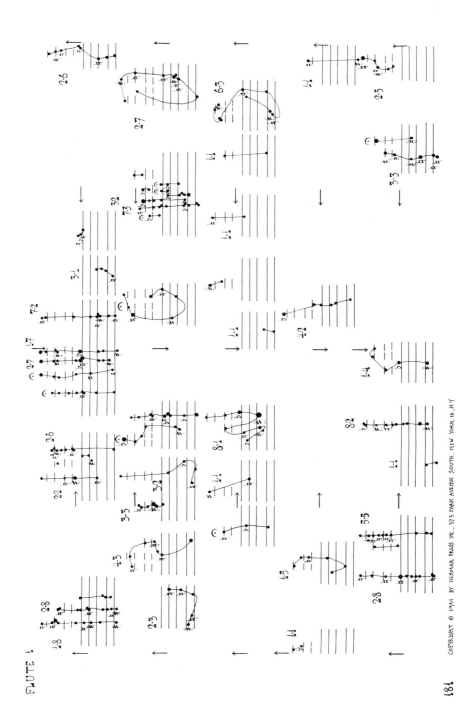

FLUTE 1

181

281

Atlas Eclipticalis consists of 86 instrumental parts which may be played in whole or in part by any combination of these instruments. It also may be performed simultaneously with Cage's *Winter Music*, and it may be performed acoustically or with the aid of contact microphones, electronically. There is no score; the conductor's part consists of directions. The instrumental parts, excerpts from which are illustrated, were composed by chance operations and by the use of star charts to select notes that are "free" of conscious choice. Cage, Feldman, and others also used "graphic" notation— ranging from variations of standard notation to purely diagrammatic indications—to induce free, random, or improvisatory choices on the part of performers in matters of pitch, duration, dynamics, color, and even instrumentation. Feldman's *The Straits of Magellan* for flute, horn, trumpet, guitar, harp, piano, and double-bass is one of a series of graphic pieces dating back to the 1950's embodying Feldman's complete rejection of musical determinism or process; only the instrumentation, the time frame, and some of the colors are fixed. Feldman's performance instructions are as follows:

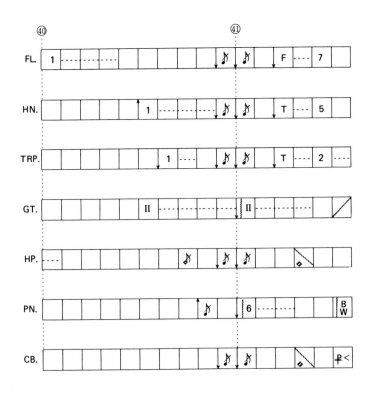

EXAMPLE 15-2. Feldman, *The Straits of Magellan,* performance instructions and final passage. Copyright © 1962 by C. F. Peters. Used by permission.

Introduction of "aleatory" or chance procedures through non-traditional compositional procedures and notations.

Each box is equal to MM 88. Numbers indicate the amount of sounds to be played within the duration of each box. Arabic numerals indicate single sounds for all the instruments except the piano, which interprets the numbers given as simultaneous sounds. Single sounds for the piano are circled. Roman numerals are used for simultaneous sounds for all other instruments. Grace notes should not be played too quickly. All sounds are to be played with a minimum of attack. Dynamics are very low throughout. Broken lines are used to sustain one sound until the next. Arrows indicate register: ↑ High. ↓ Low. Where there is no arrow, any register (or registers) may be used. Horn and trumpet with mutes, except for an occasional open sound using the standard symbol.

Symbols occurring in *The Straits of Magellan:*

F	Flutter (on one tone)
T	Double tongue (on one tone)
–	Upward slide in any register
	Downward slide in any register
	Same sound repeated seven times

Piano

◇	Fingers down without sounding, using sustaining pedal
B	Black notes ⎱
W	White notes ⎰ combinations in any register
	Same chord repeated seven times

Contra-Bass

Numbers not prefaced with a letter are played pizz.

A   Arco, P   Pont., L   con legno, ◇ harmonic, ⨏ Pont. tremolo,   ☍ Same sound repeated six times,   ⬦ tremolo (harmonic).

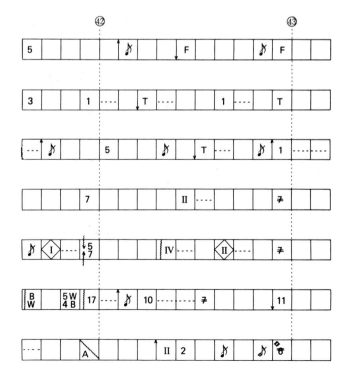

EXAMPLE 16-1. Crumb, *Night of the Four Moons*, second movement, "Cuando sale la luna . . ." ("When the moon rises . . ."). Copyright © 1972 by C. F. Peters. Used by permission.

Unusual sonorities, free performance style, and non-traditional notation in George Crumb's music.

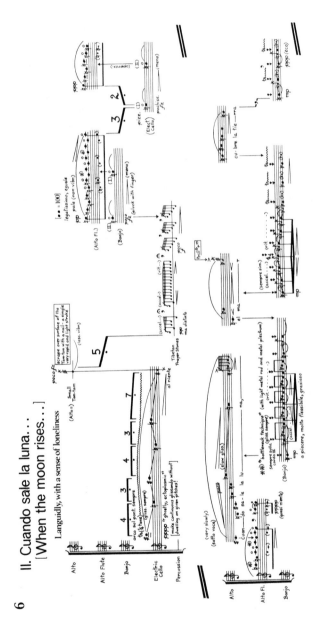

6   II. Cuando sale la luna. . .
[When the moon rises. . .]

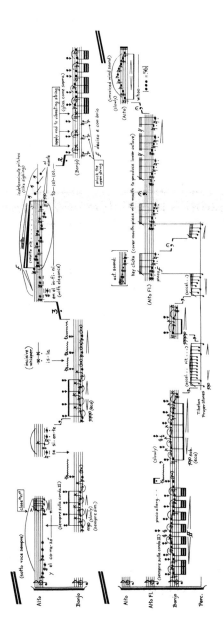

This is the complete second movement of a work by Crumb setting fragments of poetry by Federico García Lorca. Unusual instruments are used in unusual ways, including glissandos, key-clicks, harmonics, bottleneck banjo, etc. The vocal writing is also unusual, and at the beginning of the song, the singer scrapes a nail over the surface of a gong. The notation indicates a free rhythmic performance and suggests the evocative or ritualistic atmosphere of the music.

EXAMPLE 16-2. Carter, String Quartet No. 2, Introduction, meas. 1–28. Quoted by permission of Associated Music Publishers, Inc.

Individuality of the parts and one use of metrical modulation in the Introduction to Elliott Carter's String Quartet No. 2.

The cello plays accelerating or decelerating phrases (indicated both by conventional notation and by the use of a dotted line with arrow ⌒⌒⤵) with characteristic intervals of fourths and minor sixths. Violin I specializes in minor thirds and perfect fifths and a strong, virtuoso or bravura playing style (*marcato, con fantasia*, etc.). Violin II plays in a regular, even, on-beat style with various kinds of pizzicatos, staccatos, and accents, and features major thirds, sixths, and sevenths. The viola part abounds in tritones, half-steps, and minor sevenths; it is directed to be performed in a highly expressive manner with many glissandi or portamenti. One metrical modulation is indicated between measures 10 and 11, with the dotted eighth-notes pulse in Violin II becoming the new quarter-note unit of the following tempo.

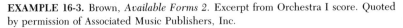

EXAMPLE 16-3. Brown, *Available Forms 2*. Excerpt from Orchestra I score. Quoted by permission of Associated Music Publishers, Inc.

Example of open-form notation with elements to be ordered in the course of performance.

Three out of five possible "events" on a page of score for one of the two orchestras. The conductor of each orchestra successively selects various events during the course of the performance and indicates his choices to the musicians by holding up the fingers of one hand.

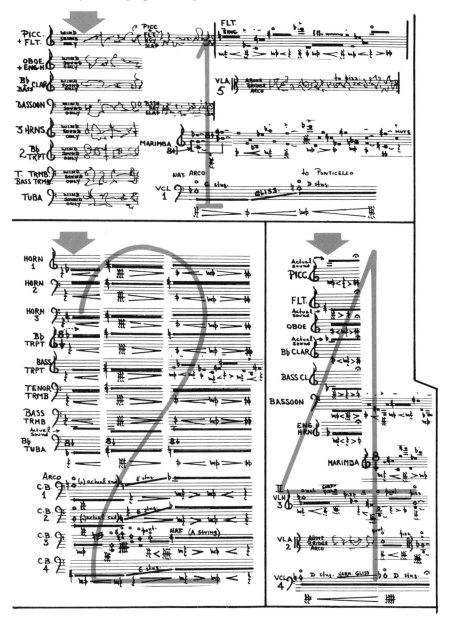

EXAMPLE 17-1. Stockhausen, *Refrain für drei Spieler.* Quoted by permission of Universal Edition.

New notation, variable elements, cluster and percussive chords in a serial structure.

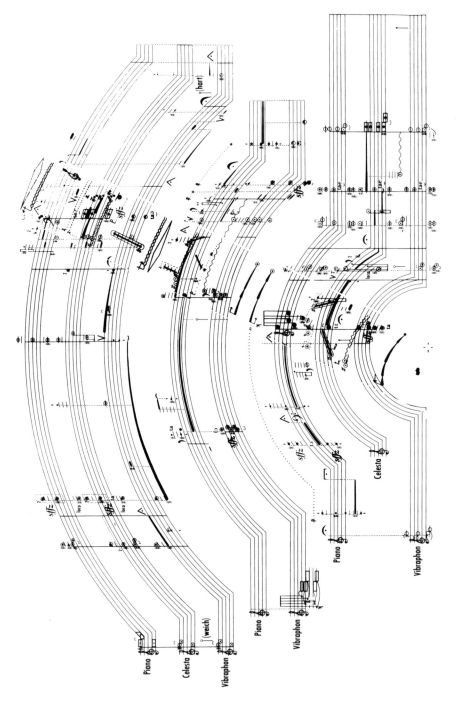

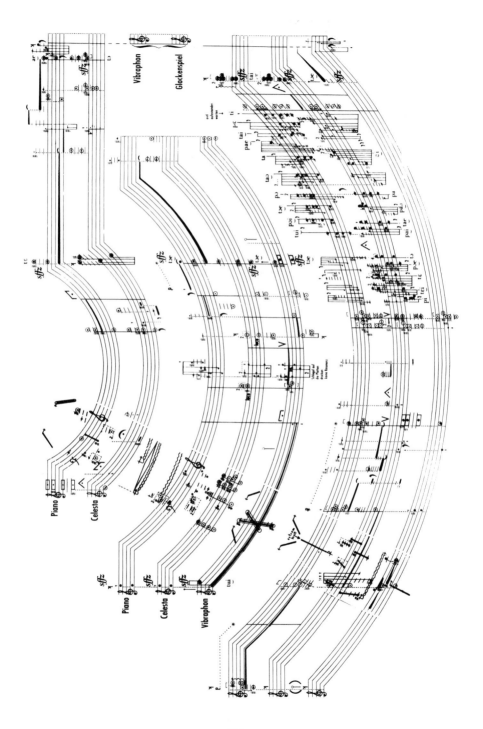

Vibraphon

Glockenspiel

Piano

Celesta

Piano

Celesta

Vibraphon

291

The first part of Karlheinz Stockhausen's *Refrain* is arranged in a circular form and overlaid with a transparent strip that rotates on a central axis and can appear in various positions. The overlay not only adds notes but can modify the performances of the music underneath. (See, for example, the bass clefs that appear on the strip on the piano stave in three places.) The three keyboard players all play percussion instruments (woodblocks, crotales, cowbells, and glockenspiel bars)—notated in red in the original score—and make vocal sounds and tongue clicks as well. The notation system, explained in a page of "rules" attached to the score, is Stockhausen's own. There are six different degrees of loudness, indicated by the size of the notes. There is no rhythmic or metrical notation; relative durations and types of attack (as well as lengths of pauses) are indicated by special notations. Special attention is paid to cut-offs, damping, sustaining, and letting vibrate different notes from each attack. (For fuller information, the original score and instructions must be examined.) *Refrain* is a piece about the attack and decay of percussive sound in live performance, and it covers a gamut of possibilities about the way ensemble sounds may be struck and die away.

EXAMPLE 17-2. Boulez, *Le marteau sans maître*, opening of the final section, "Bel édifice et les pressentiments" double. Used by permission of Universal Edition.

Composing in timbres; serialism extended through flexible tempo, rhythmic, and dynamic changes as well as extended use of fluid vocal and instrumental timbres.

Settings of and instrumental commentaries on poems by the surrealist René Char, scored for six players: flute in G (not used in this excerpt), xylorimba (sounding an octave above the written notation), vibraphone, percussion, guitar (written an octave lower than sounding), viola, and alto voice. Note the careful indication of rhythm, dynamics, and articulation, the constant changes of tempo, as well as the use of *Sprechstimme* (quasi parlando), humming (*bouche fermée*), head voice (*voix de tête*), and more traditional singing. Compare the highly coloristic, embellished fantasy in the sound of this percussion ensemble as compared to the Stockhausen example (Example 17-1).

EXAMPLE 18-1. Rochberg, *Nach Bach*. Copyright © 1967 by Theodore Presser, Inc. Quoted by permission.

Fragments of music by Bach in a collage setting.

George Rochberg's quotation technique (here illustrated in a work for piano or harpsichord) suspends bits of recognizable music—tonal, highly rhythmic—in a void of atonality and silence to produce larger musical and cognitive dissonances.

EXAMPLE 18-2. Mac Low, *5th Young Turtle Asymmetry—30 July 1967.* Copyright ©1978 by Jackson Mac Low. Published in *21 Matched Asymmetries* by Jackson Mac Low (London: Aloes Books, 1978). Reproduced by permission of the author/composer.

Text-sound notations.

    Jackson Mac Low, poet and composer closely associated with the Fluxus group in the 1960's, composed a number of "word events" and text-sound pieces, many of them employing only a set of instructions. Example 18–2, based on a picture caption in *Natural History* magazine, is intended for five simultaneous readers. Speed, duration, pacing, lengths of silences, and loudness are up to the individual readers, within certain limits. The notation gives the general shape (spaces may be silent or may contain sustained notes played on instruments) and suggests the extensions or prolongations of text sounds. Performance instructions are as follows:

    The *5th Young Turtle Asymmetry* must be performed simultaneously with the other four *Young Turtle Asymmetries* by five persons. Each must perform all five texts in a different order: 12345, 23451, 34512, 45123, or 51234. In shorter performances four or fewer may be read by each person, but all five must always be performed together.

    Blank spaces cue silences, and repeated letters cue speech-sound prolongations, at least as long as it would take individual performers to speak words printed directly above or below them.

    Performers must listen very attentively to all sounds produced by both performers and environment (audience, street, etc.) and relate consciously with them, adjusting performances—lengthening silences or prolonged sounds or changing pitches or speaking louder or softer or more rapidly or slowly—in accordance with their perceptions.

    The words of the 5 *Young Turtle Asymmetries* were drawn by chance operations from a picture caption in the article "100 Turtle Eggs," by Archie Carr (*Natural History,* LXXVI, 7 [New York: American Museum of Natural History, Aug.–Sept. 1967], p. 51):

    Young turtles, below, scuttle/to open water. Once the hatchlings/have found their way to the/sea, they embark upon a journey/whose course is a mystery./No one knows where the turtles go.

No one knows where the turtles go.

Young/nggggggggggggggggggggggggggggggggggg-
(n)gggg/turtles,

journey/iyyyyyyyyyyyyyyyyyyyyyyyyyyyyyyyyyyyyyyyyyyyyyyyyyyy-
(i)yyyyyyyyyyyyyyy/whose course is a mystery.

one/nnnnnnnnnnnnnnnnnnnnnnnnnn-
nnnnnnn/knows where the turtles go.

turtles,

journey/iyyyyyyyyyyyyyyyyyyyyyyyy-
(i)yyyyyyyyyyyyyyyyyyyyyyyyyyyyyyyyyyyyyyyyyy/whose/zzzzzzzzzzzzzzzzzzzzzzzzzzzz-
zzzzzzz/course is a mystery.

where the turtles go.

the hatchlings/zzzzzzzzzzzzzzzzzzzzzzzzzzzzzzzzzzzzzzzzzzzzzzz-
zzzzzzzzzzzzzzzzzzzzzzzzzzzzzzzzzz/have found their way to the/uhhhhhhhhhhhhhhh-
(u)hhhhhhhhhhhhhhhhhhhhhhhhhhhhhhhhhhhhhhhhhhhhhhhhhhh/sea,

they embark upon a journey/iyyyyyyyyyyyyyyyyyyyyyyyyyyyyyyyyyyyyyyyyy-
(i)yyyyyyyyyyyyyyyyyyyyyyyyyy/whose course is a mystery.

EXAMPLE 18-3. Amirkhanian, *Another Norther*. ©1976 Arts Plural Publishing (BMI). Reproduced by permission.

Text-sound notations.

   Charles Amirkhanian is a California composer and text-sound poet. The piece by him illustrated in Example 18–3 is scored for three live readers; the notation suggests the rhythmic relation between them. Each line equals a quarter note; words preceded by a hyphen are spoken off the beat. Words are used as images as well as for their pure sound value, and the rhythmic uses of repetition are an essential part of the effect.

♩ = ca. 110-120

1	2	3			
credible					
-	-	-			
credible			miracles	-	-
credible			play	xoxox	cramp
-	-	-	- play	xoxox	French
credible	credible	credible	fairly	-	cramp
credible	credible	credible	- play	credible	-
credible	credible	credible	fairly	credible	rusty
-	-	-	well	xoxox	faith
	credible		miracles	twisting	-
-		-	play	turkeys	hamper
	credible		- play	twisting	-
	credible		fairly	turkeys	cramp
-	-	-	twisting	credible	French
credible	credible	credible	turkeys	credible	cramp
credible	credible	credible	twisting	xoxox	HEY!
credible	credible	credible	turkeys	xoxox	rusty
-	-		- play	twisting	faith
		credible	fairly	turkeys	-
-	-	-	well	twisting	hamper
		credible	miracles	turkeys	-
		credible	twisting	credible	cramp
-	-	-	play	credible	turkeys
credible	credible	credible	twisting	xoxox	French
credible	credible	credible	- play	xoxox	turkeys
credible	credible	credible	twisting	twisting	cramp
-	-	-	turkeys	turkeys	French
tunic	-	-	twisting	twisting	cramp
-	-	-	turkeys	turkeys	HEY!
-	3-page	3-page			
tunic	-	-			
-	-	-			
-	3-page	3-page			
tunic	-	-			
tunic	-	-			
-	tunic	tunic			
-	3-page	3-page			
tunic	-	-			
-	3-page	3-page			
tunic	-	tunic			
-	-	-	tunic	-	-
-	3-page	-	-	-	-
tunic	-	tunic	-	3-page	3-page
-	-	-	tunic	-	-
-	3-page	-	-	-	-

tunic	tunic	-
-	tunic	tunic
tunic	-	tunic
-	tunic	-
3-page	3-page	3-page
-	-	-
3-page	3-page	3 page
-	-	-
3-page	3-page	3-page
-	-	-
3-page	3-page	3-page
miracles		
play		
- play		
fairly		
- play		
fairly		
well		

-	3-page	3-page
tunic	-	-
-	tunic	-
3-page	-	tunic
tunic	-	-
-	tunic	-
3-page	-	tunic
tunic	-	-
-	-	-
-	3-page	3-page
tunic	-	-
-	3-page	3-page
tunic	-	-
-	xoxox	-
-	-	credible
3-page	-	-
-	cramp	cramp

	credible
	-
	xoxox
	-
	credible
	credible
	xoxox
	xoxox

	rusty
	faith
	-
	hamper
	-
	cramp
	French
	cramp

miracles	credible	cramp
play	-	
- play	xoxox	
fairly	-	
- play	credible	
fairly	-	
well	credible	
	credible	rusty
	xoxox	faith
	xoxox	-
	credible	hamper
	credible	-
	xoxox	cramp
	xoxox	French
	credible	cramp
	credible	-
miracles	credible	-
play	xoxox	rusty
- play	xoxox	faith
fairly	credible	-
- play	-	hamper
fairly	xoxox	-
well	xoxox	cramp
miracles	credible	French
play	-	cramp
- play	xoxox	
fairly	xoxox	rusty
- play	credible	faith
fairly	credible	-
well	credible	hamper

EXAMPLE 19-1. Davies, *Eight Songs for a Mad King*, entry of the voice.. Copyright © 1971 by Boosey and Hawkes. Quoted by permission.

Extended vocal techniques, quotation, and post-serialism in a concert theater piece.

The text of this work, by Randolph Stow, refers to the madness of George III as he tried to teach his pet bullfinches to sing. The flute (or piccolo), clarinet, violin, and cello represent, in part, the birds; the percussionist is the King's keeper; the keyboard (piano and harpsichord) offers commentaries, quotations, comments, and asides. The extraordinary vocal part was created for Roy Hart, who developed many of the techniques; it has, however, been performed by others more or less in the same manner. Davies describes the work as an exploration of "certain extreme regions of experience," here in a quasi-theatrical form.

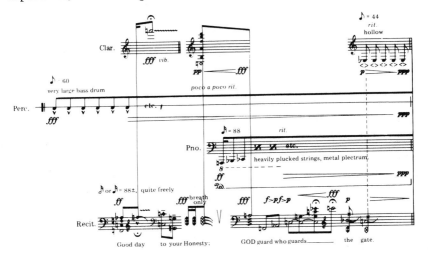

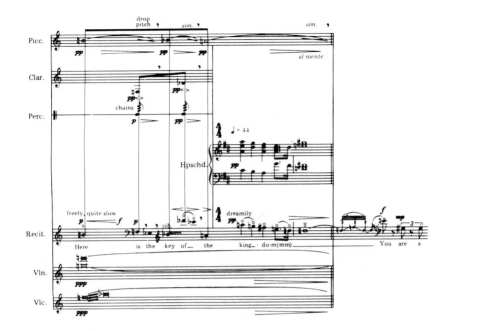

EXAMPLE 19-2. Riley, *In C*. Copyright 1964. Used by permission.

Neo-tonality in early minimalism.

Terry Riley's *In C*, one of the first works of the new minimalism, consists of 53 notated fragments to be performed by any instrumental ensemble. Not shown is a piano part called the "Pulse," consisting of the top two C's on the piano keyboard played in even eighth notes throughout. Performers repeat each musical fragment ad lib before moving on in the numbered order. The performance ends when all the performers have played fragment no. 53. The nine notes of an expanded C major are gradually introduced in the following order: C–E–F–G–B–F♯–A–B♭–D—somewhat in the manner of an East Indian modal array.

EXAMPLE 19-3. Reich, *Octet.* Copyright 1979 by the composer. Used by permission of Boosey and Hawkes.

"Minimalism"; opening of a process or pulse-music work based on sustained intervals and repetition.

Reduction of the first pages of a Steve Reich work for two woodwind players (flute, piccolo, clarinet, bass clarinet), two pianos, and string quartet. The piece changes key twice; tempo never varies. Eighth-note figures—filled in or separated by eighth-note rests—continue virtually throughout with small variants in timbre, register, rhythmic displacement, and overlays.

EXAMPLE 21-1. Sahl-Salzman, *Civilization and Its Discontents,* excerpts. Copyright © by G. Schirmer, Inc., 1985. Used by permission.

Pop, neo-tonality, and improvisational techniques in a music-theater work.

The first scene of this music-theater work uses conversational catch phrases overheard in a bar. The basic and recurring riff ("If it feels good") spawns a series of countermelodies which appear against the riff or alternate with it; the harmonic settings may be simple and static or may change on every beat. The melodic lines imply popular American singing styles, and a certain amount of rhythmic freedom in performance is possible or even desirable. Certain free sections ("Voids") employ techniques derived from music-theater improvisation (see excerpt e) in the manner of Quog Music Theater or the Natural Sound Workshop. In many cases, the notations in the printed music have been derived from the performance practice rather than the other way around.

a. Basic riff with countermelody.

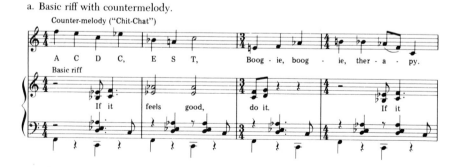

b. Countermelody (rhythmically identical to a.) in close harmony, changing on every beat.

c. and d. Derived melodic forms (not sung simultaneously) over an accompanimental vamp that is harmonically simplified (from b.) and rhythmically flattened (from a.).

e. Void I.

Free accompaniments to solo voice above.

Women (*improvisationally on high notes; free, irregular, uncoordinated; improvise similar sounds: 'luck' 'ape' 'ick' 'muck' 'pocke' etc.*)

coke toke grok zonk suck freak broke cluck sick luck nope lick choke truck blank tape fact chick

Men (*like grotesque conversations*)

blah   blah, blah   blah,   blah, blah, blah, blah   blah, blah, blah, etc.
blah, blah   blah, blah   blah   blah   blah, etc.
blah   blah   blah, blah, blah   blah   blah, blah, blah, blah, blah, etc.

Pitched instruments

Drums (timpani, roto-tom or tom-toms) (*gliss. effects where available*)

EXAMPLE 21-2. Sondheim, *Pacific Overtures*, "Someone in a Tree." Used by permission.

Excerpts from a music-theater work showing influences from non-Western music and minimalism as well as an unconventional approach to musico-dramatic form.

Stephen Sondheim's *Pacific Overtures* (book by John Weidman with additional material by Hugh Wheeler) treats the opening up of Japan to the West by Commodore Perry from the Japanese point of view. The orchestration as well as the musical style incorporates Eastern elements; there is also a close relationship with contemporary minimalism (as suggested by these excerpts). Although the rhythmic setting and prosody derive from American popular song and theater music, the static (and somewhat ambiguous or floating) tonality and the modular melodic phrases which fit and refit like pieces of a puzzle are related to contemporary new-music practice and also help to illustrate the subject of the song: the ambiguous and puzzling nature of reality. An old man, his younger self, and, later, a warrior give unexpected accounts of a historic event that they witnessed. Nearly all the musical phrases and accompaniment patterns are derivations or extensions of those shown here.

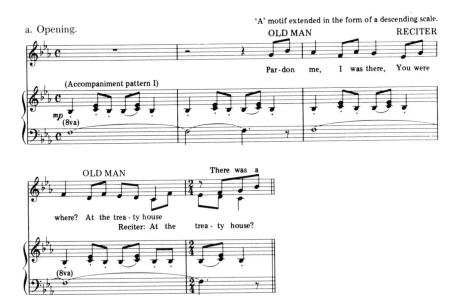

b. From Old Man's solo.

c. Old Man sings with his younger self.

INDEX

313